T0285050

The Myth of American Idealism

The Myth *of* American Idealism

How U.S. Foreign Policy
Endangers the World

NOAM CHOMSKY and
NATHAN J. ROBINSON

PENGUIN PRESS

NEW YORK

2024

PENGUIN PRESS
An imprint of Penguin Random House LLC
penguinrandomhouse.com

Brief portions of this work, by the coauthor Nathan J. Robinson, appeared in different form in *Current Affairs* during 2022 and 2023.

LIBRARY OF CONGRESS CATALOGING-IN-PUBLICATION DATA
Names: Chomsky, Noam, author. | Robinson, Nathan J., author.
Title: The myth of American idealism : how U.S. foreign policy endangers the world / Noam Chomsky and Nathan J. Robinson.
Description: New York : Penguin Press, 2024. |
Includes bibliographical references and index.
Identifiers: LCCN 2024019958 (print) | LCCN 2024019959 (ebook) |
ISBN 9780593656327 (hardcover) | ISBN 9780593656334 (ebook)
Subjects: LCSH: Hegemony—United States. | Idealism. |
United States—Foreign relations—Moral and ethical aspects. |
United States—Foreign relations—Developing countries. |
Developing countries—Foreign relations—United States.
Classification: LCC JZ1480 .C476 2024 (print) | LCC JZ1480 (ebook) |
DDC 327.73—dc23/eng/20240611
LC record available at https://lccn.loc.gov/2024019958
LC ebook record available at https://lccn.loc.gov/2024019959

Printed in the United States of America
1st Printing

Book design by Daniel Lagin

The chief ideal of the American people is idealism. I cannot repeat too often that America is a nation of idealists. That is the only motive to which they ever give any strong and lasting reaction.

—CALVIN COOLIDGE

Power always thinks it has a great Soul, and vast Views, beyond the Comprehension of the Weak; and that it is doing God Service when it is violating all His laws.

—JOHN ADAMS

We Americans are the peculiar chosen people—the Israel of our time; we bear the ark of liberties of the world. . . . God has predestined, mankind expects, great things from our race. . . . We are the pioneers of the world . . . sent on through the wilderness of untried things, to break a new path in the New World that is ours.

—HERMAN MELVILLE, *WHITE-JACKET*

Contents

Preface by Nathan J. Robinson   xi

Introduction: Noble Goals and Mafia Logic   1

PART 1

The Record: Idealism in Action

1. Disciplining the Global South   23

2. The War on Southeast Asia   63

3. 9/11 and the Wrecking of Afghanistan   85

4. Iraq: The Crime of the Century   107

5. The United States, Israel, and Palestine   135

6. The Great China Threat   167

7. NATO and Russia After the Cold War   183

8. Nuclear Threats and Climate Catastrophe   205

PART 2

Understanding the Power System

9. The Domestic Roots of Foreign Policy   235

10. International Law and the "Rules-Based Order"   249

11. How Mythologies Are Manufactured   271

Conclusion: Hegemony or Survival?   287

Notes   303

Index   383

Preface

by Nathan J. Robinson

I first encountered the work of Noam Chomsky when I was in high school, and a friend gave me his books *Hegemony or Survival* and *Failed States*. They were my first real introduction to left politics, and proved a life-altering experience. During the Bush years, as the country was gripped with war fever, Chomsky was a welcome voice of sanity, who cut through jingoistic propaganda and exposed the human toll of U.S. wars. He asked questions that hardly anybody else was asking and called attention to facts that were never mentioned in the press. From reading Chomsky, I learned to question conventional wisdom and to forensically analyze both government documents and the mainstream media.

Many hundreds of thousands of others have been similarly educated and inspired by him, especially because of Chomsky's legendary willingness to patiently engage with the public, answering thousands of letters and emails. He has changed the lives of so many who have encountered his written work, heard his talks, or interacted with him. Countless people have an anecdote about the time they emailed Noam Chomsky with a question or a request for advice and were surprised to receive a long, personal reply. That's how I, too, got to know him. I can't remember what the first email I sent him was, but I remember the feeling of delight when I received a thoughtful response.

In 2015, I founded a left magazine, *Current Affairs*, that provided an outlet for the kind of humanistic libertarian socialist worldview that Chomsky represented. I was thrilled when he became one of our early subscribers. He has always been strongly supportive of independent left media, praising countless books from small presses and plugging the work of lesser-known writers. He boosted our work by giving us public endorsements and circulating *Current Affairs* articles to his correspondents.

In 2018, I went out to interview him in Tucson, where he was teaching at the University of Arizona. After the interview, he drove me across the campus, and I was struck by how much time he had to spend hunting for parking. It was surreal to watch someone with a mind that has been compared to that of Plato and Marx, preoccupied by the search for a parking space. In 2022, another interview we did attracted a lot of attention, after Chomsky suggested that the United States bore a high level of responsibility for the war in Ukraine. Well into his nineties, he had not lost the power to provoke strong reactions with his sharp dissent from foreign policy orthodoxy.

I have always wished that some of Chomsky's ideas could be presented more systematically in a single volume. In 2022, I asked him if we could collaborate on a book. I explained to him that I would like to compile some of his most useful observations on how U.S. power is wielded around the world, and how our country's violence is obscured through self-aggrandizing mythology. This would draw insights from across his body of work into a single volume that could introduce people to his central critiques of U.S. foreign policy, including his deconstructions of the stories and propaganda used to justify our country's extreme, abhorrent militarism.[1] He readily agreed to the project, and we spent a year sending chapters back and forth. First I would assemble a series of things he had said on the topic in interviews, articles, prefaces, introductions, written correspondence, debates, and books. Then

I worked with him to edit them into a clear statement of his position, adding elaboration and further evidence, then incorporating his further comments, edits, and rewrites.

It is of course a delight and a privilege to be able to collaborate closely with one of my intellectual heroes on a major project. But as we put the book together, that joy was tempered by the darkness of much of the subject matter, and by the knowledge that we are not writing about issues of purely intellectual interest, but of urgent and dire threats. This book is not only an attempt to set the record straight. It's a plea for mass action by someone approaching the end of his own lifetime of activism.

Chomsky has never been a cynic. He may criticize the hypocrisy of those who cloak power seeking in idealistic rhetoric, but he himself remains a sincere idealist. He believes in the global spread of freedom and democracy, which is why he detests those who pervert these concepts. He believes in the moral and intellectual capacities of ordinary people and rejects the idea that it takes special genius or insight to understand world affairs.

He does not believe we should be resigned to a future of warfare and environmental destruction. We can, and must, fight for a future of world peace. Chomsky harbors a vision, in part inspired by anarchism, of a decentralized democracy in which ordinary people meaningfully participate in politics, rather than important decisions being made by a small coterie of plutocrats. Reading Chomsky's work can be a troubling experience, full as it is of atrocities and exploitation. But it is worth remembering that beneath what can look like a pessimistic framework is a deep love of humanity, a hatred of violence, and a firm belief that things can be different than they are today.

The Myth of American Idealism

Introduction

Noble Goals and Mafia Logic

Every ruling power tells itself stories to justify its rule. Nobody is the villain in their own history. Professed good intentions and humane principles are a constant. Even Heinrich Himmler, in describing the extermination of the Jews, claimed that the Nazis only "carried out this most difficult task for the love of our people" and thereby "suffered no defect within us, in our soul, or in our character." Hitler himself said that in occupying Czechoslovakia, he was only trying to "further the peace and social welfare of all" by eliminating ethnic conflicts and letting everyone live in harmony under civilized Germany's benevolent tutelage. The worst of history's criminals have often proclaimed themselves to be among humankind's greatest heroes.[1]

Murderous imperial conquests are consistently characterized as civilizing missions, conducted out of concern for the interests of the indigenous population. During Japan's invasion of China in the 1930s, even as Japanese forces were carrying out the Nanjing Massacre, Japanese leaders were claiming they were on a mission to create an "earthly paradise" for the people of China and to protect them from Chinese "bandits" (i.e., those resisting Japan's invasion). Emperor Hirohito, in his 1945 surrender address, insisted that "we declared war on America and Britain out of our sincere desire to ensure Japan's self-preservation and the stabilization of East Asia, it being far from our thought either to infringe upon the sovereignty of other nations or to embark upon territorial aggrandizement." As the late Palestinian American scholar Edward Said noted, there is always a class of people ready to produce specious intellectual arguments in defense of domination: "Every single empire in its official discourse has said that it is not like all the others, that its circumstances are special, that it has a mission to enlighten, civilize, bring order and democracy, and that it uses force only as a last resort."[2]

Virtually any act of mass murder or criminal aggression can be rationalized by appeals to high moral principle. Maximilien Robespierre justified the French Reign of Terror in 1794 by claiming that "terror is nothing other than justice, prompt, severe, inflexible; it is therefore an emanation of virtue." Those in power generally present themselves as altruistic, disinterested, and generous. The late leftist journalist Andrew Kopkind pointed to "the universal desire of statesmen to make their most monstrous missions seem like acts of mercy." It is hard to take actions one believes to be actively immoral, so people have to convince themselves that what they're doing is right, that their violence is justified. When anyone wields power over someone else (whether a colonist, a dictator, a bureaucrat, a spouse, or a boss), they need an ideology, and that ideology usually comes down to the belief that their domination is for the good of the dominated.[3]

Leaders of the United States have always spoken loftily of the country's sacred principles. That story has been consistent since the founding. The U.S. is a "shining city on a hill," an example to the world, an exceptional "indispensable nation" devoted to freedom and democracy.[4] The president is the "leader of the free world." The U.S. "is and will remain the greatest force for freedom the world has ever known," as Barack Obama put it. George W. Bush described the U.S. as "a nation with a mission—and that mission comes from our most basic beliefs. We have no desire to dominate, no ambitions of empire. Our aim is a democratic peace." The U.S. government is honorable. It is capable of *mistakes*, but not crimes. A crime would require malicious intent, of which we have none. The U.S. is continually deceived by others. It can be foolish, naïve, and idealistic—but it is never wicked.[5]

Crucially, the United States does not act on the basis of the perceived self-interest of dominant groups in society. Only other states do that. "One of the difficulties of explaining [American] policy," Ambassador Charles Bohlen explained at Columbia University in 1969, is that "our policy is not rooted in any national material interest . . . as most foreign policies of other countries in the past have been." In discussion of international relations, the fundamental principle is that we are good—"we" being the government (on the totalitarian principle that state and people are one). "We" are benevolent, seeking peace and justice, though there may be errors in practice. "We" are foiled by villains who can't rise to our exalted level. The "prevailing orthodoxy" was well summarized by the distinguished Oxford-Yale historian Michael Howard: "For 200 years the United States has preserved almost unsullied the original ideals of the Enlightenment . . . and, above all, the universality of these values," though it "does not enjoy the place in the world that it should have earned through its achievements, its generosity, and its goodwill since World War II."[6]

The fact that the United States is an exceptional nation is regularly intoned, not just by virtually every political figure, but by prominent academics and public intellectuals as well. Samuel Huntington, professor of government at Harvard, writing in the prestigious journal *International Security*, explained that unlike other countries, the "national identity" of the United States is "defined by a set of universal political and economic values," namely "liberty, democracy, equality, private property, and markets." The U.S. therefore has a solemn duty to maintain its "international primacy" for the benefit of the world. In the leading left-liberal intellectual journal, *The New York Review of Books*, the former chair of the Carnegie Endowment for International Peace states as fact that "American contributions to international security, global economic growth, freedom, and human well-being have been so self-evidently unique and have been so clearly directed to others' benefit that Americans have long believed that the [United States] amounts to a different kind of country." While others push their national interest, the United States "tries to advance universal principles."[7]

Usually, no evidence for these propositions is given. None is needed, because they are considered true as a matter of definition. One might even take the position that in the special case of the United States, facts themselves are irrelevant. Hans Morgenthau, a founder of realist inter-national relations theory, developed the standard view that the United States has a "transcendent purpose": establishing peace and freedom not only at home, but also across the globe, because "the arena within which the United States must defend and promote its purpose has be-come world-wide." As a scrupulous scholar, he recognized that the his-torical record is radically inconsistent with this "transcendent purpose." But he insisted that we should not be misled by this discrepancy. We should not "confound the abuse of reality with reality itself." Reality is the unachieved "national purpose" revealed by "the evidence of history as our minds reflect it." What actually happened is merely the "abuse of reality."[8]

Needless to say, because even oppressive, criminal, and genocidal governments cloak their atrocities in the language of virtue, none of this rhetoric should be taken seriously. There is no reason to expect Americans to be uniquely immune to self-delusion. If those who com-mit evil and those who do good always both profess to be doing good, national stories are worthless as tests of truth. Sensible people pay scant attention to declarations of noble intent by leaders, because they are a universal. What matters is the historical record.

The received wisdom is that the United States is committed to pro-moting democracy and human rights (sometimes called "Wilsonian idealism" or "American exceptionalism"). But the facts are consistent with the following theory instead: The United States is very much like other powerful states. It pursues the strategic and economic interests of dominant sectors of the domestic population.[9] In practice, this means that the United States has typically acted with almost complete disregard for moral principle and the rule of law, except insofar as complying with principle and law serves the interests of American elites. There is little evidence of authentic humanitarian concern among leading statesmen, and when it does exist, it is acted upon *only* to the extent that doing so does not go against domestic elites' interests. American foreign policy is almost never made in accordance with the stated ideals, and in fact is far more consistent with what Adam Smith called "the vile maxim of the masters of mankind" in "every age of the world," namely: "All for ourselves and nothing for other people."[10]

We might also call this the Mafia Doctrine. Its logic is straightforward and completely rational. The Godfather's word is law. Those who defy the Godfather will be punished. The Godfather may be generous from time to time, but he does not tolerate disagreement. If some small storekeeper fails to pay protection money, the Godfather sends his goons, not just to collect the money, which he wouldn't even notice, but to beat him to a pulp so that others do not get the idea that disobedience is permissible. But Godfathers, too, are known to convince themselves that they are kindly and benevolent.[11]

We might also think about this violence prerogative as the "Fifth Freedom," the one Franklin D. Roosevelt forgot to mention when he laid out his famous Four Freedoms: *freedom of speech, freedom of worship, freedom from want,* and *freedom from fear.* The United States has always claimed a fundamental additional freedom underlying the others: crudely speaking, the freedom to dominate, to undertake any course of action to ensure that existing privilege is protected and advanced. Maintenance of this freedom is the operative principle that accounts for a substantial part of what the U.S. government does in the world. When the Four Freedoms are perceived to be incompatible with the Fifth (which occurs regularly), they are set aside with little notice or concern.[12]

We can turn to a single page of history to see how Mafia logic works.

Here is an extract from a paper prepared by the National Security Council Planning Board in 1958, discussing issues arising in the Middle East. The paper poses a question facing the United States and presents the argument for two possible stances to take:

Question: Should the United States be prepared to support, or if necessary assist, the British in using force to retain control of Kuwait and the Persian Gulf?

1. The argument for such action: An assured source of oil is essential to the continued economic viability of Western Europe. Moreover, the UK asserts that its financial stability would be seriously threatened if the petroleum from Kuwait and the Persian Gulf area were not available to the UK on reasonable terms, if the UK were deprived of the large investments made by that area in the UK, and if sterling were deprived of the support provided by Persian Gulf oil. If [Egyptian president Gamal Abdel] Nasser obtains dominant influence over the Persian Gulf oil-producing areas, Western access to this oil on acceptable terms might be seriously threatened. The only way to guarantee continued access to Persian Gulf oil on acceptable terms is to insist on maintaining the present concessions and be prepared to defend our present position by force if necessary.

2. The argument against such action: If armed force must be used to help retain this area (or even if there is a public indication of willingness to use force), the benefits of any actions in the direction of accommodation with radical Pan-Arab nationalism will be largely lost and U.S. relations with neutral countries elsewhere would be adversely affected. Such accommodation would better provide the basis for continued assurance of access to Kuwait and Persian Gulf oil.[13]

Note the complete absence of any consideration of the interests of the people of Kuwait, who are effectively nonpersons, or "unpeople," a term from Orwell that Mark Curtis has updated.[14] Note, too, the absence of any discussion of *rights*. What right does the United States have to use force to help the British retain control of Kuwait and the Persian Gulf? What right do the British have to retain such control? Morally speaking, of course, the answer is "none whatsoever." But it is accepted as a basic presumption that we are allowed to use force whenever and wherever we want in order to pursue our "interests." The only necessary debate, then, is whether or not force *does* serve our interests. (There could be backlash, for instance, from Arab nationalists who resent us.) Immoral actions create public relations problems, but their immorality is irrelevant. Likewise, the Godfather might worry that excessive use of force could jeopardize certain crucial relationships. But when he shows restraint, it is not for moral reasons.[15]

At the height of John F. Kennedy's attacks on Cuba, to take another example, the pragmatic consequences for the United States were a subject for discussion, but the rights of the people under attack were simply irrelevant. In a review of internal documents, Latin Americanist Jorge Domínguez observes that: "Only once in these nearly thousand pages of documentation did a U.S. official raise something that resembled a faint moral objection to U.S. government-sponsored terrorism." A member of the National Security Council staff suggested that raids that are "haphazard and kill innocents . . . might mean a bad press in some friendly countries." The same considerations were present throughout the internal discussions during the Cuban Missile Crisis, as when Robert Kennedy warned that a full-scale invasion of Cuba would "kill an awful lot of people, and we're going to take an awful lot of heat on it." These attitudes prevail to the present, with only the rarest of exceptions. It is "U.S. interests" that matter.[16]

But the term "national interest" is itself a euphemism, for what is usually meant is the interest of a small sector of wealthy domestic elites. The American working class, whose members die in the country's wars, do not have their "interest" served in any way by the wars that kill them. Nor are their interests served by government spending money on weapons that could be used to repair school buildings. Indeed, when

American actions abroad are exposed to the judgment of public opinion, they often prove deeply unpopular with the "nation" whose "interests" they are supposedly serving. A sophisticated propaganda system must keep the public in the dark, for if the truth were known, it would become immediately apparent that the public has a very different view of its "interests" than U.S. elites have.

We should also remember this the next time we hear talk about what "the Russians" or "Iran" have done. Totalitarians wish us to think that a country speaks with one voice, that it has a "national interest." While it is the convention to refer to actions by the state as if they were actions by the country as a whole, and is unavoidable in discussions of policy, the formulation is ultimately misleading. The thousands of heroic antiwar protesters thrown in prison by Vladimir Putin have just as much claim to represent Russia as their ruler does.[17] This is why it is an error to treat this book as arguing that "the United States is terroristic and destructive," *if* the "United States" is understood to refer to some kind of collectivity of all Americans. Many in the United States have taken to the streets, and risked their lives and livelihoods, to oppose the acts of their government—when they have been permitted to learn about them, that is.

THE PRINCIPLES OF IMPERIAL GRAND STRATEGY:
WE OWN THE WORLD

The basic principles of contemporary American strategy were laid out during World War II. As the war came to its end, American planners were well aware that the United States would emerge as the dominant power in the world, holding a hegemonic position with few parallels in history. During the war, industrial production in the U.S. more than tripled; meanwhile, its major rivals were either severely weakened or virtually destroyed. The U.S. had the world's most powerful military force. It had firm control of the Western Hemisphere—and of the oceans. High-level planners and foreign policy advisers determined that in the new global system the U.S. should "hold unquestioned power" while ensuring the "limitation of any exercise of sovereignty" by states that might interfere with its global designs.[18]

Winston Churchill captured the dominant sentiment when he said that "the government of the world must be entrusted to satisfied nations," because rich countries had no "reason to seek for anything more," whereas "if the world-government were in the hands of hungry nations there would always be danger." Leo Welch of the Standard Oil Company expressed a similar aspiration when he said the U.S. needed to "assume the responsibility of the majority stockholder in this corporation known as the world," and not just temporarily, but as a "permanent obligation."[19]

From 1939 to 1945, extensive studies conducted by the Council on Foreign Relations and the State Department resulted in a policy they called "Grand Area" planning. The Grand Area referred to any region that was to be subordinated to the needs of the American economy and was considered "strategically necessary for world control." "The British Empire as it existed in the past will never reappear," mused one planner, and thus "the United States may have to take its place." Another stated frankly that the U.S. "must cultivate a mental view toward world settlement." The Grand Area had to include at least the Western Hemisphere, the Far East, and the former British Empire, which we were then in the process of dismantling and taking over. Ideally it would also include western and southern Europe and the oil-producing regions of the Middle East; in fact, it was to include everything, if that were possible. Detailed plans were laid for particular regions of the Grand Area and also for international institutions that were to organize and police it.[20]

George Kennan, head of the State Department planning staff and one of the leading architects of the post–World War II order, outlined the basic thinking in an important 1948 planning document:

We have about 50 percent of the world's wealth, but only 6.3 percent of its population. . . . In this situation, we cannot fail to be the object of envy and resentment. Our real task in the coming period is to devise a pattern of relationships which will permit us to maintain this position of disparity. . . . We need not deceive ourselves that we can afford today the luxury of altruism and world-benefaction. . . . We should cease to talk about vague and . . . unreal objectives such as human rights, the raising of the living standards, and democratization. The day is not far off when we are going to have to deal in straight power concepts. The less we are then hampered by idealistic slogans, the better.[21]

The planning staff recognized further that "the foremost requirement" to secure these ends was "the rapid fulfillment of a program of complete re-armament"—then, as now, a central component of "an integrated policy to achieve military and economic supremacy for the United States." This policy of military and economic supremacy is openly stated everywhere from the 1940s planning documents to the National Security Strategies put out by the George W. Bush, Obama, Trump, and Biden administrations. Implementing it has not just involved *ignoring* democracy and human rights, but often actively opposing them with tremendous ferocity.[22]

The U.S. planners specified the function that each part of the world was to have within the U.S.-dominated global system. The "major function" of Southeast Asia was to be "a source of raw materials and a market for Japan and Western Europe," in the words of Kennan's State Department Policy Planning Staff in 1949. The Middle East was "a stupendous source of strategic power, and one of the greatest material prizes in world history," as well as "probably the richest economic prize in the world in the field of foreign investment." That meant nobody else could interfere, and "nationalism" (the control of the country's resources by its own people) was a serious threat. As a State Department memo put it in 1958, "in a Near East under the control of radical nationalism, Western access to the resources of the area would be in constant jeopardy."[23]

Policy in Latin America, CIA historian Gerald Haines explained, was designed "to develop larger and more efficient sources of supply for the American economy, as well as create expanded markets for U.S. exports and expanded opportunities for the investment of American capital," permitting local development only "as long as it did not interfere with American profits and dominance." With regard to Latin America, Secretary of War Henry Stimson said, "I think that it's not asking too much to have our little region over here." President Taft had previously foreseen that "the day is not far distant" when "the whole hemisphere will be ours in fact as, by virtue of our superiority of race, it already is ours morally."[24]

The Latin American countries advocated what a State Department officer described as "the philosophy of the New Nationalism," which "embraces policies designed to bring about a broader distribution of wealth and to raise the standard of living of the masses." Another State Department expert reported that "Latin Americans are convinced that the first beneficiaries of the development of a country's resources should be the people of that country." These mistaken priorities ran directly counter to Washington's plans. The issue came to a head in a February 1945 hemispheric conference, where the United States put forth its "Economic Charter of the Americas," which called for an end to economic nationalism "in all its forms." The first beneficiaries of a country's resources must be U.S. investors and their local associates, not "the people of that country." There can be no "broader distribution of wealth" or improvement in "the standard of living of the masses," unless, by unlikely accident, that happens to result from policies designed to serve the interests of those with priority.[25]

The basic missions of global management have endured to this day, among them: containing other centers of global power within the "overall framework of order" managed by the United States; maintaining control of the world's energy supplies; barring unacceptable forms of independent nationalism; and keeping the U.S. domestic population from sticking their noses in.[26]

CONFRONTING THE IMPLICATIONS:
THE REALITY OF VIOLENCE FOR ITS VICTIMS

The human costs of the pursuit of dominance are for the most part kept out of the press, or not dwelt upon, and thus do not reach most of the public. Wars are sanitized. As Adam Smith pointed out, they can even become a kind of "amusement" for those who live far from the battle-field and only encounter conflicts as abstractions or collections of statistics. For those who safely inhabit "great empires," Smith said, "reading in the newspapers the exploits of their own fleets and armies" is exciting, and peace can even be disappointing, because it "puts an end to their amusement, and to a thousand visionary hopes of conquest and national glory from a longer continuance of the war."[27]

Discussions of foreign policy are often cool, abstract, and antiseptic. Feminist scholar Carol Cohn, investigating the community of "defense intellectuals" who specialize in planning for nuclear war, was disturbed by "the elaborate use of abstraction and euphemism, of words so bland that they never forced the speaker or enabled the listener to touch the realities of nuclear holocaust that lay behind the words." She found the men "likeable and admirable," but was "continually startled by . . . the bloodcurdling casualness with which they regularly blew up the world while standing and chatting over the coffee pot." Abstraction and euphemism also protect us from having to look into the eyes of the victims. They are removed from our consciousness. They do not speak.[28]

Those who see war up close know just how much worse it is than even terms like "horror" and "suffering" can convey. Ashleigh Banfield, who was ousted by NBC after speaking critically of the Iraq War, said in the lecture that got her fired that Americans did not understand what the war was really like because they were seeing curated images that didn't show the reality of civilian casualties. Journalists embedded with U.S. troops, for instance, would show soldiers firing M16s into a building, but not "where those bullets landed" or what happens when a mortar explodes. "A puff of smoke is not what a mortar looks like when it explodes, believe me," she said. But the puff of smoke was what Americans saw, with the result that "there are horrors that were completely left out of this war." Americans are never shown what it actually looks like when a U.S. drone strike hits a wedding party, or a child is crushed by a U.S. tank. They are rarely exposed to the accounts of those who have witnessed such gruesome spectacles, or to the voices of the family members who mourn the victims.[29]

Chris Hedges, who spent decades as a war correspondent for *The New York Times,* writes:

> If we really saw war, what war does to young minds and bodies, it would be harder to embrace the myth of war. If we had to stand over the mangled corpses of the schoolchildren killed in Afghanistan or Ukraine and listen to the wails of their parents, the clichés about liberating the women of Afghanistan or bringing freedom to the Afghan or Ukrainian people would be obscene. . . . Television reports give us the visceral thrill of force and hide from us the effects of bullets, tank rounds, iron fragmentation bombs, and artillery rounds. We taste a bit of war's exhilaration, but are protected from seeing what war actually does, its smells, noise, confusion, and most of all its overpowering fear.[30]

The casualties of war do not appear in U.S. armed forces recruitment material, and Donald Trump infamously specified he didn't want "wounded guys" in his military parade, because they wouldn't look good. War must be scrubbed clean.[31]

A FOG OF PROPAGANDA AND MYTH

In the United States, even to suggest that the country may have committed serious crimes can be considered scandalous and unpatriotic. For instance, when Samantha Power was nominated to be U.S. Ambassador to the United Nations in 2013, she was forced in her Senate hearing to disavow any previous comments that might imply that U.S. presidents had "committed" or "sponsored" crimes. "I would never apologize for America," Power promised Senator Marco Rubio, and affirmed that this country is a "light to the world." Power, widely regarded as a critic of U.S. foreign policy, would say only that "sometimes we as imperfect human beings do things we wish we had done a little bit differently," citing U.S. nonintervention in the Rwandan genocide. Rubio pressed her to make sure she disavowed any possible implication that the country could ever have committed a crime:

SENATOR RUBIO: So I would characterize the Rwanda situation as a crime "permitted" by the United States. Which ones did the country "commit" or "sponsor" that you were referring to?

MS. POWER: Again, sir, I think this is the greatest country on Earth. We have nothing to apologize for.

SENATOR RUBIO: So you don't have any in mind now that we have committed or sponsored?

MS. POWER: I will not apologize for America. I will stand very proudly, if confirmed, behind the U.S. placard.

SENATOR RUBIO: I understand, but do you believe the United States has committed or sponsored crimes?

MS. POWER: I believe the United States is the greatest country on Earth. I really do.

SENATOR RUBIO: So your answer to whether we've committed or sponsored crimes is that the United States is the greatest country on Earth?

MS. POWER: The United States is a leader in human rights, it's a leader in human dignity. As you know, one of the things that makes us so formidable as a leader on human rights is that when we make mistakes, and mistakes happen, for instance, in the case of Abu Ghraib in Iraq. Nobody is proud of that. Virtually every American soldier that is operating in the world is operating with profound honor and dignity. We hold people accountable. That's what we do because we believe in human rights. We believe in international humanitarian law and we observe those laws. We are, again unlike any other country, a country that stands by our principles.[32]

To be sure, there are those in the U.S. political elite who freely admit that considerations of elementary morality are absent from policymaking and believe that any savagery is justified if it serves the national interest. Tom Cotton, a Republican senator from Arkansas, writes in his foreign policy manifesto that "the goal of American strategy is the safety, freedom, and prosperity of the American people." For him, that means that whether something is good for the United States matters far more than whether it is legal, democratic, or moral. Hurting others to help ourselves is legitimate. Cotton is frank that the United States should support dictatorships when those dictatorships support the U.S.: "No one ever mistook Diem, Somoza, the shah, or Mubarak [a series of dictators supported by the United States] for the Little Sisters of the Poor. . . . But what matters, in the end, is less whether a country is democratic or non-democratic, and more whether the country is pro-American or anti-American."[33]

Yet even Cotton, who happily endorses the principle that dictatorships are good if they support us, does not reckon with what violence actually looks like in practice. He is content to talk in pleasant abstractions about freedom. He would surely prefer the public not look at the victims or think about them too much.

It would be easy, but illogical, to mistake the core claim of this book as something like: "The United States is the worst country in the world" or "The U.S. is responsible for all the problems in the world." Critics of the U.S. government have been labeled "America haters" or those who "blame America first."[34] But the core claim is actually modest: the United States is not uniquely evil. It is no worse than many other ruling powers have been.[35] It is just especially powerful, and it is captivated by a dangerous false mythology. As the global superpower, the U.S. poses unique risks; it is more consequential if a powerful country departs from a moral standard than if a weak one does.

The United States is hardly the first power in history to combine material interests, great technological capacity, and an utter disregard for the suffering and misery of the lower orders. Arrogant self-delusions are common in the history of nation-states—and dangerous, because they prevent countries from reckoning honestly with their own conduct. No one would be disturbed by an analysis of the political behavior of the Russians, French, or Tanzanians that questioned their motives and interpreted their actions in terms of long-range interests, perhaps well concealed behind official rhetoric. But it is an article of faith that American motives are pure and not subject to analysis. The long tradition of naïveté and self-righteousness that disfigures our intellectual history must serve as a warning to the world as to how our present-day protestations of sincerity and benign intent are to be interpreted.

Still, why focus on American crimes rather than the crimes of Russia or China? It is not that they don't commit major crimes. Instead, it's a very simple ethical point: It is of little moral value to condemn the wrongdoing of someone else and ignore one's own. Furthermore, we bear a responsibility for the predictable consequences of our actions. We are not responsible for the predictable consequences of somebody else's actions.

Thus, Americans should primarily criticize their government's conduct, because it is the government they are responsible for and whose behavior they have the greatest capacity to affect. Even if we conclude that the United States is responsible for only 2 percent of the preventable brutality in the world, we should still criticize primarily the U.S. government, because it is the one we can directly influence.

A moral truism that should be uncontroversial is the principle of universality: we should apply to ourselves the same standards we apply to others—in fact, more stringent ones. On the temple at Delphi, the famous maxim was inscribed: *Know thyself.* It is helpful, when assessing U.S. conduct, to ask a simple question: How would we judge a given act if it were performed by a rival power rather than ourselves? If we take this question seriously, it is not difficult to find acts that we would condemn as grave crimes if committed by others.

And so, let us try to apply basic moral standards. If we condemn terrorism, let us evaluate the actions of the United States and see whether they constitute terrorism, without treating it as axiomatic that terrorism is something only done by others. If we object to aggressive warfare and believe those who practice it ought to be sent to the Hague, let us see if we are willing to have the standard applied to ourselves. Let us test the proposition that the United States is a country committed to humanitarianism and democracy against the alternate hypothesis that the country is similar to virtually every other ruling power throughout the history of humanity, and that it acts in accordance with the Mafia Doctrine/vile maxim. Let us examine the interests and ideologies that guide U.S. decision-making and the use of power and have the courage to look honestly at what we find.

These points are not just academic. Precisely because U.S. policy decisions are so consequential and so dangerous, altering them is of the highest possible moral urgency.

POWER SYSTEMS IN GENERAL

It can be hard to break through the prevailing assumption that one must be on one side or the other, that one is either with the United States or an apologist for its adversaries.[36] But if we are to have a hope of reaching a world where people rule themselves, rather than being ruled by others, we must be able to see the illegitimate features common to nation-states around the world.

When we investigate the foreign policy of *any* state, we find first of all an official doctrine that attributes to state policy honorable intents, though occasional failure, due primarily to the machinations of evil enemies. For instance, during the Cold War, Soviet propaganda proclaimed the commitment of the Soviet Union to peace, democracy, and human rights, described the Soviet posture as defensive, and identified U.S. imperialism as the prime source of disorder and suffering throughout the world. Official U.S. doctrine was the mirror image.

The Cold War was understood as a contest between two opposite systems, and some leftists mistakenly believed the Soviet Union was a superior and more egalitarian form of society. But the similarities between the United States and the Soviet Union were just as important as the differences. Both were superpowers lacking meaningful popular control over the government. Both of their ruling ideologies (Marxist-Leninist communism and free-market capitalism) were largely false descriptions of how the societies actually operated.[37] In both, the power structure was a pyramid, with a small number of key decision-makers at the top and a mass of ordinary people at the bottom. A classic 1900s Industrial Workers of the World poster, showing the "pyramid of [the] capitalist system," is simplistic but remains roughly accurate. At the top are the leaders ("We rule you") while at the bottom are the workers, who "feed all" and "work for all." While many international conflicts concern the interests of those on the top level, the suffering and sacrifice in those conflicts falls entirely on those at the bottom level.

The purpose of this book is to demonstrate how the United States has actually wielded power in the world, what the consequences have been for many innocent people, and what are the risks that U.S. foreign policy now poses for the future of humanity. To do this, one must penetrate beneath self-serving myths and closely examine a large body of factual evidence. The only way to discover what kind of values U.S. leaders possess is to look at what they do, not what they say. And here we find a disturbing record, which includes overthrowing inconvenient foreign governments, supporting some of the most oppressive dictatorships in history, flagrantly violating both global public opinion and settled international law, and waging illegal wars with catastrophic humanitarian consequences. It is a record of election interference, nuclear threats, climate crime, and outright assassinations that would get any other country labeled a terrorist state.

We will begin by documenting U.S. conduct toward the rest of the world over the past half century, in the hopes that a thorough recounting of facts will demonstrate the size of the gap between the rhetoric and the record. The chapters are not intended to be full histories of the events in question, but evidence of the extent to which national myths have prevailed over truth. The crimes discussed are not ancient history. People who experienced them are still alive today, even if their voices go unheard. The wounds are still fresh.

We will then move on, in a brief part 2, to examine commonalities across cases. We will investigate the techniques that serve to reinforce our moral blindness, our wondrous capacity for self-adulation, and the intellectual armory that ensures that nothing is learned. First, we'll examine how the domestic structure of power helps explain U.S. conduct in the world. We will see that what is called the pursuit of the "national interest" does not, in fact, serve the interest of the overwhelming majority of the U.S. population, who are kept in the dark and excluded from meaningful decision-making. This is followed by a look at the U.S. relationship to international law, and the postwar presidents' unwillingness to subject the U.S. to the same rules we demand others conform to. Finally, we look at the role of the press and state propaganda in "manufacturing consent" for U.S. policy.

We conclude by reviewing the most pressing risks facing the world in our time, and the possibilities for averting disaster through concerted activism by popular movements. Humanity faces serious crises today that threaten the entire future of the species, in the form of climate catastrophe and the possibility of nuclear war. The challenge we face is to live up to the moral responsibilities that come with living in the most powerful state in the world at the most dangerous moment in human history.

When populations around the world are surveyed, they have ranked the United States as a greater threat to world peace and democracy than Russia or China. Much that is documented here has long been obvious to the victims of American aggression. They can only laugh when they hear U.S. presidents speak of the country's commitment to humane values.[38]

But for those in the United States, it is critically important to see through American mythology about Noble Intent. It may seem obvious that the interests of dominant elite groups are more important to foreign policy than basic moral principles, and that "American exceptionalism" is a fiction. The critical fact is that it is a *dangerous* fiction. The myth of American idealism is used to excuse behavior that has caused colossal amounts of death and destruction. It has kept us from holding our war criminals to account. It now blinds many Americans to the ways in which their country's policies threaten the violent destruction of humankind itself.

But the situation can be changed. We can act. Both "world order" and "domestic order" are based on decisions made within institutions that reflect existing power structures. The decisions can be made differently. The institutions can be modified or replaced. Those who benefit from the existing organization of state and private power will naturally portray existing arrangements as inevitable. But there is no reason to believe them. Particularly in the rich countries that dominate world affairs, citizens can easily act to create alternatives even within existing formal arrangements. These are not graven in stone.

PART 1

The Record

Idealism in Action

Large nations do what they wish, while small nations accept what they must.

—THUCYDIDES

1

Disciplining the Global South

On September 11, 1973, General Augusto Pinochet seized control of Chile from the democratically elected president, Salvador Allende. Pinochet, who was one of the most brutal dictators in recent history, conducted mass murder and torture, set up an assassination program to pursue dissidents who fled abroad, and imprisoned tens of thousands of people. He ended Chile's democracy for a generation. Per capita, if Pinochet's terror had occurred in the United States, it would have meant 150,000 deaths and a million torture victims, as well as the overthrow of the president and the end of the electoral system. The first 9/11 was pure state terrorism.

In his memoirs, former National Security Advisor and Secretary of State Henry Kissinger is frank about the U.S. role in bringing this outcome about. Allende's leftist presidency posed "a permanent challenge to our position in the Western Hemisphere." Kissinger dismisses any concerns about the legitimacy of interfering in other countries' elections or trying to engineer coups, writing that "I cannot accept the proposition that the United States is debarred from acting in the gray area between diplomacy and military intervention." He recounts that when Allende was first elected, Richard Nixon went berserk and "wanted a major effort to see what could be done to prevent Allende's accession to power: If there were one chance in ten of getting rid of Allende we should try it." Nixon's CIA encouraged and funded a plot that murdered General René Schneider, the commander in chief of the Chilean army, whose commitment to the country's constitution was seen as an obstacle to a successful coup. Nixon ordered that "aid programs to Chile should be cut; its economy should be squeezed until it 'screamed,'" that is, the lives of the Chilean people should be made as miserable as possible to punish them for voting the wrong way.[1]

Peter Kornbluh's *The Pinochet File*, released by the National Security Archive, uses declassified documents to show how the U.S. government tried to undermine and destroy Allende from the moment he was elected and lavished support on Pinochet after the coup, while lying continually about its role. The Nixon administration imposed an "invisible blockade," and "NSC records show conclusively that the Nixon administration moved quickly, quietly and politically to shut down multilateral and bilateral aid to Chile" once Allende took office, blaming the resulting economic chaos on Allende's own policies. Kissinger falsely testified to the Senate in 1974 that "the intent of the United States was not to destabilize or subvert" Allende, despite having internally recommended a course of action that "might lead to [Allende's] collapse or overthrow." Kissinger was clear in explaining to Nixon why Allende could not be allowed to succeed. "I don't see why we need to stand by and watch a country go communist due to the irresponsibility of its people. The issues are much too important for the Chilean voters to be left to decide for themselves," Kissinger said. Allende posed "some very serious threats" to U.S. interests, including the possibility of lost "U.S. investments (totaling some one billion dollars)" but also the "model effect" that Allende would have on the world if his country flourished. The "example of a successful Marxist government" would have "precedent value" elsewhere and the "imitative spread of similar phenomena" would "significantly affect the world balance and our own position in it." Nixon himself said that "our main concern in Chile is the prospect that [Allende] can consolidate himself and the picture presented to the world will be his success."[2]

Thus, just days after Allende was inaugurated, Nixon convened the National Security Council to discuss ways to "bring about his downfall." A 1970 CIA telegram said that it "is firm and continuing policy that Allende be overthrown by a coup" and promising "maximum pressure toward this end utilizing every appropriate resource," while warning that "it is imperative that these actions be implemented clandestinely and securely so that the USG [United States Government] and American hand be well hidden."[3]

Stephen M. Streeter, in a comprehensive study based on the U.S. archives, concludes that "the maximal goal of the Nixon administration was to block Allende from the presidency by either constitutional means or by promoting a military coup," while "the minimal goal became punishing Chile so that no other Latin American country would be tempted to imitate the Chilean road to socialism." Once Allende's downfall was effected, the Nixon administration immediately embraced the Pinochet junta. Kissinger told Pinochet he had done a "great service to the West" by ending Chilean democracy.[4]

The problem with Allende was that he had posed the threat of a good example. If he had succeeded in his course of independent nationalism and leftist economics, he would have inspired other countries to act similarly. This could have diminished U.S. power. Allende had to go.

After World War II, postwar planners like George Kennan realized that it would be vital for the health of U.S. corporations that the Western industrial societies rebuild so they could import U.S. manufactured goods and provide investment opportunities.

But it was crucial to restore the traditional order, with business dominant, labor split and weakened, and the burden of reconstruction placed squarely on the shoulders of the working classes and the poor. The major thing that stood in the way was the anti-fascist resistance.

The United States, therefore, actively suppressed it all over the world, often preferring to have former fascists and Nazi collaborators in power.[5] Sometimes that required extreme violence, but other times it was done by softer measures, like subverting elections and withholding desperately needed food.

U.S. planners recognized that the "threat" in postwar Europe was not Soviet aggression, although the Truman administration led the public to think otherwise. "It is not Russian military power which is threatening us, it is Russian political power," George Kennan concluded in 1947. Historian Melvyn Leffler writes, "Soviet power paled next to that of the United States," because it was an "exhausted, devastated nation," and U.S. officials, therefore, "did not expect Soviet military aggression." What was a threat was "the prospective renaissance of virulent nationalism or the development of independent neutralism." The planners "defined security in terms of correlations of power" and "defined power in terms of control over or access to resources," by which logic any threat to U.S. control of resources was a threat to national security.[6]

As Leffler writes, after the war peoples across the world "wanted a more just and equitable social and economic order," demanding "reform, nationalization, and social welfare." They now "expected their governments to protect them from the vagaries of business fluctuations, the avarice of capitalists, and the occasional disasters of the natural world," viewing this as "their due for the sacrifices they had endured and the hardships they had overcome."

In Italy, for instance, a worker- and peasant-based movement, led by the Communist Party, had held down six German divisions during the war and liberated northern Italy. As U.S. forces advanced through Italy, they dispersed this anti-fascist resistance and restored the basic structure of the prewar fascist regime. The CIA was concerned about Communists winning power legally in the crucial Italian elections of 1948. Many techniques were used, including restoring the former fascist police, breaking the unions, and withholding aid. But it wasn't clear that the Communist Party could be defeated. The very first National Security Council memorandum, NSC 1 (1948), specified a number of actions the United States would take if the communists won these elections. One planned response was armed intervention, by means of military aid for underground operations in Italy. The U.S. was willing to consider supporting a coup to stop the left, despite the known "probability [of] plunging Italy into [a] bloody civil war and seriously hazarding [the] start [of] World War III." The right to override the population is assumed.[7]

Election interference was conducted regularly. From 1948 through the early 1970s, the CIA funneled over $65 million to approved political parties and affiliates. "We had bags of money that we delivered to selected politicians, to defray their expenses," former CIA officer F. Mark Wyatt admitted.[8] In fact, between 1946 and 2000, the United States undertook over eighty election-interference operations around the world. *The New York Times* national security correspondent Scott Shane suggests that such operations, including the planting of fake news and delivering "suitcases of cash" to favored candidates, continue to this day, noting that "what the C.I.A. may have done in recent years to steer foreign elections is still secret and may not be known for decades." Shane quotes one ex-CIA officer confirming that "it never changes," and another saying "I hope we keep doing it." The issue of whether this is legitimate does not come up for public debate, though there was great hysteria about Vladimir Putin's attempt to influence the American presidential election.[9]

In Greece, British troops entered the country after the Nazis had withdrawn. They imposed a corrupt regime that evoked renewed resistance, and Britain, in its postwar decline, was unable to maintain control. In 1947, the United States moved in, supporting a murderous war to suppress the provisional government that resulted in up to 160,000 deaths. This war was complete with torture, political exile for tens of thousands of Greeks, a "reeducation" program for imprisoned leftists, and the destruction of unions and of any possibility of independent politics.

Much of the population had to emigrate in order to survive. The beneficiaries included U.S. investors and Nazi collaborators, while the primary victims were the workers and the peasants of the communist-led, anti-Nazi resistance. Our successful defense of Greece against its own population was the model for the Vietnam War—as Adlai Stevenson explained to the United Nations in 1964: "The point is the same in Vietnam today as it was in Greece in 1947 and in Korea in 1950." Reagan's advisers used exactly the same model in talking about Central America, and the pattern was followed in many other places as well.[10]

In Japan, Washington initiated the so-called reverse course of 1947 that terminated early steps toward democratization taken by General MacArthur's military administration. The reverse course suppressed the unions and other democratic forces. It purged nearly thirty thousand suspected leftists from public- and private-sector jobs as well as teaching posts, and placed the country firmly in the hands of corporate elements that had backed Japanese fascism. (The United States even covered up Japanese war crimes.) As historians John Dower and Hirata Tetsuo conclude, while the "Red Purge was aggressively pursued as part of the anti-communist policy of the Occupation . . . the reality was that it was a confrontation between labour and capital." Dower writes that over time, the U.S. "began to jettison many of the original ideals of 'demilitarization and democratization,'" and "aligned themselves more and more openly with conservative and even right-wing elements in Japanese society, including individuals who had been closely identified with the lost war."[11]

When U.S. forces entered Korea in 1945, they dispersed the local popular government, consisting primarily of anti-fascists who had resisted the Japanese, and inaugurated a brutal repression, using Japanese fascist police and Koreans who had collaborated with them during the Japanese occupation. About one hundred thousand people were murdered in South Korea prior to what we call the Korean War, including thirty to forty thousand killed during the suppression of a peasant revolt in one small region, Cheju Island. That massacre, for which there is a "a deep, deep American responsibility" (in the words of historian Bruce Cumings), was carried out by South Korean military and police under U.S. command. One eighty-three-year-old survivor of the Cheju Island massacre, asked in 2022 what he wanted from the United States, said that all he needs is a "truthful human apology, a willingness to come and hold my hands." He is still waiting.[12]

THE THREAT OF A GOOD EXAMPLE

The goal of U.S. strategy is to prevent any challenge to the "power, position, and prestige of the United States," as the respected liberal elder statesman Dean Acheson put it in 1963. The weakest, poorest countries often arouse the greatest hysteria. After all, if a tiny, powerless country defies the United States, it exposes the U.S. itself as a "paper tiger." As Michael Grow demonstrates in *U.S. Presidents and Latin American Interventions: Pursuing Regime Change in the Cold War*, countries deemed "threats" were no threat to U.S. security or even U.S. economic interests. They could, however, inspire further defiance elsewhere and undermine U.S. "credibility."[13]

Take a minor example: British Guiana, where the Kennedy administration approved a covert CIA operation aimed at influencing the national elections. The goal of this operation was to prevent Cheddi Jagan, a dentist with socialist leanings, and his party from winning the elections. They would not tolerate a "second Cuba," meaning another leftist government in the hemisphere. Declassified documents and historical records indicate that the CIA was authorized to spend substantial resources on subverting democracy. The U.S. attempted to prevent British Guiana from obtaining independence from Britain in order to stall the possibility of social democracy breaking out. American actions also included inciting violence and unrest, with reports of U.S. officials and private citizens being involved in promoting murder, arson, bombings, and creating a general atmosphere of fear. Secretary of State Dean Rusk told Britain that he had "reached the conclusion that it is not possible for us to put up with an independent British Guiana under Jagan." It is simply assumed that it is the U.S. prerogative to decide which leaders we will "put up with." Stephen Rabe, the leading historian of U.S. intervention in British Guiana, summarizes the horrendous results: "destroying a popularly elected government, undermining democratic electoral procedures, wrecking the economy of a poor nation, and inciting racial warfare. Forbes Burnham, the vicious racist embraced by the United States, made Guiana a dangerous, brutal place and a daily nightmare for the majority Indian population." British Guiana was of no economic consequence to the United States and certainly posed no threat to "national security." The intervention was pure Mafia logic: *What we say goes.* The need to humiliate those who raise their heads is an ineradicable element of the imperial mentality.[14]

Or take the Democratic Republic of Congo, a huge country rich in resources—and one of the worst contemporary horror stories. It had a chance for successful development after independence in 1960, under the leadership of Prime Minister Patrice Lumumba. But the West would have none of that. CIA head Allen Dulles determined that Lumumba's "removal must be an urgent and prime objective" of covert action, not least because U.S. investments might be endangered by what internal documents refer to as "radical nationalists." The CIA attempted to arrange Lumumba's "permanent disposal." Under the supervision of Belgian officers, Lumumba was murdered, realizing President Eisenhower's wish that he "would fall into a river full of crocodiles." Emmanuel Gerard and Bruce Kuklick, in their definitive study of the murder, conclude that "the Europeans and Americans goaded the Africans to imprison Lumumba and to secure a capital sentence," because "the West could not conceive a stand-alone African state akin to European countries in its economic and political capabilities," and "Lumumba aspired to a greatness the West would not abide." It was not the only such case. American intervention in postcolonial Africa was extensive and secretive. As Susan Williams writes in *White Malice: The CIA and the Covert Recolonization of Africa*, the years of African independence "were also the years of an intense and rapid infiltration into Africa by the CIA," and the record "reveals an extent and breadth of CIA activities in Africa that beggars belief." Congo itself was handed over to the U.S. favorite, the murderous and corrupt dictator Mobutu Sese Seko. Stuart Reid, in *The Lumumba Plot*, says that because "a seemingly pro-Soviet leader had been eliminated and replaced with a seemingly pro-American one," "in Washington's estimation, the Congo was a success."[15]

The war on Vietnam, too, emerged from the need to ensure dominance. Vietnamese nationalists would not accept it, so they had to be smashed. The threat was never that this mostly peasant population was going to conquer anyone. It was that they might set a dangerous example of national independence that would inspire other nations in the region. The real fear was that if the people of Indochina achieved independence and justice, the people of Thailand might emulate their example, and if they succeeded, Malaya would follow suit. Pretty soon Indonesia would pursue an independent path, and by then a significant part of our "Grand Area" would have been lost.

This means that in a way, there was truth to what was called the "domino theory." The publicly presented version of the theory was, of course, ludicrous, with its suggestion that Communism would come to U.S. shores if it wasn't defeated in Vietnam. The real threat is the "good example." U.S. planners from Dean Acheson in the late 1940s to the present have warned that "one rotten apple can spoil the barrel." The danger is that the "rot," namely social and economic development, might spread. This is why such minor countries, such as British Guiana or Grenada or Laos, must be kept in line.

The security arguments are too ludicrous to consider, and it is surely not the case that their resources were too valuable to lose. Rather, the concern was about a kind of "domino" effect. But under the rotten-apple theory, it follows that the tinier and weaker the country, the less endowed it is with resources, the more dangerous it is. As a George H. W. Bush National Security Policy Review on "third world threats" explained, "much weaker enemies" must not simply be defeated, but defeated decisively and quickly, because any other outcome would be "embarrassing" and might "undercut political support." A "much weaker" enemy poses no serious threat, but must be pulverized in order to reinforce the lesson. If even a marginal and impoverished country can set out on an independent path, others may follow.[16]

If you want a global system subordinated to the needs of U.S. investors, pieces of it must not wander off. Chile could send the wrong message to voters elsewhere. Suppose they get ideas about taking control of their own country. This would not do. Secretary of State John Foster Dulles described Latin Americans as "naughty children who are exercising all the privileges and rights of grown-ups" and require "a stiff hand, an authoritative hand" (though he advised President Eisenhower that to control the naughty children more effectively, it may be useful to "pat them a little bit and make them think that you are fond of them"). As historian Lars Schoultz, a leading academic specialist on human rights in Latin America, concludes, the goal of installing National Security States was "to destroy permanently a perceived threat to the existing structure of socioeconomic privilege by eliminating the political participation of the numerical majority."[17]

Sometimes the point is explained with great clarity. When the United States was planning to overthrow Guatemalan democracy in 1954, a State Department official pointed out that the country's "agrarian reform is a powerful propaganda weapon," its "broad social program of aiding the workers and peasants" having a "strong appeal" to other Central American countries with highly unequal societies. Guatemala is therefore a "threat to the stability of Honduras and El Salvador."[18]

In other words, what the United States wants is "stability," meaning security for the "upper classes and large foreign enterprises." If that can be achieved with formal democratic devices, all the better. If not, the "threat to stability" posed by a good example has to be destroyed before it infects others. This is why even the tiniest speck poses so great a threat.

CUBA: THE INFERNAL LITTLE REPUBLIC

Soon after Cuba overthrew its U.S.-supported dictator, Fulgencio Batista, this small island was subjected to vicious attack by the global superpower. Fidel Castro came to power in early 1959. By March 1960, a secret decision had been made to depose Castro. The incoming John F. Kennedy administration carried out the Bay of Pigs invasion in 1961, sending a paramilitary force to overthrow the Cuban government, in what became an embarrassing defeat.

Its failure led to hysteria in Washington. Chester Bowles, then serving in the State Department, recalled that a common attitude among high officials was "emotional, almost savage": "[Castro] can't do this to us. We've got to teach him a lesson." Kennedy launched a war to bring "the terrors of the earth" to Cuba. His brother Robert Kennedy, who was placed in charge of the operation, wanted to find Cubans who could "stir things up on [the] island with espionage, sabotage, general disorder." The Cuba Task Force launched a campaign aimed at "the destruction of targets important to the economy."[19]

The CIA's many plots to assassinate Castro are by now infamous and can easily be seen as comical (exploding cigar, toxic wetsuit, etc.). Any other nation similarly hell-bent on murdering a head of state, however, would be deemed a terrorist state. In fact, even more deranged criminal schemes were cooked up, including a CIA "proposal to have U.S. agents hijack U.S. planes or bomb U.S. targets and blame the attacks on Cuba to build a pretext for invasion." This was never implemented, but plenty of other forms of terror were. In one mission, "a seven-man team blew up a railroad bridge and watched a train run off the track, and burned down a sugar warehouse." "We were really doing almost anything you could dream up," a CIA official said later, including putting contaminants in sugar and pouring "invisible, untraceable chemicals into lubricating fluids that were being shipped to Cuba" to damage diesel engines. As Keith Bolender documents in his haunting study *Voices from the Other Side: An Oral History of Terrorism Against Cuba*,

"For half a century the Cuban people have endured almost every conceivable form of terrorism": bombings of civilian targets, attacks on villages, and even biological terrorism. "The accused," he writes, "have been primarily Cuban-American counter-revolutionaries—many allegedly trained, financed, and supported by various American government agencies."[20]

In 1962, Kennedy ordered a total embargo on Cuba. In direct violation of international law, it included a ban on drugs and food products. High officials explained internally that "the Cuban people are responsible for the regime." Therefore, the United States has the right to punish them, and furthermore, "if [the Cuban people] are hungry, they will throw Castro out." Kennedy agreed that the embargo would hasten Fidel Castro's departure as a result of "rising discomfort among hungry Cubans." A high State Department official in 1960 articulated the strategy. Because Castro could be removed "through disenchantment and disaffection based on economic dissatisfaction and hardship . . . every possible means should be undertaken promptly to weaken the economic life of Cuba [in order to] bring about hunger, desperation and [the] overthrow of the government." These economic measures would "have the effect of impressing on the Cuban people the cost of this communist orientation." The U.S. succeeded in isolating Cuba diplomatically, but efforts in 1961 to organize other Latin American countries to join Kennedy's efforts were unsuccessful, perhaps because of a problem noted by a Mexican diplomat: "If we publicly declare that Cuba is a threat to our security, forty million Mexicans will die laughing."[21]

Salim Lamrani, in his definitive study on the embargo, points out how extreme its restrictions have consistently been. The United States put "strong diplomatic pressure" on countries that declined to help isolate the island, even threatening to withhold economic aid. In 1999, the State Department successfully pressured a Jamaican company not to build a hotel complex there. The Swedish company Ericsson was fined $1.75 million for having repaired Cuban equipment, while the Treasury

Department fined an American firm $1.35 million for selling barley. (Lamrani notes again that this violates international law, which prohibits inhibiting the trade of foodstuffs, even in wartime.) The effects of the embargo policy have, of course, been severe.[22]

Particularly onerous has been the impact on the health-care system, deprived of essential medical supplies. Amnesty International showed that "the embargo had contributed to malnutrition that mainly affected women and children, poor water supply and lack of medicine." In 1992, Congress passed what was called the "Cuban Democracy Act" (CDA), initiated by liberal Democrats and strongly backed by President Clinton. A yearlong investigation by the American Association of World Health found that this escalation of U.S. economic warfare had taken a "tragic human toll," causing "serious nutritional deficits" and "a devastating outbreak of neuropathy numbering in the tens of thousands." A "humanitarian catastrophe has been averted only because the Cuban government has maintained" a health system that "is uniformly considered the preeminent model in the Third World." The UN Human Rights Council has concluded that the embargo directly produces "limitations of the enjoyment of human rights by citizens in Cuba." But these do not count as human rights violations in the prevailing doctrinal framework; rather, the public version is that the goal of the sanctions is to *counteract* Cuba's human rights violations.[23]

Notably, there has scarcely been a word of protest in elite sectors. The rest of the world, and even the majority of the U.S. population, opposes U.S. policy toward Cuba. But successive governments have maintained illegal, brutal policies toward Cuba with utter fanaticism. As Lars Schoultz noted in a 2009 study, the U.S. "has not simply declined to have normal diplomatic and economic relations with Havana for half a century" but has "spent most of these past five decades openly and actively trying to overthrow the island's government—or, in the euphemism-cloaked circumlocutions of today's Commission for Assistance to a Free Cuba, trying to 'hasten Cuba's transition.'"[24]

What was Cuba's crime toward the United States? What explained the hysterical approach, the collective punishment, the decades of support for outright terrorism? Why was the U.S. willing to defy international law and the entirety of global public opinion in an attempt to destroy a small island nation? Lamrani notes that the public explanations shifted across the decades. First it was Castro's nationalization of U.S.-owned property (i.e., giving Cuba's wealth to Cuba). Then it was Cuba's ties to the Soviet Union. (The justification had never made sense, because the relationship was as much the product of U.S. policy as its cause.) Then it was Cuba's support for liberation movements in the Global South. Finally, after the Cold War ended and destroyed the long-standing justifications for harsh policies toward Cuba, policymakers professed to be deeply concerned by Cuba's human rights abuses. (Laughable, as U.S. support for human rights abusers around the world was continuing as usual.)[25]

In fact, we know from the annals of State Department records precisely what the "Cuban threat" was, namely "successful defiance." Castro had demonstrated contempt for the interests of U.S. investors and was committed to redistributionist policies. The model, if successful, could spread, posing a threat to "U.S. interests" (i.e., U.S. business interests) around the world. John F. Kennedy had worried on the campaign trail that "the same poverty and discontent and distrust of America which Castro rode to power are smoldering in almost every Latin nation." Richard Nixon made it plain, in his memo on his 1959 meeting with Fidel Castro, that "what concerned me most" was Castro's "almost slavish subservience to prevailing majority opinion—the voice of the mob—rather than his naïve attitude toward Communism." Castro "seemed to be obsessed with the idea that it was his responsibility to carry out the will of the people whatever it might appear to be at a particular time."[26]

Arthur Schlesinger Jr., as head of a Latin American mission, reported to Kennedy that the Cuban revolution risked "the spread of the Castro idea of taking matters into one's own hands." This idea, he said, had a great deal of appeal throughout Latin America, where "the distribution of land and other forms of national wealth greatly favors the propertied classes . . . [and] the poor and underprivileged, stimulated by the example of the Cuban revolution, are now demanding opportunities for a decent living." The CIA observed that "Castro's shadow looms large because social and economic conditions throughout Latin America invite opposition to ruling authority and encourage agitation for radical change."[27]

American attempts to control Cuba date back to the Monroe Doctrine of 1823, which declared Washington's right to dominate the hemisphere. John Quincy Adams instructed his cabinet colleagues that U.S. power would increase while Britain's declined, so that Cuba (indeed the hemisphere) would fall into U.S. hands by the laws of "political gravitation," as an apple falls from a tree. As historian Ada Ferrer documents, the U.S. claimed the right "to exercise permanent, indirect rule" and to "intervene militarily in Cuba, uninvited." Indeed, as Keith Bolender explains, the U.S. was convinced that "ownership of Cuba was natural, preordained, and key to fulfilling vital national expectations." In U.S. propaganda, Cubans were consistently depicted as unable to control their own country, with the country variously portrayed as "a helpless woman, a defenseless baby, a child in need of direction, an incompetent freedom fighter, an ignorant farmer, an ignoble ingrate, an ill-bred revolutionary, a viral communist."[28]

By 1898, Adams's laws of political gravitation had worked their magic, and the United States was able to carry out the military operation known as "the liberation of Cuba," in reality the intervention to prevent Cuba from liberating itself from Spanish rule, converting it to what historians Ernest May and Philip Zelikow rightly call a "virtual colony" of the United States. Cuba's major port on Guantánamo Bay has remained an *actual* colony, held under a 1903 treaty that Cuba was forced to sign at gunpoint, and used in recent years, in violation of the terms of the so-called treaty, as a detention camp for Haitians fleeing the terror of the U.S.-backed military junta, and as a torture chamber for those suspected of having harmed, or intended to harm, the U.S.[29]

The "virtual colony" gained liberation in 1959. Within months the assault began, using the weapons of violence and economic strangulation to punish the inhabitants of "that infernal little Republic" that had so angered the racist expansionist Theodore Roosevelt that he wanted to "wipe its people off the face of the earth." To this day, Cubans refuse to comprehend that their role is to serve the master, not to play at independence. Lamrani concludes that "the state of economic siege of which the Cuban people are victims reminds us that the United States—by applying wartime measures in times of peace against a nation that has never been a threat to its national security—apparently has still not abandoned its old colonial aspiration of integrating Cuba into the U.S."[30]

OUR LITTLE REGION OVER HERE

The way to deal with a virus is to kill it and inoculate any possible victims. Cuba survived, but without the ability to achieve its feared potential. Latin America was "inoculated" with harsh dictatorships, such as the coup that established a military regime in Brazil in 1964. The generals had carried out a "democratic rebellion," Ambassador Lincoln Gordon cabled home. The rebellion was "a great victory for the free world," he exulted, which should "create a greatly improved climate for private investments." By removing what Washington saw as a Castro clone, the generals had achieved "the single most decisive victory of freedom in the mid-twentieth century." Brazil remained under military rule until 1985.[31]

A 1954 policy statement by the National Security Council lays out U.S. doctrine frankly. Recognizing a "trend in Latin America toward nationalistic regimes maintained in large part by appeals to the masses of the population," and concerned about both "anti-U.S. prejudices" and "increasing popular demand for immediate improvement in the low living standards of the masses," official policy is to "arrest the drift in the area toward radical and nationalistic regimes." Nationalism is off-limits to Latin Americans, because it entails a government that favors the population's own interest rather than the interests of the United States. The task of the U.S. is to ensure that the countries "base their economies on a system of private enterprise" and "create a political and economic climate conducive to private investment," with militaries that have an "understanding of, and orientation toward, U.S. objectives." The objectives of U.S. policy in Latin America are: "hemisphere solidarity in support of our world policies," "orderly" development, "the safeguarding of the hemisphere" through the development of military forces, the elimination of the communist "menace," access by the U.S. to raw materials, achieving support for our foreign policy elsewhere, and "standardization of Latin American military organization, training, doctrine and equipment along U.S. lines." Note the distinct absence of idealistic rhetoric about self-government and civil liberties.[32]

"Communist" was a term regularly used in American political theology to refer to people who are committed to the belief that "the government has direct responsibility for the welfare of the people," in the words of a 1949 State Department intelligence report. Or as John Foster Dulles put it, "communists" are those who appeal to "the poor people [who] have always wanted to plunder the rich." The primary threat is that it will lead nations to transform their economies "in ways which reduce their willingness and ability to complement the industrial economies of the West." (That is essentially correct and is a good operational definition of "communism" in U.S. political discourse.) So it is small wonder, with this kind of background, that John F. Kennedy should say that "governments of the civil military type of El Salvador are the most effective in containing Communist penetration in Latin America."[33]

The pattern was set. In Guatemala, for instance, democratic capitalist president Jacobo Árbenz had pursued some of the feared nationalist policies: expanding the right to vote, allowing workers to organize, and distributing uncultivated land to the poor. Naturally, this created panic. A CIA memorandum of 1953 described the situation in Guatemala as "adverse to U.S. interests" because of the "Communist influence . . . based on militant advocacy of social reforms and nationalistic policies." These "radical" policies included "persecution of foreign economic interests, especially the United Fruit Company," an action that had gained "the support or acquiescence of almost all Guatemalans." The government was proceeding "to mobilize the hitherto politically inert peasantry" while undermining the power of large landholders. To make matters worse, "a strong national movement" had formed "to free Guatemala from the military dictatorship, social backwardness, and 'economic colonialism'" that had characterized the past. The success of land reform threatened "stability" in neighboring countries where suffering people did not fail to take notice. Historian Greg Grandin notes that Árbenz was "enormously popular" and had "a mandate to extend the ideals of political democracy into the social realm." In short, the situation was dire.[34]

So the CIA carried out a successful coup, drawing "on all the advances in psychological warfare." Guatemalan democracy was ended. The country would be turned into one of the worst slaughterhouses in the hemisphere.[35]

Following the coup that destroyed Guatemalan democracy in 1954, the country was ruled by a series of brutal military officers and swiftly collapsed into civil war. During this time, as regional historian Kirsten Weld writes, "In their quest to maintain U.S. influence, protect U.S. business interests, and contain global 'communism,'" U.S. advisers in Guatemala "abetted and encouraged domestic elites' efforts to obliterate any voices calling for change in the society." The United States knew full well, as a State Department memo in 1968 conceded, that Guatemalan security forces would continue "to be used, as in the past, not so much as protectors of the nation against communist enslave-ment, but as the oligarchy's oppressors of legitimate social change."[36]

In 1977, the human rights abuses became so severe that the Carter administration ostensibly cut off military aid to the country. (In fact, between 1978 and 1980, the "human rights"–focused Carter adminis-tration gave Guatemala millions of dollars through the State De-partment's Military Assistance Program and Foreign Military Sales program.) The Reagan administration ended even the pretense of car-ing about human rights in Guatemala, and Reagan warmly embraced the country's military dictator, saying Ríos Montt had gotten a "bum rap," describing him as a "man of great personal integrity" who was "totally dedicated to democracy in Guatemala." Reagan pledged to restore mil-itary aid even as international human rights organizations documented massacres committed by the Guatemalan army. The government was in fact carrying out one of the worst acts of genocide in the modern his-tory of the Americas, with the close collaboration of U.S. military and intelligence units. Eventually, Ríos Montt was sentenced to eighty years in prison, the first time a former head of state had been convicted of genocide in their own country. "One is tempted to believe," said Guate-malan journalist Julio Godoy, "that some people in the White House worship Aztec gods—with the offering of Central American blood."[37]

A history of U.S. support for murderers in the Western Hemisphere would take many volumes.[38] As Greg Grandin writes, "by the end of the Cold War, Latin American security forces trained, funded, equipped, and incited by Washington had executed a reign of bloody terror—hundreds of thousands killed, an equal number tortured, millions driven into exile, from which the region has yet to recover." For instance, in Bolivia, president Juan José Torres was ousted in 1971 by General Hugo Banzer. Torres had established a People's Assembly representing the working class (peasants, students, teachers, miners, etc.), one of those "radical" policies that made him unacceptable to Washington. Henry Kissinger had worried that Torres would be "ultra-nationalistic, leftist and anti-U.S.," and soon ordered the CIA to "crank up an operation post-haste" to remove Torres. Banzer's coup was backed by the United States, and once in power he was bolstered by significant U.S. military aid (the Banzer government received $63 million in the first year alone). Banzer's regime arrested and tortured thousands of people, "disappeared" 155 without a trace, and drove 19,000 people out of the country. This did not stop U.S. ambassador Ernest Siracusa from describing Banzer as an "attractive," "sympathetic," "typically Catholic family man" who had no "intent" to be repressive.[39]

Torres was abducted and killed in 1976 as part of Operation Condor, a decades-long U.S.-supported program of state terrorism. Condor was a collaboration between right-wing Latin American military governments across the hemisphere that aimed to "find and kill" those deemed "terrorists" or "subversives," according to a 1976 State Department memo, which noted that "subversion" included "nearly anyone who opposes government policy." As leading Operation Condor expert John Dinges writes, drawing on declassified archives, the United States was in an "intimate embrace with mass murderers running torture camps, body dumps, and crematoriums, and who brought their terrorist operations to our own streets" (referring to the assassination of refugee economist Orlando Letelier by agents of Pinochet on the streets of Washington, DC). According to Dinges, the military governments "were not only led to believe, they were told explicitly in secret meetings that U.S. human rights policy was public and tactical only and that United States sympathies were with the regimes that had overturned democracies and were killing thousands of their own citizens."[40]

In Argentina, a 1976 coup ousted Isabel Perón, the president, paving the way for General Jorge Rafael Videla's military dictatorship, termed the "National Reorganization Process." This overthrow garnered implicit acceptance and support from the Ford administration in the United States. Videla labeled anyone a "terrorist" who "encourag[ed] others through ideas that go against our Western and Christian civilization," and responded to this pseudo-"terror" with very real terror. As

Stephen Rabe writes, Argentine security forces "abducted seven high school students in La Plata and murdered six of them because the students had the temerity to protest the elimination of subsidies for student fares on the city's buses," and "murdered a paraplegic, José Liborio Poblete, because he wrote a petition calling on companies to hire a fixed percentage of disabled workers." During Videla's rule, the United States maintained strong diplomatic ties with Argentina, evidenced by multiple official visits from Secretary of State Henry Kissinger. Rabe notes that Kissinger outright "sanctioned state terrorism" by the dictatorship, telling the Argentine foreign minister, "We understand you must establish authority," asking only that "if there are things that have to be done, you should do them quickly."[41]

THE MALIGNANCY IN MANAGUA

In the 1980s, U.S. policy toward Central America was marked by a brutal insistence on crushing any leftist or popular movements, often under the pretext of preventing the spread of communism. The U.S. intervention in Nicaragua following the overthrow of the Somoza dictatorship by the Sandinistas is a particularly egregious example. Initially, the United States attempted to maintain the status quo of "*Somocismo* without Somoza," essentially keeping the dictator's system intact with a different figurehead. Ambassador Lawrence Pezzullo hoped that "with careful orchestration, we have a better than even chance of preserving enough of the GN [Somoza's infamous militia, the Guardia Nacional] to maintain order and hold the Sandinistas in check after Somoza resigns." "We have to demonstrate that we are still the decisive force in determining political outcomes in Central America and that we will not permit others to intervene," declared Carter adviser Zbigniew Brzezinski. When this failed, the Carter administration sought to sustain Somoza's National Guard as a base for U.S. power in the region.[42]

Under Ronald Reagan, this strategy escalated into a large-scale, brutal campaign against Nicaragua. The United States waged a terrorist war, supported by economic warfare, to destabilize the Sandinista government, which was committed to improving the conditions of its people and actively involved them in the development process. This commitment posed a threat to the U.S. hegemony, as it set an example of a successful, independent, and leftist government in the region. Henry Kissinger explained: "If we cannot manage Central America" there will be doubt elsewhere "that we know how to manage the global equilibrium." Ronald Reagan, who had declared Nicaragua an "extraordinary threat" to "U.S. national security," recognized that Americans might ask themselves: "How can such a small country pose such a great threat?" He insisted we cannot "ignore the malignancy in Managua" lest it "spreads and becomes a mortal threat to the entire New World."[43]

In its early years, as Latin Americanists Thomas W. Walker and Christine J. Wade write, the "most important long-term concern of the Sandinista Revolution was to improve the human condition of the downtrodden majority of the Nicaraguan people," a project made difficult by the "terrible domestic economic situation and the huge international debt inherited from the departing dictator and his cronies." Nevertheless, the government made impressive progress in some domains, including reducing malnutrition, lowering rents, and introducing a National Literacy Crusade that saw drastic improvements in the literacy rate (and won the 1980 UNESCO award for the best program of its kind). But as Walker and Wade write, the "U.S.-sponsored surrogate war and associated forms of economic aggression" destroyed "rural schools, clinics, food storage facilities, day-care centers, and basic development projects." In the second half of the decade, the war-related expenditures consumed over half of the national budget, thus inevitably depriving social programs of badly needed resources.[44] Greg Grandin further surveys the consequences of Reagan-era policy for Nicaragua. By 1984, using a U.S. "torture manual," the Contras had "killed, tortured . . . and mutilated thousands of civilians in the countryside."

By the time the war finally concluded, tens of thousands of Nicaraguans were dead.[45]

In neighboring El Salvador, the United States long supported dictators who carried out severe repression, torture, and murder. By the late 1970s, however, there was a growth of what were called "popular organizations"— peasant associations, cooperatives, unions, Church-based Bible study groups that evolved into self-help groups, etc. That raised the threat of democracy.

In February 1980, the archbishop of El Salvador, Óscar Romero, wrote to President Carter begging him not to send military aid to the junta that ran the country. Romero said that he was deeply concerned that the United States was considering new military aid to El Salvador. If that came to pass, he said, "your government, instead of promoting greater justice and peace" will "sharpen the injustice and repression against the organizations of the people who repeatedly have been struggling to gain respect for their most fundamental human rights."[46]

A few weeks later, Archbishop Romero was assassinated while saying mass. The neo-Nazi Roberto d'Aubuisson is generally assumed to be responsible for this assassination (among countless other atrocities). On March 7, 1980, two weeks before the assassination, a state of siege had been declared in El Salvador, and the war against the population began in force (with continued U.S. support and involvement). The first major attack was a massacre at the Rio Sumpul, a coordinated military operation of the Honduran and Salvadoran armies in which between three hundred and six hundred people were butchered. Infants were cut to pieces with machetes, and women were tortured and drowned. Pieces of bodies were found in the river for days afterward. Peasants were the main victims of this war, along with labor organizers, students, priests, or anyone suspected of working for the interests of the people.[47]

Throughout Carter's last year in office and into Reagan's presidency, the death toll in El Salvador climbed steeply as a result of U.S.

involvement and support for the Salvadoran military. As NPR summarizes, "While U.S. policymakers argued the need to develop a democratic government in El Salvador, the reality was that Washington was bankrolling a corrupt military, known for kidnapping, torturing, and massacring innocent civilians." They quote journalist Victor Abalos, who reported from the country at the time: "There were always bodies being discovered in the dumps. . . . Young, old, women, men—the theme for a lot of people was that life was cheap." Because the Church had embraced the "preferential option for the poor," clergy were under particular suspicion, with Bibles being considered subversive and flyers appearing outside churches reading: "Be a patriot, kill a priest."[48]

The involvement of the Atlacatl Battalion, a unit created, trained, and equipped by the United States, reveals the depth of U.S. complicity. The battalion's actions were characterized by extreme violence, including murder, rape, and torture. It was formed in March 1981, when specialists in counterinsurgency were sent to El Salvador from the U.S. Army. From the start, the battalion was engaged in mass murder. A U.S. trainer described its soldiers as "particularly ferocious . . . We've always had a hard time getting them to take prisoners instead of ears." In December 1981, the battalion took part in an operation in which over a thousand civilians were killed in an orgy of murder, rape, and burning known as the El Mozote massacre. The Reagan administration belittled the massacre reports, the right-wing press dismissed them as "propaganda," and *The New York Times* reassigned the reporter who broke the story. As journalist Mark Hertsgaard explains, the massacre stories were threatening to the administration because they "repudiated the fundamental moral claim that undergirded U.S. policy," suggesting that "what the United States was supporting in Central America was not democracy but repression."[49]

U.S. achievements in Central America during the 1980s were a major tragedy, not just because of the appalling human cost, but because there were prospects for real progress toward meaningful democracy, with early successes in El Salvador, Guatemala, and Nicaragua.

These efforts might have worked and might have taught useful lessons to others plagued with similar problems. The threat was successfully averted.[50]

CONSTRUCTIVE BLOODBATHS: INDONESIA AND EAST TIMOR

In 1965–66, the Indonesian Communist Party was liquidated in what a CIA analysis called "one of the worst mass murders of the twentieth century." Estimates of the death toll are imprecise, because the killers subsequently ruled the country for decades and no real investigation was ever conducted. Five hundred thousand is considered a consensus estimate, though it could be as high as a million. The communists in Indonesia had been one of the most successful leftist parties in the world, and were the only mass-based political party in the country. In a short time, they were entirely wiped out, the independent nationalist Sukarno was forced from power, replaced by the murderous dictator Suharto.[51]

In *The Killing Season: A History of the Indonesian Massacres, 1965–66*, Geoffrey Robinson gives more detail about the massacres. The victims were "overwhelmingly poor or lower-middle-class people—farmers, plantation laborers, factory workers, schoolteachers, students, artists, dancers, and civil servants—living in rural villages and plantations, or in ramshackle kampungs on the outskirts of provincial cities and towns." They were murdered in "killing fields . . . dotted across the archipelago," "felled with knives, sickles, machetes, swords, ice picks, bamboo spears, iron rods, and other everyday implements." The savagery was extreme. Vincent Bevins says eyewitnesses described "the most shocking scenes imaginable, an explosion of violence so terrifying that even discussing what happened would make people break down, questioning their own sanity."[52]

In the United States, even as the atrocities were reported, the Indonesian government was celebrated. This Rwanda-style slaughter was reported as a triumph for the Free World, because by eliminating the independent left opposition, the killers had ensured Indonesia's government would be pro-Western. *Time* magazine called the decimation of the Indonesian communists "the West's best news for years in Asia," and *The Atlantic* told readers that "in attacking the communists," the "incorruptible" Suharto "was doing simply what he believed to be best for Indonesia." *The New York Times* was downright euphoric, portraying the event as part of a new "Gleam of Light in Asia." The *Times* said that despite our "political troubles in Vietnam," there were "more hopeful political developments elsewhere in Asia." While forthrightly calling it a "massacre," the *Times* said that "control of this large and strategic archipelago is no longer in the hands of men fiercely hostile to the United States."[53]

But the United States didn't just welcome this holocaust. It actively helped the killers carry it out. This was known even at the time—the *Times* report says that while "Washington is being careful not to claim any credit . . . it is doubtful if the coup would ever have been attempted without the American show of strength in Vietnam or been sustained without the clandestine aid it has received indirectly from here." Subsequent evidence confirmed the depth of U.S. involvement. Telegrams from the U.S. Embassy requested clandestine aid to "strengthen the hands of those we want to see win in the current mortal struggle for political power," and noted "small arms and equipment may be needed to deal with the PKI [the Communist Party of Indonesia]." The U.S. even provided the Indonesian army with lists of thousands of communists, with the full knowledge that they would be assassinated.[54]

In fact, since the 1940s, the United States had, according to Robinson, "worked assiduously to undermine the PKI, and weaken or remove President Sukarno," and had long been encouraging the military to seize power. Bevins summarizes the record: "U.S. strategy since the 1950s had been to try to find a way to destroy the Indonesian Communist Party, not because it was seizing power undemocratically, but because it was popular." The massacres were the payoff of a long effort to destroy the left and put Indonesia under military control. The U.S. embassy in Jakarta reported in 1958 that it was increasingly probable that "Communists could not be beaten by ordinary democratic means in elections," thus a "program of gradual elimination of Communists by police and military to be followed by outlawing of Communist Party [is] not unlikely in [the] comparatively near future." The Joint Chiefs of Staff, on the same day, urged that "action must be taken, including overt measures as required, to insure either the success of the dissidents or the suppression of the pro-Communist elements of the Sukarno government."[55]

Robert Martens, who worked as a political officer at the U.S. Embassy in Jakarta, admitted unapologetically to providing the lists of communists that helped facilitate their liquidation:

> It really was a big help to the army. They probably killed a lot of people, and I probably have a lot of blood on my hands, but that's not all bad. There's a time when you have to strike hard at a decisive moment.[56]

Howard Federspiel, then an Indonesia expert at the State Department, commented in 1990: "No one cared, so long as they were communists, that they were being butchered. . . . No one was getting very worked up about it." Bradley Simpson, director of the Indonesia/East Timor Documentation Project at the National Security Archive, concludes from the evidence that "the U.S. and its allies viewed the wholesale annihilation of the PKI and its civilian backers as an indispensable prerequisite to Indonesia's reintegration into the regional political economy," and thus "Washington did everything in its power to encourage and facilitate the Army-led massacre of alleged PKI members, and U.S. officials worried only that the killing of the party's unarmed supporters might not go far enough." Geoffrey Robinson concludes that Western states were "not innocent bystanders," but rather launched a "coordinated campaign to assist in the political and physical destruction of the PKI and its affiliates" and the imposition of Suharto. Claims that the violence "was the product of domestic political forces over which outside powers had little, if any, influence" are "untrue," because "Western powers encouraged the army to move forcefully against the Left, facilitated widespread violence including mass killings, and helped to consolidate the political power of the army."[57]

Thus the United States government was directly responsible for instigating and supporting what the CIA itself called one of the worst atrocities of the twentieth century.[58] The event is never discussed. Bevins suggests the reason. The truth that the U.S. "engineer[ed] the conditions for a violent clash" and then "assisted and guided its longtime partners to carry out the mass murder of civilians as a means of achieving U.S. geopolitical goals" is so ugly that it is impossible to acknowledge, at least for any American who wishes to continue thinking of the United States as playing a benign or positive role in the world. Bevins reflects that "what happened contradicts so forcefully our idea of what the Cold War was, of what it means to be an American, or how globalization has taken place, that it has simply been easier to ignore it."

In other words, the story is so revealing that it cannot be known. And so it isn't. The events are consigned to Orwell's memory hole, forgotten in the same way as the massacre of hundreds of thousands of Filipinos at the turn of the twentieth century, the genocidal destruction of Native Americans, and other matters not suitable to be enshrined in official history.

American support and aid for the Suharto regime continued for decades after the successful extermination campaign. In 1975, Suharto invaded East Timor, which had recently won its independence from Portugal, overthrowing the leftist government and launching a decades-long occupation that killed hundreds of thousands. People were herded into buildings or fields and killed en masse. The UN Security Council ordered Indonesia to withdraw, but to no avail. The failure was explained by then UN ambassador Daniel Patrick Moynihan. In his memoirs, he took pride in having rendered the UN "utterly ineffective in whatever measures it undertook" because "the United States wished things to turn out as they did" and "worked to bring this about." C. Philip Liechty, who served as a senior CIA officer in the Jakarta embassy during the East Timor invasion, confessed that Suharto was "given the green light" by the United States, which supplied his forces with "everything they needed." When news of the mass civilian deaths came out, the CIA tried "to cover them up as long as possible."[59]

Jimmy Carter declared in 1978 that so long as he was president, "the Government of the United States will continue throughout the world to enhance human rights," and that "no force on Earth can separate us from that commitment." Human rights, he claimed, was the "soul of our foreign policy." Nevertheless, Carter escalated arms supplies to Indonesia, which were used to crush the Timorese resistance. The official U.S. position, as expressed by the State Department to Congress, was that "we made it clear to [the Indonesians] that we understood the situation they were in; we understood the pressures they felt and their concern about the fighting that was going on and the potential for instability that would be caused by developments as they saw them." In fact, there was no fighting going on beyond Indonesia's own aggression, which was (as acknowledged by the State Department) conducted "roughly 90% with our equipment."[60]

The death toll eventually reached two hundred thousand, one of the worst slaughters relative to population since the Holocaust, with one third of the population dying, many due to famine. Clinton Fernandes, author of the comprehensive study *The Independence of East Timor*, says that "for Indonesia, the military objective of destroying the resistance overrode all other considerations," while "for Western governments, the maintenance of good relations with the Suharto regime took priority." Even though "the aircraft provided to the Indonesians by the U.S. was the primary factor in the massive death toll," protest in the West was minuscule, and there was little reporting. John Pilger says of

East Timor: "Other places on the planet may seem more remote; none has been as defiled and abused by murderous forces or as abandoned by the 'international community,' whose principals are complicit in one of the great, unrecognized crimes of the twentieth century."[61]

U.S. presidents stuck with Suharto for decades, even after the massacre of hundreds of pro-independence Timorese demonstrators in 1991 received international media coverage. A 1995 *New York Times* article explained the reasons the Clinton administration had such cordial relationships with Suharto that "the Cabinet room was jammed with top officials ready to welcome him." He has "been savvy in keeping Washington happy" through measures like "deregulat[ing] the economy" and "open[ing] Indonesia to foreign investors." The *Times* quoted a senior administration official who called Suharto "our kind of guy," contrasting him with the truculent Fidel Castro, who received a cold welcome in Washington (Castro, after all, was a dictator). The National Security Archive notes that "the Clinton Administration maintained support for Suharto until virtually the end," including by quashing an investigation into Indonesian labor practices, "and continued to view the Indonesian armed forces as the guarantors of stability," even when Suharto's military was massacring protesters against his regime. After Suharto "brutally crushed students' anti-Suharto protests and kidnapped pro-democracy activists," Bill Clinton told Suharto in a personal phone call: "Your personal leadership has produced unprecedented economic growth and prosperity for Indonesia and its people. I am convinced you can get through this present difficulty."[62]

Clinton made it clear that crushing democratic opposition was no obstacle to ongoing U.S. support. Suharto remained "our kind of guy," as he compiled one of the most horrendous records of slaughter, torture, and other abuses. But Suharto made a mistake, losing control and hesitating to implement harsh International Monetary Fund (IMF) prescriptions. In 1998, Secretary of State Madeleine Albright finally called upon him to resign to "preserve his legacy" and provide for "a democratic transition." A few hours later, Suharto transferred authority to his handpicked vice president. The rapidity of Suharto's departure following the loss of U.S. support shows just how easy it would have been for the U.S. to stop the torture of East Timor at any point.[63]

SUCCESSFUL DEFIANCE: IRAN

After World War II, nationalist currents developed in Iran. The movement coalesced around Mohammad Mosaddegh, an old-fashioned liberal of immense charisma, which appealed to Iranians of all social classes. Mosaddegh became prime minister in 1951, committed to the nationalization of Iranian oil, which had remained a British monopoly. By 1953, the United States agreed with Britain that Mosaddegh had to go. His parliamentary regime was overthrown in a coup, restoring the more compliant shah, Reza Pahlavi, to power. The CIA eventually admitted that the coup "was carried out under CIA direction as an act of U.S. foreign policy, conceived and approved at the highest levels of government."[64]

Historian Roham Alvandi and political scientist Mark J. Gasiorowski note that "both Britain and the United States publicly denied their roles in the 1953 coup so as not to embarrass the shah or endanger their close political and economic ties with Iran," and even after incontrovertible evidence emerged, denial or downplaying of the U.S. role "reached the highest levels of the U.S. government." There was also a "worry that if the U.S. public is made to feel guilty about the CIA intervention in Iran in 1953, they may be less likely to support another U.S. intervention in Iran today." Indeed, if the U.S. public understood this source of Iranian grievance against the United States, they are at dangerous risk of empathizing with an official enemy. The public must therefore be kept from learning the truth about their country's foreign policy. But internally, as State Department officer Andrew Killgore recounts, it "was regarded as [the] CIA's greatest single triumph," a "great American national victory," because "[w]e had changed the course of a whole country."[65]

The shah would remain in power for the next twenty-six years, maintained by U.S. support, even as he imprisoned, tortured, and executed dissidents and was condemned as a major human rights abuser by Amnesty International. One consequence of the coup was that U.S. oil companies took 40 percent of the Iranian concession, part of the general takeover of the world's major energy reserves by the United States. The U.S. also helped the shah pursue a nuclear program, training Iranian nuclear engineers, with U.S. officials arguing strongly that nuclear power would benefit Iran. (Once the country became an official enemy, the reasoning switched, and it was seen as impossible for Iran to have legitimate peacetime uses for a nuclear program.)[66]

The New York Times was pleased with the lesson that had been taught to Iranians and any who might try to follow their course of independent nationalism.

> Underdeveloped countries with rich resources now have an object lesson in the heavy cost that must be paid by one of their number which goes berserk with fanatical nationalism. . . . It is perhaps too much to hope that Iran's experience will prevent the rise of Mossadeghs in other countries, but that experience may at least strengthen the hands of more reasonable and more far-seeing leaders.[67]

In 1979, Iranians carried out another illegitimate act: they overthrew the tyrant that the United States had imposed and supported, and moved on an independent path, not following U.S. orders. The Carter administration considered supporting a military coup (deciding against it on pragmatic grounds), and tried "retaining as much of the Shah's regime as possible," in the words of Middle East analyst Mahan Abedin, though the strategy quickly unraveled.[68]

The United States' hostile acts toward Iranians continued through the 1980s. Saddam Hussein's Iraq invaded Iran with strong U.S. support. The war killed hundreds of thousands of people, devastating Iran, with Saddam using chemical weapons (again, with U.S. support). The Reagan administration falsely blamed Iran for the use of chemical weapons against Kurds, and blocked Congress from issuing any criticism of Saddam's chemical warfare. After the war, President George H. W. Bush's Pentagon invited Iraqi weapons scientists to the U.S. for training in bomb production, a serious threat to Iran. The U.S. public might not remember any of these events, but Iranians do.[69]

Today, the "Iranian threat" is a Western obsession. Undoubtedly, Iran is a fundamentalist regime with a horrendous human rights record. But that has nothing to do with it. There is, after all, no more extreme fundamentalist regime on Earth than Saudi Arabia. It is a missionary state that aims to disseminate its extremist Wahhabi-Salafi version of Islam around the world. In Yemen, the Saudi government is responsible for one of the most horrific humanitarian crises of our time, in inflicting mass starvation and bombing civilian targets, including a bus full of schoolchildren, with U.S.-provided weapons. (The United States even refueled Saudi planes on their bombing runs.) The regime also killed and dismembered *Washington Post* columnist Jamal Khashoggi with a bone saw. Yet Saudi Arabia still managed to retain good relations with both the Trump and Biden administrations, and Mohammed bin Salman received a friendly fist bump from Joe Biden, who was committed to "moving on" from the murder, ignoring the pleas of Khashoggi's fiancée. The Biden administration even went to court to try to prevent Khashoggi's family from successfully suing the Saudi leader. The warm embrace of the Saudi dictatorship by U.S. presidents should destroy any pretense that "human rights" or "democracy" factor into a country's status as an official enemy, or that Iran's status as an adversary is related to its government's repressive acts.[70]

The current panic about Iran focuses on Iran's possible development of nuclear weapons. But we should note a few facts. First, it is not clear that Iran is developing nuclear weapons. The Congressional Research Service observes that "official U.S. assessments [conclude that] Iran halted its nuclear weapons program in late 2003 and has not resumed it." Second, Iran resides in the neighborhood of three nuclear powers, Israel, India, and Pakistan, which are backed by the United States and have refused to sign the Nonproliferation Treaty. Finally, Iran is regularly threatened with force by both the United States and Israel, and acquiring a nuclear deterrent might well be a rational move.[71]

Israeli military historian Martin Van Creveld wrote that "the world has witnessed how the United States attacked Iraq for, as it turned out, no reason at all. Had the Iranians not tried to build nuclear weapons, they would be crazy," particularly when they are under constant threat of attack, in violation of the UN Charter. Intelligence expert Thomas Powers notes that there has been very little mainstream U.S. commentary on *why* Iran might want a nuclear weapon, with the dominant assumption simply being that "the country is run by religious fanatics crazy enough to use a bomb if they had one." In fact, Powers says, Iran probably wants a nuclear weapon for the same reason other states do: to deter attack. "As tools of coercive diplomacy nuclear weapons are almost entirely useless, but they are extremely effective in blocking large-scale or regime-threatening attack. There is no evidence that Iran has a different motive, and plenty of reason for Iran to fear that attack is a real possibility." Powers points to the long history of U.S. presidents publicly discussing the possibility of attacking Iran, and notes that the invasion of Iraq means there is very good reason to take these threats seriously. Nuclear states "cannot be casually threatened," and the regime might rationally believe nukes can "save Iran from a similar fate" as its neighbor. In considering the "Iranian threat," we must also consider the threats *against* Iran and how they compare. Iran does not assassinate Israeli scientists or carry out sabotage, but Israel does against Iran. Benjamin Netanyahu has claimed that Iran "must face a credible nuclear threat," a statement he walked back, perhaps upon remembering that Israel's nuclear weapons are illegal and supposed to be a secret.[72]

On and off since 1979, the United States has attacked the Iranian population with the use of harsh sanctions. Human Rights Watch has warned that the sanctions regime "pose[s] a serious threat to Iranians' right to health and access to essential medicines—and has almost certainly contributed to documented shortages—ranging from a lack of critical drugs for epilepsy patients to limited chemotherapy medications for Iranians with cancer." The Trump administration made it clear that the collective punishment of Iranians was the *purpose*, not an unintended consequence, of sanctions, with Mike Pompeo boasting that "things are much worse for the Iranian people [with the U.S. sanctions], and we are convinced that will lead the Iranian people to rise up and change the behavior of the regime." Biden has mostly continued the same approach, although he generously allowed Iran to access some of its own oil revenues.[73]

In 2014, a deal was reached between Iran and the five UN Security Council states, plus the European Union, to put limits on Iran's nuclear program. Nuclear-arms-control experts hailed the deal as successfully "reduc[ing] the risk of a destabilizing nuclear competition in a troubled region." In 2017, the United States certified that Iran was complying with the deal. The International Atomic Energy Agency (IAEA) affirmed Iran's compliance and concluded it had "no credible indications of activities in Iran relevant to the development of a nuclear explosive device after 2009." Nevertheless, in 2018, Donald Trump withdrew from the deal and reimposed sanctions that had been lifted under it, wrecking the agreement. Iran has repeatedly urged the United States to return to the deal, promising to rejoin "within an hour of the U.S. doing so." "We are not going to waste time on it," Biden's Iran envoy said in 2022 when asked about rejoining the deal. "It's not up for discussion," said Kurt Campbell, Biden's nominee for deputy secretary of state. Instead, "we must isolate them diplomatically, internationally." Iran must be punished for violating an agreement we sabotaged.

Iran is considered by the United States to be "the world's worst state sponsor of terrorism." One of the main crimes cited is the country's use of cyberattacks, with the State Department's Country Report on Terrorism warning that Iran "maintains a robust offensive cyber program and has sponsored cyber attacks against foreign government and private sector entities." The Office of the Director of National Intelligence's 2023 Annual Threat Assessment states that "Iran's growing expertise and willingness to conduct aggressive cyber operations make it a major threat to the security of U.S. and allied networks and data. Iran's opportunistic approach to cyber attacks makes critical infrastructure owners in the United States susceptible to being targeted."[74]

When a country is accused of "aggressive" or "offensive" behavior, very often the United States engages in the same behavior. In fact, as explained by Thomas Warrick, former deputy assistant secretary for Counterterrorism Policy for the Department of Homeland Security, in 2013, "Iran developed a cyberattack capability after the 'Stuxnet' malware that targeted Iran's Siemens industrial control systems (ICS) came to light in June 2010." Stuxnet, the "first known cyberweapon," was jointly developed by U.S. and Israeli intelligence and let loose on Iran under the Obama administration, in order to hobble the country's nuclear program. Gary Samore, the White House Coordinator for Arms Control and Weapons of Mass Destruction, all but acknowledged that the U.S. had attacked Iran with Stuxnet, saying, "We're glad they are having trouble with their centrifuge machine" and that we "are doing everything we can to make sure that we complicate matters for them." Iran has been attacked repeatedly by Stuxnet and other cyberweapons, including an attack on its banking system in 2019 by an unknown "state entity."[75] In his first months in office, President Obama "secretly ordered increasingly sophisticated attacks on the computer systems that run Iran's main nuclear enrichment facilities, significantly expanding America's first sustained use of cyberweapons." The Trump administration admitted to repeatedly using cyberattacks on Iran.[76]

The Iranian state certainly provides arms to and sponsors organizations that carry out heinous atrocities. In this respect they act like other states, including our own. But what if Iran were to murder the second-highest U.S. official, or a leading general, in the Mexico City International Airport, along with the commander of a large part of the

U.S.-supported army of an allied nation? This would be construed as an act of war, certainly a serious terroristic crime. Yet this is precisely what the U.S. did to Iranian general Qassim Soleimani, assassinating him in the Baghdad airport. The United Nations special rapporteur investigating extrajudicial and summary executions condemned the murder, saying that it "risked eroding international laws that govern the conduct of hostilities," warning that if other countries behaved similarly to the United States, a disastrous "global conflagration" would be the likely result. Yet despite being a blatant violation of international law and Iraq's sovereignty, the murder was praised in the U.S. (For Trump's Republican critics, it was "finally something to like.") American consumers can even role-play the assassination in a *Call of Duty* video game. A rogue superpower has no reason to care what the international community thinks.[77]

THE POLITICAL ECONOMY OF HUMAN RIGHTS

George Kennan, in a briefing for Latin American ambassadors, explained that one of the main concerns of U.S. policy is the "protection of our raw materials." Who must we protect *our* raw materials from? Primarily, the domestic populations of the countries who possess them. How will we protect our raw materials from that population? Kennan said we should be ruthless. The answer "might be an unpleasant one," but "we should not hesitate before police repression by the local government." This is, he said, "not shameful," because "the Communists are essentially traitors" and so "it is better to have a strong regime in power than a liberal government if it is indulgent and relaxed and penetrated by Communists." ("Communism," as we have seen, was a term applied to all who refused to take orders, whether or not they believed in communism.)[78]

Similarly, Eisenhower's panel on covert action, in the Doolittle Report, recommended that given "an implacable enemy whose avowed objective is world domination" we must embrace a "fundamentally repugnant philosophy" with "no rules," where "hitherto acceptable norms of human conduct do not apply," the only goal being to "subvert, sabotage, and destroy" the enemy. The United States has followed Kennan's and Doolittle's precepts consistently, setting aside such "vague and unreal objectives such as human rights, the raising of the living standards, and democratization." The general principle is that human rights violators are acceptable when they serve the U.S. "national interest," and not when they don't, so that even Jimmy Carter's "human rights–focused" presidency supported atrocious human rights abusers allied with the U.S. A study by Lars Schoultz showed that "U.S. aid has tended to flow disproportionately to Latin American governments which torture their citizens." It had nothing to do with how much a country needed aid, only with its willingness to serve the interests of wealth and privilege.[79]

This is no defense of the human rights records of Cuba, Iran, or the 1980s Sandinista government. Instead, it demonstrates the emptiness of the proclaimed principles. Over the past decades, the leading recipients of U.S. military aid have been Israel and Egypt. Egypt is suffering under one of the harshest dictatorships in its history, yet the Biden administration has refused to follow existing U.S. law that prohibits aid to human rights abusers, waiving the requirement in order to continue supplying Egypt with weaponry. Israel maintains an apartheid regime that has been condemned universally by international human rights organizations. The record says more than the rhetoric.[80]

The pattern of support for dictatorships thus continues to this day, including among Democratic presidents who make loud professions of commitment to human rights. In 2023, for instance, a number of human rights organizations including Amnesty International and Human Rights Watch sent a joint letter to the Biden administration with a plea for the life of Abdulhadi al-Khawaja. Al-Khawaja is the sixty-two-year-old cofounder of the Gulf Centre for Human Rights and the Bahrain Center for Human Rights. He had been imprisoned by the dictatorial

government of Bahrain for twelve years and "subjected to severe physical, sexual, and psychological torture." His health had been deteriorat-
ing, and he had been denied necessary medical care. Al-Khawaja was
on a hunger strike along with hundreds of other political prisoners in
the country. The dictatorship in Bahrain being infamously brutal, this
kind of dissent is rare.[81]

In their letter to the Biden administration, the human rights organizations implored the president to use his leverage with Bahrain to
secure the release of al-Khawaja. But they needn't have bothered sending their letter. The Biden administration happily agreed to sign a new
security pact with Bahrain, committing the United States to defending
Bahrain in military disputes with other countries. The Quincy Institute for Responsible Statecraft pointed out that the U.S. commitment
to defending Bahrain has no compelling justification. The regime does
not face an external threat. Rather, "to the extent the regime in Bahrain
faces a security threat, it involves not external aggression but instead
internal strife stemming from an unpopular Sunni regime repressing
a largely Shia population."[82]

The Biden administration, in announcing its "comprehensive security integration and prosperity agreement" with the dictatorship, boasted
of all the ways that the partnership will involve "enhancing deterrence,
including through expanded defense and security cooperation, inter-
operability, and mutual intelligence capacity-building." Only a tiny pas-
sage at the end of the announcement even mentions human rights,
explaining that both countries will continue to "engage in constructive
dialogue on the importance of universal values, human rights, and fundamental freedoms."[83]

Biden's embrace of the dictatorship must have been bitterly disappointing for Maryam al-Khawaja, the daughter of Abdulhadi al-Khawaja.
She told NPR that as her father's condition has deteriorated, so far there
had been nothing but "lip service" from the U.S. government on human
rights. The security agreement "angered and disappointed Bahraini

activists and other critics of the Gulf monarchy, which crushed an uprising that swept the kingdom in 2011, during the Arab Spring."[84]

It is clear the Biden administration simply did not care what the activists against the Bahraini dictatorship wanted. It would have been very easy to say to Bahrain: the United States is not going to commit to a military partnership while you continue to hold political prisoners. But the administration has been trying to strengthen ties with Persian Gulf states to counter China and Russia in its competition for global dominance. The human rights of Bahraini activists are considered unimportant next to the geostrategic goal of remaining more powerful than the other large countries.

The United States plainly has no problem with the violation of human rights. It all depends on the perpetrator. While Biden has signed a bill punishing China for its repression of Uyghurs, he has been happy to fist-bump a dictator like Saudi Arabia's Mohammed bin Salman and provide an endless supply of weapons to Israel to continue obliterating Gazans trapped in an open-air prison. Once we see that the ideals are applied selectively, we can ask what governs the choice to apply or not apply them in particular cases. As a general rule, the United States opposes the criminality and violence of those powers we wish to contain and supports the criminality and violence of our valued partners and allies. There is a single standard, then: whatever serves our perceived interests is good, whatever undermines them is not.[85]

2

The War on Southeast Asia

The history of the conflict that is called the Vietnam War is exemplary of how brutal, self-interested violence can be spun as altruism. In 2017, acclaimed filmmaker Ken Burns released *The Vietnam War*, a ten-part PBS documentary series. The film's narrator summarizes that the war was "begun in good faith, by decent people, out of fateful misunderstandings, American overconfidence, and Cold War miscalculation." It was continued through "tragic decisions" by presidents trying to "muddle through."

This tone was set by Anthony Lewis in 1975, who looked back on the war as built on "blundering efforts to do good" that turned into a "disastrous mistake." Similarly, Harvard historian John King Fairbank called the war a "disaster" that arose "mainly through an excess of righteousness and disinterested benevolence." *Newsweek* lamented that "the high hopes and wishful idealism with which the American nation had been born . . . had been chastened by the failure of America to work its will in Indochina." Today, Democratic rising star Pete Buttigieg calls it a "doomed errand into the jungle," and invokes the naïve title character from Graham Greene's *The Quiet American*, whose "good intentions and ignorance" make him a liability in Vietnam. ("I never knew a man who had better motives for all the trouble he caused.") There are those who think that even this is America being too hard on itself. Max Hastings, in *Vietnam: An Epic Tragedy, 1945–1975*, says that "Liberal America has adopted an almost masochistic attitude" in criticizing its government over the war.[1]

In fact, the true story of the Vietnam War was not the story of "noble motives" in pursuit of a futile objective. It was the story of crime, committed for indefensible reasons.

In 1961, when Daniel Ellsberg visited Vietnam as a member of a Pentagon task force, the main conclusion he formed was that "we weren't likely to be successful there." Ellsberg's sources indicated to him that Ngô Đình Diệm, the South Vietnamese dictator being supported by the United States, would not be able to maintain power without continuous, ever-increasing U.S. military aid. As soon as the U.S. stopped providing support, the Diệm regime would inevitably collapse. For Ellsberg, who was at the time a "dedicated cold warrior," this was disturbing news, because it meant that the U.S. would either have to accept a communist government in Vietnam or indefinitely prop up an unpopular ruler.[2]

Initially, Ellsberg questioned the wisdom, but not the morality, of U.S. policy. He viewed U.S. support for the Diệm dictatorship as strategically foolish, and was pessimistic about the prospects that the U.S. could "prevail" in Vietnam. Nevertheless, he believed the policy was well intentioned, and held on to that belief for some years after, even as the U.S. launched a full-scale invasion of South Vietnam to keep a friendly government in power. At the time, and in many ways to this day, acceptable debate on the issue was bounded on the one side by the "hawks," who felt that with sufficient dedication the United States could succeed in "defending South Vietnam," "controlling the population," and thus establishing "American-style democracy," and on the other side, by the "doves," who doubted that these noble aims could be achieved at reasonable cost. Some, like the young Ellsberg, wondered whether America could "succeed." But they did not consider whether it should succeed.

It was only when Ellsberg began working on what became known as the "Pentagon Papers," the secret internal study of U.S. decision-making on Vietnam, that he realized his view was mistaken. By studying the origins of the war in the 1940s and '50s, he came to understand that the idea of the war as a "well-intentioned mistake" could not be reconciled with the historical record, which rather showed the war to be "wrong from the start," a "crime," an "evil," "naked of any shred of legitimacy."

While the United States government had long told a story in which it was protecting "free, independent South Vietnam" from a "takeover by communist North Vietnam," in fact, the United States had actually tried to prevent Vietnamese independence and freedom from the very start. Noble Mistake theory can only be preserved by ignoring the basic facts of how the war arose in the first place. The United States opposed Vietnamese independence from France in 1945 and funded France's brutal campaign to retain possession of its colony. Then when the French were defeated, the United States took over the French role and thwarted every proposal to bring democracy to Vietnam. Ellsberg writes of how disturbed he was at our years of "diplomatic support of the French claims of sovereign ownership of a former colony that had proclaimed independence with full popular support." In fact, "we had urgently pressed the French to continue their military struggle against the independence movement and funded it almost entirely."

On September 2, 1945, in Hanoi's Ba Dinh Square, Hồ Chí Minh declared Vietnam independent from French colonial rule. Hồ's speech drew explicit parallels between the aspirations of Vietnam and the principles of the American Revolution, and his speech showed him to have closely studied the rhetoric of Thomas Jefferson. "All men are created equal," he said, yet "for more than eighty years, the French imperialists, abusing the standard of Liberty, Equality, and Fraternity, have violated our Fatherland and oppressed our fellow-citizens." He listed their offenses. "[T]hey have deprived our people of every democratic liberty. . . . They have built more prisons than schools. They have mercilessly slain our patriots; they have drowned our uprisings in rivers of blood. . . . They have robbed us of our rice fields, our mines, our forests, and our raw materials." Hồ's indictment, listing specific charges against the colonizing power, will sound familiar to Americans, with its deliberate echoes of the rhetorical structure of the U.S. Declaration of Independence. (Some of Jefferson's charges against George III were less morally compelling, such as "he has excited domestic insurrections amongst us [referring to British promises to free slaves], and has endeavored to bring on the inhabitants of our frontiers, the merciless Indian Savages.")[3]

Hồ therefore claimed Vietnam free and independent and renounced all ties to France. He appealed to the U.S. for support, citing its stated commitment to the self-determination of peoples. Having tried and failed in 1917 to win Woodrow Wilson's support for Vietnamese independence, Hồ appealed directly to President Harry Truman. In a 1946 telegram to Truman, Hồ wrote that the French were "making active preparations for a *coup de main* in Hanoi and for military aggression," and "I therefore most earnestly appeal to you personally and to the American people to interfere urgently in support of our independence and help making the negotiations more in keeping with the principles of the Atlantic and San Francisco charters." In a separate letter to Truman, Hồ warned that "millions of people will suffer" unless the United States was willing to "step out to stop that bloodshed and unlawful aggression."[4]

Hồ's pleas went unanswered. The United States did not support Vietnamese independence from France. In fact, the U.S. proceeded to aid France in its efforts to reconquer Vietnam, and soon "dollars, not francs . . . paid for almost every bomb and bullet expended on the Vietnam battlefield." Even Max Hastings, having described American feelings of moral uneasiness over the war as "liberal masochism," comments that "the interests of the Vietnamese people . . . ranked low in the priorities of President Harry Truman." Indeed, they were nonexistent. According to then serving French foreign minister Georges Bidault, the

United States went so far as to informally offer France two atomic bombs if it would help defeat the Vietnamese.[5]

American support for France was motivated by concern over the strategic resources of Southeast Asia and their significance for the global system that the United States was then constructing. Eisenhower confided to Winston Churchill his worry that "the French cannot alone see the thing through . . . [A]nd if they do not see it through, and Indochina passes into the hands of the Communists, the ultimate effect on our and your global strategic position with the consequent shift in the power ratio throughout Asia and the Pacific could be disastrous." American policymakers were not under any illusions about the fact that they were supporting French colonialism and opposing Vietnamese self-determination. Early on, the State Department noted that Hồ had established himself as "the symbol of nationalism and the struggle for freedom to the overwhelming majority of the population." By September 1948, the department deplored "our inability to suggest any practicable solution of the Indochina problem" in the light of "the unpleasant fact that Communist Ho Chi Minh is the strongest and perhaps the ablest figure in Indochina."[6]

When the Vietnamese nationalists eventually defeated their French occupiers in 1954, the United States immediately took up France's position in the struggle against indigenous nationalism. The Geneva agreement that brought an end to fighting between France and the Viet Minh had provided that the country would be unified through elections in 1956. It was quickly undermined by the United States and Ngô Đình Diệm, because it was taken for granted on all sides that elections would lead to a unified Vietnam under Viet Minh rule. "American intelligence sources were unanimous that Diệm would lose any national election," historian George Kahin concluded. The Viet Minh had agreed to the decision on the basis of "the assurance that the struggle for the control of Vietnam would be transferred from the military to the political level, a realm in which the Vietminh leaders knew their superiority over the French and their Vietnamese collaborators was even greater than it was militarily." Indeed, Eisenhower acknowledged in his memoirs that if elections had taken place, "possibly 80 per cent of the population would have voted for the Communist Ho Chi Minh." The U.S.-selected faction of South Vietnamese repeatedly stressed themselves that "frankly, we are not strong enough now to compete with the communists on a purely political basis." Thus, the regime rejected the terms of the Geneva political settlement, and refused to hold the scheduled elections.[7]

Diệm, whom Lyndon Johnson called the "Winston Churchill of Asia," controlled the population of South Vietnam with substantial violence, aided at every turn by the United States. "There can be no doubt," a 1972 study prepared for the Pentagon concludes, "that innumerable crimes and absolutely senseless acts of suppression against both real and suspected Communists and sympathizing villagers were committed. Efficiency took the form of brutality and a total disregard for the difference between determined foes and potential friends." Journalist David Hotham wrote in 1959 that Diệm had "crushed all opposition of every kind," which he had been able to do "simply and solely because of the massive dollar aid he has had from across the Pacific," concluding that "Diệm's main supporters are to be found in North America, not in Free Vietnam." "Few Americans were aware of Diệm's harsh rule," writes historian Christian Appy, "or that it became even more draconian in 1959 with the creation of roving tribunals that traveled the countryside and summarily executed anyone regarded as a threat to national security," including lopping dissidents' heads off with guillotines. State terrorism evoked renewed resistance. By 1959, Viet Minh cadres in the South received authorization from Hanoi to use violence in self-defense. The resistance threatened the quick collapse of the U.S.-imposed regime, which by then had killed tens of thousands of people and alienated much of the peasantry as well as urban elites.[8]

The Kennedy administration escalated the war in South Vietnam. In 1961–62, U.S. military forces began their direct attack against the rural society—some 85 percent of the population at the time—with extensive bombardment and defoliation. The general plan, in the words of liberal historian Stanley Karnow, "was to corral peasants into armed stockades, thereby depriving the [National Liberation Front (Viet Cong)] of their support." Several million people were driven into concentration camps ("strategic hamlets") in which they could be "protected" behind barbed wire from the guerrillas whom, the United States conceded, they were willingly supporting.[9]

There was barely any effort to pretend that the ruling government of South Vietnam had democratic legitimacy, although the U.S. media continued to claim otherwise. Indeed, the corrupt and incompetent Diệm proved unsatisfactory to the United States, and the Kennedy administration authorized a coup that resulted in his assassination. One of Diệm's early replacements told reporters that he found out he was going to be the next head of state only when his U.S. adviser "told me that a coup d'état was planned in Saigon and that I was to become president." General Maxwell Taylor spoke quite frankly about the need for "establishing some reasonably satisfactory government," replacing it if we are not satisfied, either with civilians, or with "a military dictatorship." The United States installed two former French collaborators, Nguyễn Cao Kỳ and Nguyễn Văn Thiệu, whose sole qualification for rule was that they met the U.S. condition of willingness to fight and evade political settlement. The unelected government was maintained in power solely because its aims were identical to those of the U.S. administration.[10]

It was conceded on all sides that the government imposed by the United States lacked any significant popular support. Leading U.S. government scholar Douglas Pike, in his book *Viet Cong*, said that "aside from the NLF there has never been a truly mass-based political party in South Vietnam." John Paul Vann, widely regarded as the U.S. official most knowledgeable about the situation in South Vietnam, wrote in 1965 that "a popular political base for the Government of South Vietnam does not now exist," because the existing government was simply "a continuation of the French colonial system of government with upper-class Vietnamese replacing the French."[11]

Unable to develop any political base in the south, the U.S. government proceeded to expand the war. Continuing to block all attempts at
peaceful settlement, including the proposal of the NLF to neutralize
South Vietnam, Laos, and Cambodia, the United States, finding no
other way to avoid political settlement, undertook a war of annihilation
that spread throughout Indochina, with South Vietnam always bearing
the major brunt of the American assault.

By the time of the U.S. land invasion in 1965, over 150,000 people
had already been killed in South Vietnam, most of them "under the
crushing weight of American armor, napalm, jet bombers and finally
vomiting gases," in the words of journalist Bernard Fall, or victims of
the state terrorism of the U.S.-installed regimes. From January 1965, the
United States also employed South Korean mercenaries, some 300,000
in all, who carried out brutal atrocities in the South. By 1967, Fall—himself
bitterly anti-communist—concluded that "Vietnam as a cultural and
historic entity . . . is threatened with extinction [as the] countryside literally dies under the blows of the largest military machine ever unleashed on an area of this size."[12]

Richard Nixon, rather than ending the war, escalated it, becoming
the "greatest bomber in history." He promised to "destroy the goddamn
country" with "nuclear weapons if necessary," and "bomb the living
bejeezus out of North Vietnam." U.S. forces undertook an "accelerated
pacification campaign," in actuality a mass-murder operation that demolished the NLF and much of what was left of the peasant society,
killing tens of thousands. Nixon barely pretended that the war was
about helping the people of Vietnam or checking aggression. Instead,
it was a test of U.S. "credibility." "We will not be humiliated. We will
not be defeated," he declared. Christian Appy comments that Nixon
"sounded like a desperate coach at halftime, beseeching his badly losing team to fight harder, if only for dignity." Indeed, war reporter Martha Gellhorn was horrified when she arrived in Vietnam at the way the
conflict seemed to be a sports game, and U.S. officers "sounded inhuman, like describing a deadly football game between a team of heroes

and a team of devils and chalking up the score by 'body counts' and 'kill ratio.'" A sport "won" by killing as many Vietnamese people as possible is better described as a crime against humanity.[13]

THE WAR ON THE GROUND

It is easy, in retelling this history, to discuss "what happened in Vietnam" without really discussing what happened in Vietnam. We can talk about the political decision-making behind the war without getting a true feel for what it was actually like for its victims. It is worth zooming in on what we actually did.

The most damage was inflicted from the skies, in massive aerial bombing campaigns that turned significant parts of the country into moonscapes. Huge terror operations like "Speedy Express" and "Bold Mariner" were aimed specifically at destroying the civilian base of the resistance. Over a seven-year period, U.S. and South Vietnamese aircraft flew 3.4 million combat sorties. From 1965 to 1968, the United States dropped 32 tons of bombs per hour on North Vietnam. Twenty-five million acres of farmland were subject to saturation bombing, and 7 million tons of bombs including 400,000 tons of napalm were dropped in Southeast Asia (including Laos and Cambodia) during the conflict. This is more than three times as many tons of bombs dropped in all of World War II, and the combined power of the explosives amounted to more than 640 Hiroshimas. In Quang Tri province, "only 11 of the province's 3,500 villages went unbombed," and the province's capital district was "saturated with 3,000 bombs per square kilometer." When Air Force chief of staff Curtis LeMay promised to bomb North Vietnam "back into the Stone Age," he was not bluffing. A North Vietnamese soldier said that even from a kilometer away, "the sonic roar of the B-52 explosions tore eardrums, leaving many of the jungle dwellers permanently deaf." The bomb craters "were gigantic—thirty feet across and nearly as deep. . . . The first few times I experienced a B-52 attack it seemed . . . that I had been caught in the Apocalypse."[14]

Not only were countless civilians killed, but the nonstop bombing created an atmosphere of perpetual terror for large parts of the population. Lifelong pain and trauma were inflicted on those who were maimed or lost loved ones. Whole towns were turned to rubble; farms were obliterated; women, children, and old people were incinerated. Chemical weapons including thousands of tons of CS tear gas and seventy million liters of toxic defoliants and herbicides, including Agent Orange and the lesser-known Agent Blue, were deployed as part of a deliberate strategy of killing Vietnamese farmers' crops. Biologist Arthur Westing concluded that "unprecedentedly massive and sustained expenditure of herbicidal chemical warfare agents against the fields and forests of South Vietnam . . . resulted in large-scale devastation of crops, in widespread and immediate damage to the inland and coastal forest ecosystems, and in a variety of health problems among exposed humans." Biologist E. W. Pfeiffer noted that defoliants eliminated half the mangrove forests of the country, leaving "no living green plant life anywhere," just "a solid gray scene of death." Large areas "that were once cool, moist, temperate and fertile are now characterized by compacted, leached earth and dry, blazing climate," biologist Do Quy of the University of Hanoi wrote, after "deliberate destruction of the environment as a military tactic on a scale never seen before."[15]

The defoliants, which cause cancer and birth defects, were sprayed on "a fifth of South Vietnam's jungles, over a third of its mangrove forests, as well as on rice crop." Nearly five million Vietnamese people were sprayed with these toxic chemicals, but crop destruction itself was perverse and cruel, intended to starve insurgents by ruining the lands of poor peasant farmers who supported them. As the RAND Corporation noted in 1967, "the civilian population seems to carry very nearly the full burden of the results of the crop destruction program."[16]

The destruction was apocalyptic. Nick Turse quotes two South Vietnamese generals saying that as a result of U.S. firepower "many villages were completely obliterated. . . . Houses were reduced to rubble, innocent people were killed, untold numbers became displaced, riceland was abandoned, and as much as one half of the population of the countryside fled." As early as 1962, villages in certain zones were "subjected to bombardment by artillery and air strikes in order to drive the population into the strategic hamlets," according to pro-war historian Guenter Lewy. "Driving the inhabitants" into "safety" through bombing may seem oxymoronic, but it resulted from a U.S. theory that villagers in Viet Cong–dominated areas could be persuaded to relocate to friendly territory if bombing made it in their self-interest to do so. As Turse writes, "Houses were set ablaze, whole villages were bulldozed, and people were forced into squalid refugee camps and filthy urban slums short of water, food, and shelter."[17]

Journalist Neil Sheehan confirmed that the destruction of villages and the creation of refugees was policy rather than accident, sanctioned by U.S. commanding general William Westmoreland. As Sheehan explains:

> The Americans called it "generating refugees" . . . Driving people from their homes by bombing and shelling. I was out with Westmoreland one day and I asked him, "General, aren't you disturbed by wounding all these civilians, the bombing and shelling of hamlets?" He said "Yes, Neil, it's a problem. But it does deprive the enemy of the population, doesn't it?" And I thought to myself "You cold-blooded bastard. You know exactly what you're doing."[18]

Eventually, U.S. evaluators would conclude that "putting the people behind barbed wire against their will is not the first step toward earning their loyalty and support," but Westmoreland publicly stated that making villagers homeless or putting them in camps would ensure that their villages could not be captured by guerrillas, claiming that "in order to thwart the communists' designs, it is necessary to eliminate the 'fish' from the 'water,' or to dry up the 'water' so that the 'fish' cannot survive." The "water," he said, were the villagers. By 1967 this policy had produced a million refugees.[19]

The basic facts are not disputed even by staunchly pro-war historians such as Lewy. In fact, while Lewy's work is ostensibly a strong defense of American policy, it contains shocking evidence about the
extent of U.S. destruction of Vietnam. He quotes an American officer's
assessment that "the unparalleled, lavish use of firepower as a substitute
for manpower is an outstanding characteristic of U.S. military tactics in
the Vietnam war." (In fact, when Westmoreland was asked how he intended to win the war, he did not reply with an actual military strategy.
Instead, he just said "firepower.") This "lavish use of firepower" was an
application of a maxim that the United States began subscribing to
after World War I: "Expend shells, not men." This meant minimizing
U.S. casualties at all costs, by maximizing the amount of destruction
inflicted. But while a philosophy of "risk minimization" can sound benign, the results are horrifying.[20]

Having a plane drop napalm from the air, for instance, is an easy
way to minimize risk to Americans and "expend shells," but it predictably leads to the massacre of civilians. As Ken Burns and Geoffrey
Ward say in *The Vietnam War*'s accompanying book, napalm was "an
effective weapon—a single 120-gallon aluminum tank could engulf in
flame an area 150 feet long and 50 feet wide, and its use saved untold
numbers of American and ARVN lives—but it also killed or disfigured
countless Vietnamese civilians." Lewy says the official rules of engagement allowed napalm attacks on villages only in cases where it was
"absolutely necessary," but admits that "in practice this rule does not
appear to have restricted the use of such weapons."[21]

Such destruction was greatly facilitated by the dehumanization of
the native population. Testimonies from Americans who served in Vietnam confirm that from basic training onward, "right away they told us
not to call them Vietnamese. Call everybody gooks, dinks." As for the
Viet Cong, "They were like animals. They wouldn't allow you to talk
about them as if they were people. . . . They told us they're not to be
treated with any type of mercy or apprehension."[22]

There was an important racist underpinning to the assault on Vietnam that greatly facilitated the manipulation and destruction. The refrain that "Orientals" are essentially lower animals, who don't feel pain as sensitive Westerners do and who only respect force, had its effect on policy. The head of the U.S. Information Agency in Saigon, John Mecklin, a critical supporter of U.S. involvement, wrote that Vietnamese peasants have reasoning powers "only slightly beyond the level of an American six-year-old" and mumble to each other in a vocabulary of a few hundred words. Westmoreland was openly racist, suggesting that the "Oriental" mindset meant these killings didn't matter very much: "The Oriental doesn't put the same high price on life as does the Westerner. Life is plentiful. Life is cheap in the Orient. As the philosophy of the Orient expresses it, life is not important." Burning women and children alive in their huts therefore need not trouble the American conscience.[23]

Soldiers were taught almost nothing of Vietnamese language or culture. One special forces colonel explained why there was no need for Americans serving in Vietnam to consider learning Vietnamese: "You don't need to know the gook's language 'cos he's gonna be dead. We're going to kill the bastards." Because the locals all bled together into a mob of "gooks," distinctions between civilians and combatants were often made haphazardly. Turse explains that the high civilian casualties in Vietnam resulted in part from an informal (sometimes spoken, sometimes not) "mere gook rule": the rule that if corpses were "mere gooks," nobody would be held accountable for the killings, even if the dead were civilians and the rules of engagement had been violated. Turse quotes one Marine telling another: "Shouldn't bother you at all, just some more dead gooks. The sooner they all die, the sooner we go back to the world." Vietnam veteran Tim O'Brien, in his novel *The Things They Carried*, captured the dehumanizing language in which "a VC nurse, fried by napalm, was a crispy critter," and a Vietnamese baby was "a roasted peanut" or "crunchie munchie."[24]

"Nobody cared about the Vietnamese," one anonymous soldier declared bluntly. Little fuss was made if civilians were killed, because they were often chalked up as enemy dead, with soldiers following the rule that "if it's dead and it's Vietnamese, it's VC." (Note the "it.") Even Lewy concedes that it is "clear that a steady percentage of those reported as VC dead were in fact villagers not carrying weapons."[25]

One of the most disturbing aspects of the war is the American military leadership's strategy of prioritizing "body count" above all. Westmoreland deliberately waged a war of attrition, attempting to weaken the NLF and North Vietnamese Army's resolve by killing as many of them as possible. Commanders in the field were obsessively pressured to produce as many dead Vietnamese bodies as possible. "Body count was everything," and the "pressure to kill indiscriminately" was "practically irresistible." There were "kill count" competitions, with soldiers being rewarded with leave or cases of beer for maximizing their kills. Superior officers would say things like "Jack up that body count or you're gone, Colonel." One West Point veteran remembers hearing his commander explain his strategy, which was that "he wanted to begin killing four thousand of these little bastards a month, and then by the end of the following month wanted to kill six thousand." Promotion in the officer corps could be dependent on body count, and "many high-level officers established 'production quotas' for their units."[26]

As celebrated war memoirist Philip Caputo recounted, it often seemed as if there were no traditional strategic military objectives, such as the capture of territory. The only objective was mass killing. He recounts being told:

> Your mission is to kill VC. Period. You're not here to capture a hill. You're not here to capture a town. You're not here to move from Point A to Point B to Point C. You're here to kill Viet Cong. As many of 'em as you can.

But, Caputo says, it was not clear "how you distinguish a Viet Cong from a civilian." If someone ran away, this was treated a "prima facie evidence that he, or even she, was the enemy" because "if they liked us they wouldn't run."[27]

The incredible death toll among the Vietnamese was policy, not accident. The My Lai massacre, in which hundreds of civilians were gunned down by U.S. soldiers, instantly ceases to become a mystery when we understand just how the United States went about prosecuting the war. Not only was My Lai *not* an aberration, but it would be shocking if it *were* an aberration, because war planners' goals were to carry out a massive bloodbath. This is the reality of the war characterized as a "blundering effort to do good."

THE "SIDESHOWS": LAOS AND CAMBODIA

The "Vietnam War" is a misleading name for a war that inflicted massive violence on neighboring countries as well. In Laos, the United States attacked both Laotian communist and North Vietnamese forces, flying 580,000 bombing runs between 1964 and 1973, which works out to "one planeload every eight minutes for nearly a decade." A ton of ordnance was dropped for every person in Laos, and in total the war killed one out of ten people in the country. By the end, "U.S. aircraft had dumped 2,093,100 tons of ordnance on the landlocked country, which is about twice the size of Pennsylvania, with a population then under 3 million." Laos became the most bombed country in the history of the world, exceeding the World War II bombings of Japan and Germany combined.[28]

As anthropologist and Laos expert Leah Zani notes, among American planners, the Laos operation "was considered a success," because while it did not prevent a communist government from taking charge, it "succeeded in significantly hindering the incoming communist state's capacity to build basic infrastructure and social systems" and showed "that the United States could sustain a long-term conflict with minimal American ground troops and without public or congressional support." Journalist Joshua Kurlantzick says that "Laos would prove so successful— for presidents, and for the CIA, that is—that it would become a template for a new type of large, secret war for decades to come." As a "war fought on the cheap that held the communists in Laos to a virtual stand-still for years," it "became an archetype for agency paramilitary operations—and a new way for the president to unilaterally declare war and then secretly order massive attacks, often using aerial weaponry."[29]

Laos is still one of the most war-contaminated places on Earth. For over fifty years, the bombs have continued to kill people, with more than twenty thousand Laotians dying (and many more being maimed) *after* the bombing stopped. Nearly half the victims are children. In 2021, there were over sixty explosions. The killing and maiming, of course, are only part of the damage; there is also the trauma and fear that come from living in a landscape littered with hidden bombs. Elementary school children are taught to identify the difference between types of bombs so that they don't pick them up.[30]

In 2013, *The New York Times* ran a story entitled "One Woman's Mission to Free Laos from Millions of Unexploded Bombs." It reports on the "single-minded effort" of a Lao-American woman, Channapha Khamvongsa, "to rid her native land of millions of bombs still buried there." The story notes that as a result of Ms. Khamvongsa's lobbying, the United States increased its annual spending on the removal of un-exploded bombs by an inadequate $12 million. The *Times* tells us that Ms. Khamvongsa "was spurred into action when she came across a collection of drawings of the bombings made by refugees and collected by Fred Branfman." That book displays the torment of the victims, poor peasants in a remote area that had virtually nothing to do with the Vietnam War. But the *Times* did not report on a crucial revelation made by Branfman. The article retells the standard explanation for the attack on Laos: It tells us that "the targets were North Vietnamese troops—especially along the Ho Chi Minh Trail, a large part of which passed through Laos—as well as North Vietnam's Laotian Communist allies." In fact, Branfman writes that "one of the most shattering revelations" was that "there was no military reason" for Lyndon Johnson's diverting planes into Laos. U.S. deputy chief of mission Monteagle Stearns testi-fied to the U.S. Senate Committee on Foreign Relations in October

1969 that "we had all those planes sitting around and couldn't just let them stay there with nothing to do."[31]

In 2023, ten years after the *Times* reported on Ms. Khamvongsa's mission, less than 1 percent of the unexploded bombs have been cleared. At the present rate of clearance, "it would take another 100 years to make Laos [unexploded ordnance]-free." Future generations of Laotian children will continue to have to study charts of bombs, to avoid being maimed and killed. Because the planes needed something to do.[32]

In 1970, Richard Nixon called National Security Advisor Henry Kissinger to instruct him to escalate the illegal bombing of Cambodia. Kissinger transmitted the order to General Alexander Haig: the president wanted "a massive bombing campaign in Cambodia. Anything that flies, on anything that moves." It would be hard to find a declaration with such clear genocidal intent in the archival record of any state. Ostensibly, as in Laos, the bombings were aimed at North Vietnamese military units operating out of Cambodia. Millions of tons of ordnance were deployed. We know that "in many cases, Cambodian villages were hit with dozens of payloads over the course of several hours," causing "near-total destruction." "Nothing could survive," said a U.S. official at the time. The bombings have been estimated to have killed between 50,000 and 150,000 Cambodian civilians, but experts Taylor Owen and Ben Kiernan said that "the number of casualties is surely higher" because the tonnage of ordnance dropped was five times higher than known when estimates were produced.[33]

The bombings "drove ordinary Cambodians into the arms of the Khmer Rouge, an insurgent communist group that seemed initially to have slim prospects of revolutionary success." Chhit Do, a Khmer Rouge officer, later described how the bombings served as a recruitment tool: "terrified and half crazy" from the destruction, "the people were ready to believe what they were told," and "it was because of their dissatisfaction with the bombing that they kept on co-operating with the Khmer Rouge." Kiernan concludes that the Khmer Rouge "would not have won power without U.S. economic and military destabilization of Cambodia." The "carpet bombing of Cambodia's countryside by American B-52s" was "probably the most important single factor in Pol Pot's rise." His regime committed a genocide, killing 1.7 million people in a few short years.[34]

The Khmer Rouge "killing fields" have received extensive attention in the U.S. Less frequently noted is U.S. *support* for the Khmer Rouge. Zbigniew Brzezinski said that while the regime was in power, the U.S. "encouraged the Chinese to support Pol Pot" and "winked, semi-publicly" at Chinese and Thai aid to the Khmer Rouge. Kissinger said when the Khmer Rouge came to power "we will be friends with them. They are murderous thugs, but we won't let that stand in our way."[35]

After the Pol Pot regime was overthrown and the scale of the atrocities became clear, the U.S. still backed the Khmer Rouge for a seat at the UN and "opposed efforts to investigate or indict the Khmer Rouge for genocide or other crimes against humanity." Until 1989 "all attempts even to describe the Khmer Rouge regime as genocidal were rejected by the United States as counterproductive to finding peace." This was entirely for ruthlessly strategic reasons: the U.S. saw the Khmer Rouge as convenient allies because they were opposed to the government of Vietnam.[36]

Henry Kissinger, asked about his role in Cambodia, professed himself baffled that anyone could question him: "I may have a lack of imagination, but I fail to see the moral issue involved." Others have more imagination. The deposed king of Cambodia, Norodom Sihanouk, blamed Kissinger and Nixon squarely for the rise of the Khmer Rouge, saying that the "only two men responsible for the tragedy in Cambodia" were Nixon and Kissinger, who "created the Khmer Rouge."[37]

Similarly, Francois Ponchaud, a priest who reported on the Khmer Rouge atrocities, was skeptical when a tribunal was prepared to try Khmer Rouge officials for their crimes. Ponchaud viewed the proceedings as selective and hypocritical. Citing U.S. support for the regime, he asked: "What's to be said of the international killer that was the United States, which will never be judged by anyone?"[38]

THE WAR, EVALUATED

The war on Southeast Asia that the United States first supported, then waged, from 1945 to 1975, is one of the great crimes of the twentieth century. The world's greatest technological superpower used virtually all its destructive capabilities (except nuclear weapons, which were repeatedly considered) against a small country's rural peasantry. For every American killed in the war, around forty Vietnamese died.

The U.S. war is often treated as a defeat for the U.S. It would be more accurate to call it a partial victory. On the negative side, the client regimes had fallen. On the positive side, the entire region was in ruins, and there was no fear that the "virus" of successful independent development might "infect" others. As Johnson adviser Walt Rostow commented, looking back, while what "Johnson did was more costly perhaps than it had to be," ultimately he "saved Southeast Asia and we hold the balance of power in Asia today."[39]

Documenting and analyzing particular atrocities committed in Vietnam is important, but in the final verdict, the war itself was ultimately the crime. It was not a war fought out of noble motives. American leaders were fully aware that they were not acting in the interests of the Vietnamese people or defending anything that could reasonably be called "democracy." It was a war fought because the United States feared the loss of influence and the humiliation of defeat. Policy toward Vietnam fell within the general doctrinal framework that had been established for the post–World War II global order. The United States refused to recognize Vietnamese independence after the war, supported and then took over the French effort at colonial reconquest, and finally launched a large-scale invasion that, at its height, fielded five hundred thousand troops to keep an unpopular, autocratic, U.S.-friendly government in power. By throwing its lot in with France, the United States was fully aware from the start that it was opposing the forces of nationalism and that its own clients could not withstand political competition. Resorting to peaceful means was never an option.

Americans were told that they were fighting to protect the free country of South Vietnam from aggressive invasion by North Vietnam. In fact, they were fighting to impose a dictatorial client state on South Vietnam and to subvert Vietnamese public opinion. Americans were told that they were fighting the communist *North* Vietnamese, when they were often actually fighting mostly *South* Vietnamese. In the U.S. press, the bombing of North Vietnam was extensively debated, but the much worse bombing of South Vietnam was ignored, because admitting how much we were bombing the country we were "defending" would have been difficult to reconcile with the official justifications for the war. The invasion and occupation of South Vietnam is what we correctly call "aggression" when it is conducted by an official enemy. Thus the United States was "defending South Vietnam" in the same sense in which the Soviet Union "defended Afghanistan during the 1980s."

According to the Pentagon Papers, the Defense Department's war aims were "70 percent to avoid a humiliating U.S. defeat . . . 20 percent to keep South Vietnam (and then adjacent) territory from Chinese hands, 10 percent to permit the people of South Vietnam to enjoy a better, freer way of life." But this is far too generous a view of the United States. Ten percent was a gross overestimate of U.S. concern for the Vietnamese. *No* part of American policy was designed to bring "a better, freer way of life" to the people of South Vietnam; the war was conducted in the full knowledge that it was bringing them a much worse and less free way of life. The United States obliterated the country's rural society, slaughtering peasants and driving those who survived into concentration camps.[40]

Even when the country refrained from carrying out certain atrocities, the human toll was not considered. When Assistant Secretary of Defense John McNaughton suggested destroying locks and dams to create mass starvation in 1966, the idea was discounted because "strikes at population targets" would "create a counterproductive wave of revulsion abroad and at home." Richard Nixon rebuked Henry Kissinger over Kissinger's supposed concern with civilian casualties in the bombings. ("You're so goddamned concerned about the civilians and I don't give a damn. I don't care.") Kissinger replied that he was concerned "because I don't want the world to be mobilized against you as a butcher." Kissinger himself cared not about Vietnamese lives, but about the moral judgment other countries might display, which would be a realpolitik concern. Indeed, Kissinger showed no hesitation in authorizing the most horrific war crimes, and Nixon was wrong to think that his deputy gave a damn about "the civilians."[41]

Vietnam veteran W. D. Ehrhart, who joined the antiwar movement on returning to the United States, says that the experience of war fundamentally changed his view of the U.S. role in the world. As a child, "I lived on a diet of John Wayne movies and Audie Murphy movies," and in Vietnam, "I literally expected to be welcomed with open arms by the people of Vietnam," whom he thought he would be saving from communism. In fact, he discovered that the Vietnamese "hated me," and soon realized why: "The notion I had when I was in high school was it was the Vietcong [that] terrorized the Vietnamese population, forced them to fight against the Americans on pain of death. What I began to understand in Vietnam was that they didn't need to do things like that. All they had to do was let a marine patrol go through a village and whatever was left of that village, they had all the recruits that they needed." Seeing the war up close destroyed "everything I'd ever believed about the world I lived in, the country I lived in," as he saw that "all the stuff that we were told about our country was mythology," that in fact "the Western world was trying to restore the colonial subordination of the Third World." The stories he went to Vietnam with, Ehrhart said, "had nothing to do with what this country really is."[42]

Few in the United States have faced up to the reality of what was done to Vietnam, Laos, and Cambodia by their country. Jimmy Carter, who went on to win a Nobel Peace Prize, declined to apologize for the war on the grounds that "the destruction was mutual." Because we went to Vietnam "without any desire to capture territory or impose American will on other people," Carter continued, there is no need to "assume the status of culpability."[43]

The destruction was not, of course, "mutual"—Americans did not have their towns and cities wiped out by Vietnamese bombers. But the facts of the war challenge familiar precepts about American benevolence and commitment to self-determination and justice. The erosion of this theology is a threat to the freedom of the state to engage in subversion, violence, and terror, and cannot be countenanced. Thus the actual history must be reshaped so that the state can exercise its power without the impediment of a dissident public.

9/11 and the Wrecking
of Afghanistan

S hortly after the September 11 attacks in 2001, President George
W. Bush posed a famous question: "Why do they hate us?" Bush gave
his own simple answer: "They hate our freedoms—our freedom of reli-
gion, our freedom of speech, our freedom to vote and assemble and
disagree with each other." But in a 1997 interview with a CNN journalist, the actual mastermind of the attacks, Osama bin Laden, had offered
a different answer to the question of "why they hate us." His explanation did not mention "our freedoms" or "voting." Instead, bin Laden
said that his jihad was because "the U.S. government . . . has committed
acts that are extremely unjust, hideous, and criminal," both "directly or
through its support of the Israeli occupation" of Palestine. "The mention of the U.S.," he says, "reminds us before everything else of those
innocent children who were dismembered, their heads and arms cut off
in the recent explosion that took place in Qana."[1]

Few Americans probably remember the Qana massacre, which
took place in Lebanon in 1996. The Israel Defense Forces (IDF) fired
artillery shells at a United Nations compound where 800 civilians were
taking shelter (having been ordered to flee their homes by the IDF); 106
civilians were killed in the attack, of whom half were children, plus 120

more injured, including 4 UN workers. An Associated Press report from a year after the event conveys a small sliver of the human toll: "Lina Taqi, 7, walks with a limp, moves her left arm with difficulty and rarely speaks. Her father is dead." She was "but one of the lives shattered a year ago when Israeli artillery slammed into a UN peacekeeping base packed with civilians." Lina's eight-year-old sister was killed, with "shreds of her pajamas" all that was left. Lina herself underwent six months of treatment for a shrapnel wound in the head, and would never recover the full use of her limbs. According to her mother, she would wake up at night "shaking, lost and hallucinating, sometimes wetting herself."[2]

An investigation by the United Nations secretary-general's military adviser concluded it was unlikely that the attack on the compound had been a mistake. An Amnesty International investigation found that "the IDF intentionally attacked the UN compound" despite having been informed of its position and the presence of sheltering civilians. Indeed, soldiers who were part of the Israeli artillery battery that launched the attack confessed later to the press that "no one spoke about it as if it was a mistake," saying "it was war" and the victims were "just a bunch of Arabs." The United Nations General Assembly took the modest step of voting to charge Israel for the financial costs of the damage to the UN base. The United States and Israel were the only states to vote against the resolution. Israel refused to pay the damages, saying that the Lebanese brought the cost on themselves.[3]

After the September 11 attacks, in an open "letter to America," bin Laden again gave a similar justification when answering the question "Why are we fighting and opposing you? The answer is very simple. . . . Because you attacked us and continue to attack us." Bin Laden cited, foremost, U.S. support for the Israeli occupation of Palestine, and the "oppression, tyranny, crimes, killing, expulsion, destruction and devastation" that have taken place there. "The blood pouring out of Palestine must be equally revenged. You must know that the Palestinians do not cry alone; their women are not widowed alone; their sons are not orphaned alone." Bin Laden listed other grievances, most of which related to U.S. foreign policy: "steal[ing] our wealth and oil at paltry prices because of your international influence and military threats," "support[ing] the Russian atrocities against us in Chechnya," supporting "the Indian oppression against us in Kashmir," and killing Iraqi children through economic sanctions.[4]

Bin Laden attacked America for hypocrisy, saying that the United States claims the right to possess weapons of mass destruction while denying that others have the same right, and Americans are "the last ones to respect the resolutions and policies of International Law, yet . . . want to selectively punish anyone else who does the same." He asked: "How many acts of oppression, tyranny and injustice have you carried out, O callers to freedom?" After listing his foreign policy grievances, bin Laden condemned American morality. He complained that we had "destroyed nature with your industrial waste and gases" and refused to sign the Kyoto Protocol. He accused us of "exploit[ing] women like consumer products." He professed abhorrence at American acceptance of "President Clinton's immoral acts committed in the official Oval Office," and our perceived tolerance of drug use, gambling, and sex work. (He does not acknowledge the Republican Party's stalwart efforts to advance his social agenda.)

Bin Laden's letter is certainly deranged, and drips with explicit anti-Semitism. (Bin Laden claims that "the Jews have taken control of your economy" and are "making you their servants," which is "precisely what Benjamin Franklin warned you against." Franklin's supposed warning that "the Jew" is a "great danger for the United State of America" has long been known to be a forgery.[5]) His justification for attacking civilians is unpersuasive—he says that in a democracy, ordinary citizens are responsible for the government's acts, making it fair to treat them as representatives of government policy. (He ignores the U.S. government's efforts to keep citizens in ignorance of its policies through propaganda.) He claims divine support for the archaic principle of vengeance: "Whoever has destroyed our villages and towns . . . we have the right to destroy their villages and towns." But while bin Laden was undoubtedly fanatical and homicidal, it is clear from all his public commentary that the 9/11 attacks cannot just be attributed to violent religiosity. The basic thrust of his argument is that 9/11 was an act of justified revenge, that his violence against the United States was to repay violence *by* the United States.

Bin Laden's brutal extremist tactics were fringe and entirely unrepresentative of the Muslim world. But anger at the United States was shared by others. A few days after Bush declared that they "hate our freedoms," *The Wall Street Journal* ran a series of stories that investigated the question seriously, interviewing Muslims around the world about their views on the United States. The interviewees were elite professionals. They were often pro-U.S., but shared a "perception that unlimited American power is propping up hated, oppressive regimes." Anger at the U.S. came from "America's alleged double standard in defending Israel's occupation of Arab lands while continuing to hit Iraq with economic sanctions and military attacks for what some Muslims consider essentially the same behavior." The reason "the U.S. arouses such passion and anger in the Muslim world, among all segments of society," is that its diplomacy "has seldom lived up to its cherished ideals."[6] Thus "even wealthy businesspeople are growing tired of what they see as a U.S. double standard." Said a Qatari engineer, "We don't have anything against the Americans as Americans, but these rulers are supported by the Americans."

John Esposito, director of the Center for Muslim-Christian Understanding at Georgetown University, said "this is not a clash of civilizations but a clash over American foreign policy." Esposito said that many in the Muslim world, including "businesspeople who deal with the U.S. all the time," hoped the attacks would cause the United States to rethink its policy toward the Middle East. In 2005, David Gardner of the *Financial Times* similarly reported that many in the Muslim world thought that 9/11 would make it "impossible for the West and its Arab despot clients to continue to ignore a political set-up that incubated blind rage against them."[7]

George W. Bush was not alone in preferring a more comforting story and creating an explanation for the attacks that would prevent Americans from having to scrutinize their government's policies. On September 16, 2001, *The New York Times*'s Serge Schmemann explained that the attackers acted out of "hatred for the values cherished in the West as freedom, tolerance, prosperity, religious pluralism and universal suffrage." These "fundamentalists" saw in America a land of "licentiousness, corruption, greed, and apostasy" and the Twin Towers as symbols of "Sodom and mammon." Absent was any discussion of the actual grievances listed by the perpetrator.[8]

Understanding the roots of terrorism does not justify it. In fact, those who are the most opposed to terrorist acts will do the most to try to understand their causes, in order to prevent future violence.

The horrifying atrocities of September 11, 2001, were something new in world affairs. Not since the War of 1812 had the United States been attacked within its national territory. (The case of Pearl Harbor is frequently cited as an exception, but Pearl Harbor was a military base in a colonial outpost. Hawai'i did not become a U.S. state until nearly two decades later, and the comparison between Pearl Harbor and 9/11 is analogous to the difference between an attack on a military installation in British-occupied India and an attack on London.) The United States is used to doling out violence against the people of other countries, not being on the receiving end of it.

The 9/11 attacks could have been dealt with as a crime. This would have been sane and consistent with precedent. Invading the country of the perpetrator is an atypical response to lawbreaking. When the IRA set off bombs in London, nobody called for air strikes on West Belfast (or on Boston, where a great deal of IRA funding came from). When the Oklahoma City bombing was found to have been perpetrated by a white supremacist associated with ultraright militias, there was no call to obliterate Idaho or Montana. Instead, the attacker was searched for, found, apprehended, brought to court, and convicted.

This was not the approach taken by the Bush administration. Rather than seek out and punish the guilty—and only the guilty—it launched a "global war on terror," beginning with the invasion of Afghanistan by the United States and its coalition partners, and then expanding, that led to the deaths of millions.[9] Brown University's Costs of War project found that the post–9/11 wars led to the deaths of nearly 1 million people through direct violence and an additional 3.6–3.8 million in indirect deaths, with 38 million people becoming displaced—the largest mass displacement since World War II.[10]

After the attacks, the Bush administration demanded that the Taliban, then ruling in Afghanistan, immediately hand over Osama bin Laden to the United States. The Taliban, in response, offered to put bin Laden on trial, if the United States provided evidence of his guilt. Bush refused. Nor did he consider the Taliban's offer to give up bin Laden to a neutral third country. His demand, he said, was nonnegotiable. He would not provide evidence (in fact, he had none at the time). He would not enter into talks. Historian Carter Malkasian notes that Bush did not instruct his secretary of state, Colin Powell, "to open a line to the Taliban to work things out, which would have been the normal diplomatic course of action to avoid a war."[11]

In fact, long *before* 9/11, the Taliban had reached out to the United States and offered to put bin Laden on trial under the supervision of a "neutral international organization," but the United States government showed no interest and did not respond. Milton Bearden, a CIA station chief who oversaw U.S. covert operations in Afghanistan in the 1980s, told *The Washington Post* after 9/11 that the Taliban had long been signaling to the United States that they "wanted to get rid of" bin Laden, and probably "set up bin Laden for capture by the United States," but the United States responded to the signals with threats. Relations between the Taliban and bin Laden were, in fact, "deeply contentious," and they had repeatedly placed him under house arrest.[12]

Instead of entering into extradition talks with the Taliban, Washington immediately demanded that Pakistan eliminate "truck convoys

that provide much of the food and other supplies to Afghanistan's civilian population," and caused the withdrawal of aid workers along with
severe reduction in food supplies, thereby leaving, as Samina Ahmed of
the International Crisis Group noted, "millions of Afghans . . . at grave
risk of starvation." Despite sharp protests from aid organizations and
warnings of what might ensue if the United States bombed the country,
there was little discussion of the possible humanitarian consequences
of such actions for Afghans.[13]

In the first week of October 2001, Bush launched "Operation Enduring Freedom," sending a "powerful barrage of cruise missiles and
long-range bombers against Afghanistan" to try to destroy the Taliban's government. "The Taliban will pay a price," he declared, calling
the attacks "carefully targeted." This was not the approach favored by
many scholars of terrorism, who had been "caution[ing] against a quick-
hit military response," encouraging "police work and prudence" instead. In *Foreign Affairs*, military historian Michael Howard made the
sensible suggestion that the response should be "a police operation conducted under the auspices of the United Nations . . . against a criminal
conspiracy whose members should be hunted down and brought before
an international court, where they would receive a fair trial and, if
found guilty, be awarded an appropriate sentence." But Bush himself,
according to neoconservative writer Robert Kagan, "wanted vengeance."
Colin Powell got the impression that the president "wanted to kill somebody." Indeed, on September 20, Bush told religious leaders in the Oval
Office: "I'm having difficulty controlling my bloodlust."[14]

Against one of the poorest countries on Earth, as Malkasian writes,
the United States sent "F-15E strike fighters, carrier-based F-18C fighters, black B-2 stealth bombers, and 40-year-old Vietnam-era B-52G/H
bombers . . . the propeller-driven AC-130 Specter gunship . . . carried a
150mm cannon, 25mm Gatling guns, and 40mm cannons . . . akin to a
flying artillery battery. Manned aircraft were joined by new Predator
drones." U.S. forces were soon running out of targets to bomb, because
"the Taliban had few headquarters and little infrastructure to hit."

Veteran Middle East correspondent Patrick Cockburn commented that "what the Americans never explain in Afghanistan or Iraq is why they are using weapons designed for World War Three against villages that have not left the Middle Ages—which makes heavy civilian casualties inevitable."[15]

After the bombing began, the Taliban again offered to enter talks about turning over bin Laden, on condition that the United States stop bombing the country. (They gave up the demand to see evidence of bin Laden's guilt.) The Taliban labeled the bombings a "terrorist attack," and the number of Afghan civilian deaths from the war quickly exceeded the three thousand deaths in the September 11 attacks themselves. A Human Rights Watch account from the end of October documented horrific bombings of remote Afghan villages, where residents "were adamant that there were no Taliban or Al-Qaida positions in the area." One forty-year-old mother lost her husband and all six of her children in one of the U.S.'s "carefully targeted" bombing raids. U.S. bombs struck facilities of the UN and the International Red Cross—killing multiple workers and "all but wip[ing] out the [International Red Cross's] sole complex with supplies of food and blankets for 55,000 disabled Afghans"—even though the United States had been given the locations of the facilities beforehand.[16]

NPR reporter Sarah Chayes, who filed from Afghanistan at the time, says that "the bombing was traumatizing the Afghan civilians whom it was supposed to be liberating," and the Afghan refugees she talked to "could think and talk of nothing else," having gone "mad with fear." Chayes writes of "the anguish [she] heard every day—the pleas to tell President Bush, for the love of God, to stop the bombing," but says that U.S. media at the time was reluctant to broadcast negative news about the war, with a CNN correspondent claiming to have been told not to film civilian casualties. An editor at NPR even accused Chayes of "disseminating Taliban propaganda" and said her sources must be "pro–Bin Laden."[17]

The wanton killing of innocent civilians is, of course, the opposite of a "war on terrorism." It is terrorism itself. But U.S. officials reacted with indifference. After a village was hit "with torrents of withering fire from an AC-130 aerial gunship," killing dozens of civilians, a Pentagon official remarked "the people there are dead because we wanted them dead" and "we hit what we wanted to hit." (Defense Secretary Donald Rumsfeld commented: "I cannot deal with that particular village.") Another village was wiped out in October by two thousand pounds of explosives, which missed the Taliban but killed one hundred innocent people.[18]

Afghan opponents of the Taliban were appalled by the bombing. Abdul Haq, one of the main leaders of the anti-Taliban opposition forces, expressed his vehement objection, saying that the United States "is trying to show its muscle," but didn't "care about the suffering of the Afghans or how many people we will lose." Haq argued that the American bombings were actually undercutting the efforts of anti-Taliban forces. He was not alone in his view. In October 2001, a meeting of hundreds of tribal elders and other anti-Taliban Afghan leaders unanimously demanded an end to the bombing, which, they declared, was targeting innocent people. Although they hated the Taliban, they urged that means other than slaughter and destruction be employed to overthrow the regime. It was "a rare display of unity among tribal elders, Islamic scholars, fractious politicians, and former guerrilla commanders," the press reported. They had many disagreements but unanimously "urged the U.S. to stop the air raids" and appealed to the international media to call for an end to the "bombing of innocent people." They urged that other means be adopted to overthrow the hated Taliban regime, a goal they believed could be achieved without further death and destruction.[19]

The leading Afghan women's rights organization, Revolutionary Association of the Women of Afghanistan (RAWA), issued a declaration on October 11, 2001, strongly opposing the "vast aggression on our country" by the United States, which will shed the blood of innocent civilians. The declaration called for "eradication of the plague of the

Taliban and al-Qaeda" by the "uprising of the Afghan nation," not by a murderous assault of foreign aggressors. They added that "despite the claim of the U.S. that only military and terrorist bases of the Taliban and Al Qaeda will be struck and that its actions would be accurately targeted and proportionate, what we have witnessed for the past seven days leaves no doubt that this invasion will shed the blood of numerous women, men, children, young and old of our country."[20]

Donald Rumsfeld disclaimed U.S. responsibility for *any* civilian deaths, on the grounds that "we did not start this war." This meant, he said, that "responsibility for every single casualty in this war, whether they're innocent Afghans or innocent Americans, rests at the feet of the al Qaeda [*sic*] and the Taliban." The statement was, of course, ludicrous: the Taliban had not attacked the United States, and the United States had launched the war itself in clear violation of international law. Bush himself scoffed at the notion that an unauthorized invasion of a sovereign nation was a criminal act, saying, "I don't care what the international lawyers say, we are going to kick some ass." (The applicable legal standard is that violence in self-defense is justified only in the case of armed attack, and must still be approved by the UN Security Council. The United States did not seek the approval of the Security Council, even though it would "probably" have obtained it, in all likelihood because this would have established the principle that the United States has to defer to some higher authority before carrying out the use of violence, which the Bush administration did not believe.) In fact, there were no credible grounds for the invasion whatsoever, meaning that on Rumsfeld's principle (*whoever starts a war is responsible for every casualty*), all violence that occurred as a consequence of the U.S. attack would be the responsibility of the U.S.[21]

The Taliban were toppled within six weeks and offered to surrender. Donald Rumsfeld declared, "We don't negotiate surrenders," and in November's Bonn conference, which aimed to produce a political settlement for the country, the Taliban were excluded from negotiations. Masoom Stanekzai, a senior adviser in the postwar Afghan government, later called the failure to include the Taliban a "historic mistake," and Carter Malkasian says "the mood of the time overrode wiser diplomacy." That mood, according to the leader of the U.S. delegation, was: "They have been defeated. Why should they be included?" Rumsfeld "vetoed any peace with the Taliban," warning new Afghan president Hamid Karzai that "any deal" accommodating the Taliban "would be against U.S. interests." Malkasian notes that "this narrow and inflexible approach contravened diplomatic wisdom to bring adversaries into a post-war political settlement," and set up the long war that followed. When Karzai brought up the earlier Taliban peace feelers, the Bush administration banned negotiations, even giving a "blacklist" of people that the Afghan government was forbidden from talking with. Afghan American diplomat Zalmay Khalilzad believes "America's longest war might have instead gone down in history as one of its shortest had the United States been willing to talk to the Taliban in December 2001."[22] Foreign Service officer Todd Greentree, who worked in Afghanistan, says the U.S. "violated the Afghan way of war," under which "when one side wins, the other side puts down their arms and reconciles with the side that won."[23]

The Bush administration had, of course, given little thought to the actual consequences of overthrowing the Taliban. Malkasian notes that there were no "significant investments in reconstruction, economic development, and institutions," and Ambassador Ryan Crocker summarized Rumsfeld's attitude as: "Our job is about killing bad guys . . . [once] we have killed the bad guys, who cares what happens next?" This was not a war to bring democracy or women's rights to Afghanistan, both of which were an afterthought used to justify the calamity in retrospect.[24]

In fact, Bush swiftly lost interest in Afghanistan. Plans to invade Iraq had started on September 11, 2001. The very afternoon of the day of the attacks, Donald Rumsfeld asked the CIA to produce "best info fast" so that he could "judge whether good enough [to] hit S.H. [Saddam Hussein] at same time. Not only UBL [bin Laden]." When asked about the hunt for bin Laden in March 2002, Bush replied, "I truly am not that concerned about him," a comment he later denied having made. Bush indicated that since bin Laden was no longer "running Afghanistan," he was not a priority. (Of course, not only had bin Laden never come close to "running Afghanistan," but the Taliban had found him a nuisance and offered to give him up.)[25]

Once Bush's attention was fixed on Iraq, the Afghanistan war was treated as unimportant and its mission was ambiguous. (There had never really been one, besides the desire to avenge the deaths of 9/11 victims by killing some people who resembled the people suspected of being responsible.) According to a memo from Donald Rumsfeld, when Rumsfeld asked the president if he wanted to meet "with General Franks and General McNeill," Bush replied, "Who is General McNeill?" and Rumsfeld had to explain that "he is the general in charge of Afghanistan." Bush replied, "Well, I don't need to meet with him."[26]

Plenty of money was funneled into Afghanistan. Adjusted for inflation, the amount spent exceeded Marshall Plan aid to Western Europe after World War II. At one point "the U.S. government was pumping roughly as much money into Afghanistan as the undeveloped country's economy produced on its own." But as Craig Whitlock writes, much of that money might as well have been set on fire: "U.S. officials wasted huge sums on projects that Afghans did not need or did not want. Much of the money ended up in the pockets of overpriced contractors or corrupt Afghan officials, while U.S.-financed schools, clinics and roads fell into disrepair due to poor construction or maintenance—if they were built at all." In fact, "much of the American money enriched U.S. contractors without ever entering the Afghan economy."

Whitlock explains that what the U.S. did build with that money was a "corrupt, dysfunctional Afghan government that depended on U.S. military power for its survival." Corruption was so bad that, according to the UN, by 2012, half the population was paying bribes for services, producing billions of dollars in bribes per year. According to the Institute of World Politics, militias "were using their position and closeness with the government and [the] U.S. military to control roads, secure lucrative contracts, establish themselves as regional powers, and sometimes serve both sides, cooperating with both international and Taliban forces to maximize profits."[27]

In 2009, Rodric Braithwaite reported in the *Financial Times* that among "Afghan journalists, former Mujahideen, professionals, people working for the 'coalition'" who should be "natural supporters for its claims to bring peace and reconstruction," there was in fact "deep disillusionment with the 'coalition' and its policies." Unsurprisingly, many joined the Taliban because they saw the Americans as illegitimate invaders and the Afghan government as a U.S. puppet.[28]

Whitlock notes the basic problem that "by allowing corruption to fester, the United States helped destroy the legitimacy of the wobbly Afghan government they were fighting to prop up. With judges and police chiefs and bureaucrats extorting bribes, many Afghans soured on democracy and turned to the Taliban to enforce order." The U.S.-trained Afghan Local Police were "unaccountable militias that prey on the population," and "quickly earned a reputation for brutality and drew complaints from human rights groups." They were "the most hated institution" in Afghanistan, and one official "estimated that 30 percent of Afghan police recruits deserted with their government-issued weapons so they could 'set up their own private checkpoints' and rob people." In addition to the predatory police, there were many "ghost" police—those who were on payrolls but didn't exist. Whitlock writes that while "the Afghan army and police forces looked robust on paper . . . a large percentage materialized as ghost billets, or no-show jobs," because "Afghan commanders inflated the numbers so they could pocket millions of dollars in salaries—paid by U.S. taxpayers—for imaginary personnel, according to U.S. government audits."

New York Times reporter Dexter Filkins says that none of this was a secret, and everyone in the U.S. government "knew that the Afghan government was predatory," calling it "VICE," for a "vertically integrated criminal enterprise." But Patrick Cockburn reminds us that some of the corruption came from desperation: "The police make about $120 a month. . . . The only way they can feed their families is to take bribes." Afghan soldiers and police were also doing dangerous work. At one point, an estimated thirty to forty were being killed each day, to the point where "the Afghan government kept the exact numbers a secret to avoid destroying morale." In 2019, researchers concluded that "more than 64,000 Afghans in uniform had been killed over the course of the war—roughly eighteen times the number of U.S. and NATO troops who lost their lives."[29]

NPR's Sarah Chayes wrote that the "security concerns of the Afghans" were very different from the "security concerns of the foreigners." American and NATO forces fretted about "former Taliban" while "the Afghans were worried about the quite real depredations of the government those Americans had put in power." She was critical of those who believe Afghans were simply unprepared for democracy. In fact, they simply wanted a government that was competent and didn't rob them. They were "crying out" for democracy, she said, and "want to participate in some real way in the fashioning of their nation's destiny," but were "getting precious little of any of that, thanks to warlords like Gul Agha Shirzai, whom America was helping maintain in power." U.S. policy, she said, was in fact "standing in the way of democracy."[30]

Chayes is bitterly critical of the United States for supporting some of the most brutal Afghan warlords, such as Abdul Rashid Dostum, who suffocated hundreds of Taliban prisoners of war to death in shipping containers. Akbar Bai of the Turkic Council of Afghanistan described Dostum as "the biggest butcher and criminal in the world," who "raped many people, men, women, even young girls and boys," and is accused of having ordered the murder of his former wife after she found him having sex with an underage girl. Dostum became "America's man in Afghanistan" and was placed on the CIA payroll. In the U.S.-backed government, Dostum ultimately became vice president of Afghanistan, though his presence in office was so embarrassing that the Obama administration felt obligated to bar him from visiting the United States.

Dostum ultimately fled the country to escape "criminal charges in Afghanistan for having ordered his bodyguards to rape a political opponent, including with an assault rifle."[31]

As Whitlock shows, much of the truth was kept from public knowledge. The special inspector general for Afghanistan reconstruction said there was an "odor of mendacity" to all government statements. This began under Bush, but Whitlock writes that Obama staffers "took it to a new level, hyping figures that were misleading, spurious, or downright false." In 2011, Hillary Clinton told the Senate that "life is better for most Afghans," citing statistics showing increases in school attendance, decreases in infant mortality, hundreds of thousands of farmers who had been "trained and equipped with new seeds and other techniques," and a hundred thousand microloans given to Afghan women. Yet "government auditors would later conclude that the Obama administration had based many of its statistics regarding infant mortality, life expectancy, and school enrollment on inaccurate or unverified data." The special inspector general said the administration "knew the data was bad" but used it anyway out of a desire to present a false picture of progress. Whitlock says, "Even when casualty counts and other figures looked bad, the White House and Pentagon would spin them in their favor," with any outcome presented as a win. For instance, suicide bombings were "a sign that the insurgents were too weak to engage in direct combat" while "a rise in U.S. troop deaths proved that American forces were taking the fight to the enemy."[32]

With WikiLeaks' release of the Afghan War Logs in 2010, many instances of previously unreported horrific violence by the United States and its coalition partners were disclosed to the public. In the words of *The Guardian*, what were presented as targeted strikes on "Taliban militants" were often "bloody errors at civilians' expense," including the time "a U.S. patrol . . . machine-gunned a bus, wounding or killing 15 of its passengers." There were numerous other incidents that were reported to have killed Taliban, but in fact killed innocent civilians.[33]

There were even more extreme atrocities, such as an Army staff sergeant's massacre of sixteen villagers in Kandahar province. An Australian soldier alleged to have murdered an Afghan teenager was accused in court of boasting: "I shot that cunt in the head . . . blew his brains out. It was the most beautiful thing I've ever seen." In 2015, in one of the most horrifying events of the war, a U.S. Air Force AC-130 gunship—call sign "Hammer"—attacked a Doctors Without Borders hospital in Kunduz, burning patients alive in their beds and killing a total of forty-two people. (Doctors Without Borders had provided the United States with the GPS coordinates of the trauma center beforehand.)[34]

Further humiliating and alienating Afghans was the practice of torture. As James Risen of *The Intercept* reported, the United States set up secret torture chambers and "tortured both Afghans and foreign prisoners flown to these torture rooms from all over Central Asia, Africa, and the Middle East." They "were hung by their arms for as long as two days, slammed against walls," or "forced to lie naked on tarps while gallons of ice water were poured over their bodies," with at least one person dying from the frigid temperatures. Risen notes that "no one was ever held to account for the American torture regime in Afghanistan."[35]

The use of armed drones produced yet more nightmarish results. *The New York Times* reports that "even inside the government, there is no certainty about whom it has killed," and "every independent investigation of the strikes has found far more civilian casualties than administration officials admit." Brandon Bryant, an Air Force drone operator who became a critic of their use, says the killing of a small child is "burned into my brain." He believes "total civilian deaths were much higher than the administration's estimate," because they're "deluding themselves about the impact." Those attacked have included dozens of pine nut farmers and a wedding party. Every time these horrors unfolded, U.S. officials "insisted that each strike had hit its intended target, while ignoring the claims of villagers that the missiles had killed a tribal chief or decimated a meeting of village elders." (Not everyone came out badly: U.S. defense contractors have made fortunes, and a massive drone industry has blossomed.)[36]

Of course, U.S. crimes against Afghans fueled support for the Taliban. Risen notes that "night raids," in which "U.S. and Afghan forces would burst into a home in the middle of the night and kill or capture those inside," bred so much resentment that "they sometimes led an entire village to switch its allegiance to the Taliban." Journalist Anand Gopal has identified eleven specific Taliban leaders who had left but rejoined the group "because of some kind of U.S. or government harassment." Malkasian notes that "overly aggressive and poorly informed U.S. counterterrorism operations upset Afghans and drove former Taliban back to violence."[37]

Successive U.S. presidents continued to deny the facts while continuing the war. Whitlock observes that Barack Obama pretended to have ended the war, without actually doing so. Under Donald Trump, the war "had become much less visible to Americans at home" yet was reaching "new levels of mayhem on the ground, killing and wounding record numbers of Afghan civilians." Trump escalated the indiscriminate violence, and infamously dropped the "Mother of All Bombs," the most powerful conventional explosive ever used in combat, killing a number of ISIS fighters as well as a teacher and his young son, and causing Hamid Karzai to condemn the "inhuman and most brutal misuse of our country as testing ground for new and dangerous weapons." Desperate to end the United States' costly commitment, Trump signed a deal with the Taliban that promised U.S. withdrawal if the Taliban would agree to, among other things, stop attacks on U.S. and coalition forces. The agreement was made without the participation of the Afghan government—one American official described the prevailing attitude as "Who cares whether they agree or not?"—and helped set the Taliban up to take over the country.[38]

Like Trump, Biden simply wanted to get out of Afghanistan, to take the political hit and move on. He ordered a quick but disastrous exit that abandoned many Afghans who had been core U.S. allies. *The New York Times*'s Dexter Filkins says that this was obviously "inexcusable" and "criminal," since those Afghans "fought for us and they risked their lives and many of them died for us and we have left thousands of them behind." But he concludes that the Biden administration simply didn't think it was "worth it" to put in more effort or expense, the lives of Afghans having been considered negligible to U.S. presidents since 2001.[39]

In 2021, after twenty years, the United States fired its last missile in Afghanistan. It massacred an aid worker and seven children. The U.S. military initially called it a "righteous strike," claiming it had hit terrorists who had a bomb. After a lengthy *New York Times* investigation revealed the government was lying, the Pentagon backtracked and called the killings a tragic mistake. Nobody was punished.[40]

With its mix of gruesome violence against innocent Afghans, brazen propaganda from U.S. officials, and total impunity for the perpetrators, it was certainly a fitting American end to the war.

The condition of Afghanistan after the U.S. war was appalling. The World Food Program warned at the end of 2021 that 98 percent of Afghans were not getting enough to eat, with millions facing starvation. By September 2023, the WFP claimed that they were nearly out of resources and were "obliged to choose between the hungry and the starving, leaving millions of families scrambling for their next meal." News reports out of Afghanistan are heartbreaking. There has been a significant rise in child labor as kids are sent to work to help feed families, doing jobs like picking through garbage. Some parents have been forced to sell one of their children in order to afford to feed their other children. Others have had to sell their own organs, or their children's organs.[41]

This horror was directly the fault of the United States. After the Taliban took over the country in August 2021, the United States froze $9 billion in Afghan central bank assets, which "functionally cut the country off from many foreign banks and left the Central Bank of Afghanistan unable to access its reserves and shore up the country's cash flow." The Biden administration announced that it was going to give half of the Afghans' money to American families related to the victims of 9/11—though the people of Afghanistan had nothing to do with 9/11, of course. It's an act of outright theft, as Ruth Pollard of *Bloomberg* notes: "The problem is, the U.S. doesn't own that money: Afghanistan does." *The New York Times* makes the understated observation that it is "highly unusual for the United States government to commandeer a foreign country's assets on domestic soil."[42]

Representatives of leading Afghan women's organizations wrote an open letter to Joe Biden decrying the injustice of the decision, pointing out that "the funds that the U.S. seeks to redistribute belong to the Afghan people, who were not responsible for the acts of Al Qaeda terrorists or the Taliban" and arguing that the "decision by the world's most powerful country over the resources of the world's poorest country is extremely unfair."[43] They pointed out that "thousands of Afghans have died every year in what was called the 'war on terror' by the U.S. and allies" and "taking funds from the Afghan people is the unkindest and most inappropriate response for a country that is going through the worst humanitarian crisis in its history."[44]

Obaidullah Baheer of the American University of Afghanistan described extreme anger at the decision, for the obvious reason that "Afghanistan needs a sustainable economy if it is to survive in the long run, and the federal reserves are fundamental to it." Naser Shahalemi, founder of End Afghan Starvation, is appalled by the horrific humanitarian situation. "The people of Afghanistan are starving, and they are locked out of their funds. They cannot access their bank cards. They cannot access their bank accounts . . . because of the sanctions, they've been locked away from their own money . . . it is absolutely ridiculous because we need that money for the people of Afghanistan." (The Biden administration ignored the pleas and continued to refuse to release the money.)[45]

The effects of U.S. policy have been "catastrophic for civilians," notes Laurel Miller of the International Crisis Group. "The West's immediate steps to isolate the new regime triggered Afghanistan's meltdown." David Miliband of the International Rescue Committee wrote that "the current humanitarian crisis could kill far more Afghans than the past 20 years of war." Mark Weisbrot concludes that the "Biden administration did not end the war, but continued it by other means, which are turning out to be more violent and destabilizing."[46]

Nor did we facilitate an escape from the hell we created. The Biden administration rejected over 90 percent of applications from Afghans seeking to enter the United States on humanitarian grounds. The administration imposed differing standards on Afghan refugees and Ukrainian refugees—for instance, "unlike Afghans trying to secure entry to the U.S. on humanitarian grounds, Ukrainians don't have to pay a $575 administrative fee, don't need to show proof of vaccination and don't need to have an in-person consular interview with a U.S. representative." (Public opinion research shows Afghan refugees are seen less favorably, perhaps partly thanks to press coverage depicting Ukrainians as "civilized" refugees who "look like us.")[47]

If we are even minimally morally serious, we should ask: What does the U.S. owe the people of Afghanistan, after all that we have done to them? If we actually believed the story we tell ourselves about being "the greatest force for freedom the world has ever known," how would we act?

We might begin with a few obvious changes. To deny applications from Afghan refugees is unconscionable. Laurel Miller recommends "beginning to lift sanctions on the Taliban as a group (leaving sanctions on some individuals and an arms embargo in place); funding specific state functions in areas such as rural development, agriculture, electricity and local governance; and restoring central-bank operations to reconnect Afghanistan to the global financial system." Sanctions punish the population for the crimes of its government, and have no justification.[48]

The Afghanistan war is often discussed as a kind of noble failure, another episode of the United States' good intentions going hopelessly awry. For Barack Obama, as Rajiv Chandrasekaran writes, Afghanistan was "the good war, the war that began with two fallen towers, not the war that stemmed from faulty intelligence and exaggerated claims of weapons of mass destruction." In fact, the attack on Afghanistan was a major crime, with no justification whatsoever. Neither the Afghan people nor their authoritarian Taliban government had planned or executed the 9/11 attacks (in fact, the Taliban publicly condemned the attacks and called for the perpetrators to be brought to justice).[49]

Why did the United States attack Afghanistan, then? Bush wanted to "show muscle" in the aftermath of the attacks. Michael Howard described it as the American desire for "catharsis" and "vengeance" against an "insult to American honor," which would not have been satisfied by a "long and meticulous police investigation."[50] The desire to strike back and prove strength is not an uncommon motivation in the history of U.S. foreign relations. It is more mafioso logic—using extreme violence as a means of asserting strength and discouraging opposition.

Why did we stay in Afghanistan? In part, because no president wished to "lose," even as it was increasingly clear that the U.S.-backed government could not command the popular support necessary to survive on its own. As Patrick Cockburn observed in 2012, "The problem for Washington and London is that they have got so many people killed in Afghanistan and spent so much money that it is difficult for them to withdraw without something that can be dressed up as a victory." Regardless of the "true" motives behind the war, from Bush to Biden, American presidents have shown no sincere commitment to improving the welfare of the Afghans.[51]

There are still those who defend the noble intent of U.S. policymakers. Carter Malkasian, while acknowledging the terrible consequences of U.S. refusal to engage the Taliban diplomatically or care about the consequences of their overthrow, frames the war as a "terrible trade-off" between American and Afghan well-being. "It was inadvertent," he says, and "we resuscitated a state of civil war so that we could sleep a little sounder at home," exposing Afghans to harm in order to protect Americans.

Destroying one of the world's poorest countries to "sleep a little sounder" may sound a harsh enough indictment, but Malkasian is wrong. If the Bush administration had wanted to "defend Americans from another terrorist attack," it would have pursued the criminal network responsible for the original attack. Instead, it wanted vengeance, and launched an illegal war that killed thousands of innocent people. As ugly as a "trade-off" between Afghan lives and American safety would have been, there was no such trade-off. Bush rapidly lost interest in bin Laden, American muscle having successfully been flexed. The damage was not "inadvertent"—armed drones do not spontaneously deploy of their own volition. It was born of indifference to the humanity of our victims.

Most depressingly, while those looking to redeem the crime of the Afghanistan war might point to progress on women's rights and infrastructure during the Taliban's absence, it is quite possible that had the United States never invaded, the Taliban would not be in power today. They were unpopular by 2001; Patrick Cockburn reports that "the brutality of the Taliban and their obsession with controlling people's private lives meant that they had long outlived their welcome" because "even those fond of innocent pleasures such as kite-flying were rewarded with a beating or even prison." A major source of the Taliban's renewed strength was their ability to portray themselves as freedom fighters against a government associated with American occupiers. Abdul Haq had insisted that the U.S. was actually undermining the anti-Taliban resistance through its bombing campaign, and if the U.S. had left the country alone, that resistance might someday have been able to build a government with popular support. The U.S. may well be the main reason that Afghans suffer indefinitely under strengthened Taliban rule.[52]

4

Iraq: The Crime of the Century

The United States' war on Iraq from 2003 to 2011 remains the deadliest act of aggressive warfare in this century, and perhaps the worst crime committed during the last thirty years.[1] It was, as George W. Bush said in an unintentional slip of the tongue, "wholly unjustified and brutal." At least five hundred thousand Iraqis died as a result of the war. Around three hundred thousand of those were violent deaths—people who were blown to pieces by coalition air strikes, or shot at checkpoints, or killed by suicide bombers from the insurgency unleashed by the U.S. invasion and occupation.[2]

Others died as a result of the collapse of the medical system—doctors fled the country in droves, because their colleagues were being killed or abducted. Childhood mortality and infant mortality in the country rose, as did malnutrition and starvation. Millions of people were displaced, and toxins introduced by American bombardment led to "congenital malformations, sterility, and infertility." A "generation of orphans" was created, hundreds of thousands of children having lost parents, with many being left to wander the streets homeless. The country's infrastructure collapsed, its libraries and museums were looted, and its university system was decimated. For years, suicide bombings were a daily feature of life in Baghdad and, of course, for every violent death, scores more people were left injured or traumatized. In 2007, the Red Cross said that there were "mothers appealing for someone to pick up the bodies on the street so their children will be spared the horror of looking at them on their way to school." Acute malnutrition doubled within sixteen months of the occupation of Iraq, to the level of Burundi, well above Haiti or Uganda, a figure that "translates to roughly 400,000 Iraqi children suffering from 'wasting,' a condition characterized by chronic diarrhea and dangerous deficiencies of protein."[3]

Some of the war's early proponents have gone quiet. Some have simply lied about the record. ("We were able to bring the war to a reasonably successful conclusion in 2008," wrote neoconservative William Kristol in 2015.) Others have made public displays of their regret, but cast the war as a noble and idealistic mistake. It is hard, for instance, to find more extreme pro-war statements from 2002 and 2003 than those of Andrew Sullivan, who wrote that "we would fail in any conception of Christian duty if we failed to act after all this time, if we let evil succeed, if we lost confidence in our capacity to do what is morally right."

Sullivan was unequivocal: "This war is a just one. We didn't start it. Saddam did—over twelve years ago." (The United States only ever takes defensive measures, thus Hussein is said to have "started" the war, despite never having attacked the U.S.) Time was of the essence: "To say that we are in a rush to war is an obscene fabrication, a statement of willful amnesia, a simple denial of history." In response to those who pointed out the criminality of the invasion, Sullivan insisted that "we have to abandon the UN as an instrument in world affairs." In fact, the lack of international approval only showed that the U.S. was one of the few morally serious countries in the world. It would show that "only the U.S. and the UK and a few others are prepared to risk lives and limb to enforce global norms."[4]

By 2007, however, with the war having entirely destroyed the country it was supposed to "liberate," Sullivan was professing to have been a duped innocent whose hatred of evil was so strong that it inhibited his rationality, writing that he was "far too naïve" and "caught up in the desire to fight back against Islamist evil," and that he felt rage upon learning of the "killed, tortured and maimed in the Rumsfeld-created vortex."

Sullivan's newfound concern for the killed, tortured, and maimed may be commendable (although massive human casualties were an entirely predictable consequence of the war, warned about repeatedly). But like many others who realized the war was indefensible, Sullivan retreated to the position that the war was "imprudent," "noble," and "defensible" but "[the Bush] administration was simply too incompetent and arrogant to carry it out effectively."

As in the case of Vietnam, many ostensible critics of the Iraq War were actually critics of its execution, not its intent. David Ignatius of *The Washington Post*, writing about Deputy Secretary of Defense Paul Wolfowitz, lamented that Wolfowitz's admirable, principled idealism was unfortunately a mismatch for human imperfection. Ignatius said that it was "impossible to fault on moral grounds" the case for overthrowing the Iraqi government, but the lesson is that "too much moralizing is dangerous in statecraft." The "idealism of a Wolfowitz," while "admirable," was "wishful thinking" and should be "tempered by some very hard-headed judgments about how to protect U.S. interests."[5]

The Iraq War, Ignatius wrote, was "the most idealistic war in modern times," fought solely to bring democracy to Iraq and the region, and its very idealism doomed it to failure.

Likewise, while Barack Obama felt the war was "ill-conceived" and a "strategic blunder," he did not dispute the good intentions of those who began it. Very few mainstream criticisms of the war call it what it was: a criminal act of aggression by a state seeking to exert regional control through the use of violence. A great deal of this criticism has focused on the costs of the war to the United States, with barely any attention paid to the cost to Iraq and the surrounding countries.[6]

If there is ever going to be accountability for this crime, we would do well to first understand what was done and why.

The United States' attitude toward Saddam Hussein had been consistent since his ascent to power in the 1970s, and was the same as its attitude toward other despots. Hussein's brutal rule was tolerable to the extent that he aided U.S. goals in the Middle East, and intolerable to the extent that he challenged those goals. The U.S. position varied over time, but it did not vary based on the threat Hussein posed to the safety of the people of the United States (which was nonexistent from the beginning of his rule to the end of it), or on the atrocities Hussein perpetrated against Iraqis, Kurds, and Iranians (the U.S. happily armed and assisted Hussein during the worst of his crimes). Instead, in keeping with Godfather logic, the U.S. accepted Hussein when he followed our rules and turned on him when he disobeyed. Hussein was ultimately deposed for the same reason so many other "regime change" operations have been carried out: his continued rule posed an obstacle to American power in the region, and his defiance needed to be ended, as a warning to others.

Hussein assumed full control of Iraq in 1979 and soon proved useful to the United States.[7] In 1980, he launched a war on Iran that lasted until 1988 and would ultimately kill up to a million people. The United States, eager for the punishment of postrevolutionary Iran, fully supported Hussein's war of aggression. In 1982, the Reagan administration, realizing that Iraq was "the only thing standing between Iran and the Persian Gulf oil fields," removed Iraq from the list of state sponsors of terror, to which it had been added in 1979 for its support of, among others, Palestinian militant groups. The U.S. provided logistical support, intelligence support, and over $500 million worth of equipment for Hussein's blatantly illegal war. The CDC sent Hussein samples of the germs that cause anthrax, West Nile virus disease, and botulism, which he proceeded to use for biological weapons development, and in 1988 the Dow Chemical Company "sold $1.5m-worth . . . of pesticides to Iraq despite suspicions they would be used for chemical warfare."[8]

The United States even directly participated in the war, blowing up

Iranian oil platforms and boats to, in Ronald Reagan's words, "make certain the Iranians have no illusions about the cost of irresponsible behavior." (The International Court of Justice ultimately found that the acts "cannot be justified as measures necessary to protect the essential security interests of the United States of America.") The U.S. also attacked an Iranian civilian airliner, killing all 290 people aboard, including 66 infants and children. When given the opportunity to express contrition for the calamity, George H. W. Bush said instead: "I will never apologize for the United States. I don't care what the facts are. . . . I'm not an apologize-for-America kind of guy."[9]

Iraq's warfare methods shocked the world. Hussein's army used chemical weapons to inflict horrific suffering on their Iranian opponents. According to its own official history, Iraq began using chemical weapons in 1981. Not since World War I's gas attacks had chemical weapons been used on this scale, a fact the U.S. government fully understood. When the UN Security Council tried to condemn Iraq's use of mustard gas, the U.S. blocked the measure. Even in cases where it knew Iraq would use chemical weapons, the U.S. Defense Intelligence Agency was "secretly providing detailed information on Iranian deployments, tactical planning for battles, plans for airstrikes and bomb-damage assessments for Iraq." *Foreign Policy* confirmed in 2013 that in 1988 "the United States learned through satellite imagery that Iran was about to gain a major strategic advantage by exploiting a hole in Iraqi defenses," and "U.S. intelligence officials conveyed the location of the Iranian troops to Iraq, fully aware that Hussein's military would attack with chemical weapons, including sarin, a lethal nerve agent." In fact, the CIA concealed evidence that Iraq was using chemical weapons, hoping Iran would not be able to produce such evidence itself. *Foreign Policy* notes that "senior U.S. officials were being regularly informed about the scale of the nerve gas attacks," and internal documents reveal what is "tantamount to an official American admission of complicity in some of the most gruesome chemical weapons attacks ever launched."[10]

A senior DIA official confirmed that "the use of gas on the battle-field by the Iraqis was not a matter of deep strategic concern." (Strategic concerns are the only admissible concerns, moral and legal concerns being irrelevant.) In fact, the use of chemical weapons "against military objectives was seen as inevitable in the Iraqi struggle for survival," and they "were integrated into their fire plan for any large operation." One veteran involved with the program shrugged that "it was just another way of killing people—whether with a bullet or phosgene, it didn't make any difference." In 2003, Iraq's use of gas in the Iran-Iraq war would be "repeatedly cited by President Bush . . . as justification for 'regime change' in Iraq," with Bush noting on the anniversary of an infamous massacre of Kurds that it proved Saddam Hussein was "capable of any crime," having "killed thousands of men and women and children, without mercy or shame."[11]

Bush did not discuss U.S. complicity in these crimes, nor did he show any interest in holding to account the officials in his father's ad-ministration who had aided and covered up those crimes. Saddam Hus-sein was able to carry out these attacks in part because the United States not only helped equip him, but also lied to the international commu-nity to conceal his involvement. Joost Hiltermann of the International Crisis Group wrote in 2003 that the U.S. had much to answer for when it came to the 1988 Halabja massacre, in which Hussein killed thou-sands of Kurds with chemical weapons. The U.S., "fully aware it was Iraq, accused Iran, Iraq's enemy in a fierce war, of being partly respon-sible for the attack," and the "result of this stunning act of sophistry was that the international community failed to muster the will to condemn Iraq strongly for an act as heinous as the terrorist strike on the World Trade Center." Hiltermann found it deeply cynical to use this event "as a justification for American plans to terminate the regime," when in fact the holdovers from the George H. W. Bush administration had never been held accountable for bolstering Iraq's WMD program, "giv-ing the regime a de facto green light on chemical weapons use," "turn-ing a blind eye to Iraq's worst atrocities, and then lying about it."[12]

Saddam Hussein destroyed his country, building a nightmarish totalitarian state. Stories from those who fell victim to his regime are of
the most disturbing kind imaginable. He did it, however, with U.S. protection and support. In 1990, Congress "cut off $700 million in United
States loan guarantees that the Baghdad Government uses to purchase
American wheat, rice, lumber and cattle as well as commercial goods
like tires and machinery." One Republican senator commented: "I can't
believe any farmer in this nation would want to send his products,
under subsidized sales, to a country that has used chemical weapons
and a country that has tortured and executed its children." Perhaps no
farmer would. But the Bush administration said restrictions would not
help "in achieving the goals we want to achieve in our relationship with
Iraq." After a Voice of America editorial condemned Hussein's human
rights abuses, the Bush administration expressed "regret" for the criticism but still viewed him as a "force for moderation in the region."[13]

Shortly afterward, Hussein made a critical error, however. Having
acted with impunity thus far, Hussein crossed a U.S. red line by invading Kuwait. It is not clear whether Hussein knew the United States
would object to the invasion, having been told by the U.S. ambassador,
"We have no opinion on the Arab-Arab conflicts, like your border disagreement with Kuwait," and "The issue is not associated with America. . . . All that we hope is that these issues are solved quickly."[14] *The
New York Times* reported at the time of the invasion that George H. W.
Bush had given Hussein "little reason to fear a forceful American response if his troops invaded [Kuwait]." But CIA intelligence analyst
Kenneth Pollack observed that the invasion "represented a serious
threat to America's principal objectives in the Persian Gulf region, to
ensure the free flow of oil and prevent an inimical power from establishing hegemony over the region."[15]

Critics pointed out at the time that the Bush administration appeared set on responding with threats of war and ignoring diplomatic
options. As the United States prepared to use force, *The New York Times*
reported that Hussein was considering options to "pull out of all but a

fraction of Kuwaiti territory." For the Bush administration, the *Times* said, such a concession by Hussein would be a "nightmare scenario" (the words of an administration official) because it would put the U.S. "into a position where the stakes seem too petty to fight over." Bush Sr., the paper said, wanted to convince Hussein that a partial withdrawal was "not worth trying." The U.S. was worried that some partners "remain reluctant about fighting . . . and concessions by Mr. Hussein would look appealing to them." Diplomacy was a nightmare not just because it might leave Hussein with ill-gotten gains, but because it would make "the United States look like a paper tiger that roars and roars but never bites." If we do not "bite," we lack credibility.[16]

Bush Sr. repeatedly compared Hussein to Hitler and justified the lack of interest in diplomacy with the usual "Munich" comparisons. Hussein made multiple proposals that would involve withdrawal from Kuwait (all the while pointing out that the United States itself had recently invaded Panama). All were ignored by the U.S., including one proposing that "all cases of occupation" in the region "be resolved simultaneously," meaning that Israel should be held to the same standard as Iraq. Although the Arab League had passed a resolution warning against outside intervention in the conflict, while condemning the invasion of Kuwait, Bush was set on teaching Hussein a lesson through the use of force, to show that, in Bush's words, "What we say goes." An Italian Catholic weekly, *Il Sabato*, concluded that Bush deserved the "Nobel War Prize" for his insistence on force over negotiation. In February 1990, *The Times of India* described Bush's dismissals of Iraq's withdrawal proposals as a "horrible mistake" that showed the West sought a world order "where the powerful nations agree among themselves to a share of Arab spoils." We had seen, it said, "the seamiest sides of Western civilisation: its unrestricted appetite for dominance, its morbid fascination for hi-tech military might, its insensitivity to 'alien' cultures, its appalling jingoism."[17]

The Bush Sr. administration also used propaganda to drum up public support. A PR firm pushed a false story that Iraqi soldiers had ripped babies out of incubators in a Kuwait hospital and thrown them on the floor to die. (Atrocity tales are a core component of establishing an enemy as the New Hitler.) The administration turned on a dime and condemned Hussein as a butcher and madman for the very kinds of atrocities that we had long been supporting.[18]

The Gulf War itself was a horror. Bush Sr., having promised that Hussein would "get his ass kicked" in any conflict with the United States, unleashed massive firepower against Iraq. An investigation by Middle East Watch found that "the reassuring words of allied military briefers and Bush Administration spokesmen about successful pinpoint strikes did not match the often-bloody results of allied bombing in populated areas." The U.S. was responsible for several major atrocities. It killed four hundred civilians in an attack on a Baghdad air-raid shelter, with women and children being burned beyond recognition. It also bombed a baby formula factory and then lied about the bombing, claiming the facility had produced chemical weapons. It trapped and ferociously bombed retreating Iraqi soldiers on the so-called Highway of Death, named because of the endless charred vehicles and corpses that were left along the roadside after the U.S. attack. Soldiers were told to kill "anything that moved,"[19] even if it was "a turnip truck." The U.S. killed thousands of Iraqi soldiers by using plows to bury them alive in their trenches.[20]

The Bush administration committed numerous acts of terrorism in Iraq by intentionally targeting civilian infrastructure. A *Washington Post* report from 1991 found that some targets "were bombed primarily to create postwar leverage over Iraq, not to influence the course of the conflict itself," with the intent being "to destroy or damage valuable facilities that Baghdad could not repair without foreign assistance." The *Post* noted that much of this "damage to civilian structures and interests" was presented as "collateral" and unintentional, but was in fact done deliberately.[21]

Attacking retreating soldiers, air raid shelters, and electricity-generating and water-treatment facilities, and doing so in a war waged under false pretenses, might be thought wrong, even criminal. But the Gulf War was painted in the U.S. press as a moral triumph. Bush was thrilled with the outcome because it meant that "by God, we've kicked the Vietnam syndrome once and for all." ("Vietnam syndrome" described the reluctance to use violent force that had emerged after the war on Vietnam.) The United States, he said, "has a new credibility."[22]

Once the U.S. had accomplished its objectives in Kuwait, Bush encouraged the Iraqi people to rise up and overthrow Hussein. "The Iraqi people should put [Hussein] aside," he said, to "facilitate the acceptance of Iraq back into the family of peace-loving nations." As civilian uprisings took place in Basra, Karbala, and Najaf, delegates from "two dozen Iraqi opposition groups appealed to the United States for help." But they received none, because the Bush administration had in fact quietly decided that it actually preferred a weakened Hussein to an unknown alternative.[23]

Not that the Bush administration specifically wanted Hussein himself. Any dictator would do. As New York Times chief diplomatic correspondent Thomas Friedman put it, the "best of all worlds" for Washington was "an iron-fisted Iraqi junta without Saddam Hussein," who would rule the country with the same ruthlessness as Hussein had done. The uprising, however, might have left the country in the hands of the wrong people. Rachel Bronson, director of Middle East Studies at the Council on Foreign Relations, says that "the administration got nervous because we didn't know who would take over." Thus, while knowing that Iraqi rebels had assumed they could count on U.S. support, the administration stood by as Hussein "used napalm, cluster bombs and Scud missiles to defeat the rebels, and Shiite mosques, cemeteries and religious schools were targeted for destruction." As Colin Powell explained, "Our practical intention was to leave Baghdad enough power to survive as a threat to an Iran that remained bitterly hostile to the United States." Washington and its Middle East allies held the "strikingly unanimous view [that] whatever the sins of the Iraqi leader, he offered the West and the region a better hope for his country's stability than did those who have suffered his repression," reported Alan Cowell in *The New York Times*.[24]

Hussein's suppression of the revolt caused tens of thousands of deaths. Thus: not only were Saddam's worst crimes committed when he was a favored U.S. ally and trading partner, but immediately after he was driven from Kuwait, the United States watched quietly while he slaughtered rebelling Iraqis, even refusing to allow them access to captured Iraqi arms. Idealism in action.[25]

Throughout the remainder of the 1990s, Iraq was kept in check through a mixture of sanctions and bombing. By the mid-90s, the devastation caused by the sanctions led the United Nations to institute an Oil-for-Food program to alleviate their effects, magnanimously allowing Iraq to use some oil revenue for social purposes. Denis Halliday, the distinguished diplomat who directed the program, resigned in protest after two years, charging that the sanctions were genocidal and a "form of state terrorism." Hans von Sponeck, who replaced him, also retired on the grounds that the sanctions violated the genocide convention, protesting "the continuation of a sanction regime in Iraq despite overwhelming evidence that the fabric of Iraqi society is swiftly eroding and an international awareness that the approach chosen so clearly punishes the wrong party."[26]

Stanford political scientist Lisa Blaydes, in *State of Repression: Iraq Under Saddam Hussein*, notes that the sanctions were "among the most stringent financial and trade restrictions ever inflicted on a developing country" and combined with the effects of the Gulf War created a "humanitarian disaster for the Iraqi people." Iraq was reduced to "preindustrial" levels of development. The sanctions caused the "systematic impoverishment of the entire nation," and ultimately created an effect similar to that of an ongoing "war or natural disaster that continued nonstop for fifteen years." "It was the consistent policy of all three U.S. administrations, from 1990 to 2003," she says, "to inflict the most extreme economic damage possible on Iraq." The cost to Iraqi civilians "was never a factor in U.S. policy, except insofar as it presented a political liability for U.S. administrations."[27]

In March 2003, the most awesome military force in human history attacked a much weaker country, one that turned out not only to lack weapons of mass destruction (the pretext for the invasion), but a military capable of sustaining any defense. The Iraqi forces crumbled within weeks, and U.S. media gleefully mocked the increasingly implausible assurances of Iraq's press spokesman that the invaders were being held at bay.[28]

The United States succeeded in part through the aggressive use of extreme violence. The invasion and occupation were brutal and clumsy. Human Rights Watch condemned the "widespread use of cluster munitions, especially by U.S. and UK ground forces," and noted that refusing to use the weapons "could have prevented hundreds of civilian injuries or deaths during the war." HRW reported that "American and British ground forces fired almost 13,000 cluster munitions, which spread nearly two million smaller bombs," leaving unexploded munitions "littering the landscape, waiting for people to trip over them." "The crueler it is, the sooner it's over," one colonel told *The New York Times*. "It's over for us when the last guy who wants to fight for Saddam has flies crawling across his eyeballs."[29]

Having shattered the Iraqi state with ease, thereby exposing the story of Iraq's "threat" to the U.S. as entirely hollow, the United States proceeded to establish a neocolonial regime that immediately squandered the goodwill that Iraqis had after the removal of the dictator. George W. Bush appointed L. Paul Bremer, a Harvard MBA with no knowledge whatsoever of the country, to rule over the country like an imperial viceroy. Bremer immediately moved to eliminate "Saddamism" by disbanding the country's armed forces and police, plunging the country into anarchy, and barring members of the ruling Ba'ath party from government service, thereby ensuring that no competent officials were left in their posts.[30] The Bush administration staffed its "Coalition Provisional Authority" with Republican Party loyalists unfamiliar with Iraqi culture and incapable of speaking the language. Most had never even been outside the U.S., having obtained their first passport to go to Iraq.[31]

American forces solved problems with violence. Houses were ransacked or destroyed in searches, people were shot for making sudden movements. Testimonies from Iraq Veterans Against the War's "Winter Soldier" interviews offer a disturbing look at the casual dehumanization of and violence toward the Iraqi population. Jason Washburn, a corporal who served three tours in Iraq, recounts that when a woman "looked like she was headed toward us" with a huge bag, "we blew her to pieces," only to discover it was filled with groceries. Other testimonies describe similar instances:

- "I was explicitly told by my chain of command that I could shoot anyone who came closer to me than I felt comfortable with, if that person did not immediately move when I ordered them to do so, keeping in mind I don't speak Arabic. My chain of command's general attitude was 'better them than us.' . . . [At one point our commander] ordered that everyone on the streets was an enemy combatant. I can remember one instance that afternoon when we came around a corner and an unarmed Iraqi man stepped out of a doorway. I remember the Marine directly in front of me raising his rifle and aiming at the unarmed man. Then I think, due to some psychological reason, my brain blocked out the actual shots, because the next thing I remember is stepping over the dead man's body to clear the room that he came out of. It was a storage room and it was full of some Arabic version of Cheetos. There weren't any weapons in the area except ours. The commander told us a couple of weeks later that over a hundred enemy 'had been killed,' and to the best of my knowledge that number includes the people who were shot for simply walking down the street in their own city." —Jason Wayne Lemieux, sergeant, U.S. Marine Corps

- "One time they said to fire on all taxicabs because the enemy was using them for transportation. In Iraq, any car can be a taxicab; you just paint it white and orange. One of the snipers replied back, 'Excuse me? Did I hear that right? Fire on all taxicabs?' The lieutenant colonel responded, 'You heard me, trooper, fire on all taxicabs.' After that, the town lit up, with all the units firing on cars. This was my first experience with war, and that kind of set the tone for the rest of the deployment." —Hart Viges, U.S. Army Infantry specialist, 82nd Airborne[32]

Crimes against the people of Iraq were widespread. The United States took over Hussein's infamous Abu Ghraib prison, where U.S. soldiers physically and sexually abused, tortured, and even murdered prisoners ("detainees"). American guards "beat and sodomized prisoners with broomsticks and phosphoric lights, forced them to eat out of toilets, slammed them against the wall, urinated and spat upon them, made them wear female underwear, led them around on leashes, made them sleep on wet floors, attacked them with dogs, poured chemicals on them, stripped them naked and rode them like animals." The Bush administration initially buried the reports of torture, then tried to blame low-level soldiers for the abuses, although it eventually emerged that authorization for "enhanced interrogation techniques" had come straight from the secretary of defense, Donald Rumsfeld.[33]

As in Vietnam, many atrocities occurred because U.S. soldiers were young, heavily armed, terrified, knew nothing about the country they were in, and could not tell civilians from insurgents (and didn't put in much effort to try). Dexter Filkins reports encountering two young soldiers returning from a firefight and confessing, "We were just mowing people down. We were just whacking people." When the insurgents mixed in with civilians, "we just shot the civilians too." The soldier re-counted shooting a woman after an insurgent stepped behind her, com-menting, "The chick got in the way." "He wasn't especially troubled by it," Filkins recounted.[34]

NPR reporter Anne Garrels recalls how U.S. treatment of Iraqis contributed to generating the insurgency. There was a "complete lack of cultural understanding by the troops" that caused Iraqis who were "fence-sitters" to turn against the Americans. "The occupation" was so mismanaged on the ground, it was "staggering," she says, citing "inci-dent after incident" in which innocent people were massacred by jumpy American soldiers. Jason Burke, in *The 9/11 Wars*, gives a similar ac-count of the "counterproductive behavior" of the occupiers: "Anyone accompanying [American] troops on raids could see the impact their tactics had on local populations." When searching for insurgents they "blasted the doors of the suspects' homes off their hinges with explo-sives, ransacked rooms, and forced scores of men to squat with bags over their heads for hours in the sun waiting to be 'processed.'"[35]

The 2004 assault on Fallujah was particularly heinous. Afterward, Iraqi doctor Ali Fadhil said he found the city "completely devastated," looking like a "city of ghosts." Doctors reported that the entire medical staff had been locked into the main hospital when the U.S. attack began, "tied up" under U.S. orders: "Nobody could get to the hospital and peo-ple were bleeding to death in the city." The attitudes of the invaders were summarized by a message written in lipstick on the mirror of a ruined home: "Fuck Iraq and every Iraqi in it."[36]

When Joe Carr of the Christian Peacemakers Team in Baghdad, whose previous experience had been in the Israeli-occupied Palestinian territories, arrived on May 28, 2005, he found painful similarities: many hours of waiting at the few entry points, more for harassment than for security; regular destruction of produce in the devastated re-mains of the city where "food prices have dramatically increased be-cause of the checkpoints"; blocking of ambulances transporting people for medical treatment; and other forms of random brutality. The United

States "has leveled entire neighborhoods, and about every third building is destroyed or damaged." Only one hospital with inpatient care survived the attack, but access was impeded by the occupying army, leading
to many deaths in Fallujah and rural areas. Only about a quarter of
families whose homes were destroyed received some compensation,
usually less than half of the cost for materials needed to rebuild them.[37]

There has never been, and will likely never be, a full meaningful
accounting of what was done to Iraq. Such information as we do have
has often come from illegal leaks, such as Chelsea Manning's heroic
disclosure of 2007 footage showing U.S. helicopter pilots laughing
while firing at (and killing) civilians, including two Reuters correspondents. Some of the tragedies were accidents, albeit accidents of the kind
that are inevitable when heavy firepower is used by those with little
regard for civilian losses.[38] Some were deliberate. But the war itself was
the ultimate crime.[39]

STATED JUSTIFICATIONS AND REAL-WORLD
EXPLANATIONS

The Bush administration's stated justifications for the war were based
on falsehoods, repeated endlessly by both officials and the press. The
administration terrified the American public into thinking that if Iraq
was not immediately invaded, there would soon be a "mushroom cloud"
in New York City. Outrageous lies were told over and over, such as Dick
Cheney's claim that there was "no doubt that Saddam Hussein now has
weapons of mass destruction" and "no doubt he is amassing them to use
against our friends, against our allies, and against us." In fact, as Cheney
well knew, there was not only *doubt*—as more honest officials conceded
at the time—but also no good reason to believe the claim.[40]

Some with firsthand knowledge of the intelligence were aghast at
this egregious misstatement of the facts. General Anthony Zinni recalled: "It was a total shock. I couldn't believe the vice president was
saying this, you know? In doing work with the CIA on Iraq WMD,

through all the briefings I heard at Langley, I never saw one piece of credible evidence that there was an ongoing program." The "facts were being fixed around the policy," as the head of Britain's MI6 observed in an infamous memo. Richard Clarke, the Bush administration's counterterrorism coordinator, said that "all along it seemed inevitable that we would invade . . . It was an *idée fixe*, a rigid belief, received wisdom, a decision already made and one that no fact or event could derail."[41]

There were multiple misrepresentations of the known facts about Hussein's possession of weapons of mass destruction.[42] For instance, Bush publicly asserted that "a report came out of the . . . IAEA, that they [Iraqis] were six months away from developing a weapon. I don't know what more evidence we need." There was no such report, as the IAEA itself confirmed. Colin Powell had said just two years before that Hussein had "not developed any significant capability with regard to weapons of mass destruction" and was "unable to project conventional power against his neighbors," and National Security Advisor Condoleezza Rice said in April 2001 that "we are able to keep his arms from him. His military forces have not been rebuilt." A CIA report from the same year concluded: "We do not have any direct evidence that Iraq has used the period since [the Gulf War] to reconstitute its WMD programs."[43]

Hundreds of false statements were made by Bush, Cheney, Powell, Rice, and others as they attempted to sell the public on the necessity of the war. One congressional report counts 237 "misleading" statements that departed from facts known at the time. To preclude careful assessment of the facts, they insisted that the threat was of such "unique urgency" that there could be no time for deliberation. The country posed a "grave threat to the United States," in fact a "threat to any American." All of this was calculated to create fear and panic among the American public and to cast anyone who questioned the administration's push to war as dangerous and unpatriotic. Any pause to investigate the administration's claim would mean gambling irresponsibly with human lives. Rumsfeld talked of a possible "September 11th with weapons of mass destruction." In November 2002, he warned "if Saddam Hussein were to take his weapons of mass destruction" and use them or give them to Al-Qaeda, 100,000 people could be killed.[44]

Knowing full well that Iraq was not involved in the 9/11 attacks, Bush and others nevertheless tried to convince the American public to believe in an Al-Qaeda-Hussein nexus, in the hopes that this would increase support for a war that lacked a credible justification. Administration officials were constantly putting the names "al-Qaeda" and "Saddam Hussein" together in speech, although taking care never to claim directly that Hussein had actually planned the 9/11 attacks (since this was known to be untrue). The Department of Defense even manufactured "alternative intelligence assessment[s]" to contradict the consensus of the intelligence community that there was no al-Qaeda-Hussein link. Vice President Cheney insisted: "There's overwhelming evidence that there was a connection between al-Qaeda and the Iraqi government." In fact, there was overwhelming evidence of the *opposite*.[45]

Bush later objected when it was pointed out that he had tried to make Americans channel their anger at the 9/11 attacks toward Saddam Hussein. "I didn't say that there was a direct connection between September the eleventh and Saddam Hussein." Indeed, Bush only heavily *implied* it, over and over again. In requesting authorization for the use of force against Iraq, Bush told Congress that "the use of armed force against Iraq is consistent with the United States and other countries continuing to take the necessary actions against international terrorists and terrorist organizations, including those nations, organizations, or persons who planned, authorized, committed, or aided the terrorist attacks that occurred on September eleventh, 2001." Bush also said in declaring victory in Iraq—the "Mission Accomplished" speech—that he had "removed an ally of al-Qaeda" as part of a "war on terror that began on September eleventh, 2001."[46]

The more honest hawks admitted outright that this was pure deceit. Kenneth Pollack, in his 2002 pro-war manifesto *The Threatening Storm: The Case for Invading Iraq*, discouraged readers from thinking the case for invasion was related to stopping al-Qaeda, admitting that intelligence showed that "Iraq was not involved in the terrorist attacks of September 11, 2001," and Hussein "mostly shied away from al-Qa'eda for fear that a relationship could drag him into a war with the United States that was not of his making."[47]

The "ties to al-Qaeda" justification was further called into question by the fact that Bush Jr. began planning for war against Iraq *before* the September 11 attacks, during the time when his administration paid no attention to Al Qaeda (a negligence that facilitated the 9/11 attacks). Paul O'Neill, who served as treasury secretary, confirmed that in early 2001 cabinet meetings, the administration was discussing invading Iraq and deposing Hussein: "It was all about finding a way to do it. That was the tone of it. The president saying 'Go find me a way to do this.'" O'Neill revealed documents from before 9/11 like a "Plan for Post-Saddam Iraq" and a Pentagon document titled "Foreign Suitors for Iraqi Oilfield Contracts." Indeed, in 1998, many future members of Bush's administration had declared their belief that the U.S. should "[implement] a strategy for removing Saddam's regime from power."[48]

Once the invasion began, the idea of Saddam Hussein as a threat to the United States quickly came to seem ridiculous. His army melted away, and a fleeing Hussein soon hid out in a tiny "spider hole" on a farm. The idea of Iraq as a threat to the United States was as comical as when Ronald Reagan described Nicaragua as a threat to U.S. national security. In fact, it was an impoverished country falling apart. But history teaches that there is no situation so bad that U.S. intervention cannot make it worse.

With the core argument for war having been exposed as ludicrous, the justification was switched. Suddenly, the administration discovered that their reason for invading had *not* been to find weapons of mass destruction (even though Hussein's disarmament had been called the "single question" at issue), but rather our fervent wish to bring the blessings of democracy to Iraq. As Middle East scholar Augustus Richard Norton put it, "the Bush administration increasingly stressed the democratic transformation of Iraq, and scholars jumped on the democratization bandwagon."[49]

Iraqis themselves were not buying it. A Gallup poll found that only 5 percent thought the goal of the invasion was "to assist the Iraqi people," with most assuming the goal was to take control of Iraq's resources and reorder the Middle East to serve U.S. and Israeli interests. By 2004, huge majorities saw U.S. forces as "occupiers" rather than "liberators." Iraqis of all sects and backgrounds made it clear from early on that they did not want to be occupied; public opinion polling consistently showed that the majority wanted the U.S. to leave. (In a sign of how much the U.S. respects Iraqi democracy, when the Iraqi parliament voted to expel U.S. troops in 2020, Donald Trump responded by threatening the country with sanctions.)[50]

There were good reasons to be suspicious of this sudden discovery of an altruistic purpose. First, and most obviously, the United States has never cared about liberating people from tyrannies, and in fact strongly supports friendly tyrannies. The relevant question has always been whether they serve our "interests in the region" rather than whether they are internally repressive. Iraq's crimes against Kurds and Iranians were committed during the period of U.S. support. There was no explanation offered as to why, after enabling these atrocities, the U.S. had developed a sudden concern for punishing the perpetrators, nor any talk of holding to account the U.S. officials who had helped Hussein commit mass murder. If Hussein had remained compliant, his brutality would have been treated the same way as the brutality of others, like the Saudi royal family, Suharto, Pinochet, and the shah. That is, occasionally the United States might have expressed official disapproval of the country's human rights abuses, all while continuing to extend support that would enable the continuation of those abuses.

In fact, we can resolve the question of whether the Bush administration had any humanitarian motives by looking at its attitude toward compliant dictators. For instance, *The New York Times* reported in 2005 that while Uzbekistan was ruled by an appalling Hussein-like dictator, he was warmly embraced. Before 9/11, the U.S. State Department had issued a report that was a "litany of horrors," filled with accounts of extreme uses of torture including boiling prisoners to death. Yet "immediately after the Sept. 11 attacks," Bush "turned to Uzbekistan as a partner in fighting global terrorism," giving the country "more than $500 million for border control and other security measures." No thought was given to invading Uzbekistan, despite its dreadful human rights record. In fact, the *Times* said, "there is growing evidence that the United States has sent terror suspects to Uzbekistan for detention and interrogation, even as Uzbekistan's treatment of its own prisoners continues to earn it admonishments from around the world."[51]

If the interests of Iraqis had been foremost (or anywhere) in the minds of U.S. war planners, more attention would also have been given to the dire warnings that were issued before the war about the catastrophic humanitarian consequences that could well result. With the Iraqi people at the edge of survival after the destructive sanctions of 1990–2003, international aid and medical agencies foresaw that a war might lead to a humanitarian catastrophe. In 2003, just before the war began, the Swiss government hosted a meeting of thirty countries to prepare for what might lie ahead. The United States alone refused to attend. Participants, including the other four permanent Security Council members, "warned of devastating humanitarian consequences." Former assistant secretary of defense Kenneth Bacon, head of the Washington-based Refugees International, predicted that "a war will generate huge flows of refugees and a public health crisis." Meanwhile, U.S. plans for humanitarian relief in a postwar Iraq were criticized by international aid agencies as "short on detail, woefully lacking in money, and overly controlled by the military." UN officials complained, "There is a studied lack of interest [in Washington] in a warning call we are trying to deliver to the people planning for war, about what its consequences might be."[52]

A final indication that the U.S. did not seriously care about bringing democracy to Iraq is that it consistently attempted to keep democracy from coming to Iraq. The United States in fact *resisted* transferring sovereignty of Iraq to Iraqis. Colin Powell, in rejecting the idea of UN governance for Iraq, said: "We didn't take on this huge burden with our coalition partners not to be able to have a significant dominating control over how it unfolds in the future." (Bush himself said that when Iraq was eventually allowed to elect its own leaders, he wanted "someone who's willing to stand up and thank the American people for their sacrifice in liberating Iraq.") Brent Scowcroft, former adviser to George H. W. Bush, wondered: "What's going to happen the first time we hold an election in Iraq and it turns out the radicals win? What do you do? We're surely not going to let them take over."[53]

The New York Times reported in June 2003 that Paul Bremer had canceled the first municipal election in Iraq, to have been held in Najaf, on the grounds that "rejectionists" and "extremists" were likely to win, i.e., those who opposed the ongoing occupation of their country. Marines then "stormed the offices of an obscure local political party here, arrested four members and jailed them for four days," due to the party members' "violation of a new edict by Mr. Bremer that makes it illegal to incite violence against forces occupying Iraq." Democracy is not for those who advocate violent resistance to an occupying army. The *Times* reported that hundreds of Iraqis came out to protest the cancellation of the election, and quoted the man who was "expected to win the election" saying that without elections, the Americans could expect more violent resistance. ("If they don't give us freedom, what will we do?")[54]

If all the official justifications were obvious propaganda, transparently false even at the time of invasion, one might ask what the real justifications for the war were.

Iraqis certainly thought that the war was about oil. Oil is a leading cause of war around the world, and U.S. policymakers make no secret of their strong reluctance to cede control of the world's oil supply to rival powers. Control of energy sources fuels U.S. economic and military might and provides a lever of world control. This was the rationale behind Jimmy Carter's "Carter Doctrine": "An attempt by any outside force to gain control of the Persian Gulf region will be regarded as an assault on the vital interests of the United States of America, and such an assault will be repelled by any means necessary, including military force."[55]

In explaining the first Gulf War, George H. W. Bush did not shy away from invoking oil as a justification: "Our jobs, our way of life, our own freedom, and the freedom of friendly countries around the world would all suffer if control of the world's great oil reserves fell into the hands of Saddam Hussein." Bush vowed: "We cannot permit a resource so vital to be dominated by one so ruthless. And we won't." Former CENTCOM commander John Abizaid, discussing U.S. involvement in the Middle East generally, said: "Of course it's about oil. It's very much about oil, and we can't really deny that." Indeed, if Iraq's main exports had been tomatoes and asparagus, Saddam Hussein's power within the region would have been of much less concern to the United States. Richard Haass, director of Policy Planning in the State Department under Bush Jr., wrote that "the principal reason the region matters as much as it does stems from its [oil and gas] resources and their relevance to the world economy . . . absent oil and oil's importance the region would count for much less."[56]

Bush Jr. officials have denied that they shared Bush Sr.'s stated concern with securing control over energy supplies. Rumsfeld said the war had "literally nothing to do with oil," and Bush speechwriter David Frum was emphatic that "the United States is not fighting for oil in Iraq."[57] But Kenneth Pollack explained that one of the crucial reasons *why* Hussein couldn't be permitted to wield weapons of mass destruction was that he would use the power "to advance Iraq's political interests" and might "cut or even halt oil exports altogether whenever it suited him" in order to obtain concessions from countries, including the United States.[58]

As Rumsfeld, Wolfowitz, and a number of other neoconservatives wrote in their 1998 letter to President Clinton demanding regime change in Iraq: "If Saddam does acquire the capability to deliver weapons of mass destruction . . . the safety of American troops in the region, of our friends and allies like Israel and the moderate Arab states, and a significant portion of the world's supply of oil will all be put at hazard." Republican senator Chuck Hagel, who became secretary of defense under Obama, said of the Iraq War in 2007: "People say we're not fighting for oil. Of course we are. They talk about America's national interest. What the hell do you think they're talking about? We're not there for figs." Former Federal Reserve chairman Alan Greenspan said similarly, "I am saddened that it is politically inconvenient to acknowledge what everyone knows: the Iraq War is largely about oil." Richard Clarke said that having observed the administration from the inside, while he believed multiple motivations were at work, among them were "to improve Israel's strategic position by eliminating a large, hostile military" and "to create another friendly source of oil for the U.S. market and reduce dependency upon oil from Saudi Arabia."[59]

The idea that the invasion of Iraq was just "for oil" is nevertheless simplistic. For Bush, there were many attractive reasons to depose Hussein, including his antagonistic stance toward Israel. Personal motivations can also be bound up with geopolitical ones (see, e.g., Lyndon Johnson's fear of emasculation if he went soft in Vietnam). Before the invasion, Bush said:

> One of the keys to being seen as a great leader is to be seen as a commander-in-chief. My father had all this political capital built up when he drove the Iraqis out of [Kuwait] and he wasted it. If I have a chance to invade Iraq, if I had that much capital, I'm not going to waste it. I'm going to get everything passed I want to get passed and I'm going to have a successful presidency.[60]

The younger Bush may well have thought that the key to a successful presidency is a successful war. His former press secretary wrote that he had heard Bush say that "only a wartime president is likely to achieve greatness."[61]

There were multiple perfectly rational reasons Bush had for invading Iraq, none of which had anything to do with the stated justifications. Wars distract from the domestic agenda, and the Republican Party's domestic policy platform was deeply unpopular. Even the lack of UN support for the war was an asset rather than a drawback, because by violating international law without consequence, the Bush administration could diminish the authority of the only institution theoretically entrusted with constraining U.S. use of force. As Bush administration adviser and former Reagan assistant secretary of defense Richard Perle wrote in *The Guardian*, a positive side effect of the downfall of Hussein is that he "will take the UN down with him" and "what will die is the fantasy of the UN as the foundation of a new world order." The invasion would put an end to the "liberal conceit of safety through international law administered by international institutions." Those institutions would be shown to be powerless to stop the United States. What is needed is a war with an "exemplary quality," Harvard Middle East historian Roger Owen pointed out, discussing the reasons for the attack on Iraq. The exemplary action teaches a lesson that others must heed, or else. As Perle said: "Having destroyed the Taliban, having destroyed Saddam's regime, the message to the others is, 'You're next.'"[62]

General Anthony Zinni, former chief of CENTCOM, in his personal opinion on the motives of the neoconservatives in pushing for war, gives an explanation consistent with the facts, commenting that the "neocons didn't really give a shit what happened in Iraq and the aftermath." Since "we've asserted our strength," the attitude was: "Who cares?" Not too much "idealism" here. Just pure mafioso thinking. The lives of Iraqis are meaningless. The question is whether we have successfully asserted American power.[63]

Iraq was devastated by the U.S. invasion, which incited ethnic conflict that tore apart both the country and the region. "You should see the price of your war and occupation," wrote an Iraqi blogger in 2004.

"They don't show you the hospitals overflowing with the dead and dying because they don't want to hurt American feelings." Out of the wreckage emerged the nightmarish Islamic State, which almost succeeded in taking over the country. The war, though pitched as part of a "global war on terrorism," in fact made Western countries more vulnerable than ever to terrorism. The cost was staggering, in both human lives and resources.[64]

But those responsible for the worst crime of the century have never been indicted or prosecuted. The idea is never even mentioned in U.S. discourse. In fact, a 2021 *Washington Post* Style profile said that Bush is seen in public "sharing hard candies with Michelle Obama or hanging out at a Cowboys game with Ellen DeGeneres." Bush also took up painting in his retirement, and his portraits of soldiers have been collected into a coffee table book (*Portraits of Courage: A Commander in Chief's Tribute to America's Warriors*) that attracted favorable notice in *The New Yorker*, which described his work as "surprisingly likable," "honestly observed," and of "astonishingly high quality." During the Trump years, some Democrats even looked back fondly on Bush's tenure, seeing him as a more congenial and moderate Republican. Democratic senator Harry Reid commented that "I look back on Bush with a degree of nostalgia, with some affection, which I never thought I would do."[65]

It says something disturbing about our media that a man can cause well over five hundred thousand deaths and then have his paintings flatteringly profiled, while the deaths go unmentioned. George W. Bush intentionally offered false justifications for a war, destroyed an entire country, and committed major international crimes. He tortured people, sometimes to death. Yet his public image is now that of a goofy grandpa, for whom even Democrats are nostalgic.

Bush's victims, of course, feel somewhat differently. Cindy Sheehan, whose son, Casey, was killed in the war, and who waged an admirable campaign against the war, told *The Washington Post*, "I don't think he deserves people like Ellen DeGeneres sitting next to him and giving him legitimacy like he's just some nice guy. I don't think he deserves the rehabilitation or softening of his image. I think he belongs in prison." Muntadhar al-Zaidi, the Iraqi journalist who threw his shoes at President Bush, said he did so "to express my rejection of his lies, his occupation of my country, my rejection of his killing my people."[66]

The chief architects of the war have lived prosperous and comfortable lives. Donald Rumsfeld, after leaving government service in 2007, "created the Rumsfeld Foundation to encourage public service with study fellowships and grants to support the growth of free political and economic systems abroad." Colin Powell "served as the chairman of the board of visitors of the School for Civic and Global Leadership." Paul Bremer became a skiing instructor in Vermont. Dick Cheney received a warm welcome from Democrats when he visited the Capitol on the anniversary of the January 6 uprising. And George W. Bush, of course, paints pictures of foreign leaders, soldiers, and puppies. No mainstream effort has been made to enforce international law against those who violated it.[67]

To top it off, in 2022 the navy announced a new amphibious assault vessel: the USS *Fallujah*, named to commemorate one of the most atrocious crimes of the invasion. Journalist Nabil Salih writes that "U.S. savagery didn't end" with the wholesale massacre of women and children, and "Fallujah's name, bleached in white phosphorus implanted in mothers' wombs for generations, is a spoil of war, too."[68]

George W. Bush waged what was referred to as a "global war on terror." It swiftly succeeded in exacerbating the very problem it was ostensibly launched to combat. Reducing the threat of terrorist attacks on U.S. targets was never a serious priority for the Bush administration. In an analysis of quasi-official data, terrorism specialists Peter Bergen and Paul Cruickshank found that the "Iraq effect"—the consequence of the Iraq invasion—was a sevenfold increase in terror. By fighting terrorism with terrorism, the United States handed jihadists an extraordinary recruiting tool. The CIA itself concluded that the Iraq occupation became "the cause célèbre for jihadists, breeding a deep resentment of U.S. involvement in the Muslim world and cultivating supporters for the global jihadist movement." Bin Laden could not have hoped for a more favorable outcome from the 9/11 attacks. Carter Malkasian notes that "bin Laden's dream of drawing the United States into Afghanistan came true."[69]

In the years of the "global war on terror," when individual Muslims launched violent attacks on U.S. civilian targets, the United States' own actions in the war were almost invariably cited as the reasons for the attacks. J. M. Berger, in *Jihad Joe*, which profiles scores of American Muslims who have become jihadists, says that while fundamentalist Islam is often associated with "the intent to absorb Western society into a world-spanning Islamic state ruled by a strict, often brutal, interpretation of the shariah," this motivation is in fact "nearly irrelevant to the question of radicalization," which is instead "almost always" rooted in "an urgent feeling that Muslims are under attack."[70]

At the time of 9/11, Osama bin Laden was in a tiny area on the Afghanistan-Pakistan border. Thanks to the "war on terror," terrorism spread all over the world.

The United States,
Israel, and Palestine

The following chapter was finalized early in 2023, before the October 7 attacks. Unfortunately, health reasons prevented Professor Chomsky from working with me to update the chapter to cover the most recent war. But I have decided to leave the chapter as it stood when we finished it, and added a postscript of my own covering October 7 and after. By reading the analysis as it was in early 2023, we can see the critical background to the Hamas attack on Israel and Israel's subsequent war on Gaza. Chomsky has previously quoted a placard held by an old man that reads: "You take my water, burn my olive trees, destroy my house, take my job, steal my land, imprison my father, kill my mother, bombard my country, starve us all, humiliate us all but I am to blame: I shot a rocket back." In this chapter, we recount some of the facts that fueled Palestinian rage and resistance, from the earliest years of Zionism to the shooting of peaceful protesters in 2018. We also show how the United States has stood in the way of peace. Chomsky argued long before October 7 that a "civilized reaction" to the Israel Palestine conflict would be: "The U.S. and Israel could end the merciless unremitting assault and open the borders, and provide for reconstruction—and if it were imaginable, reparations for decades of violence and repression."[1]

—Nathan J. Robinson

I f Washington, DC, crumbled to the ground, the last thing that would remain is our support for Israel," Nancy Pelosi told the Israel American Council National Conference in 2018. The close relationship between the United States and Israel is a natural one. After all, the two countries share common official origin stories: European refugees fleeing persecution came to an unspoiled virgin land, bringing the light of civilization with them. Ronald Reagan himself said that "the United States and Israel share similar beginnings as nations of immigrants, yearning to live in freedom and to fulfill the dreams of our forefathers." Some Americans see Israel as struggling with an analogous situation vis-à-vis the Palestinians as this country's founders did with its own "inconvenient" native population. The British member of Parliament and staunch Zionist Richard Crossman observed that Zionism is "much the same" as the process by which "the American settler developed the West," which leads Americans to "give the Jewish settler in Palestine the benefit of the doubt, and regard the Arab as the aboriginal who must go down before the march of progress." Americans, having "opened up a virgin country and conquered it for the white man," know "by bitter experience" what a "battle against the aboriginal" entails.[2]

But the relationship is as much strategic as spiritual. The Middle East has long been the world's major source of cheap energy, and anyone who has control over this resource is in a very strong position to play an effective role in ordering and organizing the world. Much impressed with Israel's military successes in the 1948 war, the Joint Chiefs of Staff described the new state as the major regional military power after Turkey, offering the United States the means to "gain strategic advantage in the Middle East that would offset the effects of the decline of British power in that area," in the words of historian Avi Shlaim. Ten years later, the National Security Council concluded that a "logical corollary" of opposition to growing Arab nationalism "would be to support Israel as the only strong pro-West power left in the [Middle East]." The U.S.-Israeli alliance was firmed up in 1967, when Israel performed a huge service to the U.S. by smashing secular Arab nationalism through its victory in the Six-Day War.[3]

Joe Biden was honest when he said the United States depends on Israel to "protect [our] interest in the region." Henry Jackson, who was the Senate's major specialist on the Middle East and oil, pointed out that Israel, Iran (under the shah), and Saudi Arabia "inhibit and contain those irresponsible and radical elements in certain Arab states, who, were they free to do so, would pose a grave threat indeed to our principal sources of petroleum in the Middle East." As long as Israel's actions conform to U.S. objectives, it receives the diplomatic, military, and economic support that has facilitated its takeover of valuable parts of the occupied territories and its development into a rich industrial society.[4]

American support for Israel means that Israel's actions should rightly be understood as "U.S.-Israeli" actions. When we talk about "Israeli crimes," the framing is misleading, because they are U.S.-Israeli crimes. Whatever Israel does is either implicitly or explicitly authorized by the United States, which provides economic, diplomatic, military, and ideological support, and U.S. presidents can alter Israeli policy and restrain Israel's violence when they choose to do so. When we talk about Israel, we should remember that in an important sense we are talking about ourselves. Because the U.S. arms and protects Israel, we bear responsibility for what it does.

GAZA, 2022

Najwa Abu Hamada will never have another child. Her only son, Khalil, was conceived after she had been trying to have children for fifteen years, including five unsuccessful rounds of in vitro fertilization. In August 2022, Khalil was nineteen. His mother was looking forward to his graduation and hoping he would soon get married.[5]

Khalil had just left the house when Najwa heard the bombing. Panicking, she ran outside, and saw the body of her son's best friend. "Minutes later, I found my son," Najwa recounted. "He was soaked in blood and lying on the ground. I was screaming so hard calling for an ambulance." Days later, Najwa still could not believe that after fifteen years of trying for a child, followed by nineteen years of her son's life, Khalil was suddenly gone forever. "I have no one else but him," she said.

To imagine the pain that Najwa feels is almost unbearable. But she was not the only parent in Gaza faced with the sudden death of their child that week. Fifteen children were among the dozens killed in the Israeli air strikes, which were not launched in response to violence but "preemptively."

"Their parents and I went out screaming: 'Our children, our children!' There were body parts soaked in their own blood," sixty-year-old Umm Mohammad al-Nairab told *Al Jazeera English.* Her grandchildren (Ahmad, eleven, and Moamen, five) had gone out to the supermarket across the street from the house when the airstrike hit.

In the United States, to the extent that these horrors are reported, they are usually presented without political and historical context.[6] Beyond Israel's statements about the need to launch preemptive strikes on terrorists, little information is made available to an American readership to allow them to understand why Najwa must now mourn Khalil. Nor is there discussion of our own country's complicity in the killings— complicity that arises not only through the constant supply of weaponry to Israel (the Israeli planes that drop bombs on Gaza are all American made[7]) but decades of policy that have thwarted the possibilities for a peaceful settlement to the Israel-Palestine conflict.

ORIGINS OF A CENTURY-LONG CONFLICT

The state of Israel is young, and the circumstances of its birth are important in understanding the existence of the present conflict.

The plan to establish a Jewish state in Palestine ran into a basic problem from the outset: Palestine was already inhabited by half a million people. At the dawn of the twentieth century, the country's population was 95 percent Arab, with only a small Jewish minority. The inconvenient existence of a large indigenous non-Jewish population across all of Palestine meant that those early Zionists who wanted to establish a Jewish state had to either give up the idea altogether, impose minority rule, or embark on a program of ethnic cleansing. The demographic reality of turn-of-the-last-century Palestine meant that implementing the Zionist dream would turn out to be a violent, undemocratic, and racist business. (This is one reason why not all early Zionists supported the creation of a Jewish state.) As Fawaz Turki wrote in *The Disinherited: Journal of a Palestinian Exile*, those who "admire Israeli accomplishments," its "miracle in the desert," may "find it difficult to admit that beneath the glamor lies the tragedy of another people who suffered for no reason, who were uprooted from their homeland, and who had never in their history practiced persecution in their rencontre with Jews, but who were made to pay the price of a crime that others had committed."[8]

Some early Zionists discussed Palestine as if it were essentially uninhabited, a "land without a people." In the romantic imagination of those who planned to colonize it, Palestine was a sparsely inhabited place to which Jews could move and make the desert bloom. The early Zionist leader Moshe Smilansky said Palestine appeared in stories as "a desolate and largely neglected land, waiting eagerly for its redeemers." The Eastern European Jewish essayist Ahad Ha'Am wrote in 1891 that "we abroad are used to believing that Eretz Yisrael is now almost totally desolate, a desert that is not sowed."[9]

Ahad Ha'Am and others knew, however, that this was not actually the case, and in fact "throughout the country it is difficult to find fields that are not sowed." In 1905, leading Jewish writer Hillel Zeitlin wrote that Zionist plans for settlement "forget, mistakenly or maliciously . . . that Palestine belongs to others, and it is totally settled." The same year, Hebrew linguist Yitzhak Epstein pointed out that the Zionist leaders had "overlook[ed] a rather marginal 'fact'—that in our beloved land there lives an entire people that has been dwelling there for many centuries and has never considered leaving it." The mayor of Jerusalem, Yusuf Diya al-Khalidi, corresponded with Theodor Herzl in 1899 and expressed sympathy with the Zionist project, but explained that the problem with the plan was that Palestine "is inhabited by others." His conclusion was that political Zionism was disastrous, and he pleaded: "In the name of God, let Palestine be left alone." Herzl ignored the plea, and elsewhere wrote that "both the process of expropriation and the removal of the poor must be carried out discreetly and circumspectly."[10]

Honest supporters of the Jewish state admitted at the outset that theirs was a colonial project, and would have to be carried out against the wishes of the native population. Ze'ev Jabotinsky, the founder of Revisionist Zionism, was blunt: Palestinians opposed Zionism, he said, because "they understand as well as we what is not good for them" and "look upon Palestine with the same instinctive love and true fervor that any Aztec looked upon his Mexico or any Sioux looked upon his prairie." Jabotinsky thought that "every indigenous people will resist alien settlers as long as they see any hope of ridding themselves of the danger of foreign settlement" and concluded that "that is what the Arabs in Palestine are doing, and what they will persist in doing as long as there remains a solitary spark of hope that they will be able to prevent the transformation of 'Palestine' into the 'Land of Israel.'"[11]

Because establishing the Jewish state in Palestine involved a denial of Palestinian self-determination, Jabotinsky concluded that the Arabs' "voluntary agreement is out of the question" and encouraged those who "hold that an agreement with the natives is an essential condition for Zionism" to "depart from Zionism." Zionism, he said, "is a colonizing venture, and therefore, it stands or falls on the question of armed forces." Chaim Weizmann, who became the first president of Israel, argued that "the rights which the Jewish people has been adjudged in Palestine do not depend on the consent, and cannot be subjected to the will, of the majority of its present inhabitants." In 1940, Jewish National Fund director Joseph Weitz concluded in his diaries that "there is no room for both people in this country. . . . There is no compromise on this point. . . . We must not leave a single village, not a single tribe." As Israeli historian Benny Morris put it, Zionism was a "colonizing and expansionist ideology and movement . . . intent on politically, and even physically, dispossessing and supplanting the Arabs."[12]

Jabotinsky also determined that, because Zionism "must either be terminated or carried out in defiance of the will of the native population," if it was to succeed, it would need the backing of "a force independent of the local population—an iron wall which the native population cannot break through." The Zionists found their "iron wall" in the British Empire, which officially endorsed the project to establish a Jewish homeland in Palestine in the 1917 Balfour Declaration. Balfour himself was open about the fact that the plan was to be supported regardless of the wishes of the majority of Palestinians. ("Whatever deference should be paid to the views of those who live there, the Powers in their selection of a mandatory do not propose, as I understand the matter, to consult them," because the impetus behind Zionism was "far profounder than the desires and prejudices of the 700,000 Arabs who now inhabit that ancient land.") Winston Churchill saw that a Jewish state "astride the bridge between Europe and Africa, flanking the land roads to the East" could be "an immense advantage to the British empire." He observed that the Jewish Zionists "take it for granted that the local population will be cleared out to suit their convenience."[13]

The same conclusion was reached by the U.S. government's King-Crane Commission in 1919, which heard from Zionists that they "looked forward to a practically complete dispossession of the non-Jewish inhabitants of Palestine." No military experts "believed that the Zionist program could be carried out except by force of arms." The commission noted that "nearly nine-tenths of the whole [non-Jewish population]—are emphatically against the entire Zionist program," and to subject them to it "would be a gross violation of the principle [of self-determination], and of the people's rights, though it kept within the forms of law." Presciently, the commissioners said that "if the American government decided to support the establishment of a Jewish state in Palestine, they are committing the American people to the use of force in that area, since only by force can a Jewish state in Palestine be established or maintained."[14]

The question of how to get rid of the Arabs was a matter of open discussion among Zionists, with many supporting a policy politely called "transfer" (i.e., ethnic cleansing). David Ben-Gurion, who would become Israel's first prime minister, said in 1930: "I support compulsory transfer. I don't see anything immoral in it." Benny Morris comments that "the transfer idea . . . was viewed by the majority of the Yishuv lead-ers in those days as the best solution to the problem." Morris says transfer "was inevitable and in-built into Zionism—because it sought to trans-form a land which was 'Arab' into a 'Jewish' state and a Jewish state could not have arisen without a major displacement of the Arab population."[15]

These views of Arabs were consistent with the usual view of native inhabitants by Europeans. Morris says the prevailing impression of Arabs was as "primitive, dishonest, fatalistic, lazy, savage—much as Eu-ropean colonists viewed the natives elsewhere in Asia or Africa." Amer-ican journalist Vincent Sheean—who arrived in Palestine in 1929 as a supporter of Zionism and left a few months later as a harsh critic of it—found that the Jewish settlers "had contempt [for the Arabs] as an 'uncivilized race,' to whom some of them referred as 'Red Indians' and others as 'savages.'" Portrayals of Israel as an "outpost of civilization against barbarism" (Herzl's phrase) were commonplace for the next hundred years. Ehud Barak, prime minister from 1999 to 2001, spoke for many in calling Israel a "villa in the jungle" and "a vanguard of cul-ture against barbarism." The image was shared among many Western-ers. As Edward Said put it, "so far as the West is concerned, Palestine has been a place where a relatively advanced (because European) in-coming population of Jews has performed miracles of construction and civilizing and has fought brilliantly successful technical wars against what was always portrayed as a dumb, essentially repellent population of uncivilized Arab natives."[16]

Just as American Indians were portrayed as scattered and nomadic, without real title to the land, so Arabs were portrayed as having little authentic connection to the place they inhabited. Sheean says Zionist settlers looked upon the indigenous population as "mere squatters for thirteen centuries," and believed they could, through "purchase, per-suasion and pressure . . . get the Arabs out sooner or later and convert Palestine into a Jewish national home." Sheean doubted "that the Arabs of Palestine were so different from other Arabs that they would wel-come the attempt to create a Jewish nation in their country."

Indeed, they did not welcome it, and once Palestinians understood that their dispossession was essential to the success of the Zionist enterprise, they revolted against it. In 1914, 'Isa al-'Isa described the Palestinian Arabs as "a nation which is threatened in its very being with expulsion from its homeland." As Israeli diplomat Abba Eban would later note, "If they had submitted to Zionism with docility they would have been the first people in history to have voluntarily renounced their majority status." When the Peel Commission in 1937 proposed to create a Jewish state from which two hundred thousand Arabs would be "transferred" (cleansed), Palestinian Arabs vehemently rejected the idea.[17] A massive Palestinian revolt in the late 1930s was brutally suppressed by the British Empire, with Palestinian leaders killed, jailed, and exiled. (This was the "iron wall"—the external force necessary to ensure Zionism's success—in action.)[18]

Palestinian rejection of partition in 1947 is often portrayed as unreasonable, but Zionists were quite open about the fact that they saw partition, in Morris's words, "as a stepping-stone to some further expansion and the eventual takeover of the whole of Palestine." Rashid Khalidi, responding to the commonly noted fact that Arabs rejected the UN partition plan, adds that it was "inconceivable that any people would have accepted giving up more than 55 percent of their country to a minority," as the plan provided. Historian Albert Hourani gave testimony to the Anglo-American Committee of Inquiry arguing that the Zionist plan inevitably "would involve a terrible injustice and could only be carried out at the expense of dreadful repressions and disorders, with the risk of bringing down in ruins the whole political structure of the Middle East."[19]

In 1948, during the war following the announcement of the partition plan, Israel took an important step forward in solving its "demographic problem." Some seven hundred thousand Palestinians were expelled from their homes in what became known in Palestinian memory as the "nakba" (catastrophe).[20] As Israeli novelist S. Yizhar captured it in 1949's *Khirbet Khizeh*, "We came, we shot, we burned; we blew up, expelled, drove out, and sent into exile." Zionist leader Moshe Sharett said in 1948, "We are equally determined . . . to explore all possibilities of getting rid, once and for all, of the huge Arab minority which originally threatened us." In internal discussion, Israeli government Arabists in 1948 fully expected that the refugees "would be crushed" and "die," while "most of them would turn into human dust," joining the most impoverished in the Arab world.[21]

Understanding the colonial aspects of the present-day state of Israel is critical, because Palestinian resistance is often portrayed as being grounded in irrational anti-Semitism. Israeli prime minister Ehud Barak said that negotiating with Arabs was difficult because "their culture does not contain the concept of compromise." David Ben-Gurion warned fellow Zionists that "a people which fights against the usurpation of its land will not tire so easily," bluntly telling them not to "ignore the truth among ourselves," that "when we say that the Arabs are the aggressors and we defend ourselves—that is only half the truth" because "politically we are the aggressors and they defend themselves" because "the country is theirs."[22]

Israel was born in conquest and ethnic cleansing, and Palestinian resistance has, from the start, been predictable. Instead of acknowledging the original injustice that accompanied its founding, Israel has taken the opposite approach: portraying the (much poorer, much weaker) Palestinians as aggressors in the conflict, and denying the Palestinians' right to self-determination even in their remaining territories. Some have gone so far as to treat the Palestinians as a nonentity—Golda Meir famously said, "There was no such thing as Palestinians. . . . They did not exist." The importance of denying the legitimacy of Palestinian claims to the land was made clear by Menachem Begin, who told Israelis in 1969: "If this is Palestine and not the Land of Israel, then you are conquerors and not tillers of the land. You are invaders. If this is Palestine then it belongs to the people who lived here before you came. Only if it is the Land of Israel do you have a right to live in it."[23]

Palestinians did not "turn into human dust" in 1948. They have spent seventy years struggling to achieve self-determination in the areas left to them after the establishment of the state of Israel. Since 1967, Israel has kept the Palestinians under a harsh military occupation, the character of which can be understood through a cursory glance at any of the voluminous reports from independent human rights organizations that have condemned the occupation. Amnesty International in 2017, for instance, concluded that "Israel's ruthless policies of land confiscation, illegal settlement and dispossession, coupled with rampant discrimination, have inflicted immense suffering on Palestinians, depriving them of their basic rights." Military rule "disrupts every aspect of daily life in the Occupied Palestinian Territories" and "means daily humiliation, fear and oppression . . . people's entire lives are effectively held hostage by Israel." Israel has also adopted "a complex web of military laws to crush dissent against its policies."[24]

Israel "has demolished tens of thousands of Palestinian properties and displaced large swathes of the population to build homes and infrastructure to illegally settle its own population in the occupied territories" and has "diverted Palestinian natural resources such as water and agricultural land for settlement use." Amnesty observes that "the hundreds of Israeli military closures across the West Bank such as checkpoints, roadblocks and settler-only roads, as well as the overall permit regime, make simple daily tasks for Palestinians who are trying to get to work, school or hospital a constant struggle." Israel also has "a long record of using excessive and often lethal force against Palestinian men, women, and children." There has been a "cycle of impunity" for these crimes for "over half a century."

One can present a stack of other reports from Amnesty, Human

Rights Watch, B'Tselem (the Israeli Information Center for Human Rights in the Occupied Territories), and the United Nations confirming the facts. While claiming it has the "most moral army in the world," Israel has deployed torture, extrajudicial assassination, and collective punishment in the service of a mission to "[dispossess] the Arabs of Palestine of the four fundamental elements—land, water, leaders, and culture—without which an indigenous community cannot survive," as Eqbal Ahmad put it. Benny Morris describes the difference between the image Israel projects and the human reality. "Israelis like to believe, and tell the world," he says, that the occupation is "enlightened" or "benign." The facts, he says, are "radically different," and the Israeli occupation, like other similar occupations, "was founded on brute force, repression and fear, collaboration and treachery, beatings and torture chambers, and daily intimidation, humiliation, and manipulation."[25]

The situation in Gaza in recent decades has been especially dire. Israel formally withdrew from Gaza in 2005, but has kept it under a savage blockade.[26] Gaza has become the world's largest open-air prison, its densely packed residents deprived of basic nutrition and employment. In 2012, the United Nations Relief and Works Agency (UNRWA) released a report warning that without urgent remedial action, Gaza would cease to be a "livable place" by 2020. Israel's restrictions on allowing Gazans construction materials have made it impossible for development to proceed. The Israeli plan was described by Dov Weissglas, an adviser to Prime Minister Ehud Olmert: "The idea," he said, "is to put the Palestinians on a diet, but not to make them die of hunger."[27]

To that end, health officials calculated the minimum number of calories needed by Gaza's 1.5 million residents and translated the figure into the number of truckloads of food Israel would allow to enter Gaza daily. Middle East scholar Juan Cole observed in 2012 that "about ten percent of Palestinian children in Gaza under 5 have had their growth stunted by malnutrition . . . in addition, anemia is widespread, affecting over two-thirds of infants, 58.6 percent of schoolchildren, and over a third of pregnant mothers." In 2022, Save the Children reported that "fifteen years of life under blockade has left four out of five children in the Gaza Strip reporting that they live with depression, grief and fear," and that "the mental well-being of children, young people and caregivers has dramatically deteriorated since a similar study in 2018." UN Secretary-General António Guterres has said the lives of Gazan children are "hell on earth." Israel ensures that bare survival is all that is possible. In the leading medical journal *The Lancet*, a visiting Stanford physician, appalled by what he witnessed, described Gaza as "something of a laboratory for observing an absence of dignity," a condition that has "devastating" effects on physical, mental, and social well-being.[28]

Any attempts at resistance are met with extreme reprisals by Israel. In 2006, for instance, Gazans committed a terrible crime: they voted the wrong way in an election, choosing Hamas as their governing party. The United States immediately began plotting a military coup. With constant U.S. backing, Israel increased its violence in Gaza, withheld funds that it was legally obligated to transmit to the Palestinian Authority, tightened its siege, and in a gratuitous act of cruelty, even cut off the flow of water. Israel and the U.S. made sure that Hamas would not have a chance to govern. In 2008–2009's Operation Cast Lead, Gaza was subject to relentless attack by the Israeli military—some of the poorest people in the world preyed on by one of the world's most advanced military systems (using, of course, U.S. arms and protected by U.S. diplomacy). Israeli journalist Gideon Levy described a 2006 assault on Gaza: Israel "drops innumerable missiles, shells and bombs on houses and kills entire families." At a "collapsing" hospital, Levy "saw heartrending scenes: children who had lost limbs, on respirators, paralyzed, crippled for the rest of their lives." The impact on the young is extreme: "Frightened children, traumatized by what they have seen, huddle in their homes with a horror in their eyes that is difficult to describe in words."[29]

Harvard's Sara Roy, a leading scholar on Gaza's "de-development," offered a further moving and disturbing testimony on the situation in

2012, saying that over the last half century, Gaza has gone from a restricted economy with some capacity to produce to an economy "characterized by unprecedented levels of unemployment and impoverishment, with three-quarters of its population needing humanitarian assistance." It is, she says, "catastrophic," but also "deliberate, considered, and purposeful."[30]

Israel's takeover of land and resources is illegal. The illegality of the West Bank settlements, for instance, is accepted by the UN Security Council, the International Court of Justice (unanimously, including the U.S. justice), the states party to the Geneva Convention, and the International Committee of the Red Cross (ICRC), not to mention various foreign governments and leading legal scholars. The violations of agreements, international laws, and basic civil rights are too legion to list. For instance, even though the 1993 Oslo Accords declared Gaza and the West Bank to be an inseparable territorial unity, Israel has been committed for nearly thirty years to separating the two. (Separated from Gaza, the West Bank is surrounded entirely by Israel, leaving Palestinians with no access to the outside world.)

It is also beyond serious dispute that the word "apartheid" accurately describes the situation in the Occupied Territories. Leading veterans of the South African anti-apartheid struggle like Archbishop Desmond Tutu have made the comparison with South Africa explicit. ("I have witnessed the systemic humiliation of Palestinian men, women and children by members of the Israeli security forces. . . . Their humiliation is familiar to all black South Africans who were corralled and harassed and insulted and assaulted by the security forces of the apartheid government.") But even David Ben-Gurion had warned that Israel would soon become an apartheid state if it did not rid itself of the territories and the Palestinian Arab population. Other Israeli leaders including Yitzhak Rabin and Ehud Barak similarly referred to apartheid, with Rabin saying in 1976, "I don't think it's possible to contain over the long term, if we don't want to get to apartheid, a million and a half [more] Arabs inside a Jewish state." Ehud Olmert said that "if the two-state solution collapses, and we face a South African–style struggle for equal voting rights, then the State of Israel is finished."[31]

There have been efforts at manufacturing controversy over applying the term to the Occupied Territories. When the United Nations Economic and Social Commission for Western Asia (UNESCWA) published an official report showing that "Israel has established an apartheid regime that dominates the Palestinian people as a whole," the report was removed from the UN website under pressure. Israel's UN ambassador called the label "despicable" and a "blatant lie." But plenty of Israeli officials themselves have used the term in recent years, including former attorney general Michael Ben-Yair, who said that "we established an apartheid regime in the occupied territories," and Foreign Ministry chief Alon Lie, who said that until such time as a Palestinian state is created, Israel must be considered an apartheid state.[32]

This is before we get to the reports of the mainstream human rights organizations. In its 213-page report "A Threshold Crossed," released in 2021, Human Rights Watch laid out the evidence exhaustively, noting that "Israeli authorities methodically privilege Jewish Israelis and discriminate against Palestinians," pursuing "the objective of maintaining Jewish Israeli control over demographics, political power, and land." To achieve that goal, Israeli authorities "have dispossessed, confined, forcibly separated, and subjugated Palestinians by virtue of their identity to varying degrees of intensity."[33]

Amnesty International's judgment is similarly blunt, concluding that "laws, policies and practices which are intended to maintain a cruel system of control over Palestinians, have left them fragmented geographically and politically, frequently impoverished, and in a constant state of fear and insecurity." B'Tselem reaches an identical verdict. "The entire area between the Mediterranean Sea and the Jordan River is organized under a single principle: advancing and cementing the supremacy of one group—Jews—over another—Palestinians."[34]

The day-to-day oppression of the Palestinians has been accompanied by a long-standing refusal on the part of Israel (backed by the United States) to engage in good-faith negotiations to resolve the conflict. Despite a popular narrative about Palestinian rejectionism and Arab intransigence supposedly causing Palestinians to miss numerous opportunities to have a state of their own (and certainly there have been serious failures by the Palestinian leadership), Israel has made it clear that it does not wish for a just settlement.

Israel's leaders have been blunt for decades about opposing a Palestinian state.[35] While a two-state solution roughly in accordance with the pre-1967 borders has long been the basic framework for a settlement, the 1989 Peres-Shamir coalition government responded to the explicit Palestinian National Council (PNC) peace offer by declaring that there can be no "additional Palestinian state" between Jordan and Israel ("additional" because Jordan was treated as already being a Palestinian state). Yitzhak Rabin told the Knesset in 1995 that whatever the Palestinians eventually ended up with, "We would like this to be an entity which is less than a state . . . we will not return to the June 4, 1967, lines." Benjamin Netanyahu proudly bragged that "I de facto put an end to the Oslo Accords" and indicated he was "only pretending to go along with the idea of a two-state solution." In 2015, Netanyahu declared that "there would be no Palestinian state on my watch." The 1999 platform of Netanyahu's Likud Party "flatly rejects the establishment of a Palestinian Arab state west of the Jordan river." Indeed, Ron Pundak, a key architect of the Oslo Accords, reviewing the record, concludes that "Netanyahu sabotaged the peace process relentlessly." Yitzhak Shamir admitted to intentionally using the "peace process" to stall for time: "I would have conducted negotiations on autonomy for ten years and in the meantime we would have reached half a million people in Judea and Samaria."[36] The most promising negotiations in recent history, the 2001 Taba negotiations, were called off early by Israeli prime

minister Ehud Barak. When asked why he had called off the negotiations four days early, Barak "simply denied" that there was any hope for
progress and stated, "It doesn't make any difference why I ended it."[37]

Israel could have had peace, but it chose expansion. In 1971, Israel
received an offer from Egypt for a full peace treaty. The Israeli government, led by Golda Meir, considered it and rejected it because they
wanted to colonize the Sinai Peninsula. For the past fifty years, Israel
has continued to pursue the construction of "Greater Israel," taking
over what is valuable in the West Bank step by step, while concentrating
the Palestinian population centers in ever smaller and more isolated
enclaves. Settler towns divide what is to remain under some degree of
Palestinian control—"Bantustans," as they were called by Ariel Sharon,
in a reference to the territory set aside for black South Africans during
the apartheid era. Sharon had declared in 1975 that "settlements should
be going up every day to prove to the Americans that [Israel] has no
mandate from the people to withdraw from Judea and Samaria." The
late Israeli military analyst Reuven Pedatzur noted that "every Israeli
government that has come to power, every branch of the legal establishment, all branches of the Israeli army—all have helped the settlement
enterprise in the territories to flourish."[38]

Israel's refusal to accept a peace settlement is hardly in the interests
of Israel itself, as more perceptive Israelis have long observed. Four former heads of the Shin Bet security service said in 2003 that Israel had
placed itself "on the road to catastrophe" through its rejectionism. "We
are taking sure, steady steps to a place where the state of Israel will no
longer be a democracy and a home for the Jewish people," said Ami
Ayalon, the Shin Bet chief from 1996 to 2000. Renowned Orthodox
scholar and scientist Yeshayahu Leibowitz famously warned that if Israel
did not "liberate itself from this curse of dominating another people" it
would "bring about a catastrophe for the Jewish people as a whole."[39]

The subjugation of Palestinians destroys Israel's claim to be a democratic country faithful to the rule of law. The late Moshe Negbi, a leading Israeli legal analyst, despaired at Israel's descent into a "banana

republic," believing that democracy and legal principle were being undermined by the country's court system, which has tolerated secret prisons where inmates "disappear" and given light sentences to those who torture or murder Palestinian Arabs. Likewise, diplomatic correspondent Akiva Eldar and historian Idit Zartel argue that the "ugly, racist" regime is not only destroying Palestinian human rights but "demolishes the basic norms of Israeli democracy." They review court judgments, including "very light sentences for the brutal murder of Arab children," which they claim are "destroying the entire basis of the judicial system." Benny Morris writes that "the work of the military courts in the territories, and the Supreme Court which backed them, will surely go down as a dark age in the annals of Israel's judicial system."[40]

THE U.S. ROLE

The United States has served as Israel's chief enabler, giving Israel billions of dollars in military aid each year, which the Congressional Research Service says "has helped transform Israel's armed forces into one of the most technologically sophisticated militaries in the world." Fifty-two percent of U.S. foreign military aid since 2001 has gone to Israel. (Egypt is the second-largest recipient.) American military aid for Israel is deliberately given with the intention of allowing Israel to maintain a "qualitative military edge" over its neighbors—that is, to be the strongest power in the region. The amount of aid is staggering—total "military, economic, and missile defense funding" has amounted to "$236 billion in 2018 dollars, making Israel the largest cumulative recipient of U.S. assistance since World War II." It is also illegal, as U.S. law formally prohibits aid to human rights violators; nevertheless, there has been little support for a bill in Congress designed to "ensure that U.S. funding is not used for Israel's ill-treatment of Palestinian children in its military judicial system, forced displacement of Palestinians through home demolitions and evictions, and illegal annexations of Palestinian land."[41]

The United States has also aided Israel by preventing the implementation of an agreement that would end the conflict with Palestinians. Since the issue of Palestinian national rights in a Palestinian state reached the agenda of diplomacy in the mid-1970s, "the prime obstacle to its realization"[42] has undoubtedly been the U.S. The history here is not controversial, even if it is unknown in this country. In 1976, the U.S. vetoed a UN resolution calling for a two-state settlement on the international borders, which was backed by the major Arab states and the Palestinian Liberation Organization (PLO). In the years since, the U.S. has (virtually alone) continued to block the international consensus on a diplomatic resolution, and instead chosen to support Israel's continued expansion into illegally occupied Palestinian territory.

For decades, the UN General Assembly has voted in favor of a resolution affirming "the right [of the Palestinian people] to their independent State of Palestine," and stressing "the urgency of achieving without delay an end to the Israeli occupation that began in 1967" and reaching a peace settlement based on a two-state solution. Only Israel, the United States, and a few other small nations vote against the resolution, which in 2020 passed by 163 to 5. To anyone interested in resolving the question of which party is the obstacle to peace, a look at the text and vote count of the "Peaceful settlement of question of Palestine" resolution provides a definitive answer.[43]

When the Geneva Accord was introduced in December 2002, detailing proposals for a two-state solution, "the United States conspicuously was not among the governments sending a message of support," and Israel rejected the accord. Likewise, all the countries of the Arab League have offered full peace with Israel (the "Arab Peace Initiative") in exchange for Israel's withdrawal to its 1967 borders and a just settlement of the conflict, but Israel has rejected the offer, and the U.S. has declined to pursue it. Ron Pundak, in a balanced review of the diplomatic history, concludes that "the American government seemed sometimes to be working *for* the Israeli Prime Minister, when it tried to convince (and pressure) the Palestinian side to accept Israeli offers." Aaron David

Miller, as U.S. adviser to Arab-Israeli negotiations from 1988 to 2003, said there was "a clear pro-Israel orientation to our peace process planning" and confessed that "not a single senior-level official involved with the negotiations was willing or able to present, let alone fight for, the Arab or Palestinian perspective."[44]

The record of Security Council vetoes concerning Israel is another illustration. George W. Bush vetoed UN resolutions calling for a UN observer force in the territories to reduce violence, condemning all acts of terror and violence and establishment of a monitoring apparatus, expressing concern over Israel's killing of UN employees and destruction of a UN World Food Program warehouse, reaffirming the illegality of deportation, expressing concern over the Separation Barrier cutting through the occupied West Bank, condemning the assassination of the quadriplegic cleric Sheikh Ahmed Yassin (and half a dozen bystanders) in March 2004, and condemning an Israeli military incursion into Gaza that killed many civilians and caused extensive property damage.[45]

Bush's successor Barack Obama was no less devoted to the relationship, calling it "sacrosanct" and "nonnegotiable." In a 2012 speech at AIPAC, Obama accurately bragged that he had been more deferential to Israel than any previous administration, citing his provision of military aid and protection of Israel at the UN against investigations into its human rights abuses. Ben Rhodes, a Deputy National Security Advisor in the Obama administration, wrote in his memoir that Palestinians received "little more than rhetorical support from us," and that while it was clear that "Netanyahu wasn't going to negotiate seriously" about peace, Obama "would always side with Israel when push came to shove."[46]

Indeed, the Obama administration made the remarkable move in 2011 of vetoing a UN Security Council resolution calling to limit settlement expansion, even though the United States officially opposes settlement expansion (thus vetoing a resolution affirming the U.S.'s own stated position). Though Obama was reportedly "shocked" when shown maps revealing Israel's "systematic . . . cutting off [of] Palestinian population centers from one another," he made no effort to condition U.S. assistance to Israel on Israel's compliance with international law and stated American policy. *Financial Times* Middle East specialist David Gardner accurately described Obama as "the most pro-Israel of presidents: the most prodigal with military aid and reliable in wielding the U.S. veto at the Security Council." In fact, Obama's language on Israel was so closely in line with that of Israel's right-wing government that Netanyahu's militantly nationalist and outright racist foreign minister Avigdor Lieberman effusively praised Obama's 2011 UN speech, saying, "I am ready to sign on [to] this speech with both hands."[47]

The Trump administration somehow managed to be even more supportive of Israel's ongoing crimes. As a Peace Now report noted, during the four years of Trump's administration, the "American position on Israeli settlements . . . shattered the international consensus around a two-state solution, [and] promoted annexation in all but name," which led to "high levels of settlement unit approvals, transgressions of informal international red lines in highly sensitive areas like the Jerusalem environs and Hebron, and the building of over 30 new outposts." As political scientist Jerome Slater notes, among other things, Trump closed the PLO's offices in Washington, supported Israel's annexation of the Golan Heights, ended economic assistance to Palestinians, moved the U.S. embassy to Jerusalem and recognized it as Israel's "undivided" capital (thereby "effectively denying the Palestinians the right to establish their capital in East Jerusalem"), stopped calling the West Bank "occupied," and declared that the Israeli settlements were no longer considered illegal.[48]

Under Trump's "peace plan," Israel would have been allowed to annex the Jordan River Valley and all of the West Bank settlements, 30 percent of the territory, while the Palestinians "would receive a 'state' comprising non-contiguous separated enclaves in the rest of the West Bank, as well as some territory in the Negev desert, adjacent to the Gaza Strip, along Israel's southern border." After Palestinians balked at what Trump called the "deal of the century," Trump's son-in-law Jared

Kushner (the "architect of Trump's Middle East peace plan") said that Palestinians "are proving through their reaction that they are not ready to have a state," but "the hope is that over time, they can become capable of governing."[49]

The Trump administration made special efforts to ensure Israel's dispossession of Palestinians became permanent and irreversible. As *Politico* reported, Trump "assured that the dream of a Palestinian state is nearly dead." The Biden administration made no significant changes. Joe Biden has been staunchly supportive of Israel for the duration of his political career. In office, he put "virtually no diplomatic muscle" into a push for a Palestinian state, declining to revive peace talks and accepting most of Trump's policies as the new reality. Both Trump and Biden continued the basic pattern of U.S. policy since 1967: successive administrations have pretended to be "honest brokers" committed to fairly adjudicating the conflict, while consistently backing Israel's rejection of a political settlement in line with the broad international consensus. Israel's wrongdoing is the direct responsibility of the United States, which funds it and prevents international law from being followed. The miseries of apartheid in the West Bank and the horror of air strikes on Gaza are the result of American policies.[50]

GAZA, 2018

In 2018 and 2019, tens of thousands of Palestinians staged a remarkable act of civil protest. Every Friday they gathered at the border between Gaza and Israel to demonstrate in favor of their right to return to the territory from which their families were expelled in 1948, as well as against the blockade of Gaza and the recognition of Jerusalem as the capital of Israel. Just marching in the vicinity of the border fence constitutes civil disobedience, for it has been declared a "no-go zone" by Israel, i.e., part of Gaza that Gazans themselves are forbidden from setting foot in.[51]

Though the protests were overwhelmingly nonviolent, Israeli forces

opened fire on demonstrators with live ammunition. Over the months
of demonstrations, Israeli snipers fatally shot hundreds of Palestinians,
and wounded (in many cases permanently maiming) thousands of others. Those hit included journalists, medics, children, and the disabled.
Human rights organizations overwhelmingly condemned the killings.
A witness described the horror:

> What was notable was the amount of injured people. And the slow,
> methodical shooting. Every few minutes . . . you would hear a shot
> ring out and you would see someone fall. And then another shot
> and another person fell. It went on for hours. . . . There was a con-
> stant stream of bloody bodies being carried back towards the am-
> bulances. It was surreal and endless. It became almost normal, it
> was happening so often. A shot, a person falling, people carrying
> the body away. The number of wounded was astonishing. I couldn't
> say how many people I saw who were shot because it was so high.
> I have covered wars in Syria, Yemen, Libya. I have never seen any-
> thing like this. The slow methodical shooting. It was just shocking.[52]

The UN General Assembly passed a resolution calling the shoot-
ings "excessive, disproportionate and indiscriminate." In 2019, the UN
Human Rights Council released a report on Israel's 2018 conduct in
Gaza. It found that Israel shot a schoolboy "in the face as he distributed
sandwiches," shot a footballer in the legs (ending his football career),
killed a mechanic standing three hundred meters from the border, shot
a student journalist wearing a "PRESS" vest, fatally shot a man running
away from the fence, and shot a man smoking a cigarette standing hundreds of meters from the fence. A university student was shot in the
head and killed as he spoke on the phone. A member of the Palestinian
cycling team, wearing his cycling kit and watching the demonstration,
was shot in the leg, ending his career. The most upsetting crimes in the
report are the murders of disabled people. Israeli snipers shot and
killed a double amputee in a wheelchair (whose legs had been ampu-

tated after a previous Israeli bombing), and two men who walked with crutches.[53]

Israel was, of course, unapologetic. Benjamin Netanyahu simply waved away the new UN report, saying that "the council has set new records of hypocrisy and lies out of an obsessive hatred for Israel" and Israel will continue to "fiercely defend its sovereignty and citizens against Hamas attacks and Iran-backed terror organizations."[54]

In the United States, *The New York Times* ran a front-page story on how Palestinians' deaths made Israelis feel (they "hoped every bullet was justified") while suggesting that Gazans exploited their own suffering for "political" ends (it's a place "where private pain is often paraded for political causes"). A *Times* op-ed from an editor of the *Jewish Journal* was entitled "Israel Needs to Protect Its Borders. By Whatever Means Necessary."[55]

The United States, predictably, blocked a Security Council resolution calling for an inquiry into the killings of the protesters. Israel once again suffered no consequences.[56]

In the U.S., politicians are still expected to show deference to Israel. Even Democratic politicians on the far left of the spectrum frequently feel obligated to insist that under no circumstances would they reconsider U.S. military support for Israel.[57] In 2019, Minnesota congresswoman Ilhan Omar caused a furious political controversy when she criticized the influence of pro-Israel lobbying and claimed members of Congress were expected to show "allegiance" and "pledge support" to Israel. In response, Omar was accused of hating Jews. Bret Stephens of *The New York Times* said Omar "knows exactly what she is doing" and intentionally evoked stereotypes about Jewish conspiracies. Meghan McCain nearly came to tears on *The View* as she described Omar's remarks as "very scary." *National Review*'s Kevin Williamson said Democrats have a "major problem in the form of Jew-hating weirdos."[58]

If Palestinians are ever going to achieve justice and self-determination, unanimous political support for Israel's crimes must change. For over a hundred years, the colonization of Palestine has been based on slowly establishing facts on the ground that the world would ultimately come to accept. The policy has succeeded so far, and will persist so long as the United States continues to provide military, economic, diplomatic, and ideological support.

The Israel-Palestine conflict is often portrayed as complicated. In fact, it is relatively simple.[59] The conflict is centered in territories that have been under harsh military occupation for fifty years. The conqueror is a major military power, acting with massive military, economic, and diplomatic support from the global superpower. Its subjects are alone and defenseless, many barely surviving in miserable camps, who have suffered brutal terror of a kind familiar in colonial wars and have in turn committed terrible atrocities. The United States has long had a choice: will it insist that Israel operate in accordance with basic democratic values and international norms, or will it fund and encourage the immoral, illegal, and self-destructive project of building a permanent apartheid state? Only through domestic public pressure in the U.S. can the pattern of this country's policies be disrupted.

POSTSCRIPT BY NATHAN J. ROBINSON, APRIL 2024

Noam Chomsky has long argued that Israel has fatefully chosen "expansion over security," by which he means that by maintaining an occupation and thwarting the establishment of a Palestinian state, Israel has been endangering itself: "Israel was much more insecure trying to hold a hostile population inside it than it would be under a political settlement which would reduce tensions and leave a demilitarized Palestinian state on its borders." Self-proclaimed defenders of Israel were nothing of the kind, he said, because the oppression of Palestinians fueled rage and resentment, made Israel a pariah state, and created moral degeneration within Israel. He insisted that anyone truly interested in Israel's security would be pressing it to end its occupation and the siege of Gaza.[60]

On October 7, Hamas soldiers broke out of Gaza's "open-air prison" and perpetrated a horrific massacre of both soldiers and civilians in Israel. Approximately twelve hundred people were killed, including young children and the elderly. Hundreds of hostages were taken back to Gaza, leaving agonized family members behind. Israel's promised "mighty vengeance" came swiftly. Gaza is only twenty-five miles long by five miles wide, but Israel dropped tens of thousands of bombs on the strip, obliterating entire neighborhoods. Schools, hospitals, bakeries, ambulances, and refugee camps were attacked. Soon, over half the population was starving and nine out of ten Gazans were not eating every day. Within months, more children had been killed in Gaza than in all the world's conflict zones combined in 2023. By the spring, the Palestinian death toll was over thirty thousand, with most of the population having been forced to flee their homes. *New York Times* columnist Nicholas Kristof said the killings of civilians were so extensive as to be comparable to the Rwandan genocide. When Gazans tried to return to their demolished houses to see what they could salvage during a brief ceasefire, Israeli troops opened fire on the refugees.[61] The scenes were gruesome: children with amputations and horrific burns, dealing simultaneously with severe infections and the trauma of seeing their families die, and dead infants left to decompose in hospital beds after an ICU was forcibly evacuated by Israeli forces.[62]

The statements of top Israeli officials made it clear that preserving civilian lives was not a high priority. "Are you seriously asking me about Palestinian civilians?" former prime minister Naftali Bennett asked a TV news presenter who wondered about the effects of Israel cutting off Gaza's power supply. Some, echoing World War II–era rhetoric that there "are no civilians in Japan," said that the population of Gaza should be considered combatants, because they had voted for Hamas. (First, this was not true, because most Gazans are under eighteen and were not alive when Hamas was elected. Second, this was the very logic that both Hamas and Osama bin Laden had used to justify their own attacks on civilian populations.)[63]

Israeli magazine +972 quoted intelligence sources saying the massive bombing campaign was meant to "create a shock" that would "lead civilians to put pressure on Hamas." As *The Guardian* summarized the findings, Israel was "deliberately targeting residential blocks to cause mass civilian casualties in the hope people would turn on their Hamas rulers." One intelligence source explained that "nothing happens by accident. . . . When a 3-year-old girl is killed in a home in Gaza, it's because someone in the army decided it wasn't a big deal for her to be killed—that it was a price worth paying in order to hit [another] target." A separate +972 report quoted Israeli intelligence sources saying that sometimes "hundreds" of civilians were knowingly killed in order to attack a single Hamas commander, and there were virtually no restraints. "Whatever you can, you bomb," and "the emphasis was to create as many targets as possible, as quickly as possible," with little regard for who was killed, even when entire families were wiped out.[64]

Some Israeli officials invoked Allied atrocities against Dresden and Hiroshima to justify the pummeling of Gaza. Indeed, after two months the destruction in the northern part of Gaza was more extensive than the bombing of Dresden, an infamously brutal attack that had deliberately targeted the civilian population. A *Haaretz* analysis of the deaths found that the percentage of civilian casualties was "significantly higher than the average civilian toll in all the conflicts around the world during the 20th century." More aid workers were killed in Gaza in 2023 than were killed in all the world's combat zones combined in any previous year over the last three decades. Grotesquely, some in Israel (including the official state Twitter account) promoted false claims that Palestinians were faking their injuries in an elaborate charade called "Pallywood." Meanwhile, West Bank settlers took advantage of the moment to attack Palestinians in the Occupied Territories, seizing land and killing hundreds, including many children.[65]

There were plenty of outright calls for ethnic cleansing. Former justice minister Ayelet Shaked said Israel should "take advantage of the destruction that we will wreak upon them" to disperse forcibly the entire population of Gaza into other countries. Benjamin Netanyahu planned to "thin" the population of Gaza to a "minimum." The Intelligence Ministry floated a plan for depopulating the strip and driving refugees into neighboring countries, and Netanyahu lobbied countries to take in hundreds of thousands of Gazans being driven from their homes. "The Gazans must be kicked out of here," said Deputy Speaker of the Knesset Nissim Vaturi. The agriculture minister said the government was "rolling out the Gaza Nakba," referring to the 1948 mass expulsion. The Center for Constitutional Rights documented many instances of rhetoric and actions that suggest the entire Gazan population must be punished for October 7. Israeli major general Ghassan Alian, the head of the Coordinator of Government Activities in the Territories (COGAT), for instance, said, "Human animals must be treated as such. There will be no electricity and no water [in Gaza], there will only be destruction. You wanted hell, you will get hell." Ninety-five-year-old Israeli Army reservist Ezra Yachin, called upon to "boost morale" among the troops, exhorted them: "Don't leave anyone behind. Erase the memory of them. Erase them, their families, mothers and children. These animals can no longer live." Some similar calls came from within the United States, such as the U.S. congressman who called for cutting off all humanitarian aid to Gaza and making it "like Nagasaki and Hiroshima."[66]

Oren Zini, chief of staff of the IDF Northern Brigade in Gaza, calling the strip "a wasp's nest," said he "object[ed] to the entry of all sorts of things to the other side that might help them recover. I believe in suffocating it." "Gaza has to be wiped off the map, in order to send a message to all our enemies and those who seek us harm," said Knesset member Yitzhak Kroizer. Giora Eiland, an adviser to the Israeli defense minister and former head of the National Security Council, gave a shockingly overt justification for the mass murder of civilians in November, saying that killing off the population with disease would help lower the cost of winning for Israel. "Severe epidemics in the south of the Gaza Strip will bring victory closer and reduce casualties among IDF soldiers," he said, arguing that "the way to win the war faster and at a lower cost for us requires a system collapse on the other side and not the mere killing of more Hamas fighters." He wrote that "creating a severe humanitarian crisis in Gaza is a necessary means to achieve the goal," promising that "Gaza will become a place where no human being can exist." The general soon got his wish, as severe disease began to spread among Gazan refugees crowded into tents, with eight hundred people sharing a single toilet.[67]

The terrorization of civilians was justified in the name of eliminating Hamas and preventing a repeat of October 7, and opponents of a ceasefire argued that Israel could not have its hands tied in its effort to ensure its own security. But the justification did not make sense. As centrist Democratic congressman Seth Moulton argued, "Israel so far killed about 5,000 Hamas terrorists but in the process they've recruited about 100,000 new adherents." The reality was that Israel's strikes were less about security and far more about a desire to avenge and punish. Israel created "kill zones" in which anyone who crossed an invisible line would be shot, then deemed to have been a "terrorist." As David Klion of *Jewish Currents* writes, "The key driver of this war that no one ever outright names is the Israeli public's desire for vengeance." Indeed, internal Israeli intelligence sources told +972 that "vengeance" and "hysteria," not sound military strategy, appeared to be guiding the target selection procedures in Gaza.[68]

As usual, the U.S. government fully supported Israel. Joe Biden's administration said there were no "red lines" for Israel. In other words, Israel could do anything, even violate the laws of war, and still receive firm U.S. support. The United States was one of the only countries in the world not to call for a ceasefire at the United Nations. The Biden administration even helped Israel by casting doubt on Palestinian death statistics (entirely groundlessly). And despite the Biden administration's insistence that it was trying to press Israel for humanitarian concessions, it refused to consider curtailing weapons aid, and in fact soon requested billions of dollars in additional arms transfers to Israel (while keeping the specifics of what it was transferring a closely guarded secret). The Biden administration continued to supply Israel with two-thousand-pound bombs, even as it publicly insisted it wanted Israel to use smaller munitions. The administration's inflexible commitment to complete support of Israel, even as the casualties mounted in Gaza, led many members of Biden's own State Department to revolt and sign a letter of protest, and several to resign.[69]

As the body count in Gaza mounted into the tens of thousands, the testimonies coming from Gazans were heartbreaking and disturbing. Ahmed Moghrabi, a doctor in one of Gaza's last remaining functional hospitals, pleaded with the world to stop the violence. "No words can describe what is going [on] here," he said. It was "massacres all over," and "horror, horror, horror," with entire families being wiped out, children being burned to the bone, and starvation to the point where he could barely keep his own two-year-old daughter alive. "Please stop the genocide against us," he implored. "I beg you." A doctor who visited Gaza said that what he saw there "was not war—it was annihilation." A UNICEF spokesperson said there was "nothing left" of cities, and "the depth of horror surpasses our ability to describe it."[70]

In the face of this, the Biden administration continued to send weapons to Israel and repeatedly blocked UN Security Council resolutions calling for a ceasefire, which had 13 votes in favor and 1 against. (Eventually, after immense public protest, the Biden administration abstained from a ceasefire resolution, allowing it to pass, but then insisted it was "nonbinding" and made no effort to enforce it.) The UN General Assembly also passed a ceasefire resolution that had 153 votes in favor and only 10 against (the motion was therefore opposed by only 5 percent of the world's population, with the U.S. comprising 4 percent of that). The Biden administration staunchly supported Israel in genocide proceedings against it at the International Court of Justice, dismissing accusations that Israel was engaged in genocide and defending its occupation of Palestine. Yet again the U.S. stood alone in its defiance of global public opinion. *Politico* reported that one reason the Biden administration didn't want to stop the fighting is that "there was some concern in the administration about an unintended consequence of the pause: that it would allow journalists broader access to Gaza and the opportunity to further illuminate the devastation there and turn public opinion on Israel." Once again, if the people of the U.S. knew what was being done by their "democratic" government, they wouldn't like it, therefore they must not be told.[71]

In April 2024, seven World Central Kitchen aid workers were killed by an Israeli strike, after delivering food to Gazans. There was a great deal of evidence that the strike was intentional. The workers were in clearly marked vehicles and had coordinated their movements with the IDF. The killing of the aid workers resulted in the suspension of hunger relief operations in Gaza by the WCK and other aid organizations.

The day of the strike, the Biden administration approved yet another arms transfer to Israel. After it happened, the Biden administration yet again refused to attach conditions to weapons aid. Former State Department official and Israel-Palestine negotiator Aaron David Miller stated bluntly that Biden's policies are grounded in an imbalance of empathy, with Palestinian lives counting for less to the U.S. president. This has long been obvious to Palestinians, who rightly condemn the hypocrisy of a country that enables Palestinian suffering while publicly professing its desire for peace and justice.[72]

The Great China Threat

"China is our enemy," Donald Trump declared repeatedly. "These are not people that understand niceness." Accordingly, between 2017 and 2021 the Trump administration "took a sledgehammer" to U.S.-China relations, which "reached their lowest point in decades." Trump officials spoke of China using the most extreme McCarthyite language. Secretary of State Mike Pompeo said the "threat from the CCP" was "inside the gates" and could be found in "Des Moines and Phoenix and Tallahassee. . . . [The CCP] will stop at nothing to undermine the very way of life we have here in America and in the West." Donald Trump's former chief strategist Steve Bannon wrote, "China has emerged as the greatest economic and national security threat the United States has ever faced." FBI Director Christopher Wray warned in July 2020 that "the Chinese threat" endangered "our health, our livelihoods, and our security."[1]

How is China endangering the "way of life we have here"? Wray explained that "the scope of the Chinese government's ambition" is nothing less than "to surpass our country in economic and technological leadership." William Barr claimed China was engaged in an "economic blitzkrieg," which would see it ascend to the "commanding heights of the global economy and to surpass the United States as the world's preeminent technological superpower." This is the true nature of the "China threat": that the United States will no longer rule the world. A basic premise of our foreign policy is that we are fully entitled to do so indefinitely.[2]

This becomes explicit in the Trump administration's strategy documents. The 2017 National Security Strategy (NSS) warns that "China seeks to displace the United States in the Indo-Pacific region, expand the reaches of its state-driven economic model, and reorder the region in its favor." How could the United States—which is not located in the Indo-Pacific region—be "displaced" there? But the NSS does not touch on the question of why the United States, rather than the much more populous country of China, is entitled to dominance in Asia. China and Russia, says the NSS, are "contesting our geopolitical advantages," and we are locked into a "Great Power competition." This also means we must "restore the readiness of our forces for major war" by drastically increasing the capacity of our military to annihilate large numbers of human beings quickly. The NSS recommends we "overmatch" the "lethality" of all the world's other armed forces in order to "ensure that America's sons and daughters will never be in a fair fight."[3]

The Trump administration's "Strategic Framework for the Indo-Pacific" explains that one of the U.S.'s top interests in the Indo-Pacific is to "maintain U.S. primacy" and sustain "diplomatic, economic, and military preeminence in the fastest-growing region of the world," so that China does not develop a new "sphere of influence." In other words, we have to make sure that the largest Asian country does not have more power and influence in Asia than the much smaller United States.[4]

As China grows, efforts to maintain "primacy" over its own region will require increasingly aggressive confrontation, something both major parties in the United States seem committed to. Even as he campaigned, Joe Biden was engaged in "attempts to out-hawk Mr. Trump" on China, to the point of releasing anti-China campaign material that was criticized by some as racist. Biden called Xi Jinping a "thug" and wrote in *Foreign Affairs* that "the United States does need to get tough on China."[5]

Once in office Biden essentially maintained much of Trump's foreign policy, including on China. In some cases Biden was even more harsh. A *Politico* report warned that "Biden's actions to crack down on Beijing's tech development will do more to hinder the Chinese economy—and divide the two nations—than Trump ever did" and constitute "the most aggressive American action yet to curtail Beijing's economic and military rise." An *Atlantic* commentary said that voters who want to punish China in 2024 should choose Biden, not Trump, because "Biden has hit China harder than Trump ever did" and "inflicted acute damage on the country's economy and geopolitical ambitions." The entitlement to wreck the economies of other countries is, as usual, assumed.[6]

"Behind the scenes, there is very little difference in approach by these two presidents toward China," says diplomatic correspondent Michael Hirsh. *Politico* quotes Clete Willems, an architect of Trump's China policy, saying that "[the Biden] administration views Chinese indigenous innovation as a per se national security threat . . . and that is a big leap from where we've ever been before." Secretary of State Antony Blinken has said that "the most serious long-term challenge to the international order" is "the one posed by the People's Republic of China." The 2022 National Defense Strategy, like Trump's, pledges to combat "the growing multi-domain threat posed by the PRC" and pledges to "prioritiz[e] the PRC challenge in the Indo-Pacific." To that end, the Biden administration continued "surging troops and military hardware into the region and encouraging its allies to enlarge their arsenals," according to Stephen E. Biegun, who served as deputy secretary of state in the Trump administration. In fact, the present course was initiated by Barack Obama's "pivot to Asia," which promised, among other things, to "[prioritize] Asia for our most advanced military capabilities." Obama declared "the United States is a Pacific power, and we are here to stay."[7]

The New York Times tells us that both "the Trump and Biden administrations have had to grapple with the question of how to maintain America's global dominance at a time when it appears in decline." The United States is thus quite open, under presidents of both parties, about seeking to limit China's role in global affairs and impede its development. A desire to "maintain global dominance" is treated as a perfectly legitimate and benign aspiration.

It has long been the presumption of U.S. planners that we are entitled to have our way in Asia. After the Chinese communist revolution in 1949, American politicians began debating the "loss of China," with accusations flying back and forth as to who "lost" it.[8] The terminology contains a tacit assumption that the United States owned China. The idea of China being out of our control was horrifying. Today, the U.S. is attempting to prove to China that it has no hopes of becoming a regional hegemon in its own backyard, using a "military-first" approach. The U.S., UK, and Australia have announced they will "will co-operate on the development of hypersonic weapons, expanding a trilateral security pact designed to help Washington and its allies counter China's rapid military expansion." And as Michael Klare observes, the 2022 National Defense Authorization Act "provides a detailed blueprint for surrounding China with a potentially suffocating network of U.S. bases, military forces, and increasingly militarized partner states . . . to enable Washington to barricade that country's military inside its own territory and potentially cripple its economy in any future crisis." The Department of Defense tells us that "Beijing views the United States as increasingly determined to contain the PRC." Because our Indo-Pacific policy is built explicitly around containing the PRC, it should not be surprising that Beijing feels that way.[9]

Those who characterize China as a threat can immediately produce a substantial list of its misdeeds to justify the charge. There are, of course, serious human rights abuses in China, including its suppression of dis-

sent and the repression of the Uyghur population. It has unquestion-
ably violated international law in the South China Sea. Trump's national
intelligence director John Ratcliffe said China "robs U.S. companies of
their intellectual property, replicates the technology and then replaces
the U.S. firms in the global marketplace." A July 2022 NID report warns
of sinister Chinese influence efforts "to expand support for PRC interests among state and local leaders [in the United States] and to use these
relationships to pressure Washington for policies friendlier to Beijing."
The Trump administration, at the urging of Senator Chuck Schumer,
formally labeled China a "currency manipulator." William Barr said
China practices "modern-day colonialism" by "loading poor countries
up with debt, refusing to renegotiate terms, and then taking control of
the infrastructure itself."[10]

The problem with the list of charges, however, is that they either
plainly pose no threat to the United States or are actions we ourselves
claim the right to engage in.

For instance, China's hideous mistreatment of the Uyghurs is
deeply morally objectionable. But it is difficult to see how the Uyghur
repression makes China a threat to others. And as we have seen, the
invocation of human rights arguments is entirely based on the arguments' usefulness to U.S. power. Saudi crimes are not used as the basis
for establishing a "Saudi threat," but China's crimes are used to prove
it is a unique menace.

Some charges against China are exaggerated, like the idea of its
neocolonial "debt trap" that supposedly exploits countries through
predatory lending practices.[11] (Some international debt traps are quite
real, however.[12]) Others might as well be lists of events in American history. As the Associated Press notes, to charge China with intellectual
property theft is to condemn "the very sort of illicit practices that
helped America leapfrog European rivals two centuries ago and emerge
as an industrial giant." Alexander Hamilton, whose life is celebrated in
a popular patriotic musical, advocated "a federal program to engage in
industrial theft from other countries on a grand scale." Peter Andreas,

author of *Smuggler Nation: How Illicit Trade Made America,* notes that "only after becoming the leading industrial power did [the U.S.] become a champion of intellectual-property protections." Similarly, our condemnations of economic warfare and influence campaigns ring hollow, given that the United States exercises its economic power through possessing the global reserve currency, and the CIA is quite open about conducting influence operations abroad.[13]

Kyle Haynes of *The Diplomat* asks us to imagine a situation in which "an emerging great power is rapidly expanding its military capabilities" and "unilaterally abrogates decades-old norms and agreements by militarizing a strategically vital waterway," while "seeking to coercively expel the reigning global hegemon from the region." This could be a description of China today. But it's an equally accurate description of the period in which the United States came to rule the Western Hemisphere. China is simply rejecting the principle that we are allowed to "kick away the ladder." The term is used to describe the pattern whereby countries climb the ladder of development through whatever unscrupulous means they please—including violence, deceit, and the theft of higher technology—and then impose a "rules-based order" to prohibit others from doing the same.[14]

The actual China "threat" is very well described by Paul Keating, former prime minister of Australia. "By its mere presence," China is "an affront to the United States." China has never actually threatened the U.S., Keating notes, but it "represents a challenge to United States preeminence." The "threat" posed by China, then, is that China exists.[15]

If China is a threat to us, then what are we to China? When China established its first overseas military base—in Djibouti—it was treated as part of a plan to "shift global power dynamics, eroding U.S. dominance, and relegating Europe to the sidelines of international affairs." What, then, should China make of our own seven hundred fifty overseas bases across eighty nations? When China reached a security agreement with the tiny Solomon Islands, raising the possibility of its opening a second overseas base, the United States immediately began to "turn the screws" on the Solomon Islands, in what Chinese officials (accurately) called an "attempt to revive the Monroe Doctrine in the South Pacific."[16]

China scholar Lyle Goldstein, having reviewed a series of official PRC articles called China's Atlantic Strategy, reports that "one of the things they said very clearly was, 'The Atlantic is absolutely critical to the United States, and the United States is coming to our backyard and poking around in the South China Sea, so we have to go to their backyard.'" Is turnabout fair play, or do the rules apply only to our competitors? For instance, China has indeed violated the UN Convention on the Law of the Sea. But the United States hasn't even signed the convention. China's actions toward Taiwan are menacing. But the United States has claimed the right to depose governments around the world.[17]

Such points as these are often labeled "whataboutism"—distracting attention from one set of crimes by pointing to another. (In this case, examining our own crimes and not just those of our official enemies.) In fact, they are evidence that we do not seriously care about the ideals we profess. China, of course, sees this plainly. "The attacks on China mirror exactly what the United States has been doing," said Zhao Lijian, a spokesman for the country's foreign ministry.[18] Zhao argued that the U.S. "has no respect for the international order underpinned by the UN Charter and international law," and is a "saboteur of the international order" because it "wantonly withdraws from treaties and organizations," placing "its domestic law above international law and international rules." Zhao pointed out the long history of illegal violence perpetrated by the U.S., commenting that "in the eyes of the United States, international rules must be subordinate to and serve its interests." The attitude, he said, is: "When international rules happen to be consistent with U.S. interests, they are cited as authority. Otherwise they are simply ignored."

It is difficult to see how anyone could argue with the Chinese position. One reason China is disinclined to listen to the United States' pious pronouncements on military aggression, human rights, and international law, then, is that so much U.S. history is a history of military aggression, human rights abuse, and brazen violations of international law.

But what about Taiwan? Surely here is an instance in which China is posing a serious threat—not to us directly, but to the principle of self-determination. In recent years, China's rhetoric about reunifying Taiwan with China has become increasingly bellicose, and there are ominous signs that as China's military capacity grows, so does the risk that it will go to war to subsume Taiwan. Lyle Goldstein notes the increasing prevalence of rhetoric out of China that "the PLA [People's Liberation Army] has the will and capability to ensure national unification." A PLA video quotes a Chinese navy captain saying: "We have the determination and ability to mount a painful direct attack against any invaders who would wreck unification of the motherland, and would show no mercy."[19]

The situation is serious. But the history matters. Taiwan's background is complex, but it was part of China before being ceded to Japan in 1895. Before and during World War II, Japan used Taiwan as a military base, its "unsinkable aircraft carrier." In 1945, Japan surrendered Taiwan to the Republic of China (ROC), although there was controversy over its sovereignty for some years afterward. When the People's Republic of China (PRC) defeated the ROC in the Chinese Civil War in 1949, Chiang Kai-shek's ROC forces retreated to Taiwan and set up a government in exile. For the next decades, both the PRC and the ROC claimed to be the legitimate government of *all* China, both the mainland and Taiwan, and during the 1960s and '70s, Chiang's government in Taiwan was still planning to reinvade the mainland. The United States long endorsed the position that Taiwan was part of China, and only ceased to recognize Taiwan as the legitimate government of all China when it became clear that the PRC was not going away. Taiwan does not yet define itself as an independent country and still technically considers mainland China to be part of its own territory. In recent decades, Taiwan itself has seen a diminution in residents who identify as Chinese rather than Taiwanese, and an increased sense of the island as its own nation rather than the Republic of China. (In fact, Taiwanese officials used to *dislike* the country being referred to as Taiwan, precisely because it implied it was a separate nation rather than the legitimate Chinese state.)[20]

It is easy to portray the conflict over Taiwan today simply as the story of a large aggressor wanting to dominate a small neighbor. But the history makes the story more complicated. In the aftermath of a civil war, if the defeated party retreats to a small part of the country, it is predictable that a complicated sovereignty dispute will arise. Over time, Taiwan has clearly gone from being a disputed part of China to a nation of its own that deserves self-determination. But when we look at the situation from the PRC's perspective, we can see why certain U.S. actions in support of Taiwan may actually be counterproductive. First, Taiwan has been used by both Japan and the ROC to wage or plot war against the mainland. The more the PRC associates the cause of Tai-wanese independence with the U.S. strategy to encircle China with hos-tile countries to maintain U.S. power in the region, the PRC may become determined to crush any prospect of Taiwanese independence. To give another analogy: If Puerto Rico sought independence, we can ponder whether a favorable U.S. response to the cause of independence would be made more or less likely if China declared its intention to de-fend Puerto Rico militarily and used Puerto Rico to combat U.S. hege-mony in the Caribbean.

To ensure the self-determination of Taiwan, we should avoid taking steps that make it more likely that Beijing would decide to try to pursue unification through force. We should do our best to preserve the peace-ful status quo, because if China did decide to seize Taiwan, it is not clear the United States could successfully defend the island, and any U.S.-China war would be a humanitarian and economic catastrophe of un-precedented magnitude, especially for the people of Taiwan. As the old proverb goes, "When elephants fight, it is the grass that suffers," and if Taiwan is used as a piece in a power tussle between the United States and China, the Taiwanese will inevitably end up the worst off of the three.[21]

In fact, there is good reason to believe a war over Taiwan can be avoided. The Taiwanese themselves, when polled, are far more likely to say that they do not think the situation will end in war, and "some Taiwan politicians think that the U.S.'s increasingly bitter competition with China is adding to the risk." The *Financial Times* quoted Taiwanese experts saying, "Washington needed to better explain its growing alarm over the perceived risk of a Chinese attack." The Taiwanese and Chinese governments have actually met on cordial terms in fairly recent memory, and in previous years, millions of Chinese tourists have visited Taiwan. There is even a conceivable peaceful path to eventual independence by which the status quo is maintained until permanent Taiwanese autonomy is essentially an established fact. (Note, though, that outright independence is controversial even in Taiwan, and the shape of the ideal long-term outcome is unclear; but whatever it is, it should certainly not be determined by U.S. aspirations for Taiwan.)[22]

Following the path to a lasting peaceful and just settlement will require the United States to refrain from actions that make China feel it needs to assert its might or that make it see a failure to pursue reunification through force as a humiliating capitulation to the U.S. We must avoid creating the impression that we consider China an enemy and Taiwan a crucial ally against that enemy. We should certainly avoid entering into an arms race with China that turns the region into a powder keg.

Unfortunately, U.S. support for Taiwanese self-determination may have little to do with a principled belief in democracy and everything to do with preserving our power in Asia. Instead, Chris Horton of *The Atlantic* explains why the United States is so invested in the cause of Taiwan: "It is difficult to overstate Taiwan's strategic importance to both the United States and an increasingly assertive China." If the island becomes part of China, "China would instantly become a Pacific power, control some of the world's most cutting-edge technologies, and have the ability to choke off oil shipments to Japan and South Korea— leverage it could use to demand the closure of U.S. military bases in both countries."[23]

The U.S. government could forgo opportunities that help to reduce tensions if they are seen as aiding China. For instance, Lyle Goldstein says that there are opportunities for diplomacy, but they involve fostering warmer relations between China and Taiwan. But instead of trying to facilitate amicable cross-strait relations, we encourage Taiwan to become a missile-covered "porcupine" that can resist a Chinese invasion. U.S. officials have deliberately taken steps they know will anger China—such as Biden promising he would go to war with China over the island, and Nancy Pelosi's self-aggrandizing visit. In doing so, we may flatter ourselves that we are supporting Taiwanese self-determination, but we are actually increasing the likelihood of war. For fifty years, the U.S. has accepted the "One China" policy, acknowledging that "all Chinese on either side of the Taiwan Strait maintain there is but one China and that Taiwan is a part of China," with neither side making moves to undermine it. It could continue, in the absence of reckless and provocative moves by the U.S.[24]

In fact, China's sensible long-term strategy regarding Taiwan is not to invade, which would severely harm its own prospects, and perhaps spark a suicidal war. (It also hasn't shown signs of actually planning to invade.) Yet alarmingly, there are those in the United States who think war with China over Taiwan is all but inevitable. "To us, it's only a matter of time, not a matter of if," said the director of intelligence of the U.S. Indo-Pacific Command. Rather than war being unthinkable, a diplomatic solution is unthinkable.[25]

American tension with China is sometimes characterized as displaying the classic "security dilemma" of international relations, "whereby military programs and national strategies deemed defensive by their planners are viewed as threatening by the other side," in the words of Paul Godwin of the Foreign Policy Research Institute. Stephen M. Walt warns that "remarkably, plenty of smart, well-educated Westerners—including some prominent former diplomats—cannot seem to grasp that their benevolent intentions are not transparently obvious to others." In other words, China cannot see that we are only trying to deter its own aggression by building a regional military alliance, flooding the surrounding territory with high-precision weaponry aimed at China, labeling China an "enemy," sending increasing numbers of warships to patrol its coast (ostensibly to enforce the Law of the Sea Convention, which we have not signed), sending Australia a fleet of nuclear submarines to counter China, and conducting military exercises near China's shores. China is not expected to act the way we would act if Chinese warships were steadily gathering in the Gulf of Mexico and conducting military exercises. Chinese military drills are interpreted by us as hostile, but the United States organizing the largest maritime warfare exercise in the world as a warning to China should not be interpreted by China as hostile. They are supposed to accept that we only ever engage in "defense," while it is other countries that engage in "aggression."[26]

But U.S. actions are not, in fact, best characterized as "defensive" at all. Perhaps China is not tragically misinterpreting our policy, but has simply read our publicly available strategy documents. They see that U.S. planners wish to maintain control of the Indo-Pacific and deny China the right to do in the Eastern Hemisphere what we have done in the Western Hemisphere. They might open *The Wall Street Journal* and read the "Henry Kissinger Distinguished Professor of Global Affairs" arguing that to protect the "world America built," we must undertake a new "urgent, enduring effort to contain an advancing rival," even if this means new "Cold War–style tensions and crises" (i.e., the constant threat of human civilization coming to an abrupt and violent end). The Chinese government may also read in our new National Defense Authorization Act that the secretary of defense is tasked with "strengthen[ing] United States defense alliances and partnerships in the Indo-Pacific region so as to further the comparative advantage of the United States in strategic competition with the People's Republic of China." They might hear our talk of the "rules-based order" and then remember that Barack Obama, speaking of the Trans-Pacific Partnership, said, "The

THE GREAT CHINA THREAT 179

rule book is up for grabs. And if we don't pass this agreement—if America doesn't write those rules—then countries like China will." In 2012, they saw leading "moderate" Republican Mitt Romney pledging to "ensure that this is an American, not a Chinese century" and arguing that "security in the Pacific means a world in which our economic and military power is second to none."[27]

China surely notices that in "stark contrast to what Biden said he would do as president," as *Politico*'s Michael Hirsh writes, Biden is escalating nuclear threats against China, adopting a "Trumpian" policy, and "in some ways taking an even more aggressive stance than his predecessor did." These aggressive stances are, according to an analysis in *Foreign Affairs,* causing China to build up its own nuclear forces in response, because China fears "that the United States has lowered its threshold for nuclear use."[28]

The United States may be incapable of seeing its own actions as anything other than idealistic and benevolent, but our own government has clearly stated our intention to prevent a "fair fight" and maintain the ability to annihilate anyone who challenges our power. As political scientist John Mearsheimer explained in 2005, the increasing tension as China grows more powerful comes about because "the U.S. does not tolerate peer competitors" and "is determined to remain the world's only regional hegemon." The United States intends to rule the world, even if that requires escalating the threat of a war that will be possibly terminal to human civilization.[29]

The starting point for reducing tensions with China, then, is to look in the mirror and ask whether each demand we make of it is fair, and whether we are willing to do unto others as we ask them to do unto us. We might consider whether a good relationship is ever likely if we continue trying to ring China with hostile sentinel states in an attempt to contain its power. We might also consider whether China has certain legitimate grievances against the demands made by the United States. On climate change, for instance, we are depending on China not to behave as destructively as we have. The average American is a far worse carbon polluter than the average Chinese person, and the U.S. and Europe are responsible for the bulk of historical emissions, meaning that China must be far less irresponsible as it develops, to avoid accelerating the catastrophe. When we ask China not to expand the reach of its military across the globe, or not to contemplate the overthrow of governments it feels threaten its interests, or to treat U.S. intellectual property claims as universal, we are asking for it to show more restraint than we have. These requests may be sound—if all countries acted like the U.S., the world would quickly be destroyed—but they should be made with humility.

The situation we face now is dangerous. An arms race is under way. For many years, China kept a relatively low level of nuclear weapons, and proudly so. Now it is accelerating production of weapons that can only be either (1) a massive waste of resources (if unused) or (2) a genocidal horror (if used). Even Henry Kissinger—hardly a man of peace—warned that the United States and China are stumbling toward a World War I–like calamity. Of course, in the age of thermonuclear weapons, the potential for destruction is far, far greater than it was in 1914.[30]

It does not have to be this way.

The idea that China poses a military threat to the United States *itself* is so absurd that Lyle Goldstein says it is "almost a joke in Washington." China does, however, pose a threat to the United States' ability to maintain its desired level of economic dominance in Asia. If we are unwilling to share the Earth, conflict is assured.

There are undoubtedly deep areas of contention between the United States and China that will take long, laborious negotiations to resolve. Perhaps there will be compromises that please nobody. But war is simply not a thinkable option in the twenty-first century. Martin Luther King, Jr. was correct when he said the choice is: "We must learn to live together as brothers or perish together as fools." A Third World War must not happen under any circumstances. What is needed is diplomacy and negotiations on contested matters, and real cooperation on such crucial issues as global warming, arms control, and future pandemics—all severe crises that know no borders.

China, for its part, has implored the United States not to adopt a "Cold War mentality," arguing that it is "irresponsible" to hype up the threat and saying we must "cast away imagined demons." China has accused the U.S. of trying to "reignite a sense of national purpose by establishing China as an imaginary enemy." Indeed, it wouldn't be the first time that the Chinese have been blamed for America's domestic problems. The editors of *Yellow Peril!: An Archive of Anti-Asian Fear* helpfully review the history of U.S. politicians whipping up fear of Asiatic enemies to prove that the "horrid, pestilent other is causing all our problems." The "they" threatening our way of life is ever-changing, but in every case resolvable conflicts of interest become "epic civilizational contests between imagined diametrically opposed foes."[31]

We should be cooperating with China. Our fates are intertwined. There is no choice but to get along. Yet relations have been falling apart. After Pelosi's visit to Taiwan, China launched new military exercises that could lead to deadly errors and escalation and broke off talks with the U.S. about climate change, among other matters.[32]

There is little hope for the planet if the two leading powers cannot even discuss how to solve our most urgent problems. This is the road to disaster. The United States needs to stop needlessly stoking conflict, think about how things look from the Chinese perspective, and work sincerely to understand and collaborate with a country of 1.4 billion people we have to share a planet with.

NATO and Russia
After the Cold War

In the 1990s, after the dissolution of the Soviet Union, the purpose of the North Atlantic Treaty Organization (NATO) became unclear. Having been created in 1949 at the outset of the Cold War, the organization's continued presence after the end of the Cold War was difficult to justify. NATO had existed, after all, to protect the West against the Soviet hordes menacing Western civilization. Without any looming Soviet hordes, what was NATO for? Clinton-era State Department official Strobe Talbott notes that at the time "many commentators and some political leaders were asking whether NATO, having served its original purpose, should go into honorable retirement."[1]

Instead, NATO's mission changed. It became a U.S.-run intervention force with a worldwide mandate to secure the West's strategic interests. Part of its mission was to maintain control of the international energy system. NATO secretary-general Jaap de Hoop Scheffer instructed a NATO meeting in June 2007 that "NATO troops have to guard pipelines that transport oil and gas that is directed for the West," and more generally have to protect sea routes used by tankers and other "crucial infrastructure" of the energy system. NATO therefore laid claim to a worldwide jurisdiction.[2]

At one time, there was a somewhat vigorous debate in the United States over whether NATO's role in the post–Cold War world was constructive, or whether expanding the organization would be perceived as a hostile attempt to exert power and keep Russia in check. George Kennan, the architect of containment, warned that expanding NATO was a "tragic mistake" that would spark "a new cold war." At a time when "no one was threatening anyone else," continuing to add countries to NATO would needlessly make Russia feel menaced, and it would "react quite adversely." Kennan predicted that when that Russian reaction came, those who supported NATO expansion would point to the response as proof of a Russian threat, even if it was a predictable consequence of NATO expansion itself. (Indeed, political scientist Richard Sakwa argued that in our time "NATO exists to manage the risks created by its existence.")[3]

Kennan was far from the only one issuing the warning. In 1994, Charles Kupchan, who had served on Clinton's National Security Council, similarly argued that "an expanded NATO would lead Russia to reassert control over its former republics and to remilitarize." Kupchan was unequivocal: expanding NATO would mean the "chance to build a European security community that included Russia would be lost." In 1995, political scientist Michael Mandelbaum, writing in *Foreign Affairs*, said that the pivotal question in determining whether NATO expansion was positive was "its effect on the peaceful coexistence of Ukraine and Russia." Reviewing the record, Ted Galen Carpenter of the Cato Institute wrote that "analysts committed to a U.S. foreign policy of realism and restraint have warned for more than a quarter-century that continuing to expand the most powerful military alliance in history closer and closer to another major power would not end well."[4]

As predicted, the relationship between NATO and Russia has grown more contentious as NATO has continued to expand, despite periods of cooperation. By 2022, NATO was fighting what even some U.S. officials called a "proxy war" with Russia in Ukraine. Mainstream commentators have even argued that the United States faces the serious prospect of a "third world war" with Russia. Today, NATO weapons are pouring into Ukraine, raising the possibility of escalation into nuclear war between great powers.[5]

NATO's new role was demonstrated in 1999, with its bombing campaign in Yugoslavia during the Kosovo war. The attacks have been widely presented as a successful example of "humanitarian intervention," in which the United States acted on a "moral imperative" to stop an atrocity.[6]

The Kosovo bombing is worth examining more closely, however, because it was both a serious breach of international law and a major contributor to the deterioration of relations between Russia and the United States. It is also consistently misunderstood and misrepresented as a great humanitarian triumph, one of the clearest demonstrations of the American willingness to use violence for altruistic purposes. The editors of *The New York Times* concluded that "the West can be proud of its role in ending terror and mass expulsions from Kosovo," while former NATO secretary-general Javier Solana described the success as unqualified: "With no casualties of its own, NATO had prevailed. A humanitarian disaster had been averted. About one million refugees could now return to safety. Ethnic cleansing had been reversed." Samantha Power claims that "the United States and its allies likely saved hundreds of thousands of lives."[7]

The truth is somewhat different. In a *Foreign Affairs* review of NATO's actions, Michael Mandelbaum describes the intervention as a "perfect failure" insofar as the goal was a humanitarian one. "Western political leaders declared they were fighting for the sake of the people of the Balkans," but the population "emerged from the war considerably worse off than they had been before," Mandelbaum comments. NATO's bombing campaign was ostensibly intended to stop Serbian abuses of Kosovar Albanians. But the veracity of many reported abuses from *before* the bombings was later called into question, and the worst crimes were conducted *in reaction* to the bombings. The intervention made the situation far worse than it had been, with NATO triggering Serbian reprisals against the Albanians the operation was supposed to protect.[8]

As summarized by Christopher Layne and Benjamin Schwarz in *The Washington Post*, "The U.S.-led NATO bombing precipitated the very humanitarian crisis the administration claimed it was intervening to stop." Power herself conceded that "from the moment NATO began bombing, Serbian regular military units teamed up with police and militia to do something unprecedented and unexpected: They expelled virtually the entire Albanian population at gunpoint." Power says that the U.S. "miscalculated" what the Serbian reaction would be, and "allied planners failed to predict that Milošević would respond to bombing by retaliating so violently and audaciously against the Albanian population in Kosovo."[9]

But Wesley Clark, who commanded the NATO operation, said that Serbian retaliatory atrocities were "entirely predictable" and "fully anticipated." He had told the White House before the operation that if NATO attacked, "almost certainly [Serbia] will attack the civilian population." In early March, Italian prime minister Massimo D'Alema had warned Bill Clinton of the huge refugee flow that would follow the bombing; Clinton's national security adviser Sandy Berger responded that in that case "NATO will keep bombing," with still more horrific results. U.S. intelligence also warned that there would be "a virtual explosion of refugees" and a campaign of ethnic cleansing, reiterating earlier predictions of European monitors. The bombings themselves were also often indiscriminate, and resulted in approximately five hundred civilian deaths. NATO bombed houses, a refugee column, a refugee camp, a passenger train, a bus, and the Chinese embassy. The latter incident killed three Chinese nationals, sparked massive protests in China, and seriously damaged U.S.-Chinese relations. As with our destruction of the Iranian airliner and the saturation bombing of North

Korea, Americans retain little awareness of incidents that fuel other countries' resentment of us.[10]

The bombing campaign fulfilled the crazed fantasies of *New York Times* columnist Thomas Friedman, who openly encouraged war crimes in the pages of the paper of record:

> Let's at least have a real air war. The idea that people are still hold-
> ing rock concerts in Belgrade, or going out for Sunday merry-go-
> round rides, while their fellow Serbs are "cleansing" Kosovo, is
> outrageous. It should be lights out in Belgrade: every power grid,
> water pipe, bridge, road and war-related factory has to be tar-
> geted. Like it or not, we are at war with the Serbian nation (the
> Serbs certainly think so), and the stakes have to be very clear:
> Every week you ravage Kosovo is another decade we will set your
> country back by pulverizing you. You want 1950? We can do 1950.
> You want 1389? We can do 1389 too.[11]

In multiple instances, according to Amnesty International, "NATO forces failed to suspend their attack after it was evident that they had struck civilians." Human Rights Watch documented ninety separate incidents involving civilian deaths over the course of the seventy-eight-day bombing campaign, including multiple incidents where bombings targeted illegitimate civilian infrastructure like bridges and a heating plant. NATO committed one major war crime by deliberately targeting a television station, killing journalists and a makeup artist. Tony Blair justified targeting the television station, saying that it was part of the "apparatus of dictatorship," and NATO's military spokesman said the station had "filled the airwaves with hate and with lies."[12]

Human Rights Watch documented NATO's uses of cluster bombs in populated civilian areas, and was particularly critical of NATO for lying about its actions, with its public deceptions "suggest[ing] a resis-tance to acknowledging the actual civilian effects and an indifference to evaluating their causes." In 2009, Amnesty's Balkans expert was scathing about NATO's conduct, noting that "civilian deaths could have been significantly reduced during the conflict if NATO forces had fully adhered to the laws of war," and pointing out that "ten years on, no public investigation has ever been conducted by NATO or its member states into these incidents," and nobody had been held to account for obvious crimes.[13]

In addition to killing innocent people and worsening the humanitarian crisis, the bombings were indisputably illegal under international law. The UN Charter prohibits the use of force except in self-defense, or as approved by the UN Security Council. NATO's actions had not been endorsed by the UN Security Council and were not in self-defense, thus they violated the UN Charter. (Arguably, they also violated NATO's own charter, which commits it to following international law and using force defensively.) Those who advocated the intervention did not invoke credible legal justifications, instead suggesting that force was so morally necessary that international law could be disregarded. Susan Sontag, writing in *The New York Times*, responding to the argument that there was no right to invade a sovereign state, asked: "Are national borders, which have been altered so many times in the last hundred years, really to be the ultimate criterion?" President Clinton, in his memoirs, does not attempt to supply any legal justification for the attacks, instead simply explaining why he felt they were necessary. The Independent International Commission for Kosovo used the remarkable phrase "illegal but legitimate" to describe the attack.[14]

But many around the world *did* take international law seriously. As international relations specialist Michael MccGwire summarized, "The world at large saw a political-military alliance that took unto itself the role of judge, jury and executioner . . . [which] claimed to be acting on behalf of the international community and was ready to slight the UN and skirt international law in order to enforce its collective judgment." Indeed, UN secretary-general Kofi Annan said that NATO's decision to bomb without UN approval constituted a threat to the "very core of the international security system." India's prime minister demanded a halt to the air strikes and asked: "Is NATO's work to prevent war or to fuel one?" *The Washington Post* reported during the campaign that all around the world, especially in developing countries, the Kosovo campaign was creating large-scale resentment of the United States over its assumption of a right to drop bombs wherever it deemed necessary. Nelson Mandela said in 2000 that it was deeply wrong for the U.S. and Britain to assume they could be "policemen of the world" without obtaining the consent of others. Kosovo and the 1998 Iraq bombings, Mandela said, were threatening to shatter the entire foundation of international law. "They're introducing chaos into international affairs," Mandela warned, giving other countries license to do whatever they want.[15]

Even though the bombings were inhumane, worsened the crisis, and ran roughshod over the basic principles of international law, one might still argue that they were done out of benevolent humanitarian motives. One could contend that international law is meaningless and can be ignored when there are significant moral imperatives requiring the use of military force. We know, of course, that the United States *actively aids* atrocities when they serve "vital interests." At the very same time that NATO was violating international law for moral reasons in Kosovo, it was assisting the atrocities of member state Turkey against the Kurds. But even Power concedes that NATO's decision to intervene was "not purely humanitarian" and would likely not have occurred if there weren't ulterior motives of maintaining "credibility." She writes that "Operation Allied Force would probably not have been launched without the perceived threat to more traditional U.S. interests." Milošević had been making Clinton "look silly" and "humiliating" the United States.[16]

The United States, she says, had also spent billions of dollars on the region and didn't want to "see its neighborhood investment squandered." John Norris argues that what motivated U.S. policymakers was "not the plight of Kosovar Albanians." Milošević had proved difficult to control and therefore needed to be kept in line. NATO went to war "because its political and diplomatic leaders had enough of Milošević," who was imposing "humiliation and frustration" on Western leaders. Madeleine Albright said that Milošević "was jerking us around." Nobody jerks the Godfather around.[17]

Diplomatic options for averting the need to use force, as usual, were not pursued. Lord Gilbert, Britain's second most-senior defense minister during the conflict, later said that NATO "forced Slobodan Milošević into a war" by deliberately offering him "absolutely intolerable terms" in negotiations. Gilbert said that "certain people were spoiling for a fight in NATO at that time." MccGwire suggests that one reason they might have been spoiling for a fight was "the importance of demonstrating the continuing relevance of the [NATO] alliance on its fiftieth anniversary, and the opportunity presented by the Kosovo crisis to further the out-of-area issue and to establish NATO's right to act without specific UN endorsement."[18]

NATO's subversion of international law and assumption of a right to bomb without Security Council permission outraged the Russian government. Boris Yeltsin demanded of Clinton: "On what basis does NATO take it upon itself to decide the fates of peoples in sovereign states? Who gave it the right to act in the role of the guardian of order?" John Norris explains that when NATO "made clear that it would use force no matter what Russia thought," it "fuelled intense public resentment" and hurt the country's national pride, as well as signaling a possible future willingness "to involve itself in Russia's internal affairs without a UN mandate." Yeltsin had previously complained during NATO's 1995 bombing of Bosnia, warning that it was "the first sign of what could happen when NATO comes right up to the Russian Federation's borders. . . . The flame of war could burst out across the whole of Europe."[19]

As NATO grew in size and military capability, Russian leaders stated repeatedly that they saw the organization as a security threat to them, and did not understand what purpose the organization could conceivably have beyond creating a security order that excluded Russia. Madeleine Albright, in her memoir, writes that "Yeltsin and his countrymen were strongly opposed to enlargement, seeing it as a strategy for exploiting their vulnerability and moving Europe's dividing line to the east, leaving them isolated." Strobe Talbott, a proponent of expansion, nevertheless warned: "Many Russians see NATO as a vestige of the cold war, inherently directed against their country. They point out that they have disbanded the Warsaw Pact, their military alliance, and ask why the West should not do the same."[20]

Both publicly and privately, Russian leaders have been intensely hostile to the expansion of NATO, especially when NATO declared in 2008 that Georgia and Ukraine would ultimately become members. This, *Politico*'s Europe columnist Paul Taylor writes, "marked the culmination of the 'unipolar moment,' when the U.S. believed it could reshape the world along Western lines, ignoring warnings by leaders like former French president Jacques Chirac, that 'Russia should not be humiliated,' and German chancellor Angela Merkel, that Moscow's 'legitimate security interests' should be taken into account." Diplomatic cables released by WikiLeaks show that expansion was considered a major issue for Russian security. The U.S. ambassador to Russia, William Burns, who became Biden's CIA director, wrote in a 2007 cable that "NATO enlargement and U.S. missile defense deployments in Europe play to the classic Russian fear of encirclement." (That "classic fear" comes about in part because in the twentieth century, Russia was invaded twice by future NATO member Germany.) Burns later said that Ukraine's and Georgia's entry into the alliance would represent "an 'unthinkable' predicament for Russia."[21]

Dimitry Trenin of the Carnegie Endowment for Peace warned in a 2008 cable that "Ukraine was, in the long term, the most potentially destabilizing factor in U.S.-Russian relations, given the level of emotion and neuralgia triggered by its quest for NATO membership." Burns reported being told by Russia's deputy foreign minister that "Russia's political elite firmly believes that the accession of Ukraine and Georgia represented a direct security threat to Russia." Not only that, but Russian leaders saw expansion as a betrayal of the assurances given by the George H. W. Bush administration to Mikhail Gorbachev, when Secretary of State James Baker famously said: "We understand that not only for the Soviet Union but for other European countries as well it is important to have guarantees that if the United States keeps its presence in Germany within the framework of NATO, not an inch of NATO's present military jurisdiction will spread in an eastern direction." Robert Gates, who served as defense secretary under both George W. Bush and Barack Obama, concluded in his memoir that the United States was "recklessly ignoring what the Russians considered their own vital national interests." Moving to incorporate so many former Soviet states into NATO was a "mistake" that damaged relations with Russia, Gates said, and the attempt to bring Georgia and Ukraine into NATO, he said, was a "monumental provocation."[22]

One can argue that Russia's view of NATO was paranoid and delusional, that NATO's purpose is purely defensive and Russia had no reason to object to expansion. But NATO has engaged repeatedly in illegal and aggressive warfare. We have already reviewed the case of Kosovo, where NATO violated international law, targeted civilian infrastructure, lied about its conduct, and refused to investigate its crimes. In 2001, NATO countries illegally attacked Afghanistan, the disastrous consequences of which have also already been reviewed. Multiple NATO countries illegally invaded Iraq in 2003, of course. Then in 2011, NATO, acting under a UN mandate to protect civilians in Libya, instead launched military operations aimed at outright regime change. The head of the UN's Support Mission for Libya commented afterward that "it is impossible to believe that there would have been the necessary votes in the Security Council, let alone the withholding of vetoes by Russia and China, if the full extent of the military campaign had been foreseen." Indeed, Russia and China were scathingly critical of NATO's broad interpretation of its mandate, though their objections were ignored. The Libya bombing plunged the country into catastrophe, and NATO countries refused to acknowledge or take responsibility for the civilian deaths they caused.[23]

To understand the Russian attitude, it helps to imagine how U.S. policymakers would react if a military alliance led by China began, over the course of decades, slowly admitting the countries of the Western Hemisphere and providing them with weaponry and training. The United States has reacted to fears that countries are slipping out of its control with violence and even outright regime change. There was no reason not to expect a similar response from Russia to what Gates called a "monumental provocation."

In the case of Ukraine, the West took the worst of all possible courses for Ukrainians. NATO declared that Ukraine would ultimately become a member, infuriating Russia, though it had no intention of actually admitting Ukraine to the alliance. John Mearsheimer, in 2015, declared that the West was "leading Ukraine down the primrose path, and the end result is that Ukraine is going to get wrecked." Still, the United States continued along the same course, with the U.S. deepening military cooperation between NATO and Ukraine and signing a new strategic partnership agreement that, as Branko Marcetic notes from the leaked diplomatic cables, was "viewed as an escalation in Moscow." Putin told Biden directly that "the eastward expansion of the Western alliance was a major factor in his decision to send troops to Ukraine's border."[24]

On February 24, 2022, Vladimir Putin announced what he called a "special military operation" in Ukraine, a euphemism for a full-scale invasion. In an accompanying speech explaining the justifications for the war, Putin led with, and spent the most time on, what he argued were "fundamental threats" to Russia created by "irresponsible Western politicians." Putin made clear that he was "referring to the eastward expansion of NATO," claiming that while he had long been "trying to come to an agreement with the leading NATO countries," the alliance "continued to expand despite our protests and concerns" and was now "approaching our border," showing a "contemptuous and disdainful attitude toward our interests and absolutely legitimate demands."[25]

Putin's decision to launch a criminal war of aggression against a neighboring state cannot be excused. There is no extenuation, no justification, and there is zero merit to Putin's argument that U.S. hypocrisy justifies his own criminality. However, U.S. policy toward Russia over the last several decades made this decision more probable. As Thomas Friedman admitted in *The New York Times*, "If [Russia] had been included rather than excluded from a new European security order [it] might have had much less interest or incentive in menacing its neighbors." It was an enduring "mystery," Friedman said, why the United States "would choose to quickly push NATO into Russia's face when it was weak." Could different U.S. policies have prevented the war? It is impossible to know. But we do know that every warning about Russian red lines was disregarded. When Putin had amassed troops along the Ukrainian border and demanded a commitment from Joe Biden that Ukraine would not join NATO, Biden responded, "I don't accept anybody's red lines."[26]

The invasion of Ukraine was the culmination of a long conflict that had been becoming progressively more dangerous for years. In eastern Ukraine, pro-Russian separatists had been at war with the Ukrainian government for eight years. In 2021, international affairs expert Anatol Lieven warned that "the most dangerous problem in the world" was looming in Ukraine. The existing dispute over the status of majority-Russian-speaking eastern parts of Ukraine threatened to spiral out of control, and could, if not resolved, drag the United States and Russia into a ghastly war. Fortunately, Lieven wrote, the underlying conflict, while it was the world's most dangerous, was also in principle one of the "most easily solved." But that easy solution, he cautioned, would require the U.S. to change its existing policies toward Ukraine, using skillful diplomacy to bring about a peaceful negotiated solution.[27]

The United States, Lieven argued, needed to push for the implementation of the Minsk II agreement reached in 2015 and endorsed unanimously by the UN Security Council. The U.S., Lieven wrote, should drop the goal of NATO membership for Ukraine and pressure the Ukrainian government to agree to autonomy for the Donbas region. A natural settlement for the issue would have declared Ukraine to be a neutral country, without participation in any military alliance. Former U.S. ambassador to Russia Jack Matlock similarly concluded that "there would have been no basis for the present crisis if there had been no expansion" of NATO.[28]

The United States, however, declined to push for a settlement. It refused to consider revoking the commitment to admit Ukraine into NATO, even though it was obvious that the commitment was mostly theoretical. In fact, in December 2021, NATO reaffirmed that it was ultimately planning to integrate Ukraine. Even as the U.S. warned of an impending invasion, it made no diplomatic efforts to influence Russia's behavior. A Russia specialist at the RAND Corporation even said in January 2022 that "the louder Moscow protested, the more determined western capitals became to deny Russia what was seen as a veto over alliance decision-making."[29]

One reason there was little inclination to negotiate was that a Russian invasion of Ukraine would be much worse for Russia than the United States. Atlantic Council researcher John Deni wrote in *The Wall Street Journal* in December 2021 that there were "good strategic reasons for the West to stake out a hard-line approach, giving little ground to Moscow." Deni wrote that a Russian invasion would ultimately "forge an even stronger anti-Russian consensus across Europe," "further weaken Russia's economy," "sap the strength and morale of Russia's military," and "reduc[e] Russia's soft power globally." Deni was critical of the West for being in a "reactive mode, hoping to avoid a war in Europe that could result in tens of thousands of casualties." Instead, "the West ought to stand firm, even if it means another Russian invasion of Ukraine." There was no incentive for the U.S. to negotiate with Russia when it could "leverage the Kremlin's mistake" (no incentive, that is, other than avoiding "tens of thousands of casualties").[30]

There are parallels here with the U.S. attitude toward the Soviet occupation of Afghanistan in the 1980s. Zbigniew Brzezinski, national security adviser to President Carter, claimed that CIA aid to the mujahideen began before the Soviet invasion, and that the United States knew that the aid "was going to induce a Soviet military intervention." From the perspective of the U.S., Brzezinski said, a Soviet invasion would be a good thing. "We now have the opportunity of giving to the USSR its Vietnam war," Brzezinski says he told Carter. Even though the conflict killed up to two million Afghans and produced millions more refugees, Brzezinski later said he had no regrets. "Regret what? That secret operation was an excellent idea." By "drawing the Russians into the Afghan trap . . . Moscow had to carry on a war that was unsustainable for the regime."[31]

Anatol Lieven recalls a conversation he had with a U.S. diplomat in Islamabad in 1989, at the end of the war, in which the American attitude was made clear. When Lieven asked why we were still funding the extremists of the Afghan mujahideen, the U.S. official replied that "getting the Russians to leave is not enough—we want to inflict the kind of humiliation on them that they inflicted on us in Vietnam." Lieven was appalled that "there wasn't a single scrap—not the slightest element—of concern for Afghanistan or the Afghan people," and it "was totally irrelevant to him how many of the Afghan people died in the process.[32]

Once the war in Ukraine started, the Biden administration took steps that weakened any possibility for a negotiated settlement. Alexander Ward, a national security reporter for *Politico*, cautioned in March 2022 that the West's attitude toward Russia was foreclosing all "obvious ways out" and could make "a historically dangerous situation worse." Because there was no offer to *lift* sanctions under certain conditions, the sanctions did not create an incentive for Putin to end the war. As Daniel

Drezner wrote in *The Washington Post*, "If the goal is to compel, then the sanctioners need to be explicit about what Russia can do to get the sanctions lifted." The Biden administration made clear that its goal was not just to push Russia out of Ukraine, but to "weaken" Russia to the point where it was militarily incapable of aggression.[33]

Diplomacy quickly became a forbidden word in U.S. politics and media. When a group of progressive Democrats in Congress released a mild letter encouraging the Biden administration to "make vigorous diplomatic efforts in support of a negotiated settlement and ceasefire," they instantly came under a firestorm of criticism, including from fellow Democrats, one of whom said she was "dismayed that some of my [Democratic] colleagues think that we can negotiate with Putin." The progressives quickly retracted the letter, saying nothing again about a negotiated settlement to end the war. In April 2022, an extraordinary article in *The Washington Post* reported what it called the "awkward reality" that "for some in NATO, it's better for the Ukrainians to keep fighting, and dying, than to achieve a peace that comes too early or at too high a cost to Kyiv and the rest of Europe." Headlined NATO SAYS UKRAINE TO DECIDE ON PEACE DEAL WITH RUSSIA—WITHIN LIMITS, it noted that NATO countries did not think it was purely up to Ukraine to decide when and how to end the war. It was completely Ukraine's choice—unless they made the wrong choice.[34]

Opposition to diplomacy was not uniform within the U.S. government. General Mark Milley, chairman of the Joint Chiefs of Staff, had internally called for "press[ing] Ukraine to seek a diplomatic end to its war with Russia" and publicly argued that "when there's an opportunity to negotiate, when peace can be achieved, seize it." *The New York Times* reported that Milley's view was "not shared" by Biden or others on his staff, creating what one U.S. official called "a unique situation where military brass are more fervently pushing for diplomacy than U.S. diplomats."[35]

When allies hesitated in the pursuit of a military solution, the United States brought pressure to bear. In early 2023, Germany was reluctant to send tanks to Ukraine, because in the words of a German defense policy expert at the European Council on Foreign Relations, in the country "there is a big belief that weapons are no solution, you don't solve conflicts with arms." As German officials fretted that sending tanks was inconsistent with the country's post–World War II commitment to stay out of the business of mass killing, and that it could further escalate the war, *The Washington Post* editorial board was apoplectic: "Biden cannot let this stand," they wrote. After intense pressure from the U.S. (but not from the German electorate, which was divided on the issue), Germany gave in and agreed to supply tanks.[36]

The war created an ugly domestic atmosphere in the United States, reminiscent of World War I, when sauerkraut became "liberty cabbage" and orchestras stopped playing Wagner. Former State Department and CIA analyst Graham E. Fuller described a "a virulent anti-Russian propaganda barrage whose likes I have never seen during my Cold Warrior days." Democratic representative Eric Swalwell even suggested that "kicking every Russian student out of the United States [should] be on the table." The Ukraine war was covered by the media far more than the U.S. invasion of Iraq, with Ukrainian victims of Russian aggression receiving the kind of sympathetic treatment that Yemeni, Afghan, and Iraqi victims of U.S. aggression never did.[37]

Some could hardly contain their glee at the war's benefits to the United States. Timothy Ash, in a commentary for the Center for European Policy Analysis (CEPA), wrote that "when viewed from a bang-per-buck perspective, U.S. and Western support for Ukraine is an incredibly cost-effective investment." Senator Mitt Romney, in an address to Americans explaining the rationale for supporting Ukraine, was clear that a major factor behind U.S. policy is taking advantage of the chance to weaken a rival power. "We are, by virtue of supporting Ukraine in this war, depleting and diminishing the Russian military," he said, declaring that "weakening Russia is a very good thing."[38]

Similarly, a RAND Corporation analysis, while ultimately concluding that a long war is ultimately *not* in the interests of the U.S. (due to the risk of catastrophic nuclear escalation), still notes that "protracted conflict, as perverse as it might seem, has some potential upsides for the United States." Ash writes excitedly that the war "provides a prime opportunity" for the U.S. to "erode and degrade Russia's conventional defense capability" with "little risk to U.S. lives." It would be an "absolutely incredible investment" and a "bargain," because it would be like "Vietnam or Afghanistan" for Russia: "A Russia continually mired in a war it cannot win is a huge strategic win for the U.S. Why would anyone object to that?"[39]

Who could object, other than those who end up dying gruesome deaths in an avoidable war? But as a bonus, Ash wrote, the war would be an economic boon for the United States, "pushing NATO partners to quickly increase [military] spending." Given the U.S.'s "advantage in defense equipment, a sizable share of this additional military outlay will be spent on U.S. equipment," making the war highly profitable for U.S. weapons manufacturers. Plus, because "wars are shop windows for defense manufacturers," "any buyer in their right mind will want the technology made by the winner," thus "Putin's misjudgment has merely provided a fantastic marketing opportunity for [Russia's] Western competitors." (Indeed, *The Wall Street Journal* reported that BAE Systems was receiving a flood of interest for M777 howitzers after a successful "performance on Ukrainian battlefields revive[d] interest in the weapon," and *The New York Times* said in December 2022 that a "new boom for arms makers" had been sparked by the war in Ukraine.) David Ignatius of *The Washington Post* said in mid-2023 that the West shouldn't "feel gloomy" about the destruction of Ukraine, because "these 18 months of war have been a strategic windfall, at relatively low cost (other than for the Ukrainians)." Likewise, a commentary for the Atlantic Council argued that the West was reaping "multiple benefits" from aiding Ukraine, because "the West is able to dramatically reduce Russia's military potential without committing any of its own troops or sustaining casualties." The war was a shot in the arm for U.S. power.[40]

Eliot Cohen, a neoconservative Johns Hopkins professor, writing in

The Atlantic, said that "spending some tens of billions of dollars to shatter the land and air forces of one of our chief opponents, Russia, is a bargain." Cohen said that all diplomatic resolutions should be off the table, that we should "stop talking about talks," and rejected the view "that it is time to think about how to bring the war in Ukraine to a close." Instead, Cohen said, we should adopt the "Chicago way" used to deal with Al Capone. He quoted *The Untouchables*: "You wanna know how to get Capone? They pull a knife, you pull a gun. He sends one of yours to the hospital, you send one of his to the morgue." (In other words, be even more ruthless and murderous than the most ruthless and murderous gangster.) Veteran U.S. diplomat Chas Freeman, pointing out that U.S. policy choices were virtually "guarantee[ing] a long war," noted that a lot of people in the United States seem to think that a long war is "just dandy": "What's so terrible about a long war? If you're not Ukrainian, you probably see some merit in a long war." Freeman commented acidly that the U.S. stance appeared to be that it would "fight Russia to the last Ukrainian." Indeed, U.S. senator Lindsey Graham commented: "I like the structural path we're on. As long as we help Ukraine with the weapons they need and the economic support, they will fight to the last person."[41]

Many Europeans started to grumble, as *Politico* reported, that "the country that is most profiting from this war is the U.S. because they are selling more gas and at higher prices, and because they are selling more weapons." A diplomat described a growing impression among European countries that "your best ally is actually making huge profits out of your troubles." Similarly, in many countries of the Global South, there are those who doubt that the U.S. policy toward Ukraine has been made for reasons of principle. Few countries other than Europe, Canada, the United States, Australia, and Japan imposed sanctions on Russia over the war, and only a handful of other countries have offered military aid to Ukraine. This is in part because the war is perceived by many around the world not as a battle between democracy and authoritarianism but as a great-power conflict not worth getting involved in.

Countries in Africa, Latin America, and the Middle East find U.S. rhetoric about resisting aggression to be laughable hypocrisy.[42]

The war in Ukraine has brought the world closer to a catastrophic great-power confrontation than at any time since the Cold War. "It is as if the world has learned nothing from Europe's terrible twentieth century," lamented Richard Sakwa in the lead-up to the present conflict. The war has been horrific for Ukrainians, killing tens of thousands of people, physically maiming many more, displacing millions, shattering the economy, and ruining entire cities.[43]

It is right to ask, when an aggressor attacks another country, what we ought to do to help. When Ukrainians ask for assistance in resisting Russian occupation, they should receive it. But we should also critically examine the U.S. role in making war more likely, and ask what ought to be done to bring the war to an end as quickly as possible. Taking diplomacy off the table encouraged a long war that will be in nobody's interest—though it will maintain Ukraine as a "showroom" for U.S. weapons, demonstrating their capacity to kill more and more people.

It has become common to treat criticism of U.S. policy toward Russia as "apologism" for Vladimir Putin's homicidal insanity, or to argue that a belief in negotiation means Ukraine should "surrender."[44] Neither argument is valid. Just as it is no defense or rationalization of terror attacks to prove that the Iraq and Afghanistan wars increased the probability of terrorism toward the United States, it is no rationalization of Putin's war to show that U.S. refusal to take Russia's stated interests into account made a violent reaction more likely. Putin's war is Putin's responsibility, but as always, the question that those in the United States should ask is: How does U.S. policy affect likely outcomes? If Russia had been incorporated into a post–Cold War security order, or if the U.S. had pressured both Russia and Ukraine to adhere to the Minsk II agreement on Ukraine, it is possible that the people of Ukraine could have been spared a hideous war.

In 2023, leading Ukrainian politician David Arakhamia said that at the beginning of the war, Russia had "promised Kyiv peace in exchange for refusing to join NATO" and was "prepared to end the war if we agreed to—as Finland once did—neutrality." All the talk of "denazification," he said, was just "seasoning," the central sticking point being NATO. Russia, too, claims that a peace deal was nearly reached at this point. At that time, former UK prime minister Boris Johnson came to Kyiv and told the Ukrainians they should refuse any deal, that they should "just fight." Former Israeli prime minister Naftali Bennett says the U.S. and UK blocked a peace deal. As the war progressed, U.S. media continued to present whatever facts could be twisted to show Putin intended to conquer the world, but ignored Russia's regular offers to negotiate a ceasefire, with the United States claiming, despite the evidence, that Russia had shown no interest in negotiating. It is impossible to know if diplomacy could have achieved a just peace, because it was never tried.[45]

The Ukrainians took their Western partners' advice to "just fight." The resulting war reached five hundred thousand casualties within a year. The Ukrainian population was so decimated that the average age of soldiers was forty-three. A World War I–style stalemate emerged on the front lines, with mounting death tolls for few territorial gains. The entire global food supply was threatened as the resources of the Black Sea region were cut off. The threat of escalation to nuclear war became more severe than at any time since the Cold War, and efforts to address the climate catastrophe were set back dramatically. By 2024, it increasingly looked like Ukraine might eventually have to take an unfavorable peace deal and give up hope of regaining its territory. After proudly waving the Ukrainian flag for a year, the United States began to lose interest in helping Ukraine, its attentions focused elsewhere.[46]

As Ukraine is devastated, some are doing fine. The U.S. military and fossil fuel industries are drowning in profit, with great prospects for many years ahead. *The Wall Street Journal* reports that the Ukraine war has been good for the U.S. economy, a huge boost to arms manufacturers, with the Biden administration pointing to Ukraine aid's effect in "building America's defense industrial base, jump-starting and expanding production lines for weapons and ammunition, and supporting jobs in 40 states." Plus, for a small fraction of its colossal military budget, the United States is severely degrading the forces of a major military adversary. In the geopolitical dimension, Vladimir Putin's criminal aggression handed the United States its fondest wish: driving Europe deeper into the U.S.-run NATO-based system.[47]

Undermining rival powers is explicitly part of U.S. national policy. James Mattis, in delivering the 2018 National Defense Strategy, stated directly that "Great Power competition—not terrorism—is now the primary focus of U.S. national security," and the Defense Department's "principal priorities are long-term strategic competitions with China and Russia." China is undeterred, continuing to expand its loan and development programs through Eurasia, extending to the Middle East, Africa, and even Latin America, much to Washington's discomfiture. Meanwhile, the world outside of the Anglosphere and Western Europe has been unwilling to join what most see as a U.S.-Russia proxy war fought with Ukrainian bodies. The Global South does not admire the nobility of the U.S. defense of Ukraine, seeing the rhetoric as hypocritical and the fight as a contest for dominance between superpowers. New alliances are forming, along with commercial interactions and novel financial arrangements that are not dependent on the United States and its fierce reprisals by sanctions and other means.[48]

Nuclear Threats and
Climate Catastrophe

In the twenty-first century, there are two problems for our species' survival—nuclear war and environmental catastrophe—and we are hurtling toward them knowingly. Moreover, the world faces these threats in significant part because of choices made by U.S. corporations and the U.S. government over the course of decades. Our own country's actions have helped to create a situation of unprecedented peril.

The climate crisis is unique in our history and is getting more severe every year. If major steps are not taken within the next few decades, the world is likely to reach a point of no return. The nuclear weapons issue is talked about less, but is a major threat to our existence, increasing over time as we enter a risky new era of "Great Power competition." Since the bombing of Hiroshima in 1945, we have been surviving under a sword of Damocles. Without understanding and addressing these two threatening crises of our time, organized human life will not survive our century.

Human history is filled with records of horrific wars, tortures, massacres, and abuses. But today we face threats that are altogether different in terms of their sheer scale. For the first time, our entire species faces *collective* disasters. The environmental and nuclear weapons threats are truly existential, and what we choose to do will determine the fate not only of our species but of all the other species on Earth.

THE OMNICIDAL MADNESS OF NUCLEAR WEAPONS

It has been argued that we live in the most peaceful time in human history. Harvard psychologist Steven Pinker, who says that we are in a "long peace," writes that "as one becomes aware of the decline of violence, the world begins to look different. The past seems less innocent; the present less sinister." But this is exactly backward. The idea of a "long peace" depends on minimizing the many millions of deaths in warfare that have occurred since the end of World War II, including the countless bloodbaths for which our country is directly responsible. It is more accurate to describe this era as by far the most dangerous time in human history, with extreme violence a greater threat than ever before.[1]

The possession of thousands of nuclear warheads by the world's most powerful countries places the entire world under constant risk of annihilation. We may not enjoy contemplating it, we may try to get on with our lives without considering it, but the nuclear threat hangs over us at every moment, everywhere we are. The idea that we are in a period of "peace" is a dangerous illusion.

Nuclear weapons are not just lying around unused in the background. They are in use at every moment to frighten adversaries, just as a robber who points a gun at a store owner is using the gun, even if he doesn't fire it. What is misleadingly and euphemistically called "deterrence" is more accurately understood as "the constant threat of extreme violence." Situations look more peaceful than they are if we do not understand the role of threats.[2]

With thousands of nuclear warheads held by the great powers, escalating tensions among those powers that could lead to a global war, and plans under way for the massive increase of an already out-of-control arms race, we face the possibility of *terminal war*, a war that would end human civilization altogether. And there are powerful forces pushing us closer and closer to the brink. The possession of civilization-destroying weapons by states, and the fact that those states are controlled by rulers over whose decisions we have little control, means we are all in peril.

On August 6, 1945, the United States demonstrated that human intelligence would soon be capable of destroying virtually all life on Earth. Things didn't quite reach that point until 1953, with the development of thermonuclear weapons, but the trajectory was clear: nuclear weapons gave states staggering new destructive capabilities and plunged the whole world into unprecedented danger.

The dropping of atomic bombs on Hiroshima and Nagasaki was not terribly different from the firebombing of Tokyo, in terms of their savagery and disregard for innocent lives. Atomic weaponry merely made the mass murder of civilians more efficient. But the bombings did demonstrate how far human technological capacities had outstripped human moral capacities. They showed how the godlike power to smite whole cities could be unleashed by a country that saw itself as humane and righteous.[3]

Regrettably, the calamity of the Second World War, and the horrifying reality of the Hiroshima and Nagasaki bombings (the true disturbing facts of which were suppressed in the United States) did not lead humanity to put a definitive end to great-power conflict and warmaking, or to eliminate the weapons and forbid their use. Instead, it sparked an arms race that nearly ended life on Earth for good.[4]

The frantic warnings of leading scientists were generally ignored. J. Robert Oppenheimer, the "father of the atomic bomb," publicly opposed developing the hydrogen bomb, saying that "no world has ever faced a possibility of destruction—in a relevant sense annihilation—comparable to that which we face." Oppenheimer was smeared as "more probably than not [an] agent of the Soviet Union," and his career was destroyed. Joseph Rotblat, another Manhattan Project physicist, had refused to continue working on the bomb when it was clear Nazi Germany had stopped their own efforts at developing nuclear weapons. Rotblat dedicated his life to trying to eliminate nuclear weapons. Naturally, he, too, was accused by the American right "of being a servant or unwitting tool of the Soviet Union."[5]

The 1955 Mainau Declaration, signed by dozens of Nobel laureates including Werner Heisenberg and Max Born, warned that "science is giving mankind the means to destroy itself," and "it is a delusion if governments believe they can avoid war for a long time through the fear of [nuclear] weapons." Thus "all nations must come to the decision to renounce force as a final resort," or they will "cease to exist." The same year, a manifesto penned by Bertrand Russell and Albert Einstein brought together some of the world's leading scientists to warn that humanity faced a "stark and dreadful and inescapable" dilemma, namely: "Shall we put an end to the human race; or shall mankind renounce war?"[6]

The UN General Assembly's first-ever resolution, in 1946, called directly for "the elimination from national armaments of atomic weapons and of all other major weapons adaptable to mass destruction." The Soviet delegate, warning that any use of nuclear weapons "brings untold misery," and "the rules of warfare must not allow the extermination of innocent civilian populations," proposed a multilateral treaty providing that "all stocks of atomic energy weapons whether in a finished or unfinished condition" would be immediately destroyed. But the United States was unwilling from the start to consider giving up a formidable means of coercing others.[7]

The United States began developing plans for potential nuclear attacks against the Soviet Union years before the Soviets had nuclear weapons of their own. Physicists Michio Kaku and Daniel Axelrod, in *To Win a Nuclear War: The Pentagon's Secret War Plans*, document plans made by the Truman administration in the late 1940s for nuclear strikes against Soviet cities, with a Joint Chiefs of Staff memo arguing that "offense, recognized in the past as the best means of defense, in atomic warfare will be the only general means of defense." The Truman ad-

ministration did not hesitate to use nuclear weapons as a means of diplomatic coercion. Secretary of War Henry Stimson commented as the
bomb was being developed that it would be a "master card" giving the
U.S. a "royal straight flush" in diplomacy.[8]

The decision to embrace the continued use of nuclear weapons was
never approved by the U.S. public. In September 1946, a poll showed
that over two thirds of Americans wanted the UN to "prevent all countries, including the United States, from making atomic bombs." As the
U.S. was announcing its plans to build a hydrogen bomb, 68 percent of
Americans agreed there ought to be efforts toward an arms control
agreement with the Soviet Union.[9]

Fueled by paranoia about Soviet plans for world domination and an
unbending commitment to maintaining global power, the United States
initiated an arms race that reached almost unfathomable extremes. At
one point, the U.S. possessed over thirty thousand nuclear warheads,
and the Soviet Union ultimately reached forty thousand, enough to
turn the whole planet into a wasteland many times over.

The worst nearly happened. The history of nuclear weapons is full of
alarming "close call" incidents. Take the Cuban Missile Crisis. In October
1962, the United States discovered Soviet ballistic missiles in Cuba, leading to a tense thirteen-day standoff between the U.S. and the Soviet Union.
The crisis ended when Soviet leader Nikita Khrushchev agreed to dis-
mantle the missile installations in exchange for the U.S. promising not
to invade Cuba and secretly removing U.S. missiles from Turkey.

Why did Khrushchev make the reckless decision to put missiles in
a domain that the United States insists it controls? There were two primary reasons. First, the U.S. was conducting a murderous terrorist war
against Cuba, which could have potentially escalated into an invasion.
This made the missile deployment partly a defensive move against a
significant military threat. Years later, Robert McNamara recognized
that Cuba was justified in fearing an attack. "If I were in Cuban or Soviet

shoes, I would have thought so, too," he observed at a major conference on the missile crisis on the fortieth anniversary. Second, while Khrushchev had proposed a mutual reduction in offensive military capabilities, the Kennedy administration had responded with an unprecedented peacetime military buildup, despite already being well ahead in military capabilities.[10]

Kennedy refused Khrushchev's proposal for public withdrawal of the missiles from Cuba in exchange for withdrawal of U.S. Jupiter missiles from Turkey; only the withdrawal from Cuba could be public. Kennedy insisted on secrecy for the removal of the American missiles in order to maintain the principle that while the United States could station lethal missiles near Soviet borders, the converse was not permissible. The Kennedy administration thus resisted what they knew to be a reasonable trade. It is hard to think of a more horrendous decision in history—and for this, Kennedy is still highly praised for his cool courage and statesmanship. His stance almost led the world to catastrophic destruction. As historian Christian Appy writes, "According to Kennedy's own reasoning, what brought the world to the brink of nuclear war was not the presence of nuclear missiles in Cuba, but his insistence that they be removed," his compulsion "to demonstrate his steely resolve to stand tough against the Communists" to avoid the risk of being "viewed as a paper tiger, as much by his own people as by Khrushchev and the world."[11]

The crisis that brought the world closest to the brink of apocalypse began with Kennedy's attack against Cuba, with a threat of invasion in October 1962. It ended with the president's rejection of Russian offers that would seem fair to a "rational" person, but were unthinkable because they would have undermined the fundamental principle that the United States has the unilateral right to deploy nuclear missiles anywhere. To establish that principle, the American president considered it entirely proper to face a high risk of a war of unimaginable destruction and to reject simple and admittedly fair ways to end the threat.[12]

The lesson should not need spelling out. The U.S. insistence on maintaining dominance, on refusal to grant other countries the rights claimed for ourselves, is not just unprincipled. It is dangerous. And in 1962 the uncompromising insistence on maintaining hegemony nearly led to the destruction of modern civilization. There is no reason it could not happen again.

Indeed, plenty of times over the course of the Cold War, automated systems in the United States and the Soviet Union warned of imminent nuclear attacks that nearly set off an automated response but for human intervention. In 1983, for instance, the Reagan administration had been simulating attacks on the Soviet Union and debating installing Pershing missiles in Europe (with a ten-minute flight time to Moscow), causing the Soviet government to believe that the U.S. was preparing an imminent nuclear first strike. This meant the Soviet Union was on hair-trigger alert, "very nervous and prone to mistakes and accidents," because they were "geared to expect an attack and to retaliate very quickly to it." At this tense moment, a Soviet automated warning system detected incoming ballistic missiles. A single Soviet military officer, Stanislav Petrov, who disobeyed protocol and did not pass the warning on to the next level, is thought by some to have saved the world by stopping a process that could have ended in a massive Soviet nuclear attack.[13]

It was not the only such incident. General Lee Butler, former head of the U.S. Strategic Command (STRATCOM), reflected after the Cold War that we had so far survived the nuclear weapons era "without a holocaust by some combination of skill, luck, and divine intervention, and I suspect the latter in greatest proportion." Butler called the U.S. strategic plan of 1960, which called for an automated all-out strike on the communist world, "the single most absurd and irresponsible document I have ever reviewed." Daniel Ellsberg, who worked as a RAND Corporation nuclear planner in the '60s, was similarly horrified by a secret document he discovered that outlined contingency plans for the killing of hundreds of millions of Soviet civilians—what he called an outright "omnicide."[14]

The United States and the Soviet Union developed both the capacity and the plans for destroying each other and the world, and then maintained systems that could easily have triggered this apocalypse with only a few simple mistakes or misunderstandings. Even if the ultimate disaster was a low-probability event, over a long period, low-probability events cease to be low probability.[15]

We are still doing it. Irresponsible nuclear policy didn't end with the Cold War. In the Clinton era, STRATCOM produced an important study entitled "Essentials of Post–Cold War Deterrence," concerned with "the role of nuclear weapons in the post–Cold War era." A central conclusion: that the United States must maintain the right to launch a first strike, even against nonnuclear states. Furthermore, nuclear weapons must always be at the ready because they "cast a shadow over any crisis or conflict," enabling us to gain our ends through intimidation. STRATCOM went on to advise that "planners should not be too rational about determining . . . what the opponent values the most." Everything should simply be targeted. "It hurts to portray ourselves as too fully rational and cool-headed. . . . That the U.S. may become irrational and vindictive if its vital interests are attacked should be a part of the national persona we project." It is "beneficial [for our strategic posture] if some elements may appear to be potentially 'out of control,'" thus posing a constant threat of nuclear attack. This is Richard Nixon's "madman theory," formalized in strategy.[16]

Even Democratic presidents who have indicated support for disarmament have done precisely the opposite in practice. Barack Obama issued pleasant words about working to abolish nuclear weapons, then crafted plans to spend $1 trillion on the U.S. nuclear arsenal over thirty years. Obama's programs to modernize nuclear weapons increased "killing power" sufficiently to create "exactly what one would expect to see if a nuclear-armed state were planning to have the capacity to fight and win a nuclear war by disarming enemies with a surprise first strike," as explained in the *Bulletin of the Atomic Scientists*.[17]

The Biden administration's 2022 Nuclear Posture Review (NPR) is open about the fact that threatening the use of nuclear weapons is a core part of U.S. foreign policy, not just meant to deter nuclear attacks by other countries. The NPR says that "our nuclear posture is intended to complicate an adversary's entire decision calculus, including whether to instigate a crisis, initiate armed conflict, conduct strategic attacks using non-nuclear capabilities, or escalate to the use of nuclear weapons on any scale" and "thus undergirds all our national defense priorities" including "deterring regional aggression." The 1968 Treaty on the Non-Proliferation of Nuclear Weapons, which the United States has ratified, places an obligation on its parties to pursue "general and complete disarmament under strict and effective international control." The NPR instead says that "for the foreseeable future, nuclear weapons will continue to provide unique deterrence effects that no other element of U.S. military power can replace." Indeed, when "deterrence" is understood to mean "the use of the threat of annihilation to attain compliance," the NPR is correct that pointing civilization-destroying weapons at other countries has a coercive power that cannot be replicated. All of this is a violation not only of the UN Charter but the obligation under the Non-Proliferation Treaty to make "good faith" efforts to eliminate nuclear weapons entirely.[18]

China, which unlike the United States has a formal policy that it would never be the first country to use nuclear weapons (U.S. doctrine is that they can be used first if our "vital interests" are at stake), has strongly objected to the U.S. posture, saying that the U.S. logic of "seeking absolute military superiority" inevitably "stimulate[s] a nuclear arms race," and that by "strengthening the role of nuclear weapons in its national security policy and lowering the threshold for their use, the U.S. has increasingly become a source of risk of nuclear conflict."[19]

But the amount of mainstream debate within the United States on whether the existing nuclear policy encourages proliferation and endangers the world is approximately zero.

Since the United States first obliterated two civilian populations in 1945, there have been global popular movements to restrict or eliminate nuclear weapons. Lawrence Wittner, in *Confronting the Bomb: A Short History of the World Nuclear Disarmament Movement*, shows that these movements succeeded in bringing about the arms control measures that do exist, and that *without* popular pressure, there would have been little inclination on the part of successive U.S. administrations to take any steps at all toward reducing nuclear weapons stockpiles. In 1956, Henry Cabot Lodge Jr., U.S. ambassador to the United Nations, grumbled that the atomic bomb had developed "a bad name . . . to such an extent that it seriously inhibits us from using it," and Eisenhower told his Joint Chiefs of Staff that "the current state of world opinion" would not permit the greater use of nuclear threats. It was public opinion, not the humanitarian instincts of policymakers, that curtailed proliferation and use.[20]

The government treated protesters with immense hostility. For instance, when the Nuclear Freeze movement arose in the 1980s, President Reagan's national security adviser Robert McFarlane later recalled seeing it as serious political threat, and a "movement that could undermine congressional support for the [nuclear] modernization program." David Gergen, who was the White House communications director at the time, says the prevailing view within the administration was that the Freeze movement was "a dagger pointed at the heart of the administration's defense program." Wittner shows that the administration engaged in a major effort to discredit the Nuclear Freeze campaign, with the president publicly declaring that "foreign agents" had helped to create it in order to ensure the "weakening of America."[21]

The activists were tenacious and heroic. They are also mostly forgotten. In 1981, for instance, a group of women in the UK set up the Greenham Common Women's Peace Camp outside a base being built to house nuclear cruise missiles. The women repeatedly disrupted construction on the base, and at one point thirty thousand women gathered to join hands around the base. The missiles were eventually removed, but the Peace Camp remained as an antinuclear protest until 2000.[22]

Antinuclear activism has been strong around the world, especially in those countries that were subjected to some of the over two thousand nuclear tests that have been conducted by the nuclear powers since 1945. Wittner reports on some of the initiatives in the Pacific nations. In Fiji, for instance, "church, union, and student organizations established the Fiji Anti-Nuclear Group to work for the creation of a nuclear-free Pacific," while "in Tahiti, thousands of people marched through the streets protesting French nuclear tests and demanding independence from France." Marshall Islanders staged an occupation to resist U.S. plans to extend its military rights. In Palau, the people of the island voted to enshrine their opposition to nuclear weapons in the constitution, despite U.S. efforts to influence the vote. The efforts of peace activists did bear fruit, in the form of the Partial Test Ban Treaty of 1963, the Nonproliferation Treaty of 1968, the Anti-Ballistic Missile Treaty of 1972, the Biological Weapons Convention of 1972, and the Chemical Weapons Convention of 1993.

All of their successes are now under threat.

Elaine Scarry has argued convincingly that the existence of nuclear weapons is necessarily deeply undemocratic. When a tiny number of people hold the fate of the Earth in their hands, she writes, we live in what is more accurately described as a "thermonuclear monarchy." To better understand the situation, Scarry asks us to envisage a hypothetical world in which each country sits on a "flexible floor," i.e., a trapdoor into the Earth. Imagine, she says, that with the push of a button, the trapdoor could be opened, and the country and all its people would vanish forever into the abyss. In a situation where a small group of people possess access to this button, at any time able to extinguish hundreds of millions of others, we would correctly describe the situation as incompatible with democracy, if democracy is defined as *popular control over the fate of one's community*. As General Lee Butler asked: "By what authority do succeeding generations of leaders in the nuclear-weapons states usurp the power to dictate the odds of continued life on our planet?"[23]

And yet this is the situation we are in. "I can go back into my office and pick up the telephone and in twenty-five minutes seventy million people will be dead," Richard Nixon once observed. Nixon was speaking accurately: he personally held the fate of countless millions in his hands, whether they liked it or not. Nor did Nixon hesitate to contemplate actually using this hideous killing machine. "If the president had his way," Henry Kissinger commented, "there would be a nuclear war each week!" Indeed, according to a high-ranking CIA official, in 1969, after North Korea shot down a U.S. spy plane over the Sea of Japan, Nixon drunkenly ordered a tactical nuclear strike in response. Kissinger had to tell the Joint Chiefs of Staff "not to do anything until Nixon sobered up in the morning."[24]

Former Clinton secretary of defense William J. Perry has pointed out how few constraints there are on a president who wishes to use nuclear weapons: "If a president decides to launch, he has the authority to do it, he has the equipment to do it, and, if it goes, there's no way of calling it back and there's no way of just destroying it in flight." Former director of National Intelligence James Clapper confirmed in 2017: "Having some understanding of the levers that a president can exercise, I worry about, frankly, the access to the nuclear codes." Speaking of Donald Trump specifically, Clapper said that under existing systems, if Trump had wanted to launch a nuclear attack on North Korea "in a fit of pique," there would be "very little to stop him," because there's "very little in the way of controls over exercising a nuclear option." Clapper found this "pretty damn scary."[25]

Ben Rhodes, former deputy national security adviser to Barack Obama, said that we lack "some check, some process, some chain of command, some congressional notification, some form of break in which people can stop and consider even for just a brief period of time: Do we really want to do this?" The only barrier between ourselves and nuclear war is the president, that one person "has completely, with their own discretion, the capacity to destroy life on Earth." During the Nixon administration, when Nixon's drunkenness and paranoia were becoming evident, Senator Alan Cranston phoned the defense secretary and warned of "the need for keeping a berserk president from plunging us into a holocaust." But then as now, the world's fate depends on the president not going berserk.[26]

We know exactly how to overcome the threat of apocalypse: eliminate the weapons. Steps short of that can be taken to alleviate the threat, among them implementing Nuclear-Weapon-Free Zones (NWFZ). These exist in much of the world, including Central Asia and across the Southern Hemisphere. For instance, the 1996 Treaty of Pelindaba created an African Nuclear-Weapon-Free Zone across the entire continent of Africa. Under its protocols, the nuclear weapons states are "invited to agree not to use or threaten to use a nuclear explosive device against any Treaty party" or to "test or assist or encourage the testing of a nuclear explosive device anywhere within the African zone." The United States has yet to ratify the treaty.

The most important step would be establishing a Nuclear-Weapons-Free Zone in the Middle East. This would end the alleged Iranian nuclear threat (and the pretext for the U.S.-Israeli bombings, assassinations, and sabotage in Iran). That crucial advance in world peace has long been blocked by the United States, however, because it would interfere with Washington's protection of Israel's nuclear arsenal. In 2015, Benjamin Netanyahu thanked the Obama administration for blocking an Egyptian proposal to ban nuclear weapons from the entire Middle East. Establishment of NWFZs is an important step toward reducing the nuclear weapons threat, and if the U.S. were a functional democratic society, in which public opinion influenced policy, the issues could be resolved. A 2007 poll of Iranians and Americans found them to be in agreement on nearly all the major questions related to nuclear proliferation, including on Iran's right to nuclear power but not nuclear weapons, elimination of all nuclear weapons, and a "nuclear-weapons-free zone in the Middle East that would include both Islamic countries and Israel."[27]

There are other steps that can be taken. The United States has consistently rejected the idea of committing to a "no first use" policy, even though polls show two thirds of Americans support such a pledge. In 2021, the UN's Treaty on the Prohibition of Nuclear Weapons came into force. It is the first binding agreement to comprehensively prohibit these weapons and aims eventually to eliminate them entirely. Nearly one hundred countries have signed it. Unfortunately, negotiations were "boycotted by all nuclear-weapons-possessing states, most NATO countries, and many military allies of nuclear weapons states." The U.S. could demonstrate true international leadership by moving toward accepting the treaty and calling on the other nuclear states to do the same. But it hasn't.[28]

Regrettably, that level of civilization still seems beyond the range of the most powerful states, which are careering in the opposite direction, upgrading and enhancing the means to terminate organized human life on Earth. George W. Bush withdrew the United States from the Anti-Ballistic Missile Treaty, in what James Acton of the Carnegie Endowment for International Peace says was clearly an "epic mistake." The Bush administration also stood alone in rejecting an international cessation of the production of fissionable materials for weapons purposes (FISSBAN). In November 2004, the UN Committee on Disarmament voted in favor of a verifiable FISSBAN. The vote was 147 to 1 (United States), with two abstentions: Israel and Britain. President Trump dismantled the Reagan-Gorbachev INF [Intermediate-Range Nuclear Forces] Treaty and immediately tested weapons that violate the treaty. We are not turning back. According to the Arms Control Association, Biden's 2021 budget request planned to continue "the expensive and controversial nuclear weapons sustainment and modernization efforts it inherited from the Trump administration."[29]

The Non-Proliferation Treaty creates a legal obligation for the nuclear powers to carry out good-faith measures to eliminate nuclear weapons. But the United States has led the way in refusal to abide by these obligations. Mohamed ElBaradei, head of the International Atomic Energy Agency, emphasizes that "reluctance by one party to fulfill its obligations breeds reluctance in others." Former president Jimmy Carter blasted the United States as the major culprit in this erosion of the NPT. American leaders, he said, while claiming to oppose proliferation, "not only have abandoned existing treaty restraints but also have asserted plans to test and develop new weapons," as well as threatening first use of nuclear weapons against nonnuclear states.[30]

When Harry Truman left office, he commented that "the war of the future would be one in which man could extinguish millions of lives at one blow, demolish the great cities of the world, wipe out the cultural achievements of the past—and destroy the very structure of civilization that has been slowly and painfully built up through hundreds of generations. Such a war is not a possible policy of rational men." Robert McNamara, toward the end of his life, warned of "apocalypse soon," saying that he regarded "current U.S. nuclear weapons policy as immoral, illegal, militarily unnecessary and dreadfully dangerous," creating "unacceptable risks to other nations and to our own," including the "unacceptably high" risk of "accidental or inadvertent nuclear launch," and of nuclear attack by terrorists. Former Clinton defense secretary William Perry regards "the probability of a nuclear calamity [as] higher today" than during the Cold War, when we escaped global apocalypse by sheer luck. Former senator Sam Nunn also raised the alarm, writing that "we are running an unnecessary risk of an Armageddon of our own making." Under current policies, "a nuclear exchange is ultimately inevitable," international relations expert Michael MccGwire concluded in 2005.[31]

Given the risk, it would be wrong, even criminal, to fail to do what can be done to constrain the production and use of these terrible weapons. But we must also bear in mind that unless we address the nationalistic and militaristic drives that push us toward catastrophic confrontation with other powers, we are simply delaying a terminal conflict. Only the timing is in doubt.

WRECKING THE EARTH:
THE U.S. AND GLOBAL CLIMATE POLICY

In July 2022, British firefighters had their busiest day since World War II. A record-breaking heat wave produced catastrophic wildfires, which swept through towns and villages around the country. Firefighters faced "unprecedented" difficulties trying to put out eleven hundred fires in London alone, as temperatures soared above 104°F. In some places, entire streets were turned into charred ruins, and people's homes were utterly destroyed within minutes. It was, said some who saw it, like a "scene from the Blitz," with cottages turned to ash and their residents left to rebuild their lives from scratch.[32]

The event was not freakish or aberrational. It was entirely predictable. Global warming has increased the frequency and intensity of heat waves in Britain and is leading to "a dramatically increasing trend in the number of summer days . . . with very high fire weather indices." The "scenes from the Blitz" will become more common, as what were previously "once in a century" fire threats become annual occurrences.[33]

The month after the British wildfire disaster, it began to rain unusually hard in Pakistan. The rain did not let up, and soon Pakistan was experiencing one of the worst natural disasters in history, with a third of the country submerged under floodwaters. Twenty-seven thousand schools and fifteen hundred public-health facilities were destroyed or damaged, along with hundreds of bridges and dams and thousands of miles of roads. The prime minister reported that "village after village has been wiped out" and "millions of houses have been destroyed." UNICEF reported that in early 2023, "as many as 4 million children were still living near contaminated and stagnant flood waters, risking their survival and well-being. [. . .] Frail, hungry children are fighting a losing battle against severe acute malnutrition, diarrhea, malaria, dengue fever, typhoid, acute respiratory infections, and painful skin conditions." The flooding is estimated to have caused $15 billion in damages, in a poor country, making it one of the costliest disasters ever to befall a population.[34]

Like the British wildfires, the flooding in Pakistan was not a freakish "act of God" but an expected result of climate change. The monsoons are intensifying because of moisture in the atmosphere, and rising temperatures are also melting Pakistan's thousands of glaciers, further swelling rivers and exacerbating the problem.[35]

This, of course, is only the beginning.

The scientific literature on the climate crisis is harrowing. It shows that we are careering toward disaster, and that early warnings were too conservative. In November 2019, a group of more than 11,000 scientists from 153 countries issued a public warning that Earth is facing a "climate emergency." They showed that many of our "planetary vital signs" (temperatures, sea level, ice mass, rainforest loss rate, biodiversity loss, etc.) are reaching critical levels. If the Earth was an individual, it would be one in immediate need of emergency care for multiple deadly ailments.[36]

Dire warnings from climate scientists abound. "Things are getting worse," says Petteri Taalas, secretary-general of the World Meteorological Organization. "The only solution is to get rid of fossil fuels in power production, industry and transportation." Susan Joy Hassol, director of Climate Communication, said, "I haven't ever seen a time when we've broken so many records all at the same time," pointing to "smashed records in temperature, sea ice loss, and wildfire" in 2023. Raymond Pierrehumbert, professor of physics at Oxford and lead author of the Third Assessment Report from the IPCC (Intergovernmental Panel on Climate Change), says that "we are in deep trouble" and "it's time to panic." We must move to net zero carbon emissions quickly because "there is no plan B." UN secretary-general António Guterres did not overstate matters when he said in November 2022 that "we are on a highway to climate hell with our foot still on the accelerator." Israeli climatologist Baruch Rinkevich says that people "don't fully understand what we're talking about," noting that "everything is expected to change: the air we breathe, the food we eat, the water we drink, the landscapes we see, the oceans, the seasons, the daily routine, the quality of life." He concludes, sadly, "I'm happy I won't be alive."[37]

The plausible scenarios involve suffering on an unimaginable scale. Half of the species on Earth may be wiped out as their environment changes in ways they cannot adapt to. The damage already done to animal populations has been horrifying enough. A billion or more people may be displaced from their home region, a series of refugee crises many times greater than the Pakistan flood catastrophe. Lethal temperatures could make much of the world unfit for life. (Beetles and bacteria might do all right.)[38]

Atmospheric CO_2 is now at levels last seen millions of years ago, when global sea levels were twenty meters higher than today. Jeremy Lent, summarizing the World Scientists' Warning to Humanity, notes that "whether it's CO_2 emissions, temperature change, ocean dead zones, freshwater resources, vertebrate species, or total forest cover, the grim charts virtually all point in the same dismal direction, indicating continued momentum toward doomsday." Twelve researchers writing in *BioScience* warned frankly that life on Earth is "under siege" and "time is up," with "an alarming and unprecedented succession of climate records" being broken. "The truth is that we are shocked by the ferocity of the extreme weather events in 2023."[39]

Nevertheless, they conclude with a call to action rather than despair: "this is our moment to make a profound difference for all life on Earth, and we must embrace it with unwavering courage and determination to create a legacy of change that will stand the test of time." Says lead author William Ripple, "Our situation is not hopeless." But we have no time to waste.

The climate crisis is man-made, but responsibility does not fall equally on everyone. The rich countries, especially the United States, are substantially more to blame for the problem than many of the victims. Our policy choices have imposed a dire cost on others. The thirty-three million Pakistanis displaced by flooding suffer from the effects of the crisis, but they did almost nothing to cause it. Pakistan has produced only 0.4 percent of the greenhouse gas emissions that have created this threat.

To clearly understand responsibility for the problem, it is only necessary to look at comparative emissions totals. By 2020, the 230 million residents of Pakistan were responsible for only 5 billion tons of carbon emissions, while the 330 million residents of the United States had produced over 400 billion tons. The majority of total carbon emissions have been from Western countries, with the contributions from the U.S. and Europe dwarfing the responsibility of China and India. Citizens of those countries live far less carbon-intensive lifestyles than do their counterparts in the U.S. As anthropologist Jason Hickel notes, the countries of the Global North are responsible for 92 percent of all the emissions that exceed the boundaries of planetary sustainability, while the majority of the Global South remains "well within their fair share of the boundary," meaning they have "not contributed to the crisis at all." Still, these are the countries that will suffer the most, including "82–92 percent of the economic costs of climate breakdown, and 98–99 percent of climate-related deaths." Hickel concludes that it "would be difficult to overstate the scale of this injustice.[40]

It is also the case that not all residents of a country contribute equally to the crisis. The top 1 percent of income earners in the world generate 16 percent of the global carbon, and the top 10 percent of income earners generate about half of the total. Economist Solomon Hsiang notes that the effects of climate change are poised to further increase inequality, because warming does not have the same negative impacts everywhere. Hotter countries near the equator, where global heating will have the most catastrophic effects, already tend to be poorer, while some wealthier cold places "often benefit, since warming can actually improve human health and economic productivity." Thus the destructive behavior of the wealthy will wreck the lives of the poor, delivering consequences that many of the perpetrators are comparatively insulated from.[41]

In other contexts, we often apply terms like "theft," "arson," even "murder" to describe deliberate actions by one party that destroy the lives and property of another. The term "carbon colonialism" has been coined to describe the way in which Western countries have improved their standards of living through burning fossil fuels, with the benefits accruing to the global 1 percent and the catastrophic costs falling on everybody else.[42]

The encouraging thing is that the outlines of a solution are known, because the causes of the problem are understood. Three quarters of greenhouse gas emissions are caused by fossil fuel use, so preventing catastrophic heating requires the elimination of fossil fuels. This is why a growing list of scientists, civil society organizations, and governments have endorsed the Fossil Fuel Non-Proliferation Treaty initiative, which has proposed an international treaty for the phasing out of existing fossil fuel production and a global transition to renewable energy sources that would meet the demands of justice. The United States, however, has shown no interest in signing on to the treaty and moving it forward.[43]

In the United States, we have a clear domestic plan for the transition to renewable energy. The Green New Deal (GND) resolution introduced by Representatives Alexandria Ocasio-Cortez and Ed Markey lays out a basic framework for government action to keep the U.S. to its emission-reduction targets, while creating well-paying jobs. There is solid research explaining how it could work and how it could be funded. Economist Robert Pollin, who has done extensive work on the practical requirements, explains that the GND's goals are not implausible or pie in the sky, but in fact quite workable. Pollin notes that it is an "entirely reasonable and not an especially difficult proposition to build a zero-emissions U.S. economy by 2050." Nor does the GND end up being a net loss for society. In fact, it would be a net gain. *Not* to pursue the GND, when faced with the urgency of the catastrophe, is therefore indefensible.[44]

Of course, the GND only addresses the domestic component. But because the United States has among the worst per-capita emissions in the world, adopting the GND could demonstrate its willingness to rein in its destructive behavior and be willing to work constructively with the rest of the world on fair solutions. Instead, however, U.S. politicians have consistently placed the interests of the domestic fossil fuel industry over the future of humanity.

In the United States, the major institutions of society seem determined to make the problem worse. The Republican Party in particular is openly committed to blocking any meaningful climate action. Donald Trump, who has insisted climate change is a hoax conjured up by the Chinese, called for rapidly increasing fossil fuel use. In office, he shredded environmental regulations. The Trump administration's 2018 review of fuel-efficiency standards argued that because global warming would worsen regardless of U.S. efforts, there was no need for fuel efficiency to reduce carbon output. Trump attempted to make sure federal agencies would, as *The New York Times* reported, "no longer have to take climate change into account when they assess the environmental impacts of highways, pipelines and other major infrastructure projects."[45]

The Republican leadership has been frank about its intention to undermine the global Paris Agreement, the main existing international agreement to limit carbon emissions, adopted in 2015. One reason, which they hardly conceal, is that the Republicans wanted to smash anything done by the hated Obama. Another reason is the principled opposition to any external constraints on U.S. power. But the decision also follows directly from the party leadership's uniform rejection of any efforts to confront the looming environmental crisis—a stand traceable in large part to the historic service of the party to private wealth and corporate power.

In GOP-run states, there is even an effort to punish banks that seek to address the climate crisis. Republicans are introducing "Energy Discrimination Elimination" legislation to ban the release of information on investment in fossil fuel companies. Republican attorneys have called on the Federal Energy Regulatory Commission to keep asset managers from purchasing shares in U.S. utility companies if the companies are involved in programs to reduce emissions—that is, to save us all from destruction.[46]

The Democratic Party, despite rhetoric about the importance of climate change, has not been much better at taking the action necessary to avoid catastrophe. In a campaign speech in 2008, Barack Obama said that future generations would tell their children that "this was the moment when the rise of the oceans began to slow and our planet began to heal." But in office Obama acted much as his predecessor had, sabotaging global climate talks and escalating fossil fuel production. After the 2009 Copenhagen climate summit, which failed in large part due to the U.S.'s unwillingness to propose an acceptable deal, *Vanity Fair* observed that "the Obama administration's refusal to offer more than 4 percent emissions cuts by 2020 was seen by many other countries, rich and poor alike, as evidence that the U.S. under Obama was not that different than it had been under George W. Bush." *Forbes* commented on the "irony" that George W. Bush, "widely viewed as a Texas oil man, presided over eight straight years of declining U.S. crude oil production," while Obama, "who is not viewed as a friend of the oil and gas industry . . . has presided over rising oil production in each of the seven years he has been in office." Obama was proud of his destructive record, boasting in 2012 that "under my administration, America is producing more oil today than any time in the last eight years. . . . We are drilling all over the place."[47]

Far from embracing the GND, Democratic leaders disparaged it. "The green dream, or whatever they call it," scoffed Nancy Pelosi. California senator Dianne Feinstein waved away activists by falsely claiming that "there's no way to pay for it" and pointing out that many of the bill's teenage supporters could not vote.[48]

Of course, the big business lobbies are even worse. The Chamber of Commerce, American Petroleum Institute, and others have long been carrying out a massive publicity campaign to convince Americans that climate change is a hoax. The fossil fuel industry has been engaged in a decades-long campaign of sowing doubt, trying to ensure nothing whatsoever is done to prevent the catastrophe. ExxonMobil's chief lobbyist was caught on tape not only admitting that the company had funded efforts to discredit the science, but that they pushed policies (like a carbon tax) that they knew would never be adopted, in order to further stymie any efforts at dealing with the problem. The lobbyist said that while Exxon did indeed "fight aggressively against some of the science" and join "shadow groups to work against some of the early efforts [to address climate change]," there was "nothing illegal about that," and "we were looking out for our investments, we were looking out for our shareholders." In other words, the structure of a capitalist enterprise, which pursues profit even at the expense of a livable planet, is to blame. Sadly, corporate power is so great that within our current institutional framework we have to bribe those who are destroying the environment if we want them to desist. This is nothing new. As the United States was mobilizing for war eighty years ago, Secretary of War Henry Stimson explained: "If you are going to try to go to war, or to prepare for war, in a capitalist country, you have got to let business make money out of the process or business won't work." If something is in the public's interest, but not in the interests of the corporate sector, they will fight to prevent the problem from being solved.[49]

The industry's effort to protect its profits at the expense of the species' future has been effective. The Paris Agreement does not mention fossil fuels, and fossil fuel lobbyists are permitted to crawl all over the UN's climate summits, ensuring that the resulting agreements do nothing to threaten the bottom lines of major corporations. Things have devolved to the point where 2023's UN COP28* climate conference was chaired by a fossil fuel executive, who used his position to lobby for new oil and gas projects. (Biden climate envoy John Kerry called the selection a "terrific choice.") Climate scientist Peter Kalmus wrote despairingly that the UN process had become a "sick joke," as over one thousand fossil fuel lobbyists flooded the conference to ensure that the necessary steps to protect humanity's future could not be taken. Kalmus said he was "almost at a loss of finding words to adequately describe the corruption and the evil at COP28."[50]

Even as the leading scientific bodies make clear that catastrophe is looming unless we begin immediately to reduce fossil fuel use, phasing it out by midcentury, the move to increase oil production is still discussed as if it were rational rather than suicidal. Petroleum industry journals are euphoric about the discovery of new fields to exploit. The business press debates whether the U.S. fracking industry or OPEC is best placed to increase production. In *The Wall Street Journal*, we read that "South America has long been the world's sleeping energy giant, with massive oil-and-gas reserves still untapped," but "now it is rumbling awake, with huge implications for the global market." The article mentions climate change exactly once, pointing out that the UN climate conference committed countries "to transition[ing] away from fossil fuels but essentially allowed governments to choose their own paths to get there," then notes that "the recent activity in South America indicates countries in this region don't intend to dial back soon." The consequences of refusing to "dial back soon" go entirely unmentioned. Meanwhile, in the United States, both oil and natural gas production reached an all-time high in 2023 and "show no indications of slowing."[51] In Biden's first twenty-one months in office, the U.S. both produced more crude oil than under Trump and approved 74 percent more oil and gas wells than Trump did during the same time period.[52]

---

*COP stands for Conference of the Parties of the United Nations Framework Convention on Climate Change.

The New York Times observes that while Biden campaigned on addressing climate change, as president he "has taken a much different tack," to the point where he has "hectored oil companies to increase production." Biden decided to skip the COP28 summit, sending the vice president instead, in a "significant snub by a president who has vowed to fight global warming." Even Biden's signature piece of "climate" legislation, the Inflation Reduction Act, was a "boon for [the] fossil-fuel sector." To "contain" the "threat" of China, by "breaking Chinese dominance of the batteries and critical minerals needed to fuel the transition," Biden jeopardized electric vehicle production by reducing the number of cars that qualify for subsidies, "disqualify[ing] a vehicle from receiving the credit if even one of its suppliers has loose ties to Beijing."[53]

Some Democratic groups have even encouraged Biden to brag about the increased oil production, touting it as a "moderate" policy achievement. As climate scientist Bill Hare told the Associated Press, this continued expansion of fossil fuel production is "hypocritical and not at all consistent with the global call to phase down fossil fuels." Peter Kalmus says he is losing his faith in humanity when he sees the continuation of an obviously disastrous course, even though the knowledge and capacity are available. As a climate scientist, he says, "I'm terrified by what's coming down the pipe," and given our current trajectory, "huge amounts of the Earth will become uninhabitable." Kalmus says he believed that at this frightening level of heating, with disaster so obvious, "everyone would wake up and realize that none of our hopes and dreams will come to fruition if we don't have a habitable planet." But the hoped-for mass awakening has yet to occur.[54]

American media coverage of the climate catastrophe has been almost universally abysmal. In the financial industry's paper of record, *The Wall Street Journal*, one can find an endless parade of denialist propaganda on the opinion pages, with headlines like CLIMATE CHANGE ISN'T

THE END OF THE WORLD; CLIMATE SCIENCE IS NOT SETTLED; CLIMATE CHANGE DOESN'T CAUSE ALL DISASTERS; CLIMATE CHANGE BARELY AFFECTS POVERTY; FOSSIL FUELS WILL SAVE THE WORLD (REALLY); EVEN WITH CLIMATE CHANGE, THE WORLD ISN'T DOOMED; CLIMATE CHANGE SAVES MORE LIVES THAN YOU'D THINK; CLIMATE CHANGE IS AFFORDABLE; and WE'RE SAFER FROM CLIMATE DISASTERS THAN EVER BEFORE.

But even in the liberal *New York Times*, climate change coverage has been poor. Not only does the *Times* run fossil fuel ads, publish "sponsored" articles written by the fossil fuel industry, and even *make* ads for the fossil fuel industry through its in-house advertising firm, but a comprehensive study by Berkeley researchers shows that few of the paper's climate articles made mention of the most basic salient facts about the situation: that warming is happening now, that it is caused by record levels of CO_2, that burning fossil fuels has caused these record levels, that there is a scientific consensus about this, and that warming is permanent.[55]

Sometimes, *Times* stories about warming-induced disasters exclude all mention of the role of fossil fuels. For instance, in its coverage of Colorado's extreme wildfires during the winter of 2022, the *Times* mentioned that "a severe multiyear drought nurtured the brittle-dry conditions that allowed the fire to sweep through residential areas," but did not mention that our burning of fossil fuels is *causing* such extreme drought and worsening wildfires. Yet fire scientist Jennifer Balch, director of the Earth Lab at the University of Colorado Boulder, was unequivocal when discussing the Colorado fires: "I want to be crystal clear about this. Climate change is playing a role in this disaster—absolutely."[56]

The tragedy of the climate crisis is that if it had been dealt with back when it first came to public attention in the 1980s, it needn't have been a calamity threatening the future of the species. Instead, with both U.S. political parties entirely subservient to industry interests, and a concerted campaign of denial and doubt-sowing, a serious problem turned into an existential crisis that will cause untold suffering for billions of people around the globe. It is a horrendous injustice, in which the wealthiest people in the wealthiest countries inflict misery on the poorest people due to an unwillingness to take the basic measures to ensure civilization can sustain itself.

The IPCC's 2023 report was by far the most dire warning it has yet produced. The report made clear that we must take firm measures now, with no delay, to cut back the use of fossil fuels and to move toward renewable energy. The warnings received brief notice, and then our strange species returned to devoting our scarce resources to the pursuit of our own destruction.[57]

But the game is not over. There is still time for radical course correction. The means are understood. If the will is there, it is possible to avert catastrophe. Here, too, however, popular mobilization is essential. We need people who take responsibility for safeguarding the welfare of future generations. To adopt the phrases used by indigenous people throughout the world: Who will defend the Earth? Who will uphold the rights of nature? Who will adopt the role of steward of the commons, our collective possession?

PART 2

Understanding the Power System

Between a monarchy and the most democratic republic there is only one essential difference: in the former, the world of officialdom oppresses and robs the people for the greater profit of the privileged and propertied classes, as well as to line its own pockets, in the name of the monarch; in the latter, it oppresses and robs the people in exactly the same way, for the benefit of the same classes and the same pockets, but in the name of the people's will. In a republic, a fictitious people, the "legal nation" supposedly represented by the state, smothers the real, live people. But it will scarcely be any easier on the people if the stick with which they are being beaten is labeled "the people's stick."

—MIKHAIL BAKUNIN

9

The Domestic Roots
of Foreign Policy

If we hope to understand anything about the foreign policy of any state, it is a good idea to begin by investigating the domestic social structure. Who sets foreign policy? What interests do these people represent? What is the domestic source of their power? It is a reasonable surmise that the policies will reflect the special interests of those who design them. Countries have internal power structures, with some groups having vastly more power than others. And in this country, as leading international relations theorist Hans Morgenthau once observed, "the concentrations of private power which have actually governed America since the Civil War have withstood all attempts to control, let alone dissolve them [and] have preserved their hold upon the levers of political decision."[1]

The broad American public has little influence over U.S. foreign policy. In fact, the divergence between public opinion and state action is frequently sharp. For instance, a large majority of Americans have long opposed U.S. government policy on Israel, support the international consensus on a two-state settlement, think the U.S. should stay neutral in the conflict, and think that the United States should deny aid to both of the contending parties—Israel and the Palestinians—if they do not negotiate in good faith toward this settlement. The U.S. government simply defies public opinion.[2]

Plenty of similar examples can be offered. In 1984, the American public was polled on whether they supported Ronald Reagan's decision to mine Nicaragua's harbors. By a staggering 67 percent to 13 percent, respondents disapproved. In 2001, of Americans who had heard of global warming, 88 percent supported the Kyoto Protocol. The Bush administration rejected it. Two-thirds of the U.S. population is opposed to the embargo against Cuba, including 59 percent of Republicans. The embargo remains in place. Government spying programs are disapproved of by the public. In 2023, a poll showed that only "28% of adults support the government listening to phone calls made outside of the U.S. without a warrant." Nevertheless, the practice is routine and legal. In December 2023, at a time when the overwhelming majority of Americans wanted a permanent ceasefire between Israel and Hamas, the president, and almost all of Congress, refused to call for one.[3]

Here, we're assuming the policy options are actually known to the public. But frequently, the public is simply kept in the dark about what the government is doing and is therefore incapable of having any opinion at all. In cases like the ravaging of East Timor, the bombings of Cambodia and Laos, or the drone assassinations around the world, the public had no idea what was done in its name. The policies are not subject to public discussion, let alone put to a vote. "The people aren't asked or told—they're ignored," says economist Jeffrey Sachs.[4]

"The public is lied to—lied to about the situation on the battlefield, lied to about the real reason for going to war, and so forth," says international relations scholar John Mearsheimer. Summarizing an extensive study of how policy is made, Mearsheimer says, "what we discovered is that public opinion . . . matters hardly at all in the decision-making process. A small number of elites get together and they make the decisions." This is as true of democracies as autocracies. (In fact, Mearsheimer says the leaders in democracies lie to the public far more often than leaders in autocratic countries, because the public has a mechanism of expelling the leaders and thus must be manipulated more.)[5]

Typical is the example of Robert McNamara, who confessed to his aides on a flight home from Vietnam that despite pouring troops into the country, "there's been no improvement," meaning the "underlying situation is really worse." Upon getting off the plane, McNamara told assembled journalists exactly the opposite: "Gentlemen . . . I've just come back from Vietnam, and I'm glad to be able to tell you that we're showing great progress in every dimension of our effort. I'm very encouraged by everything I've seen and heard on my trip."[6]

In *The Foreign Policy Disconnect*, Benjamin Page and Marshall Bouton documented the way that "year after year, decade after decade, there have been many large gaps between the foreign policies favored by officials and those favored by the public." For example, the public generally prefers cooperative, peaceable foreign policies, including strengthening the UN, expanding arms control, accepting the World Court's jurisdiction, giving up the U.S. power to veto otherwise unanimous Security Council decisions, and dealing with countries using diplomacy rather than force. They note that U.S. repudiation of international agreements has repeatedly "flown in the face of the public's wishes."[7]

The persistence of these beliefs is especially remarkable when we consider how much effort is put into *manipulating* public opinion. The American public was generally supportive of the Bush administration's attack on Iraq, but *only* because they believed the president's falsehoods about the threat Iraq posed to the United States. Then, when they discovered the truth and turned against it, they were seen as a nuisance, to be ignored. In fact, Dick Cheney was open about the Bush administration's contempt for public opinion:[8]

MARTHA RADDATZ, ABC: Two thirds of Americans say [the Iraq War is] not worth fighting.

DICK CHENEY: So?

RADDATZ: So? You don't care what the American people think?

CHENEY: No. I think you cannot be blown off course by the fluctuations in the public opinion polls.[9]

When presidents do not feel that the public would support their policies, the public is simply kept in the dark. The history of the CIA is a litany of atrocities that have seldom been subjected to public debate. The agency's MK-ULTRA project involved experiments in mind control and torture that journalist Stephen Kinzer explains were "essentially a continuation of work that began in Japanese and Nazi concentration camps." The CIA "actually hired the vivisectionists and the torturers who had worked in Japan and in Nazi concentration camps to come and explain what they had found out so that we could build on their research." The United States has tested biological weapons on its own people without their knowledge, including a 1966 experiment that released clouds of bacteria onto New York subway passengers. Over a decade of bio-weapons tests, the Pentagon "exposed troops and perhaps thousands of civilians to the compounds," releasing "substances [that] included E. coli and other agents that were later found to be harmful or fatal to young children, the elderly and those with compromised immune systems." The history of the FBI is its own sordid story, including attempting to blackmail the nation's most prominent civil rights leader into killing himself.[10]

Documentary evidence of this kind of activity is long kept secret on grounds of "national security," usually remaining classified until the point when nobody will care much once it is released. When eventually declassified, it becomes clear there was never any "threat to national security" from its being revealed. The threat was that the public might assume it lived in a democracy and want to change the agency's conduct. Henry Kissinger made this explicit in 1983 when he explained his support for secret operations against the Nicaraguan government: "I am sympathetic to the covert operations if we can still conduct them the way their name implies. But if covert operations have to be justified in a public debate, they stop being covert and we will wind up losing public support." If the public were allowed to know its own government's policy, it would not support the policy. This is taken as a reason for keeping the policy secret rather than a reason for ending it.[11]

Why is there so little correlation between the public's preferences and actual policy?

It's not complicated. In highly unequal countries, the public's role in decision-making is limited. In the United States, as elsewhere, foreign policy is designed and implemented by small groups who derive their power from domestic sources. A study in the *American Political Science Review* found that "U.S. foreign policy is most heavily and consistently influenced by internationally oriented business leaders," while "public opinion" has "little or no significant effect on government officials." Top advisory and decision-making positions relating to international affairs are heavily concentrated in the hands of representatives of major corporations, banks, investment firms, the few law firms that cater to corporate interests, and the technocratic and policy-oriented intellectuals who do the bidding of those who own and manage the private empires that govern most aspects of our lives, with little pretense of public accountability and not even a gesture to democratic control.[12]

The problem is not new. Adam Smith describes, in his day, the "merchants and manufacturers" as "an order of men, whose interest is never exactly the same with that of the public, who have generally an interest to deceive and even to oppress the public, and who accordingly have, upon many occasions, both deceived and oppressed it." He said they make sure to design policy so that their own interests are served, however grievous the impact on others, including on the general population.

Concentration of wealth yields concentration of power, particularly as the cost of elections skyrockets, which forces political parties even more deeply into the pockets of major corporations. This political power quickly translates into legislation that increases the concentration of wealth. So fiscal policies like tax policy, deregulation, rules of corporate governance—all political measures designed to increase the concentration of wealth and power—yield more political power to do the same thing.

In his book *Golden Rule*, political scientist Thomas Ferguson argues that where the major investors in political parties and elections agree on an issue, the parties will not compete on that issue, no matter how strongly the public might want an alternative. He contends that for ordinary voters to influence electoral choices they would have to have "strong channels that directly facilitate mass deliberation and expression." These would include unions and other intermediate organizations that might, through their collective power, cause the interests of ordinary voters to be given greater weight in the political system.[13]

For example, polls regularly indicate that, except in periods of war and intense war propaganda, the public wants a smaller defense budget and favors a spending shift from defense to education and other civil functions. But because the major investors agree that a large defense budget is desirable, the two dominant parties compete only on whether one or the other is stinting on military expenditures, with both promising to enlarge the amount. And the mainstream media do the same, limiting debate to the terms defined by the two parties and excluding discussion of the desirability of large cuts. The U.S. corporate community has favored an immense defense budget because of the great benefits its members derive from military spending through weapons contracting and subsidies to research.[14]

Even within the narrow range of issues that are submitted in principle to democratic decision-making, the centers of private power exert an inordinately heavy influence in obvious ways, through control of the media and political organizations and by putting forward the people who ultimately get elected. Things have not changed much since Richard Barnet's 1969 study of the top four hundred decision-makers in the postwar national security system, which found that most "have come from executive suites and law offices within shouting distance of one another in fifteen city blocks in New York, Washington, Detroit, Chicago, and Boston."[15]

As philosopher John Dewey put it, "Politics is the shadow cast on society by big business" (adding that "attenuation of the shadow will not change the substance"). The business world has tight organizations, ample resources, and a high level of class consciousness. Its members see themselves as fighting a bitter class war, and have done so for a long time. Business has long understood that what it calls the "public mind" is "the only serious danger confronting the company," as an AT&T executive once put it. Political decisions are made by a very small sector of extreme privilege and wealth. The opinions of most of the population simply don't matter in the political system. They are essentially disenfranchised. Shifting coalitions of investors account for a large part of political history. There is little role for unions or other civic organizations that might offer a way for the general public to play some role in influencing programs and policy choices.[16]

In the United States now, there is essentially one political party, the business party, with two factions. The Republican Party is totally dedicated to serving private power, private wealth, and corporate power, having long ago abandoned any pretense of being a normal parliamentary party. Norman Ornstein of the American Enterprise Institute and Thomas E. Mann of the Brookings Institution describes today's Republicans as "a radical insurgency—ideologically extreme, scornful of facts and compromise, dismissive of the legitimacy of its political opposition"— a serious danger to society. The party marches in lockstep with the very rich and the corporate sector. Because votes cannot be obtained on the platform of helping the rich get richer, the party uses its extremist positions on "cultural" issues as a battering ram in the neoliberal assault on the population. Its core agenda is still to privatize, to deregulate, and to limit government, while retaining those parts that serve wealth and power, like the military. On the other side, the Democrats have essentially abandoned whatever commitment they had to working people and the poor, becoming a party of affluent professionals and Wall Street donors.[17]

One of the great achievements of the doctrinal system has been to divert anger from the corporate sector to the government that implements the programs the corporate sector designs, such as the highly protectionist corporate/investor rights agreements that are uniformly misdescribed as "free trade agreements" in the media and commentary. With all its flaws, the government is, to some extent, under popular influence and control, unlike the corporate sector. It is highly advantageous for the business world to foster hatred for pointy-headed government bureaucrats and to drive out of people's minds the subversive idea that the government might become an instrument of popular will, a government of, by, and for the people.[18]

The result is that even more decision-making power is placed in the hands of the unaccountable private tyrannies that comprise the corporate world. That is the goal of the current efforts to weaken those elements of the national government that serve public needs, while expanding those that serve business power, notably the Pentagon system, which was designed in large measure as a device to transfer public funds to advanced sectors of industry under the guise of "security," and continues to serve that function.

In our own time, corporations and financial institutions generally set policy, no matter how grievous the impact on others, including the U.S. population. This is not to say that there are not other influences at work, such as nationalism and even machismo. The essential point is that those in power do not care about U.S. "security." Foreign policy and domestic policy are only driven by a search for "security" in a very special sense: security for those groups who comprise Adam Smith's "masters of mankind," those who own the society and are the principal architects of policy.

Throughout U.S. history, many have justified limiting the role of the public in decision-making. This goes back to the founding generation.

John Jay famously said that "those who own the country ought to govern it." James Madison was as much of a believer in democracy as anybody in the world at that time. Still, he felt that the United States system should be designed so that power was in the hands of the wealthy, because they were the responsible men. Decisions should be delegated to "the wealth of the nation," "the more capable set of men," who understand that the role of government is "to protect the minority of the opulent against the majority." Madison had faith that the "enlightened Statesman" and "benevolent philosopher" who were to exercise power would "discern the true interest of their country" and guard the public interest against the "mischief" of democratic majorities. He worried that if everyone had a free vote, the poor would get together and take away the property of the rich. "The mass of people . . . seldom judge or determine right," as Alexander Hamilton put it during the framing of the Constitution, expressing a common elite view.

The fears expressed by the "men of best quality" in the founding generation have never subsided. They were expressed by the influential moralist and foreign affairs adviser Reinhold Niebuhr. He wrote that "rationality belongs to the cool observers," while the common person follows not reason but faith. The cool observers, he explained, must recognize "the stupidity of the average man" and must provide the "necessary illusion" and the "emotionally potent oversimplifications" that will keep the naïve simpletons on course. It remains crucial to protect the "lunatic or distracted person," the ignorant rabble, from their own "depraved and corrupt" judgments, just as one does not allow a child to cross the street without supervision.[19]

On this theory, there is no infringement of democracy if a few corporations control the information system: in fact, that is the essence of democracy. The leading figure of the public relations industry, Edward Bernays, explained that "the very essence of the democratic process" is "the freedom to persuade and suggest"—what he calls "the engineering of consent." Bernays expressed the basic point in 1928, when he said that the "conscious and intelligent manipulation of the organized habits and opinions of the masses is an important element in democratic society." He said that "intelligent minorities . . . need to make use of propaganda continuously and systematically."[20]

The "intelligent minorities" have long understood this to be their function. As explained by William Shepard in his presidential address to the American Political Science Association in 1934, government should be in the hands of "an aristocracy of intellect and power," not directed by "the ignorant, the uninformed, and the anti-social element." In *The Encyclopedia of the Social Sciences* in 1933, leading political scientist Harold Lasswell explained that we must not succumb to "democratic dogmatisms about men being the best judges of their own interests." We must find ways to ensure that they endorse the decisions made by their farsighted leaders.

Walter Lippmann described a process he called "the manufacture of consent." There are two classes—those who make the decisions and the public. The former are the "men of best quality," who alone are capable of social and economic management. They are the "insiders," who have access to information and understanding and are able to take the responsibility for "the formation of a sound public opinion." This specialized class should be protected from "ignorant and meddlesome outsiders," i.e., the general public, so they can effectively serve what is called "the national interest."

What Lippmann defines as "the task of the public" is much more limited. It is not for the public, Lippmann observes, to "pass judgment on the intrinsic merits" of an issue or to offer analysis or solutions. "The public must be put in its place," he writes, so that we may "live free of the trampling and the roar of a bewildered herd," whose "function" is to be "interested spectators of action," not participants. Participation remains the purview of "the responsible men."[21]

When the "bewildered herd" attempt to be more than spectators and take part in democratic action, the specialized class reacts with panic. That is why there is so much hatred among elites for the 1960s, when groups of people who had historically been excluded began to organize and take issue with the policies of the specialized class, particularly the war in Vietnam but also social policy at home. In 1975, the Trilateral Commission published a revealing report called *The Crisis of Democracy*. In it, Samuel Huntington, the head of the Government Department at Harvard, spelled out the problem plainly: the United States was becoming too democratic. He explained that the country was suffering from "an excess of democracy." Previously marginalized groups had forgotten that their proper function was to be spectators: "The effective operation of a democratic political system usually requires some measure of apathy and non-involvement on the part of some individuals and groups."[22]

Huntington wrote that because groups like "the blacks" were overloading the system with their "demands," it was time to consider "potentially desirable limits to the indefinite extension of political democracy." Matters are rarely stated this plainly, but the attitude is common: it doesn't matter what the public thinks. They are not the ones who should set foreign policy. They should demonstrate "apathy and non-involvement." The attitude that the rabble need to be kept away from important decisions persists. A *Wall Street Journal* contributor explains that "democracy works well only when it is enabled and fortified by a great many institutions that are not in themselves democratic—or that at least aren't supposed to be democratic."[23]

We know that foreign policy would look much different in an authentically democratic society. But concentrated power centers pursue their agenda relentlessly, using every opportunity to press their plans forward, and in the harshest possible way. In particular, they use crises, whether earthquakes, or wars, or September 11 and its aftermath, to exploit the atmosphere of fear and anguish. They hope that their popular adversary will be distracted, and frightened, while they continue to push their programs without pause.

Never has a population so safe ever been so terrified of external threats. In fact, if we look at history, we find regular echoes of Senator Arthur Vandenberg's 1947 advice to the president that he should "scare

[the] hell out of the American people" about the Soviet Union. Dean Acheson, one of the creators of the postwar order, praised the NSC-68 of 1950, a founding document of the Cold War, which called for a huge military buildup and an imposition of discipline on our dangerously free society so that we could defend ourselves from the "slave state" that wants "total power over all men [and] absolute authority over the rest of the world." When Richard Nixon met Fidel Castro, he reported that Castro cautioned him about a "very disturbing attitude on the part of the American press and the American people generally." This country, he said, "should be proud and confident and happy. But everyplace I go you seem to be afraid—afraid of Communism, afraid that if Cuba has land reform it will grow a little rice and the market for your rice will be reduced—afraid that if Latin America becomes more industrialized American factories will not be able to sell as much abroad as they have previously." Nixon concluded that Castro was simply "incredibly naïve about Communism."[24]

On the domestic front, the Cold War was convenient for both Soviet and U.S. leaders. It helped the military-bureaucratic ruling class of the Soviet Union entrench itself in power, and it gave the United States a way to compel its population to subsidize high-tech industry. The technique used was the old standby, the fear of a great enemy. This does not mean that the "Evil Empire" was benign; it was an empire, and it was brutal. But each superpower controlled its primary enemy—its own population—by terrifying it with the (quite real) crimes of the other. In crucial respects, then, the Cold War was a kind of tacit arrangement between the Soviet Union and the United States under which the U.S. conducted its wars against the Third World and controlled its allies in Europe, while the Soviet rulers kept an iron grip on their own internal empire and their satellites in Eastern Europe—each side using the other to justify repression and violence in its own domains.

This kind of fearmongering persists, with a revolving cast of enemies, both foreign and domestic, used to frighten the population into accepting state policies that ultimately harm us. Fear of terrifying enemies about to crush us is a constant theme in American culture, from the "merciless Indian savages" spoken of by the Declaration of Independence to today's fear of migrants, China, or "cultural Marxism." Yet the main serious threats the United States faces are those of its own making, i.e., the climate and nuclear perils.[25]

Nobody has taken Vandenberg's lesson to heart more than Donald Trump, for whom "scaring the hell out of the American people" (about antifa, Iran, leftist "vermin," etc.) is indispensable to maintaining power. Meanwhile, Trump's actual agenda involves pouring taxpayer funds into the pockets of the fossil fuel producers so that they can continue to destroy the world as quickly as possible. Trump has shown political genius in tapping the poisonous currents that run right below the surface of American society. He has skillfully nourished the white supremacy, racism, and xenophobia that have deep roots in American history and culture, now exacerbated by fear that "they" will take over "our" country with its shrinking white majority. The fearmongering is working. A George Washington University study reveals that Republicans feel that "the traditional American way of life is disappearing so fast that we may have to use force to save it," and more than 40 percent agree that "a time will come when patriotic Americans have to take the law into their own hands."[26]

Much of the general population recognizes that the organized institutions do not reflect their concerns and interests and needs. They do not feel that they participate meaningfully in the political system. They do not feel that the media are telling them the truth, or even reflect their concerns. The political system increasingly functions without public input, and the public assumes that the decisions are going on independently of what they may do in the polling booth. They do not even get to *ratify* the decisions presented. Ratification would be a very weak form of democracy in which voters are asked to pass judgment on a policy that has already been decided. A really meaningful democracy would give the public the lead role in *forming* those decisions, in creating those positions, reflecting everyone's active participation and deliberation.

From what we know of public preferences, we could expect a radically different set of policies, foreign and domestic, if authentic democracy existed in the United States.

Despite the popular interest in peace, the United States spends more on the military than most other peer nations combined. With this monstrous military budget, we not only endanger the world but severely harm ourselves, wasting enormous resources that could do much to deal with the crises we face. In an important speech in 1953, Dwight Eisenhower explained that military expenditures were a theft from society: "Every gun that is made, every warship launched, every rocket fired signifies, in the final sense, a theft from those who hunger and are not fed, those who are cold and are not clothed." Military spending could pay for hospitals, schools, and homes. Eisenhower lamented the waste of "the sweat of [our] laborers, the genius of [our] scientists, the hopes of [our] children," pointing out that "we pay for a single destroyer with new homes that could have housed more than eight thousand people." Eisenhower even proposed that to avoid the socially self-destructive endless expansion of the armed forces, "there should be a limitation, by absolute numbers or by an agreed international ratio, [on] the sizes of the military and security forces of all nations."[27]

In 2023, Joe Biden proposed a huge military budget. Congress expanded it beyond even Biden's wishes. As Eisenhower explained so many years ago, this should properly be understood as a major attack on society, an act of theft. Instead it is called "national security." But the security of the population is simply not a concern for policymakers. Security for the rich, the corporate sector, and arms manufacturers: yes. But not for the rest of us.[28]

International Law and
the "Rules-Based Order"

The 1989 United States invasion of Panama is not well remembered
domestically, though it is remembered in Panama, where a national holiday commemorates the lives of the victims. Hundreds of
Panamanian civilians were killed during the operation, which was the
largest U.S. combat operation since the invasion of Vietnam. The invasion "saw the impoverished Panama City neighborhood of El Chorillo
pulverized to the point of being referred to by ambulance drivers as
"Little Hiroshima." TV networks and newspapers in the United States
gave almost no coverage to Panamanian deaths, instead focusing almost exclusively on the deaths of U.S. soldiers.[1]

The invasion, called "Operation Just Cause," was a classic attempt
to punish successful defiance. Panamanian dictator Manuel Noriega
had been a U.S. asset during the 1980s but had ceased to be compliant
and had been harassing U.S. troops stationed in the country. Noriega
"ostentatiously thumbed his nose at the United States," as intelligence
expert Thomas Powers summarized it. Like Saddam Hussein, he had
become a nuisance. The United States turned against Noriega because
he wasn't cooperating with their support for the Contras in Nicaragua.
But his criminal charges stemmed from activity in the early 1980s,

when the U.S. was still praising the amazing "free" elections he won in 1984. (In fact, he used murder, fraud, and secret funding from Washington to assure that his candidate would win. Secretary of State George Shultz flew down to praise Noriega for "initiating the process of democracy"—not such a strange comment in light of the Reaganite concept of "promoting democracy.")[2]

Importantly, the invasion was blatantly illegal. It was condemned by the UN General Assembly, which passed a resolution that "strongly deplores the intervention in Panama by the armed forces of the United States of America, which constitutes a flagrant violation of international law and of the independence, sovereignty, and territorial integrity of States." Other legal experts agreed that the invasion was a "gross violation" of international law. George H. W. Bush, in explaining the invasion to the country, offered no claim to legality. He didn't have to, because the "what we say goes" principle applied.[3]

The crimes of the first half of the twentieth century led to dedicated efforts to save humanity from future wars. These efforts produced a broad international consensus on the principles that every state should follow, formulated in the United Nations Charter, which in the United States is "the supreme law of the land." The charter opens by expressing the determination of the signatories "to save succeeding generations from the scourge of war, which twice in our lifetime has brought untold sorrow to mankind." In fact, by that point war wasn't just a "scourge." After the development of nuclear weapons, it threatened the total destruction of all humankind. The charter therefore required straightforwardly that members "shall settle their international disputes by peaceful means" and refrain "from the threat or use of force against the territory or political independence of any state." Under the charter, force can lawfully be deployed only when authorized by the Security Council, or under Article 51 of the charter, which permits the "right of individual or collective self-defense if an armed attack occurs against a

Member of the United Nations, until the Security Council has taken measures necessary to maintain international peace and security."

Any other resort to force is a war crime. In fact, the aggressive use of force is the "supreme international crime," in the words of the Nuremberg Tribunal. As international law specialists Howard Friel and Richard Falk point out, "International law presents clear and authoritative standards with respect to the use of force and recourse to war that should be followed by all states," and if "under exceptional circumstances" any departure is allowed, "a heavy burden of persuasion is on the state claiming the exception." That should be the conventional understanding in a decent society. And so it appears to be among the general American population, though, in sharp contrast, the idea receives little support within elite opinion.[4]

The UN Charter is the founding document of modern international law. Its basic principles have been consistently reaffirmed since its inception. They are clear and sound. The use of force requires authorization. Notably, individual states do not possess a "right of intervention," for reasons explained by the World Court in 1949, which said that "the alleged right of intervention" cannot "find a place in international law," because it "would be reserved for the most powerful states, and might easily lead to perverting the administration of justice itself."[5]

The United States has had scant regard for the constraints imposed by international law. For instance, every year since 1992, the United Nations General Assembly adopts a resolution condemning the U.S. embargo against Cuba. The resolution condemns the United States embargo for violating the principle of "non-intervention and non-interference in [states'] internal affairs and freedom of international trade and navigation." In 2022, the thirtieth consecutive year the resolution had been passed, the vote was 185–2, with only the U.S. and Israel voting against it. UN member states called the embargo "cruel, inhumane and punitive," and Cuba's Caribbean neighbors argued that the blockade "was stifling not only Cuba's growth but that of the entire region."[6]

A country with basic respect for the rule of law would, in the face of such overwhelming opposition from the entire international community, change its policy. Instead, the U.S. issues the same challenge to the UN that Andrew Jackson infamously gave to the Supreme Court: they have made their decision, now let them enforce it. This defiance persists under Democratic and Republican presidents alike.

To take another example, in the 1980s, Nicaragua had a strong legal case against the United States. Tens of thousands of people had died in the civil war fueled by U.S. support for the Contras, and the country was substantially destroyed. The attack was accompanied by a devastating economic war, which a small country isolated by a superpower could scarcely sustain.

So Nicaragua went to the World Court, which ruled in their favor, ordering the United States to desist and pay substantial reparations. Nicaragua dealt with the problem of being terrorized by a foreign power in exactly the right way. It followed international law and treaty obligations. It collected evidence, brought the evidence to the highest existing tribunal, and received a verdict.

The United States dismissed the court judgment and immediately escalated the war. So Nicaragua then went to the Security Council, which considered a resolution calling on all states to observe international law. The U.S. alone vetoed it. Nicaragua next went to the General Assembly, where they got a similar resolution, which passed with the U.S. and Israel opposed two years in a row (joined once by El Salvador). Nicaragua's foreign minister Miguel d'Escoto protested that "to dispense with the rule of law in international relations is tantamount to condemning humanity to a future of suffering, death and destruction." But U.S. policy is not guided by whether or not a given course of action "condemns humanity to a future of suffering, death, and destruction."[7]

The United States has consistently undermined efforts to apply universal global standards of justice to its own actions. The U.S. has refused, for instance, to join the International Criminal Court (ICC), for fear that Americans could be prosecuted for crimes they commit (an intolerable outcome). In fact, it has gone further and resorted to extreme measures to undermine the court. The U.S. put major pressure on countries to sign agreements promising never to turn a U.S. citizen over to the ICC, pulling assistance from those countries that refused to enter such agreements. In 2002, the U.S. threatened to use its Security Council veto to block the renewal of UN peacekeeping operations unless the UN agreed to permanently exempt U.S. nationals from ICC jurisdiction. The 2002 American Service-Members Protection Act prohibits federal, state, and local authorities from cooperating with the ICC, and even prohibits military aid to countries that are parties to the ICC (with exceptions for favored allies). The law was dubbed the Hague Invasion Act because it authorizes the president to use "all means necessary and appropriate" to secure the release of any "U.S. or allied personnel" detained by the ICC, presumably including invading the Hague if this was "necessary."[8]

American refusal to recognize the ICC rebounded against it when Vladimir Putin invaded Ukraine, at which point U.S. politicians, including Joe Biden, began demanding that Putin be put on trial for war crimes. Former Democratic senator Chris Dodd and former National Security Council legal adviser John B. Bellinger III, writing in *The Washington Post*, argued that it did not constitute a "double standard" for the U.S. to encourage the ICC to prosecute others while refusing to be bound by its jurisdiction, because the ICC should "not investigate every allegation of misconduct" but only those "not addressed by the nations that commit them." Indeed, it conforms to the "single standard," which is that the world's laws do not apply to the United States, a country that has already addressed any and all misconduct it may have committed.[9]

We have seen that where there are international laws in place, the United States defies them when it so chooses. But the U.S. has also stymied efforts to create new international agreements that make the world safer. Take cluster munitions, for instance. There is a consensus among human rights groups that cluster munitions are an inherently barbaric weapon, because they leave hundreds of tiny unexploded "bomblets" strewn across the battlefield, which kill and maim for years after the cessation of war. Veteran national security journalist Jeremy Scahill describes witnessing the effects. In a marketplace in Serbia, he saw the aftermath of the use of cluster bombs, which "shred everything in [their] path into meat and limbs." The result of any bombing is horrifying to see, he says, but cluster bombs are especially brutal, and he saw what had happened to children who picked up bomblets days after the initial attack.[10]

Well over one hundred countries have agreed to the Convention on Cluster Munitions, promising never to develop, stockpile, or use these weapons under any circumstances. The United States has refused to join. The Institute for Policy Studies notes that as a global consensus against the use of cluster bombs has developed, the U.S.—the largest manufacturer and user of them—has defended them as a valid tool of warfare. U.S. defense secretary Robert Gates called them "legitimate weapons with clear military utility," while Richard Kidd, the director of the Office of Weapons Removal and Abatement in the U.S. State Department, said that "cluster munitions are available for use by every combat aircraft in the U.S. inventory; they are integral to every Army or Marine maneuver element and in some cases constitute up to 50 percent of tactical indirect fire support." We both produce and use these weapons despite the condemnation of human rights groups. In Afghanistan between 2001 and 2002, the U.S. dropped over twelve hundred cluster bombs. Of course, this did not stop the U.S. from criticizing Russia for using cluster munitions in Ukraine, with the U.S.'s UN ambassador saying Russia was using "banned" weapons that had "no place on the battlefield." (The transcript of her remarks was later edited to condemn only cluster munitions used against civilians.)[11]

There is no shortage of examples. The United States refuses to join 167 other countries in being a party to the Law of the Sea Convention, and has made the Biological Weapons Convention toothless by opposing methods for verifying compliance. Other crucial treaties left unratified by the U.S. include the Convention on the Elimination of All Forms of Discrimination Against Women (CEDAW), the Convention on the Rights of the Child (CRC), the International Convention for the Protection of All Persons from Enforced Disappearance (ICPPED), the Anti-Personnel Mine Ban Convention, the Convention on the Rights of Persons with Disabilities, and the Kyoto Protocol. In the case of the Genocide Convention, the U.S. took forty years to ratify the convention, and even then only did so with the express reservation that the U.S. was exempt from being accused of genocide. The issue is the same in every case: the U.S. is happy to accept restrictions on the power of other states, but reserves the right to act as it pleases.[12]

The United States has also used its veto power in the Security Council to thwart UN action on issues that the rest of the world supports. Its first veto was in support of the racist regime of Southern Rhodesia, which the UN was trying to sanction. In 2023, the U.S. vetoed a Security Council resolution "to condemn all violence against civilians in the Israel-Hamas war and to urge humanitarian aid to Palestinians in Gaza."[13]

In *Foreign Affairs,* the leading establishment journal, David Kaye reviews one aspect of Washington's departure from the rest of the world: rejection of multilateral treaties "as if it were sport." He explains that some treaties are rejected outright, as when the U.S. Senate "voted against the Convention on the Rights of Persons with Disabilities in 2012 and the Comprehensive Nuclear-Test-Ban Treaty (CTBT) in 1999." Others are dismissed by inaction, including "such subjects as labor, economic and cultural rights, endangered species, pollution, armed conflict, peacekeeping, nuclear weapons, the law of the sea, and discrimination against women." Rejection of international obligations "has grown so entrenched," Kaye writes, "that foreign governments no longer expect Washington's ratification or its full participation in the institutions treaties create. The world is moving on; laws get made elsewhere, with limited (if any) American involvement." While not new, the practice has indeed become more entrenched in recent years, along with quiet acceptance at home of the doctrine that the United States has every right to act as a rogue state.[14]

Respect for domestic law by American presidents has been little better. Presidents typically regard constitutional restraints on executive power as merely suggestive.

For instance, under the United States Constitution, nobody is supposed to be deprived of their liberty without "due process of law." However, in a small island prison at Cuba's Guantánamo Bay, the United States has imprisoned hundreds of foreign nationals without even giving them the pretense of due process. Over many years and thanks to the relentless efforts of lawyers, most of the "detainees" have been released, but to this day thirty remain in limbo. Both Democratic and Republican presidents have continued this policy. In fact, there is no reason to *have* a prison at Guantánamo Bay other than to avoid the domestic legal processes that guarantee some elementary rights to criminal defendants.[15]

The wars waged by U.S. presidents are frequently illegal. Barack Obama, for instance, attacked Libya in flagrant violation of the War Powers Resolution, which requires congressional authorization for military engagements. The administration's justification for not getting approval was laughable: A White House spokesman insisted that the administration's bombing of the country did "not amount to hostilities" because no soldiers were put on the ground. Thus overthrowing the Libyan government did not, according to the administration, qualify as "hostilities." *ProPublica* observed that in ignoring the law Obama was simply following a "well-worn path" for presidents, who have never recognized Congress's authority to constrain executive power to kill people.[16]

Barack Obama claimed the right to kill American citizens, without any semblance of due process, even when they were far away from any battlefield. He personally approved a kill list (or "disposition matrix," as it was known in the parlance of Orwellian euphemisms) that went unreviewed by any court. *The New York Times* reported on the dystopian internal deliberations. It is "the strangest of bureaucratic rituals," in which "members of the government's sprawling national security apparatus" pore over possible suspects and "recommend to the president who should be the next to die" in a kind of "grim debating society." Reassuringly, the *Times* tells us that as "a student of writings on war by Augustine and Thomas Aquinas, [Obama] believes that he should take moral responsibility for such actions," although he did not apparently question whether life-and-death decisions should be in the hands of an enlightened philosopher-king rather than the courts. This "strangest of bureaucratic rituals" is, after all, possible only by eliminating the basic legal guarantees that date back to the Magna Carta.[17]

In a democratic society where the people are sovereign, the representatives of the people (in the legislative branch) are supposed to make the laws, and the president (in the executive branch) is supposed to execute them. In the United States, however, presidents frequently assume that they are not bound by the law. "If the president does it, it's not illegal," to quote Richard Nixon's infamous phrase.

To take another disturbing example: U.S. law explicitly bars aid to countries that systematically use torture. This law is sound and humane. But presidents simply defy the law. The United States supported Saddam Hussein when he was one of the world's leading torturers. Leading recipients of U.S. aid include Israel, Egypt, and Turkey, which have all been cited by human rights organizations for their use of torture.

Examples of support for human rights abusers are legion. In 2021, Amnesty International condemned "the United States role in fueling ceaseless cycles of violence committed against the people of Colombia," noting that "the United States government has been an agonizing party to the killing, disappearances, sexual violence and other torture, and horrendous repression of dozens of mostly peaceful demonstrations." The U.S. "believed that the Colombian military was behind a wave of assassinations of leftist activists and yet spent the next two decades deepening its relationship with the Colombian armed forces." During the Clinton administration, Turkey carried out monstrous acts of ethnic cleansing. Tens of thousands were killed, thousands of towns and villages were destroyed, hundreds of thousands were driven from their homes. The main support for the state crimes came from Washington: Clinton provided 80 percent of the arms as atrocities increased.[18]

In 2023, human rights organizations pleaded with the Biden administration to withhold military aid from Egypt, on the grounds that Egypt remained a serial human rights violator. Eleven members of the House Foreign Affairs Committee sent a letter to Biden imploring him to deny the aid, citing Egypt's jailing of "journalists, peaceful civil society activists, human rights defenders and political figures." By the text of the law, Biden was *required* to withhold aid from Egypt, but the administration simply "waived" the law. *The New York Times* says the administration concluded that "national security interests outweigh congressionally mandated benchmarks for Egyptian progress on human rights." Of course, nobody ever says how our "national security" is served by giving Egypt hundreds of millions of dollars without imposing any of the human rights requirements that Congress has demanded. Egypt has certainly learned the lesson that it need not make any human rights concessions to the United States, because the money will keep flowing regardless. Biden's administration concluded, according to the *Times*, that "America's relationship with the most populous country in the region is too important to risk fracturing despite pleas from human rights activists for a much harder line from Washington." But this is not a decision that the executive should get to make. The law prohibits aid to human rights abusers, regardless of how Biden feels about the consequences.[19]

It can be difficult to know when presidents are breaking the law. Edward Snowden exposed government surveillance programs far beyond the scope of anything Congress had authorized, which may well have been unconstitutional. By allowing the people to understand what their government was doing, Snowden performed a public service. He ought to have received a promotion. Instead, he has long been sought for prosecution, and will probably spend his life in exile. Government whistleblowers who expose major wrongdoing by the state are routinely prosecuted, with Barack Obama having been one of the most ruthless in applying criminal charges (despite once promising "the most transparent administration ever"). Jeremy Scahill points to the continuity between the Bush-Cheney absolutist view of presidential power and the view of the Obama administration: Obama "had an opportunity to roll back some of the executive branch power grabs" of the previous president; instead he maintained and even escalated them, "using the full power structure of the executive branch in the same excessive way that was being used under Bush and Cheney."[20]

The defiance of domestic law reaffirms that when we speak of the actions of the U.S. state, we are not speaking of the collective will of the American people. Even when the people, through their representatives, succeed in putting restraints on the executive, the executive frequently ignores the restraints.

THE POSTWAR PRESIDENTS

American violations of international law have been egregious and constant. They are committed by both Democratic and Republican presidents, and the facts are well documented. A brief run through some selected examples from the historical record will suffice to show that if the Nuremberg standards were consistently applied, every president since the Second World War would have to be convicted and sentenced.

In the case of Truman, we have not only the bombings of Hiroshima and Nagasaki, but the massive firebombing of Japanese cities that took place *after* the Nagasaki bombings, once the Japanese had offered to surrender. The bombings, "the heaviest conventional bombing of the war," were intended as a "finale," without any military justification whatsoever. Earlier we reviewed the case of Greece, where the

United States fueled a murderous war of counterinsurgency, success-fully demolishing the anti-Nazi resistance and restoring the old order, including leading Nazi collaborators, at the cost of some 160,000 lives, plus tens of thousands of victims of torture chambers.[21]

Under Eisenhower, the bombings of North Korea in 1951 and '52 were an outright war crime. *The Washington Post*'s Blaine Harden ex-plains that "after running low on urban targets, U.S. bombers destroyed hydroelectric and irrigation dams in the later stages of the war, flood-ing farmland and destroying crops." Curtis LeMay, in an official Air Force history, comments, "Over a period of three years or so, we killed off—what—20 percent of the population." Dean Rusk, the eventual sec-retary of state, says the United States destroyed "everything that moved in North Korea, every brick standing on top of another." People were hanged for less than that at Nuremberg, but this wasn't the only terrible crime from the Eisenhower years. There was also the CIA-led coup against democratically elected prime minister Mohammad Mossadegh of Iran and the overthrow of Jacobo Árbenz of Guatemala, which led to civil strife and mass killings.[22]

Little more needs saying about the crimes against Vietnam, Laos, and Cambodia during the Kennedy, Johnson, and Nixon years. Ken-nedy, whose *Camelot* government is still looked upon nostalgically by many liberals, first sent the Air Force to start bombing Vietnamese vil-lages and authorized the use of napalm. Kennedy also laid the basis for the huge wave of repression that spread over Latin America with the installation of neo-Nazi dictators who were always supported directly by the United States. In the case of Johnson, the invasion of the Domin-ican Republic should be included. After the ousting of the U.S.-supported dictator, Johnson sent the Marines to "prevent the Dominican Republic from going Communist." He then ordered FBI director J. Edgar Hoover to "find me some Communists in the Dominican Republic," in order to justify the invasion. (Johnson wanted to prevent liberal intellectual Juan Bosch from being restored to power.) Again, a plain violation of the UN Charter.[23]

Richard Nixon's crimes in Indochina need no further review, but one underreported horror was the Nixon administration's support for one of the worst genocides of the twentieth century, the Pakistani killings of Bengalis in 1971. As *The Washington Post*'s Ishaan Tharoor explains, after Bengali nationalists scored an election victory, a crackdown by the Pakistani military "turned into a mass slaughter" in which "hundreds of thousands of women were raped" and "whole villages were razed, and cities depopulated." The Nixon White House, however, "stood on the side of Pakistan's generals—clear Cold War allies" and "covertly rushed arms to the Pakistanis—in violation of a congressional arms embargo." Support for the genocide could not be excused on the grounds of ignorance; Kissinger received multiple "messages and dissent cables from U.S. diplomats in the field, warning him that a genocide was taking place with their complicity."[24]

Gerald Ford was not in office for long, but still managed to commit major crimes. Ford and Secretary of State Kissinger gave Indonesia approval for its invasion of East Timor, which killed two hundred thousand people. Ford presided over U.S. support for Operation Condor, which undermined left-wing governments across Latin America and propped up right-wing dictatorships. Ford attempted to thwart the Church Committee's investigation into U.S. covert operations, including illegal spying on domestic dissidents, illegal experiments on human subjects involving psychological torture, and assassination plots against foreign leaders. He warned the committee that to "make public the report on the subject of assassinations" would "result in serious harm to the national interest." Note, again, that the public must be kept from making an informed decision about foreign policy, the "national interest" not being something the people of the nation are entrusted to pass judgment on.[25]

In the Carter years, major crimes included support for the Indonesian invasion of East Timor, already discussed, plus U.S. assistance to the Somoza regime in Nicaragua. In fact, it is a real tribute to the propaganda system that the press can still refer to a "human rights campaign"

262 THE MYTH OF AMERICAN IDEALISM

during the Carter administration, a presidency that sponsored and supported the Somoza family in Nicaragua, the shah of Iran, Marcos in the Philippines, Park in South Korea, Pinochet in Chile, Suharto in Indonesia, Mobutu in Zaire, the Brazilian generals, and their many confederates in repression and violence.

For Reagan, we do not need to make the case, because the World Court already issued its decision in *Nicaragua v. United States*, even if the U.S. ignored it. But it's worth mentioning the invasion of Grenada, which was condemned by the UN General Assembly as "a flagrant violation of international law." Reagan claimed the usual right to deploy violent force around the world wherever he pleased, and supported the white supremacist government of South Africa, even as that country became a pariah state. In 1988, the Reagan administration declared Nelson Mandela's African National Congress to be one of the "more notorious" terrorist groups in the world. While greatly honored internationally, Mandela remained on the U.S. terrorist list until 2008, when at last a congressional resolution allowed him to enter the "land of the free" without special dispensation.[26]

The major crimes of the George H. W. Bush years have already been extensively covered. The invasion of Panama was an act of outright aggression in plain violation of the UN Charter and was condemned internationally. We have also discussed the overlooked crimes of the Gulf War and the resort to violence over diplomacy.

Within a few months of Bill Clinton's arrival in office, he sent missiles to bomb Baghdad, without any credible pretext and in obvious violation of the UN Charter. During his administration, about half of military aid and training to Latin America went to Colombia, which had the worst human rights record in the hemisphere, and killed thousands. There was also Clinton's 1993 missile attack on Iraq, in which three missiles hit a residential neighborhood. The legal justifications for this strike were entirely spurious, but such violations are so routine that the attack is a mere footnote to the Clinton presidency. In 1998, Clinton also bombed Sudan's Al-Shifa pharmaceutical plant, destroying a crucial supply of medicine for a poor country. Clinton claimed the plant was producing chemical weapons, a claim for which no evidence was presented, but instead of taking his case to the United Nations, he bombed a sovereign country. Years later, *The New York Times* reported that the Sudanese still resented the attack, and the fact that "no apology has been made and no restitution offered."[27]

The major crimes of the George W. Bush years have also been extensively covered. But the administration's use of torture deserves more attention. In 2011, Amnesty International released a report called "Bringing George W. Bush to Justice," which showed conclusively that acts of torture were carried out by the CIA in severe violation of international law. Bush himself, they said, was responsible, having personally "decided that the protections of the Geneva Conventions of 1949 . . . would not be applied to [Taliban or al-Qaeda] detainees." Under the UN Convention Against Torture, Amnesty found, states had an obligation to investigate and prosecute Bush.[28]

The view is shared by other analysts. U.S. Army Major General Antonio Taguba, author of a major internal report on human rights abuses, concluded: "There is no longer any doubt as to whether the current administration has committed war crimes. The only question that remains to be answered is whether those who ordered the use of torture will be held to account." Human Rights Watch, in an extensive report called "Getting Away with Torture," said that within days of the 9/11 attacks, the Bush administration began crafting policies that "violated the laws of war, international human rights law, and U.S. federal criminal law." These included "tactics that the U.S. has repeatedly condemned as torture or ill-treatment when practiced by others." The administration sent detainees to undisclosed locations where they "were beaten, thrown into walls, forced into small boxes, and waterboarded." Some in Guantánamo "were forced to sit in their own excrement, and some were sexually humiliated by female interrogators." David Hicks, an Australian national who was held in Guantánamo, reported thinking: "How can they treat another human like this? How can they be so cruel?" as he recalled the "fear of pain, fear of the beatings, fear of the strange mind games I am subjected to." HRW made clear that these abuses "did not result from the acts of individual soldiers or intelligence agents who broke the rules" but were the result of deliberate decisions by U.S. leaders to ignore the rules.[29]

There is no doubt whatsoever that the techniques used were torture, despite Bush administration euphemisms. A pro-war columnist who underwent waterboarding for a *Vanity Fair* article reached an unequivocal conclusion: "If waterboarding does not constitute torture, then there is no such thing as torture."[30]

The list continues. Soon after Barack Obama came into office, he was awarded the Nobel Peace Prize in anticipation of his future contributions to peace. It was hoped that as a former constitutional law professor, Obama would break from his predecessor's lawlessness. In his Nobel acceptance speech, which was devoted in substantial part to a defense of U.S. military power, Obama affirmed that "the words of the international community must mean something" and "those regimes that break the rules must be held accountable." Obama cited as proof of his commitment to international law the fact that he had "ordered the prison at Guantánamo Bay closed." (Obama did not close the prison at Guantánamo Bay.[31])

Obama's commitment to enforcing rules against regimes that break them was immediately put to the test. He had a mountain of evidence that his predecessor's government had committed heinous acts of torture in violation of both domestic and international law. A report prepared by the International Human Rights Clinic at Harvard Law School, and submitted to the United Nations Committee Against Torture, described the torture program as "breathtaking in scope." But Obama soon decided that rather than enforce the law, he would "look forward as opposed to looking backwards." The victims, of course, trapped in the past by the trauma of losing family and friends, may keep sourly "looking backwards," but the United States has moved on. While Obama acknowledged that "we tortured some folks," he worried that investigating the CIA would make operatives feel as if their conduct were being scrutinized: "I don't want them to suddenly feel like they've got to spend all their time looking over their shoulders." As Murtaza Hussain wrote in *The Intercept*, this "don't look backward attitude" (which would be absurd applied to any other crime) guaranteed complete impunity for *future* wrongdoing, and by failing to prosecute Bush officials, "demonstrated that even if government officials perpetrate the most heinous crimes imaginable, they will still be able to rely on their peers to conceal their wrongdoing and protect them from prosecution."[32]

Obama also conducted illegal drone strikes around the world, claiming the right to assassinate anyone he had personally determined to be unworthy of life. When Malala Yousafzai met with Obama in 2013, she warned him that "innocent victims are killed in these acts, and they lead to resentment among the Pakistani people," meaning that ultimately "drone strikes fuel terrorism." The same conclusion was reached in an NYU-Stanford study, which summarized the impact on Pakistanis, above whom "drones hover twenty-four hours a day," a presence that "terrorizes men, women and children, giving rise to anxiety and psychological trauma among civilian communities." There are numerous negative effects: humanitarian workers are reluctant to assist victims for fear of second strikes, people are afraid to gather in groups, family members are afraid to attend funerals, and children are kept at home. The entire fabric of the community is disrupted. Farea Al-Muslimi, a Yemeni man educated in the United States, told the Senate in 2013 that his efforts to promote the image of the United States in Yemen were in vain, because "when they think of America they think of the terror they feel from the drones that hover over their heads ready to fire missiles at any time."[33]

In 2013, thirteen-year-old Zubair uh Rehman told Congress that he "no longer love[s] blue skies," after seeing his mother blown to pieces in a U.S. drone strike. The drone "had appeared out of a bright blue sky." Zubair came to "prefer gray skies" because "the drones do not fly when the skies are gray."[34]

The criminality became more extreme under Donald Trump, who makes no secret of his thuggish disposition (he once boasted of having sent federal agents to murder an antifa activist). Civilian casualties from drone strikes increased significantly. With the assassination of Qassim Soleimani of Iran, Trump also claimed the right to unilaterally order the assassination of high officials in other countries.[35]

On the grounds that the Venezuelan government oppresses its people, the Trump administration imposed measures that inflicted even worse harm on the Venezuelan people. As Mark Weisbrot and Jeffrey Sachs showed in a study of the sanctions' effects, they "reduced the public's caloric intake, increased disease and mortality (for both adults and infants), and displaced millions of Venezuelans who fled the country as a result of the worsening economic depression and hyperinflation." The sanctions caused an estimated forty thousand deaths across a two-year period, and fell hardest on the poorest Venezuelans. Importantly, Weisbrot and Sachs conclude that "these sanctions would fit the definition of collective punishment of the civilian population as described in both the Geneva and Hague international conventions, to which the U.S. is a signatory. They are also illegal under international law and treaties which the U.S. has signed, and would appear to violate U.S law as well." Yet the issue of impeaching Donald Trump over his deadly, illegal Venezuela sanctions was never even raised for public discussion.[36]

Vladimir Putin was universally condemned within the United States for trying to keep Ukraine within the Russian sphere of influence by military force. Ukraine, it is argued, has the right to choose its alliances, and Russia does not have the right to dictate whether Ukraine enters NATO or not. Russia certainly cannot use Ukraine's slip from the Russian orbit as an excuse for regime change. All sound arguments. But let us consider an admission made by Mike Pompeo, who served as secretary of state under Donald Trump, in his memoir. Writing of Venezuela, Pompeo says that "we couldn't tolerate" a country near Florida "putting out the welcome mat" for countries like Russia and Iran, because it constituted "a twenty-first-century violation of the Monroe

Doctrine." Pompeo admits that economic pressure was used to try to depose the existing government, and the "military option" (i.e., invading Venezuela) was even considered. The military option did not go unexercised because of the Trump administration's respect for the UN Charter. Rather, Pompeo says, other means were expected to be sufficient to force regime change, such as destroying the government's ability to export oil.[37]

Joe Biden's term in office is not yet concluded as of this writing, but there are plenty of serious documented violations of international law, including his illegal air strikes on Syria, failure to uphold the rights of asylum seekers, transfer of cluster bombs to Ukraine, and support (against almost unanimous condemnation by the rest of the world) for Israel's war on Gaza. Biden has subverted congressional approval processes to transfer arms to Israel and gone against the entire rest of the world to shield Israel at the UN. Biden's climate policies, while better than Trump's, have nevertheless resulted in record oil production, an achievement the administration is proud of, despite its role in wrecking the Earth.[38]

In a world where the basic principles of the UN Charter were enforced, and violators tried and convicted, none of these leaders would have escaped conviction for serious crimes. Furthermore, we have a Constitution. That Constitution says that treaties entered into by the government are the supreme law of the land. One of those treaties is the UN Charter. It has an article, 2.4, that says *the threat or use of force* in international affairs is banned. This means every leading political figure has violated the Constitution.

The matter is never even raised for public discussion.

Rather than follow international law, the United States has laid out an alternative vision to the UN-based order. It calls this the "rules-based order." This phrase is used not to refer to the enforcement of international law as made by the UN, but the adoption of an obscure set of "rules." In practice, the "rules" are set by the dominant global power, which across most of the world is the United States. As international relations scholar Stephen M. Walt writes, "When U.S. officials say 'rules-based order,' they mean the *current* order, whose rules were mostly made in America." The U.S. has strong reasons to oppose the UN-based order, whose basic principle is that the threat or use of force is barred in international affairs, except in special circumstances. Attacking countries with no credible pretext, launching terrorist wars, trying to overthrow a parliamentary government by imposing harsh sanctions, or simply declaring that "all options are open" if a country does not meet certain demands—all are explicit violations of Article 2 of the UN Charter.[39]

Michael Byers observes in *War Law: Understanding International Law and Armed Conflict* that there is scarcely any effort to conceal "the tension between a world that still wants a fair and sustainable international legal system, and a single superpower that hardly seems to care [that it] ranks with Burma, China, Iraq and North Korea in terms of its adherence to a seventeenth-century, absolutist conception of sovereignty" for itself, while dismissing as old-fashioned nonsense the sovereignty of others.[40]

It is worth noting that just because something is a violation of law does not mean it is wrong, and just because something is legal does not mean it is not a "crime." We know the United States is responsible for major crimes in the layman's sense of this term. What we may reasonably ask is whether the acts that are documented beyond dispute are also crimes in the lawyerly sense, recognizing that when we raise this question, the *law* is also on trial. If we find that international law does not condemn certain atrocities as criminal in the technical sense, a rational person will regard the law, so understood, with all the respect accorded to the divine right of kings.

International law is in many ways inadequate and unfair. (Why should the United States, and a few other powerful countries, have veto power at the Security Council and be able to keep the wrongdoing of allies from being condemned?) Nevertheless, the basic principles of the UN-based order that were introduced after the Second World War remain sound to this day, and a country committed to "rules" ought to consider following them.[41]

As we have seen, the United States freely violates treaties when it pleases, and when the International Court of Justice ruled that the United States had acted unlawfully in supporting the Nicaraguan Contras, the U.S. simply refused to recognize the court's jurisdiction and blocked enforcement of the judgment. Anything to ensure that we are not subject to the same rules as everybody else. No justifications for this are ever offered. None are thought to be needed. The right to rule is assumed.

How Mythologies
Are Manufactured

In his unpublished preface to *Animal Farm*, George Orwell made astute observations about how censorship of "unpopular ideas" can occur even where there is broad freedom of speech. Orwell is today famous for his critique of the way thought is controlled by force in totalitarian dystopias. His useful discussion of *free* societies is less known. In such societies, he says, censorship is not coerced by the state. Yet it nevertheless exists, and is effective at silencing those who dissent from "prevailing orthodoxy." Explaining how it works, Orwell cited the internalization of the values of subordination and conformity, and the control of the press by "wealthy men who have every motive to be dishonest on certain important topics."[1]

Orwell was perceptive about how a democratic society could nevertheless produce intellectual conformity and stifle unpopular views. The press can be free in the sense that the government does not interfere with it. But if those who own the press choose not to elevate certain viewpoints, those viewpoints stand little chance of reaching the public. Those kinds of choices are made every day, and we can rationally expect information to reflect the biases and interests of those who own the media. Philosopher John Dewey identified a similar mechanism. Speaking of "our un-free press," he observed the "necessary effect of the present economic system upon the whole system of publicity; upon the judgment of what news is, upon the selection and elimination of matter that is published, upon the treatment of news in both editorial and news columns." We should ask "how far genuine intellectual freedom and social responsibility are possible on any large scale under the existing economic regime."[2] (Not far, he thought.)

The United States is a remarkably free country when it comes to what it is legally permissible to say. Nevertheless, the mechanisms described by Orwell still operate, and shape what is actually heard and read. The major media corporations are not uniform in the views they present, nor do they reflexively endorse all state policies, but they do reliably reflect the assumptions and viewpoints of U.S. elites. They contain spirited criticism and debate, but only in line with a system of presuppositions and principles. These constitute a powerful elite consensus, which the individual actors have internalized mostly without conscious awareness.

One such unstated assumption, ubiquitous in U.S. political discourse, is the view that the United States has an inherent right to dominate the rest of the world. In fact, leading liberal commentator Matthew Yglesias calls this an "uncontroversial premise," and says that outside of a few fringe "left-wing intellectuals," the U.S. right to rule is considered axiomatic. "The United States has been the number one power in the world throughout my entire lifetime," he says, and "the notion that this state of affairs is desirable and ought to persist is one of the least controversial things you could say in American politics today." Yglesias himself accepts the premise, seeing no need to argue for it because it is so uncontroversial. He might have added that not only does no "elected official" challenge the view, but it is hardly ever challenged in the U.S. media. Even when there are debates over the wisdom of U.S. uses of force, rarely is any question raised of whether the U.S. has the *right* to use force.[3]

Take Iraq. Once the invasion of Iraq began to produce an out-of-control bloodbath, there was plenty of criticism of the war in the U.S. media. But as Anthony DiMaggio documents in a useful study of media coverage of the "war on terror," criticisms from mainstream liberal commentators focused on whether the war was being waged effectively, not whether the war was legitimate in the first place. Bob Herbert of *The New York Times* described the war as "mismanaged," "not sustainable," and "unwinnable," with "no coherent strategy." The editors of the *Los Angeles Times* criticized a "terribly botched occupation," the botching rather than the occupation being the problem. Paul Begala, the Democratic strategist, said Bush "didn't have enough troops" in the country. DiMaggio observes that these seemingly "anti-war" criticisms are in fact *pro*-war criticisms, because they highlight "military errors that, if corrected, might contribute to a more smoothly functioning occupation and war effort." But, DiMaggio asks, "if the war is imperial and immoral, designed to secure control over oil rather than promote democracy, then why attack the administration for not effectively fighting it? Why complain that the war is 'unwinnable' or 'mismanaged' when Americans should not be trying to 'win' or 'manage' a repressive imperial war in the first place?"[4]

It is permissible to suggest that the United States has made mistakes in attempting to achieve its goals, but there is no debate about the goals. So, for example, *The New York Times*, in an editorial assessing the Vietnam War after its conclusion, defined the scope of the debate. "There are those Americans," the *Times* wrote, "who believe the war . . . could have been waged differently," while others believe that "a viable non-Communist south Vietnam was always a myth." The "ongoing quarrel," they say, has not been resolved. The hawks said we could have won. The doves said we couldn't. A debate on these grounds can be had.[5]

The words "misguided," "tragic," and "error" recur in commentary. But what of another possible position: one that asserts that the United States had no legal or moral right to intervene in Vietnam to begin with. The U.S. did *not* "hope that the people of South Vietnam would be able to decide on their own form of government," but prevented democracy from breaking out. It had no right to support France's attempt to reconquer the country, or to violate the 1954 Geneva Accord and oppose the reunification of Vietnam through elections. The question "Could we have won?" is debated in the press, while the correct ones—"Did we have the right to try?" "Were we engaged in criminal aggression?" and "When will there be war crimes trials for those who waged an illegal war of aggression?"—are not. These questions are excluded from the debate, for which the *Times* sets the ground rules.

Julian E. Zelizer, a professor of history and public affairs at Princeton University, gives expression to the dominant view in *Foreign Policy*, writing that the "one constant" in our history is that "presidents frequently make oversights, miscalculations, and even egregious mistakes in handling national security." Oversights. Miscalculations. Mistakes. The ends are not questioned. Only the means of achieving them, which might be reckless. One can go through the history of U.S. wars and see similarly narrow disputes over tactics that presume the legitimacy of U.S. global power. The spectrum runs from those who argue the war is being waged successfully to those who regard it as mismanaged. (This is the same spectrum of debate that exists in Russia around the war in Ukraine. There is harsh criticism of Putin for not prosecuting the war effectively, but not for waging it in the first place.) It is wrong to think that debates over whether a war is *winnable* or a *blunder* are actually debates about the war itself. After all, even Hitler's generals could have criticized his war for its *mistakes*; that is, its failure to achieve the desired objectives. They could have done so with no less fanatical a commitment to Nazism than the Führer himself. In the German case, we recognize that strategic criticisms are not criticisms of the underlying objective; in fact, they are premised upon support of it. Yet in the United States, much passes for criticism of our foreign policy that is in fact mere strategic criticism, accepting the bipartisan consensus that the United States is constitutionally incapable of committing crimes.[6]

The kind of liberal "dovishness"—questioning tactics but not goals—could be found in the press as the U.S.-backed Contras were terrorizing

Nicaragua in the 1980s. *The Washington Post,* for example, criticized support for the Contras on tactical grounds. The fact that Nicaragua was a Soviet-style menace requiring confrontation was "a given." Echoing the Reagan administration, the paper's editorial board considered the Sandinistas "a serious menace—to civil peace and democracy in Nicaragua and to the stability and security of the region," and agreed that we must "contain . . . the Sandinistas' aggressive thrust." But they felt that the "contra force is not a useful instrument to bring to bear." It was not the "best available way" to undermine the Nicaraguan government. The *legitimacy* of our use of force was simply not up for discussion.[7]

The Afghanistan war gave rise to the same kinds of concerns among liberal critics. MSNBC is considered a liberal network, supportive of the Democratic Party. Rachel Maddow, for a long time its leading host (and a self-described "national security liberal"), was plenty critical of the U.S. war in Afghanistan. But on tactical grounds. Maddow concluded that "if you believe that our actions, our American actions in 2010 cannot make it more likely . . . that there's a real government in Afghanistan, then asking Americans to die in Afghanistan is wrong." In other words, the moral considerations center on the likelihood of our success, not the rights of Afghans.[8]

When U.S. wars are over, there is virtually no national self-examination, except over whether the wars were *blunders.* As we have seen, popular narratives about the Vietnam War are exemplified by Ken Burns's description that it was "begun in good faith by decent people out of fateful misunderstandings, American overconfidence, and Cold War miscalculation." As the carnage escalated in Iraq, Nicholas Kristof of *The New York Times* wrote that "Iraqis are paying a horrendous price for the good intentions of well-meaning conservatives who wanted to liberate them."[9]

As U.S. media critics Adam Johnson and Nima Shirazi observe, the media's retrospective characterization of the United States' uses of force is that they were "unpleasant, imperfect, mistaken, but ultimately incidental by-products of a noble and righteous empire that, above all, meant well." They show that once our wars become unpopular, "a cottage industry of punditry and pseudo-history emerges," pushing the ideas that "it was an accident, they were mistaken, they had bad intelligence, they were driven by concerns for freedom and democracy." Johnson and Shirazi liken the situation to a lawyer trying to get a client convicted of manslaughter instead of first-degree murder, which is necessary because in U.S. mythology, enemy states are "Bond villains" who do evil things, while we are innocent do-gooders.[10]

Many crucial issues and questions are simply not raised. Afghanistan and Iraq have all but disappeared from view. When we read that the United States has conducted a drone strike in Iraq, we are not told that the Iraqi government vigorously objected to the violation of its sovereignty, and there is no debate on the matter. Countries suffering from the long-term effects of our "interventions," from Haiti to Laos, are covered superficially or not at all. The "unpeople" of the world might as well not exist.[11]

TERRORISM: ANATOMY OF A PROPAGANDA CONCEPT

In *City of God*, St. Augustine recounts the story of Alexander the Great meeting a pirate. Alexander confronted the pirate, asking him why he felt entitled to "hostile possession of the sea." The pirate responded with "bold pride": "What do you mean by seizing the whole earth? Because I do it with a petty ship, I am called a robber, while you who does it with a great fleet are styled emperor." Identical behavior can get one labeled a pirate or a great emperor.

For an obvious example of unstated ideological assumptions in U.S. political discourse, we can look at uses of the word "terrorism." Terrorism is defined by the Department of Defense as "the unlawful use of violence or threat of violence, often motivated by religious, political, or other ideological beliefs, to instill fear and coerce governments or societies in pursuit of goals that are usually political." This definition is unusable, however, because it is immediately obvious that it would render the United States a terrorist state. George W. Bush, who unlawfully used violence, motivated by ideological beliefs, to coerce societies in pursuit of political goals, would indisputably be one of the world's leading terrorists. Likewise the respected statesman Henry Kissinger and the Nobel Peace Prize winner Barack Obama.

There are other official definitions.[12] None of them are ever actually used in U.S. political discourse, because each of them leads to the same conclusion: respected American political figures are terrorists. Lyndon Johnson was a terrorist. Richard Nixon was certainly a terrorist when he launched the "Christmas bombings" (Operation Linebacker II) in 1972, dispatching two hundred B-52 bombers to drop twenty thousand tons of bombs on North Vietnam. The bombings were intended to force the North Vietnamese to come back to the negotiating table, even though they had only left after the Nixon administration scuttled its own prior offer.[13] The bombings destroyed the Bạch Mai hospital, killing dozens of staff, and leaving "medical and pharmaceutical books . . . strewn all over a mass of torn iron, fractured concrete beams and broken walls." "They're going to be so god damned surprised," Richard Nixon had said as he launched the attack.[14]

Even a cursory examination of how the word "terrorism" is actually used in the United States reveals, therefore, that there is an implicit premise: terrorism is, by definition, something done *to* us or our allies. It cannot be done *by* us or our allies. The idea of terrorism by the U.S. is *doctrinally inadmissible*, regardless of the facts.

The United States currently designates Cuba, for instance, as one of a small number of "state sponsors of terror." In fact, the U.S. is responsible for decades of terrorism against Cuba. (Cuba was briefly removed from the list by Barack Obama, then added back on under Donald Trump. Joe Biden has so far kept Cuba on the list, despite the fact that the groundless terror list designation "creates additional obstacles to delivering humanitarian aid at a time when the country is grappling with shortages of basic goods and medical supplies.") The

United States also refuses to extradite those who have terrorized other countries, including accused criminals from Haiti and Cuba. Under the Bush-era principle that countries "harboring" terrorists may be violently attacked, the Haitian and Cuban governments could legitimately begin bombing Washington.[15]

The Washington Post accused Vladimir Putin of "aerial terrorism" over missile attacks on Ukraine, describing it as "terror bombing." When Russian-backed Ukrainian separatists downed a civilian airliner (recklessly, but seemingly not deliberately), Hillary Clinton was quick to call it an act of "terrorism." But we can note what is *not* terrorism: the U.S. "shock and awe" bombing campaign in Iraq, or the U.S. downing of an Iranian civilian airliner (also reckless but seemingly not deliberate), or the Dresden-like decimation of Gaza.[16] "Terrorism" never includes a bombardier on a B-52 mission over Indochina wiping out entire villages, nor the higher authorities who authorize the attack.

Flicking through the history of the last half century, we find example after example. Attacks by Palestinians on Israeli civilians are reported in the U.S. press as "terrorist attacks." Attacks on Palestinians by Israeli settlers? These are simply "cases of settler violence." When the Nicaraguan Contras were directed by their CIA and Pentagon commanders to attack civilian targets, *New Republic* editor Michael Kinsley, at the liberal end of mainstream commentary, argued that we should not be too quick to dismiss the justifications for terrorist attacks: a "sensible policy" must "meet the test of cost-benefit analysis," measuring "the amount of blood and misery that will be poured in, and the likelihood that democracy will emerge at the other end." It is understood that U.S. elites have the right to conduct the analysis and pursue the project if it passes their tests.[17]

In 1986, disabled American Leon Klinghoffer was murdered by Palestinian Liberation Front members on the hijacked cruise ship *Achille Lauro*. The murder "seemed to set a standard for remorselessness among terrorists," senior *New York Times* correspondent John Burns wrote, capturing the general horror at a despicable crime. Yet no such standard is set by many similar cases, such as when British reporters found "the flattened remains of a wheelchair" in the remnants of the Jenin refugee camp after Ariel Sharon's spring 2002 offensive. "It had been utterly crushed, ironed flat as if in a cartoon," they reported: "In the middle of the debris lay a broken white flag" held by a disabled Palestinian, Kemal Zughayer, who "was shot dead as he tried to wheel himself up the road. The Israeli tanks must have driven over the body, because when [a friend] found it, one leg and both arms were missing, and the face, he said, had been ripped in two." Another act of un-terror, which does not enter the annals of terrorism along with Leon Klinghoffer. His murder was not under the command of a "monster," but rather a "man of peace," as Ariel Sharon was called by George W. Bush.[18]

The word has no place in honest discourse. And yet we find it used casually over and over. "We must recognize," communications scholar Michael Stohl observes, "that by convention" the use of force by great powers is "normally described as coercive diplomacy and not as a form of terrorism," though it commonly involves "the threat and often the use of violence for what would be described as terroristic purposes were it not great powers who were pursuing the very same tactic." Only one qualification must be added: the term "great powers" must be restricted to favored states; in the "conventions" under discussion, Russia is granted no such rhetorical license.[19]

The unprincipled use of the term "terrorism" is just one example of how violence done by official enemies is evaluated differently than comparable acts of violence done by the United States and its allies. The media has an implicit hierarchy of victims, in which some are considered worthier of attention than others. *Newsday* editor Anthony Marro admitted in the context of the Iraq War that "we pay more attention to Americans' deaths" than the deaths of Iraqis. Once the Ukraine war started, reporters were remarkably open in treating its victims as more human than those of other conflicts. A CBS correspondent described the horror of seeing conflict unfold in "a relatively civilized, relatively European" place where you "wouldn't expect that, or hope that it's going to happen."[20]

Coverage also varies according to who was doing the killing and where the United States itself stood in the conflict. In the 1980s, the killing of Polish priest Jerzy Popiełuszko by communists created a flurry of U.S. media attention. The murder of Salvadoran priest Óscar Romero, an opponent of U.S. support for the dictatorship, attracted far less. These kinds of paired examples reveal a systematic pattern of bias.[21]

Since 1986, the media watchdog agency Fairness and Accuracy in Reporting (FAIR) has carefully monitored the U.S. press for examples of such bias. Their case studies offer conclusive evidence that Washington's foreign policy consensus is reflected in mainstream media coverage. A few of their findings:

- During the Iraq War, FAIR studied cable news and found that 64 percent of guests were in favor of the war, while only 10 percent of guests were antiwar.[22]
- In conflicts between Israel and Palestine, deaths are covered unequally, with seven times as many mentions of each Israeli death as each Palestinian death, and Palestinians' legal rights were downplayed or ignored.[23]
- U.S. media frequently notes when violence around the world is committed with "Iranian-made weapons," but does not take similar note of killings carried out with U.S.-made weapons.[24]
- "Renouncing violence" is a demand made of Muslims but not the U.S. state.[25]
- Chinese imperialism in Hong Kong receives coverage, but there is little comparable coverage of U.S. domination of other countries.[26]
- The war in Afghanistan can be discussed for hours without any substantial attention being paid to how U.S. policies have worsened conditions there.[27]

- When Donald Trump launched air strikes on Syria, there was zero opposition in the press, with *The New York Times* even running the ludicrous headline: "On Syria Attack, Trump's Heart Came First."[28]
- The U.S.-supported Saudi war in Yemen has been all but ignored.[29]
- There was more media coverage of a holiday ad for Peloton than of the new Pentagon budget.[30]

There is plenty of evidence of how nationalistic biases and reliance on government sources warp U.S. media coverage of foreign conflicts. Take, for instance, *The New York Times*'s coverage of China, a U.S. competitor. "Chinese aggression" is treated as an established fact in the U.S. press,[31] with "U.S. aggression" considered impossible. In a story entitled "China Sends Spy Balloons over Military Sites Worldwide, U.S. Officials Say," we read that "American intelligence agencies have assessed that China's spy balloon program is part of a global surveillance effort that is designed to collect information on the military capabilities of countries around the world." The article quotes an expert claiming China has "violated the sovereignty of countries across five continents" with its spying program.

But for an honest press, there would be an obvious and important context to discuss, namely: What spying programs does the *United States* carry out against China? After all, in order to evaluate whether China's behavior is especially nefarious, we have to know whether it is behavior we claim the right to engage in ourselves. As foreign policy scholar Van Jackson explains, U.S. espionage in China has been far more serious than the Chinese balloon that floated briefly over the United States before being shot down. In fact, in 2010, the Chinese leadership "discovered that the CIA had extremely high-level human intelligence plants in the party apparatus, including in security and intelligence ministries." It saw this U.S. infiltration "as an extreme threat to regime security," which led to a "huge acceleration in Chinese assertiveness." Jackson finds it strange that "nobody in American foreign policy talks about the fact that China stumbled on to the CIA having infiltrated them at the highest levels. Talk about surveillance, we're worried about a balloon!"[32]

The selection of topics is also critical. Some are simply not covered and therefore go undiscussed. For instance, the media's coverage of the war in Ukraine has been extensive, with endless sympathetic profiles of Ukrainian fighters and civilian victims appearing in *The New York Times*. There is no comparable coverage of Yemeni victims of Saudi aggression, Kurdish victims of Turkish aggression, or Iraqi victims of U.S. aggression. Palestinian victims of Israeli violence receive vastly less coverage than Israeli victims of Palestinian violence. The value of a life is not determined objectively (with all persons treated equally) but in accordance with the priorities of U.S. foreign policy.[33]

THE LANGUAGE OF PROPAGANDA

In "Politics and the English Language," Orwell wrote of how "defense of the indefensible" becomes possible through euphemism. The bombardment of vulnerable villages may be called "pacification." Robbing peasants of their land and driving them away might be called "transfer of population." Misdeeds are cloaked in vague, pleasant phrases, a practice that is "needed if one wants to name things without calling up mental pictures of them." To make any sense of political discourse, therefore, we must continually translate it into plain English. The choice of terminology distorts the framework of thought, so that it is difficult to understand what is happening or talk about matters of human significance in a coherent way.[34]

One could draw up a glossary of propaganda, decoding Orwellian expressions found in U.S. political discourse. Foreign policy in particular is a domain where horrors are concealed beneath anodyne terminology. We have already seen how the word "terrorism" is used opportunistically rather than in accordance with a neutral definition. Sometimes words are used to soften our actions ("detained" for imprisoned, "enhanced interrogation" for torture, "lethal aid" for cluster bombs, etc.).

A "deterrence posture" refers to the way in which violent annihilation is threatened. Words like "equilibrium" and "stability" are used as euphemisms for the maintenance of American power positions. "We were determined to seek stability," one scholar wrote, through "our efforts to destabilize a freely elected Marxist government in Chile." The inconsistency disappears when we realize that "stability" means "support for U.S. interests."[35]

Notice that Russia has "oligarchs," while the same class of people in the United States are described as "businessmen." We can similarly be on guard for selective uses of the term "dictator." The phrase "security" does not refer to the security of the population; rather to the security of the "principal architects of policy"—in Adam Smith's day, "merchants and manufacturers," in ours, megacorporations and great financial institutions, nourished by the states they largely dominate. When Western states and intellectuals use the term "international community," they are referring to themselves. For example, NATO's bombing of Serbia was undertaken by the "international community" according to consistent Western rhetoric, although those who did not have their heads buried in the sand knew that it was opposed by most of the world, often quite vocally. Those who do not support the actions of wealth and power are not part of "the global community."[36]

In a highly unequal society, bias toward the interests of the American domestic elite is not the product of a conscious conspiracy. Rather, as Edward Herman explained, it "is built into the structure of the system, and flows naturally and easily from the assorted ownership, sponsor, governmental and other interest group pressures that set limits within which media personnel can operate, and from the nature of the sources on which the media depend for their steady flow of news." Journalists do not conspire to censor themselves. They are usually perfectly sincere and committed to their work. They may believe what they say, but if they held different beliefs, they wouldn't be in their positions.[37]

Those who step outside the limits will swiftly find out *how* discourse is kept within certain narrow confines. Phil Donahue despite robust ratings, was fired from his job as an MSNBC host in 2003 because he questioned the Iraq invasion. Network executives felt he would present a "difficult public face for NBC in a time of war." Chris Hedges recounts that at *The New York Times*, after he issued "warnings in public forums about the chaos and bloodbath" the Iraq invasion would trigger, he was formally reprimanded, while another reporter who supported the invasion was not.[38]

"I think the press was muzzled and I think the press self-muzzled," said CNN's Christiane Amanpour. She admitted that "certainly television—and perhaps to a certain extent my station—was intimidated by the administration and its foot soldiers at Fox News," and there was "a climate of fear and self-censorship in terms of the kind of broadcast work we did." *New York Times* reporter Elisabeth Bumiller was frank about the lack of interest in asking difficult questions of the government. "We were very deferential," she says, because "it's frightening to stand up there . . . on prime-time live TV asking the president of the United States a question when the country's about to go to war. . . . No one wanted to get into an argument with the president at this very serious time."[39]

CBS's Dan Rather was similarly honest in admitting that he was incapable of producing coverage untainted by nationalism.

> Look, I'm an American. I never tried to kid anybody that I'm some internationalist or something. And when my country is at war, I want my country to win, whatever the definition of "win" may be. Now, I can't and don't argue that that is coverage without a prejudice. About that I am prejudiced.[40]

Some have forcefully defended their work. Judith Miller, who produced the most infamous *New York Times* articles that repeated false government claims in the lead-up to the Iraq War, says that the role of a *Times* journalist *is* to uncritically repeat government propaganda: "My job isn't to assess the government's information and be an independent intelligence analyst myself. . . . My job is to tell readers of *The New York Times* what the government thought about Iraq's arsenal." Readers are, presumably, supposed to become "independent intelligence analysts" themselves if they hope to discover the truth.[41]

There has nevertheless been some self-reflection among journalists since the debacle of the Iraq War, focusing in particular on the question of whether reporters should repeat the claims of anonymous government sources. But over a decade later, anonymous sources were still in heavy use, with the phrase "intelligence and military officials said" appearing in newspapers as a synonym for "is true." Cable news guests often have direct ties to the military-industrial complex. Opinions remain confined within a narrow range; the same mechanisms that silenced Phil Donahue in 2003 continue to operate.[42]

Propaganda is to a democracy as the bludgeon is to a totalitarian state. In his "First Principles of Government," David Hume observed that the rulers must ultimately rely on controlling thought: "It is therefore, on opinion only that government is founded; and this maxim extends to the most despotic and most military governments, as well as to the most free and most popular." If rulers are to remain in power, they must keep public opinion on their side. In a dictatorship, opinion can partly be controlled by throwing dissidents in jail. In a relatively free and democratic society, thought control operates differently.[43]

The U.S. press has helped the state manufacture new enemies. In case after case, we see the U.S. media reinforcing and spreading the basic doctrines of U.S. foreign policy, portraying our aggression and terror as self-defense and dedication to inspiring visions. Our current adversaries are portrayed as diabolical and bent on our destruction.

Our prior wrongdoing is consigned to the memory hole or recast as another "noble mistake." As Harold Pinter argued in his Nobel Literature Prize address: "The crimes of the United States have been systematic, constant, vicious, remorseless, but very few people have actually talked about them." It's as if, he said, "it never happened," and "even while it was happening it wasn't happening." The U.S., he says, "has exercised a quite clinical manipulation of power worldwide while masquerading as a force for universal good."[44]

We have so much information and yet we know so little. The internet has allowed for the rise of alternative channels of information and somewhat shaken the monopoly of corporate media, but the platforms through which information is spread are still operated in the interest of corporate profit. As a result, it is still the case that the general public doesn't know much about what's happening in the world, and doesn't even know that it doesn't know. A genuinely democratic media, operated in the interest of the public, could change this, and there are proposals for how one could be built. Until then, consumers of media should remember that their lack of knowledge is an important part of what allows the powerful to maintain their position.[45]

Conclusion

Hegemony or Survival?

The United States has a particularly blood-soaked history. By some measures, the country has been engaged in wars for 93.5 percent of all years between 1775 and 2018. The Founders explicitly regarded the country as an "infant empire," and its early history was marked by an annihilationist conquest of the land's native inhabitants. Beneath rhetoric about how the "country we love" is "clear-eyed," "big-hearted," and "optimistic that unarmed truth and unconditional love will have the final word"—in the words of an Obama State of the Union address— lies power, backed by violence.[1]

"Much that passes as idealism . . . is disguised love of power," Bertrand Russell said. Indeed, U.S. history can be traced along two parallel tracks: the track of rhetoric, appearing in newspapers and presidential speeches, and the track of fact, as experienced in the lives of the victims. In every age the press is full of pious statements. Meanwhile, beyond the annihilation of the Indigenous population, the U.S. conquered the Hawaiian Kingdom and the Philippines, seized half of Mexico, intervened violently in the surrounding region, and (since World War II) extended its resort to force throughout much of the world. The number of victims is colossal.[2]

In one high-level postwar document after another, U.S. planners stated their view that the primary threats to the new U.S.-led world order were "nationalistic regimes" that are responsive to "popular demand for immediate improvement in the low living standards of the masses" and production for domestic needs. The planners' basic goal, repeated over and over again, was to prevent such "ultranationalist" regimes from ever taking power—or if, by some fluke, they did take power, to remove them and to install governments that favor private investment, production for export, and the right to bring profits out of the country.

Opposition to democracy and social reform is never popular in the victim country. Thus the United States expects to rely on force and makes alliances with the military—"the least anti-American of any political group in Latin America," as the Kennedy planners put it—in order to crush any indigenous popular groups that get out of hand.

Under some conditions, forms of democracy are indeed acceptable. But democratic decision-making will only be accepted if it is consistent with strategic and economic plans. The United States has consistently opposed democracy if its results can't be controlled, tolerating social reform only when the rights of labor are suppressed and the climate for foreign investment is preserved. As Thomas Carothers, who worked in the Reagan State Department on "democracy enhancement" projects, concluded, Washington "sought only limited, top-down forms of democratic change that did not risk upsetting the traditional structures of power with which the U.S. has long been allied." What mattered was not whether a government was democratic but whether it was aligned with "U.S. interests." A fascist coup in Colombia, inspired by Franco's Spain, brought little protest from the U.S. government; neither did a military coup in Venezuela, nor the restoration of an admirer of fascism in Panama. But the first democratic government in the history of Guatemala, which modeled itself on Roosevelt's New Deal, elicited bitter U.S. antagonism. Things didn't change much in the years to follow.

When the rights of investors are threatened, democracy has to go; if these rights are safeguarded, killers and torturers will do just fine.[3]

The basic dilemma facing policymakers is sometimes candidly recognized at the dovish liberal extreme of the spectrum, for example, by Robert Pastor, President Carter's national security staffer for Latin America. He explained why the administration had to support the murderous and corrupt Somoza regime in Nicaragua, and, when that proved impossible, to try at least to maintain the U.S.-trained National Guard even as it was massacring the population "with a brutality a nation usually reserves for its enemy." The reason was the familiar one: "The United States did not want to control Nicaragua or the other nations of the region, but it also did not want developments to get out of control. It wanted Nicaraguans to act independently, *except* when doing so would affect U.S. interests adversely."[4]

There are numerous cases of outright aggression. Plotting the (sometimes successful, sometimes not) overthrow of governments, such as those of Guatemala, Chile, Iran, Cuba, Haiti, and British Guiana, to name just a few. Over and over again, there have been possibilities of diplomacy and negotiation, which might not have succeeded, but which looked promising. But these were abandoned and dismissed in favor of force and violence. The current arms race with China, and the possibility that the war in Ukraine could have been avoided, are particularly tragic examples of how the U.S. preference for threats over cooperation is leading us constantly into new disasters and creating a vastly more dangerous world.

Even in cases where the United States was not the aggressor, the country's resort to extreme force has produced totally unnecessary carnage. The Pacific war in World War II was brutal on both sides, but numerous racist atrocities against the Japanese have gone largely unacknowledged. The firebombings of Japanese cities (which destroyed sixty-nine cities and killed up to half a million people) were calculated to *maximize* the number of civilian casualties, with U.S. military tacticians even producing "flammability maps" of cities to ensure that as many people as possible were burned alive. Philosopher A. C. Grayling, in a careful evaluation of the Allied area bombings of civilian populations, concludes that they have to be considered "moral crimes." Curtis LeMay was right to point out that had the Allies lost the war, they would likely have been prosecuted as war criminals, but postwar criminal trials were constructed in such a way that only crimes that we did not commit ourselves were considered crimes. Nuremberg prosecutor Telford Taylor observed that "there was no basis for criminal charges against German or Japanese" leaders for aerial bombardment because "both sides had played the terrible game of urban destruction—the Allies far more successfully." As it turns out, the operational definition of a "crime of war" is a criminal activity of which the defeated enemies, but not the victors, are guilty.[5]

Throughout all of this, the myth of American idealism has persisted. The internal records often reveal that U.S. decision-makers were motivated by nothing of the kind, that they wanted to serve "national" economic interests or protect "credibility." And yet the unshakable belief in American goodwill and generosity continues to stultify political thinking and debase political discourse. Sometimes, foreign policy is portrayed as vacillating between "Wilsonian idealism" and "Kissingerian realism." In practice, the distinctions are mostly rhetorical. Every great power toys with the rhetoric of benign intentions and sacrificing to help the world. Our belief in our own exceptionalism is the most unexceptional thing about us.

Also ready on the shelf is the doctrine of "change of course." True, we made errors in the past, a result of our innocence and excessive goodwill. But that is behind us, and we can therefore keep to the grand vistas that lie ahead, ignoring all of history and what it might suggest about the functioning and behavior of institutional structures that remain unchanged. The doctrine is invoked with impressive regularity, always with sober nods of approval for the profundity of the insight.

There is a striking bipartisan consensus on the legitimacy of U.S. dominance. After Joe Biden came into office, *The New York Times* observed in a headline that "On U.S. Foreign Policy, the New Boss Acts a Lot Like the Old One," citing Biden's menacing of China, warm embrace of the murderous Saudi crown prince, and continuing support for Israel despite international condemnation of the occupation of Palestine. The *Times* quoted Donald Trump's former deputy secretary of state making the accurate comment that "continuity is the norm, even between presidents as different as Trump and Biden."[6]

ON GOOD INTENTIONS

No ruling powers have ever thought of themselves as evil. They believe they are good, and it is their opponents who are evil. We must make sure we are not falling into the trap of believing we are on the right side simply because we have been told so. Instead we must confront the ugly truth and pay attention to the victims of our country's actions. A reigning doctrinal system pervades the media, journals of opinion, and much of scholarship. An honest inquiry reveals that striking and systematic features of our international behavior are suppressed, ignored, or denied. It reveals further that our role in perpetuating misery and oppression, even torture and mass slaughter, is not only significant in scale, but is also a predictable and systematic consequence of long-standing geopolitical conceptions and institutional structures.

But even if one chooses to maintain the belief in the good intentions behind U.S. violence, intent is not particularly morally significant. After all, we rarely consider intentions when evaluating enemy states. We do not measure the legitimacy of the invasion of Ukraine on the basis of whether Vladimir Putin truly believed it was full of Nazis. His sincerity is considered an irrelevant factor, because his actions were criminal. The Chinese famine of 1958–61 is not usually dismissed on the grounds that it was a "mistake" and that Mao did not "intend" to kill tens of millions of people. Nor is it mitigated by speculations about his personal reasons for the orders that led to the famine. In the case of adversaries, we often blame them for the predictable consequences of their actions, regardless of whether they felt themselves to be doing good. We recognize that even the worst monsters may have convinced themselves that they are engaged in something morally worthy.[7]

We know that those who conquer and suppress describe themselves as doing it for the victims' own good. Instead of saying they wanted easily exploitable, cheap labor for their own benefit, enslavers said they were acting for the benefit of the enslaved. John C. Calhoun, defending slavery as a "positive good," said, "Never before has the black race of Central Africa, from the dawn of history to the present day, attained a condition so civilized and so improved, not only physically, but morally and intellectually." Do we care whether Calhoun was sincere in believing this? Does it mitigate anything if he was?[8]

Instead of focusing on what we meant to do, then, we should look at what we have done. We distinguish ourselves from the "terrorists" by pointing to the fact that when *they* shoot civilians, they do so intentionally, whereas *we* and our allies only ever do so inadvertently. Our victims are "collateral damage." Of course, this explanation doesn't make much difference to the victims. But also: Does it matter whether one who drops a bomb on a village intends to kill the villagers or just to flatten their houses?

The application of a double standard (or rather, the aforementioned single standard, namely that we can never be malevolent by definition) results in extraordinary intellectual contortions. If Fidel Castro had organized or participated in multiple assassination attempts against the United States president, or tried to destroy livestock and crops, he would be the very symbol of barbarian evil. Yet we claimed the right to do just that to Cuba. We also took it for granted that we had the right to put missiles in the Soviets' backyard. But when they tried to exercise the same right, we nearly started World War III. The inconsistencies are barely noticed.

To ask serious questions about the nature and behavior of one's own society is often difficult and unpleasant. Difficult because the answers are generally concealed, and unpleasant because the answers are ugly and painful. But we must engage in the exercise, because the danger of maintaining our delusions continues to grow.

In 1999, political analyst Samuel P. Huntington warned that for much of the world, the United States is "becoming the rogue super-power," seen as "the single greatest external threat to their societies." A few months into George W. Bush's first term, Robert Jervis, president of the American Political Science Association, warned that "in the eyes of much of the world . . . the prime rogue state today is the United States." Yet Americans find it difficult to conceive of their country as aggressive or a threat. We only ever engage in *defense*.[9]

Whenever you hear "defense," it's usually correct to interpret it as "offense." The imperial drive is often masked in defensive terms: it is not that we are seeking to dominate an integrated world system, but rather that we must deny strategic areas to the Kremlin, or China, thus protecting ourselves and others from their "aggression." The masters of the Soviet Union affected a similar pose, no doubt with equal sincerity and with just as much justification. The practice has respectable histor-ical antecedents, and the term "security" is a conventional euphemism. The planners merely seek to guarantee the security of the nation, not the interests of dominant social classes.

The United States is already far in the lead in conventional forces and weapons of mass destruction, outspending the next ten countries combined. It continues to fuel a vast global arms race, and is trying to move to a new frontier that hasn't yet been militarized: outer space. This would violate the Outer Space Treaty of 1967, which has so far prevented the militarization of space (the United States and Israel abstained from reaffirming it in the UN). The goal, as U.S. Space Command documents explain, is to dominate "the space dimension of military operations to protect U.S. interests and investments." The U.S. is also leading the way in developing and deploying new kinds of autonomous weapons systems that make their own decisions about when and whom to kill. The danger here could not be more extreme, though it goes mostly undiscussed.[10]

There is an alternative path to the one we have pursued, namely to take stated ideals seriously and act on them. The United States could commit itself to following international law, respecting the UN Charter, and accepting the jurisdiction of the International Criminal Court and the World Court. It could sign and carry forward the Kyoto Protocol. The president could actually show up to international climate conferences and take the lead in brokering deals. The U.S. could stop vetoing Security Council resolutions and have a "decent respect for the opinion of mankind," as the Declaration of Independence mandates. It could scale back military spending and increase social spending, resolving conflicts through diplomatic and economic measures rather than military ones.

For anyone who believes in democracy, all of these are mild and conservative suggestions. They are mostly supported by the overwhelming majority of the population. They just happen to be radically different from existing public policy.

THE RESPONSIBILITY TO ACT

Once we see the consequences of the attempt to impose U.S. hegemony through force, we have an obligation to oppose it. It is the fundamental duty of the citizen to resist and to restrain the violence of the state. It is cheap and easy to deplore the crimes of others, while dismissing or justifying our own. An honest person will choose a different course.

Those who have the capacity to act have a duty to act. Living in a free society where extraordinary wealth is available confers, at the very least, a responsibility to understand how power works and ask basic moral questions.

Even those who are not "heroes" by nature are capable of resistance. Mass popular movements have always been comprised of everyday people who have the courage and intellectual integrity to face the moral challenges of their time. The world is full of suffering, distress, violence, and catastrophes. Each person must decide: Does something concern you, or doesn't it?

Many who have access to privilege may be reluctant to forgo the ample rewards that a wealthy society offers for service to power and to accept the sacrifices that the demands of honesty may well entail. Even in the most humane and democratic society it requires considerable courage to refuse to take part in crimes against peace.

Fortunately, such courage is not lacking. The history of the world is not just a bleak compendium of atrocities, but also the story of resistance by those who refused to accept cruelty and oppression as natural, normal, or inevitable. Wherever there is injustice, there are also people trying to stop it.

In the United States, mass movements have achieved striking successes. In the nineteenth century, workers tried to create an independent labor movement based on the principle that "those who work in the mills should own them." Under conditions immeasurably more difficult and repressive than those existing today, they tried to secure better conditions for themselves and each other. They were ultimately defeated, but their work had lasting effects. These same years saw the rise of mass education, a major contribution to democracy (hence, unsurprisingly, a main target of today's assault on democracy). Emerging out of the ashes of Wilson-era repression, the militant labor movement of the 1930s led America to social democracy while Europe was succumbing to fascism (another process now being reversed under assault). Instead of fascism, they delivered Social Security and the guaranteed right to collective bargaining.[11]

During the 1960s, large groups of people chose to enter the political arena to press their demands rather than remain passive and apathetic. The movements they began—for Black civil rights, women's liberation, LGBTQ rights, environmental protection, and an end to the Vietnam war—made the United States a better country, in ways that are permanent. Today, there is greater sensitivity to racist and sexist oppression, more concern for the environment, more respect for other cultures and for human rights. There is much to learn from studying the words and actions of those who launched the Mississippi Freedom Summer, the American Indian Movement, the Free Speech Movement, the Chicano Movement, the Movimiento Estudiantil in Mexico, and the other major global uprisings that tried to reapportion power.

We have also seen a significant effort to improve public understanding of the country's history and present-day injustices. Out of the activism of the 1960s came Black Studies and Women's Studies programs that drew attention to perspectives that had been entirely left out of mainstream scholarship. Major contributions like Howard Zinn's *A People's History of the United States* (and the companion *Voices* volume) lifted the veil on the standard patriotic histories and aired aspects of the country's past that many would rather not discuss. Exposure of these truths creates backlash, with an effort to censor and purge this supposedly dangerous material. "Critical race theory," for instance, is now used as a scare phrase to refer to any study of the systematic structural and cultural factors that gave this country a four-hundred-year history of racist repression. There is an organized effort to ensure that young people are only exposed to propagandistic narratives that uncritically celebrate and venerate the United States.[12]

Today, thanks to the efforts of activists, there is more popular revulsion at U.S. crimes around the world. For instance, in 1963, when the Kennedy administration launched a direct attack against South Vietnam, there was almost no protest in the United States. By the late 1960s, public outrage had grown so substantial that one reason the military hesitated to send more forces to Vietnam was that they were expected to be needed at home—to quell public uprisings. That greater public scrutiny of U.S. conduct has endured. Activist pressure helped limit, and ultimately end, U.S. support for South African apartheid. The Reagan administration's support for atrocities in Central America was clandestine in part because it was known that there was little public support for the policy.

In 2003, when the Bush administration launched its criminal war against Iraq, it immediately sparked the largest antiwar protests in history. Protesters could not stop the war, but there was clear evidence of an increased unwillingness to tolerate atrocities—an example of the "civilizing effects" of the 1960s. To muster public support for the Iraq invasion, it was necessary for the Bush administration to launch a huge propaganda offensive depicting a weak country as the ultimate evil and an imminent threat to our very survival. Popular resistance in this country can impose certain constraints on state violence.[13]

We can recount the stories of plenty of individuals who saw matters clearly and summoned the personal courage to act, even at the risk to their own freedom. In the United States, Chelsea Manning exposed U.S. war crimes in Iraq, landing herself in solitary confinement for years and being driven repeatedly to the brink of suicide. Edward Snowden knew that when he exposed the reach of the U.S. surveillance state, he would be driven into permanent exile. In Israel, nuclear technician Mordechai Vanunu endured nearly two decades in prison (including eleven years in solitary confinement) for blowing the whistle on his country's secret nuclear program. Rachel Corrie, an American student in Israel, became a martyr for peace when she was killed by an Israeli bulldozer, which she was trying to stop from demolishing a Palestinian home. Berta Cáceres, a Honduran environmental activist and Indigenous leader, was murdered for organizing protests to stop the plunder and destruction of her community. (One of her murderers was, unsurprisingly, trained by the U.S. government.[14])

But the stories of heroic individuals give a false impression of how movements succeed. Necessary social change happens because of large numbers of dedicated people, most of whose names are never known, working together at all levels, day in and day out. History books, which pick out only a few famous leaders, mislead us. In reality, from the abolition of slavery to the democratizing movements of the 1960s, to Black Lives Matter and the democratic socialist movement today, as the late Howard Zinn put it, "what matters are the countless small deeds of unknown people, who lay the basis for the significant events that enter history."

In our own time, there is much to be inspired by. The Palestinians who risked Israel's (U.S.-funded) bullets to demonstrate on the Great March of Return showed incredible courage. The Kurds of Rojava have not just resisted a hostile (U.S.-supported) military, but have experimented with a remarkable new social model that emphasizes popular participation in government and women's liberation. The Zapatistas of Mexico also offer an example of authentic democratic politics. There are extraordinary popular movements for justice across the Global South.

We have seen examples of how movements can achieve significant policy changes. The environmental movement of the 1960s succeeded in forcing a Republican administration to take important steps toward reining in pollution. Today, the Sunrise Movement is at the forefront of activism on climate and has engaged in civil disobedience. They successfully pressured the Biden administration to improve its climate policies. The popular movements of our time, many nourished by the Bernie Sanders campaigns of 2016 and 2020, have forced the Biden administration to adopt progressive stances that would previously have been out of the range of the politically possible. While Biden's record on labor issues remains underwhelming, he is the first president since Franklin Roosevelt to take a strong public stand in favor of unionization. This is not just out of personal conviction, but because a newly energized and popular labor movement forced him to do so. This is how the New Deal came about, too—through a combination of militant labor action, CIO organizing, sit-down strikes, and a sympathetic administration.

The record of crimes can be numbing. It is easy to feel hopeless, to see an immovable hegemon. But there are ample opportunities to help create a more humane and decent world, if we choose to act upon them. Those who want to shift policy in a progressive direction must grow and become strong enough so that they can't be ignored by centers of power. We can learn a great deal from the long and hard struggles for social justice in past years, and we can and must move forward to build on their achievements and to surpass them.

We live entangled in webs of deception—often self-deception. But with a little honest effort, it is possible to extricate ourselves. If we do, we will see a world that is rather different from the one presented to us by a remarkably effective ideological system. We will also learn that the system of thought control can collapse very quickly, as happened during the Vietnam War, with consequences that persist today. The main achievement of hierarchy is to get the "unpeople" to accept that oppression is natural. The first step toward making change is to recognize the forms of oppression that exist. The lessons of history teach us a good deal, but nothing more clearly than the fact that we often remain quite unaware of the forms of oppression of which we are victims, or sometimes agents, until social struggle liberates our consciousness and understanding.

We now need what the great antiwar activist A. J. Muste called "revolutionary pacifism." Muste urged that "one must be a revolutionary before one can be a pacifist"—by which he meant that we must cease to "acquiesce [so] easily in evil conditions," and must deal "honestly and adequately with . . . the violence on which the present system is based, and all the evil—material and spiritual—this entails for the masses of men throughout the world."[15]

We citizens of democratic societies must develop critical thinking skills as a form of intellectual self-defense, to protect ourselves from manipulation and control. We can do it. There's nothing in the social sciences or history or whatever that is beyond the intellectual capacities of an ordinary fifteen-year-old. We have to do a little work. We have to do some reading. But there is nothing too deep to grasp.

We are at a unique moment in history. Decisions that must be made right now will determine the course of our species' future (if there is to be one). We have a narrow window to implement the measures necessary to avert the cataclysmic destruction of the environment. Unfortunately, the "masters of mankind" in the world's most powerful state have been hard at work to close that window and to ensure that their exorbitant short-term profit and power will remain untouched as the world goes up in flames.

World-destroying nuclear weapons are being accumulated, and the countries in possession of these weapons are unable to cooperate and talk openly of the possibility of war with one another. The *Bulletin of the Atomic Scientists'* "Doomsday Clock," which provides experts' best estimate of the risk of civilization-wide disaster, has recently been set to ninety seconds to midnight, the closest it has come to termination. The analysts who set the clock cited the two most salient reasons: the growing threat of nuclear war and the failure to take the required measures to prevent global heating from reaching a point where it will be too late. Ninety seconds may be too generous an appraisal, unless those who want to save the world from worse horrors act quickly, firmly, and decisively.[16]

There is a lack of public understanding of the urgency of the situation. A Pew Research Center poll offered respondents a set of issues to rank in order of urgency. Nuclear war did not even make the list. Climate change was ranked close to last; among Republicans, only 13 percent said mitigating climate change should be a top priority.[17]

An extraterrestrial observer looking at our species would say that our primary trajectory is toward suicide, that we are collectively running toward a cliff. Human civilization, having started almost ten thousand years ago in the Fertile Crescent, may now be approaching its inglorious end. It may turn out that higher intelligence was a kind of "evolutionary mistake." One of the theories put forward for why no intelligent life has so far been discovered elsewhere in the universe—the "Fermi paradox"—is that intelligent life may be a kind of lethal mutation that annihilates itself whenever it arises. We are a new species, having been around for a mere second in the evolutionary time scale, and so far we seem intent on proving the theory that intelligence leads to self-destruction.

We are now engaged in an experiment to determine whether our humanity's moral capacity reaches far enough to control our technical capacity to destroy ourselves. Unfortunately, the prospects look grim, and the observer might well conclude that the gap between moral capacity and technological capacities is too immense to prevent species suicide.

But the observer could be mistaken. It's up to us to prove this judgment wrong.

We don't know that honest and dedicated effort will be enough to solve or even mitigate the problems we face. Still, we can be quite confident that the lack of such efforts will spell disaster. Freedom and democracy are by now not merely values to be treasured, but are quite possibly the prerequisite to survival. We therefore have only two choices. One is to say, "It's hopeless. Let's give up." This guarantees that the worst will happen. The other is to say, "We want to make things better, so we will try."

Given the urgency of the crises we face, there is no time to lose.

Notes

PREFACE

1. The best approximation of that before now has been *Understanding Power*, an extremely well-edited collection of interviews, which unfortunately is now thirty years out of date. Individual Chomsky books dive deeper into each of the subjects covered in the present work, and provide more context and supporting evidence for claims made here. Chomsky's critique of media is expanded upon in *Requiem for the American Dream* and Chomsky and Herman's *Manufacturing Consent: The Political Economy of Mass Media*. See also Chomsky's *Necessary Illusions*; *Letters from Lexington: Reflections on Propaganda*; *Media Control*; and *Propaganda and the Public Mind*. On the domestic power structure, see also Chomsky and Marv Waterstone's *Consequences of Capitalism*. On Vietnam, see *American Power and the New Mandarins*; *At War with Asia*; *For Reasons of State*; and *Rethinking Camelot*. (The latter does an excellent job destroying the myth that John F. Kennedy was a dove and exposes the moral bankruptcy of liberal Kennedy nostalgia.) On misleading popular images of the Cold War, see *World Orders Old and New*. On Central America, see *Turning the Tide* and *Deterring Democracy*. On Israel-Palestine, see *Fateful Triangle* and *Middle East Illusions*. The interview books *On Palestine* and *Gaza in Crisis* (both with Ilan Pappé) are also informative. On Iraq and Afghanistan, see *Hegemony or Survival* and *Failed States*. On Cuba, see *On Cuba* (with Vijay Prashad). On the colonization of the Americas, see *Year 501: The Conquest Continues*. On anarchism and political philosophy, see *Chomsky on Anarchism*. On education, see *Chomsky on Mis-Education*. For Chomsky's critique of intellectuals, see the essays "The Responsibility of Intellectuals" and "Foreign Policy and the

Intelligentsia," the former of which is available as a stand-alone book, while the latter can be found in *Towards a New Cold War*, which also includes Chomsky's satisfying evisceration of Henry Kissinger's memoirs. For an accessible introduction to Chomsky's insights on linguistics and cognitive science, see *What Kind of Creatures Are We?* For Chomsky's views on a broad range of subjects, see *The Essential Chomsky* (edited by Anthony Arnove), as well as the numerous books of interviews with Chomsky by David Barsamian and C. J. Polychroniou. A short introduction to Chomsky's linguistic and political analysis can be found in *Problems of Knowledge and Freedom*, which contains two lectures, "On Interpreting the World" and "On Changing the World," both of which are vital tasks.

INTRODUCTION: NOBLE GOALS AND MAFIA LOGIC

1. Heinrich Himmler, "Himmler's Posen Speech—'Extermination,'" October 4, 1943, Jewish Virtual Library; "Decree of the Government of the Reich on the Protectorate of Bohemia and Moravia," March 16, 1939, in *Foreign Relations of the United States, Diplomatic Papers, 1939, Vol. 1* (Washington, DC: U.S. Government Printing Office, 1956), 45–47, 51–52.
2. Hirohito, Emperor of Japan, "Surrender Address," radio broadcast, August 14, 1945; Edward Said, *Orientalism* (1978; repr.: London: Penguin, 2003), xvi.
3. Maximilien Robespierre, "On the Moral and Political Principles of Domestic Policy," February 5, 1794; Andrew Kopkind, *The Thirty Years' War* (London and New York: Verso, 1995), 61.
4. Madeleine Albright famously said that "if we have to use force, it is because we are America; we are the indispensable nation," interview on *Today*, NBC, February 19, 1998.
5. "Remarks by President Obama at the 70th Anniversary of D-Day," Normandy, France, June 6, 2014; George W. Bush, "State of the Union Address," January 20, 2004.
6. Charles E. Bohlen, *The Transformation of American Foreign Policy* (New York: W. W. Norton, 1969), 95–96; Michael Howard, "The Bewildered American Raj; Reflections on a Democracy's Foreign Policy," *Harper's Magazine*, March 1985, 56–57.
7. Samuel Huntington, "Why International Primacy Matters," *International Security* 17, no. 4 (Spring 1993): 82; Jessica T. Mathews, "The Road from Westphalia," *New York Review of Books*, March 19, 2015. The U.S. vacillates, Mathews writes, between "narrowly promoting its own security" and "idealistically serving the interests of others," i.e., it is defensive or benevolent but never aggressive.
8. Hans J. Morgenthau, *The Purpose of American Politics* (New York: Vintage, 1964).
9. Economic and strategic interests are not the only motivation, of course. There are highly irrational influences as well, such as pride, fear of emasculation, or straightforward bigotry. When Lyndon Johnson was asked why he was continuing the war on Vietnam, he is reported to have pulled out his penis, showed it to the journalist, and replied, "This is why." Famously, the British brigadier general

who perpetrated the Amritsar massacre in 1919 claimed he resorted to live ammunition because he didn't want the crowd to laugh at him. Robert Dallek, *Flawed Giant: Lyndon Johnson and His Times* (New York: Oxford University Press, 1998), 491; Ferdinand Mount, "They Would Have Laughed," *London Review of Books*, April 4, 2019.

10. Adam Smith, *An Inquiry into the Nature and Causes of the Wealth of Nations*, Bk. III, Ch. IV.

11. Note that Godfathers, too, may do people kindnesses. They may love their children. To say that the United States operates in the world much like a Mafia kingpin is not to say that no humanitarian act can ever be found across the entire historical record. Al Capone himself once sponsored a soup kitchen.

12. Franklin D. Roosevelt, Annual Message to Congress, January 6, 1941.

13. "Paper Prepared by the National Security Council Planning Board," July 29, 1958, *Foreign Relations of the United States, 1958–1960, Near East Region; Iraq; Iran; Arabian Peninsula, Vol. XII* (Washington, DC: U.S. Government Printing Office, 1956).

14. Curtis uses *unpeople* to mean those whose lives are deemed expendable or worthless by policymakers. See Mark Curtis, *Unpeople: Britain's Secret Human Rights Abuses* (London: Vintage, 2004).

15. The language can even be gangsterish. Lyndon Johnson is reported to have told the Greek ambassador: "Fuck your parliament and your constitution. America is an elephant. Cyprus is a flea. Greece is a flea. If these two fleas continue itching the elephant, they may just get whacked good. . . . We pay a lot of good American dollars to the Greeks, Mr. Ambassador. If your Prime Minister gives me talk about democracy, parliament and constitution, he, his parliament and his constitution may not last long," quoted in Philip Deane, *I Should Have Died* (New York: Atheneum, 1977), 113–14. Indeed, Greek democracy was soon overthrown, and the country was ruled by a right-wing junta supported by the U.S.

16. Jorge I. Domínguez, "The @#$%& Missile Crisis: (Or, What Was 'Cuban' About U.S. Decisions During the Cuban Missile Crisis?)," *Diplomatic History* 24, no. 2 (2000), 305–15; "Memorandum from Gordon Chase of the National Security Council Staff to the President's Special Assistant for National Security Affairs (Bundy)," September 12, 1963; in *Foreign Relations of the United States, 1961–1963, Cuban Missile Crisis and Aftermath, Vol. XI*; Ernest R. May, Philip D. Zelikow, eds., *The Kennedy Tapes: Inside the White House During the Cuban Missile Crisis* (New York: W. W. Norton, 2002), 47.

17. "Russia: 20,000 Activists Subject to Heavy Reprisals as Russia Continues to Crack Down on Anti-War Movement at Home," Amnesty International, July 20, 2023.

18. Larry Shoup and William Minter, *Imperial Brain Trust* (New York: Monthly Review Press, 1977), 130.

19. Winston S. Churchill, *The Second World War, Vol. V: Closing the Ring* (New York: Houghton Mifflin, 1951), 337; Leo Welch, "Speech at the National Trade Convention," November 12, 1946, quoted in Carl Marzani, *We Can Be Friends: Origins of the Cold War* (New York: Topical Books, 1952), 107.

20. Shoup and Minter, *Imperial Brain Trust,* 163, 164.

21. George Kennan, "Report by the Policy Planning Staff," February 24, 1948, *Foreign Relations of the United States, 1948, General; The United Nations, Vol. I, Part 2.*

22. Shoup and Minter, *Imperial Brain Trust,* 130.

23. Under Secretaries' Meeting, April 4, 1949, UM D-26, Office of the Executive Secretary, quoted in Michael Schaller, "Securing the Great Crescent: Occupied Japan and the Origins of Containment in Southeast Asia," *Journal of American History* 69, no. 2 (September 1982): 403; "Memorandum by the Under Secretary of State (Acheson) to the Secretary of State," October 9, 1945, on *Foreign Relations of the United States: Diplomatic Papers, 1945, The Near East and Africa, Vol. VIII* (Washington, DC: U.S. Government Printing Office, 1969); "Memorandum from the Assistant Secretary of State for Near Eastern, South Asian, and African Affairs (Rountree) to Secretary of State Dulles," March 24, 1958, in *Foreign Relations of the United States, 1958–1960, Near East Region; Iraq; Iran; Arabian Peninsula, Vol. XII.*

24. Gerald Haines, *The Americanization of Brazil* (Wilmington, DE: Scholarly Resources, 1989). The U.S., Haines writes, had "assumed, out of self-interest, responsibility for the welfare of the world capitalist system." Stimson quoted in Gabriel Kolko, *The Politics of War: The World and U.S. Foreign Policy* (New York: Random House, 1968), 471; President William Howard Taft quoted in Jenny Pearce, *Under the Eagle: U.S. Intervention in Central America and the Caribbean* (Boston: South End Press, 1981), 17.

25. David Green, *The Containment of Latin America: A History of the Myths and Realities of the Good Neighbor Policy* (Chicago: Quadrangle Books, 1971), 175–76; "U.S. Economic and Industrial Proposals Made at Inter-American Conference," *New York Times,* February 26, 1945.

26. "Overall framework of order" is a phrase of Henry Kissinger's, quoted in Donald Brandon, "Henry Kissinger's Approach to Foreign Policy," *Worldview* 12, no. 3 (March 1969): 9.

27. Adam Smith, *An Inquiry into the Nature and Causes of the Wealth of Nations,* Bk. V, Ch. III.

28. Carol Cohn, "Sex and Death in the Rational World of Defense Intellectuals," *Signs* 12, no. 4 (1987): 687–718.

29. Ashleigh Banfield, Landon Lecture, Kansas State University, April 24, 2003; Michael Isikoff, "Yemenis: Drone Strike 'Turned Wedding into Funeral,'" NBC News, January 7, 2014; "Iraqi Child Crushed by U.S. Tank," *Al Jazeera English,* November 3, 2003.

30. Chris Hedges, *The Greatest Evil Is War* (New York: Seven Stories Press, 2022), ebook.

31. Aaron Blake, "John Kelly's Full-Throated Confirmation of Trump's Ugliest Comments, Parsed," *Washington Post,* October 2, 2023.

32. Nominations of the 113th Congress, First Session. Hearings Before the Committee on Foreign Relations, United States Senate, One Hundred Thirteenth Congress, First Session, May 7 Through December 17, 2013. Power had previously

written that as "the most potent empire in the history of mankind," we needed "a historical reckoning with crimes committed, sponsored, or permitted by the United States" such as "the CIA-assisted coups in Guatemala, Chile, and the Congo; the bombing of Cambodia; and the support for right-wing terror squads in Latin America." Samantha Power, "Force Full," *New Republic*, March 2, 2003.

33. For a longer reflection on Cotton's book, *Only the Strong*, see Nathan J. Robinson, "We Can't Overstate the Danger of Tom Cotton's 'Might Makes Right' Foreign Policy," *Current Affairs*, April 17, 2023.

34. The "blame America first" epithet was made famous during the Reagan administration by Ambassador Jeane Kirkpatrick during her speech at the 1984 Republican National Convention.

35. For instance, take our predecessor in imperial domination, Britain. Historians like Caroline Elkins and Shashi Tharoor are now beginning to lift the veil on the hideous record of centuries of British imperialism. British wealth and global power derived from piracy (such heroic figures as Sir Francis Drake), despoiling India by guile and violence, hideous slavery, the world's greatest narcotrafficking enterprise, and other such gracious acts. France was no different. Belgium broke records in hideous crimes. Today's China is hardly benign within its much more limited reach. Exceptions would be hard to find. As in the U.S., even during the period of Britain's worst atrocities, British intellectuals were praising themselves as the most moral people in the world. John Stuart Mill, as an agent of the East India Company, was aware of the murderous, criminal destruction inflicted by the British Empire. Yet when Mill wrote about the principles that should guide intervention in foreign countries, he made an exception for Britain. Britain, he said, is an angelic country. "Not only does this nation desire no benefit to itself at the expense of others, it desires none in which all others do not as freely participate." In fact, he said, we in Britain are so magnificent that other countries can't understand it. They heap "obloquy" upon us because they can't see that the actions we take are for the benefit of mankind. They "look out in all quarters for indications to prop up the selfish explanation of our conduct." When we slaughter Indians, and conquer more of India to increase our control of the opium trade, so we can break into China by force, they criticize us. But nevertheless, he said, we have to put their criticism aside, recognize that they are just not capable of understanding our magnificence and go ahead with our humane actions. Shashi Tharoor, *Inglorious Empire: What the British Did to India* (N.p.: Scribe, 2018); Caroline Elkins, *Legacy of Violence: A History of the British Empire* (New York: A. A. Knopf, 2022); John Stuart Mill, "A Few Words on Non-Intervention," 1859, in *The Collected Works of John Stuart Mill, Vol. XXI: Essays on Equality, Law, and Education* (London: Routledge, 2014).

36. For an extreme example of this kind of binary thinking, see a 2023 Harvard Harris Poll that asked respondents whether they "side more with Israel or Hamas," obliging them to choose between endorsing the indiscriminate bombing of Gaza or the atrocities of October 7, Harvard CAPS Harris Poll, October 19, 2023.

37. The Soviet Union was not communist in any meaningful sense, and the United States is not a practitioner of free market economics. For elaboration, see Noam Chomsky, *World Orders Old and New* (New York: Columbia University Press, 1994), *passim*.

38. Rob Schmitz, "Poll: Much of the World Sees the U.S. as a Threat to Democracy," NPR, May 5, 2021.

CHAPTER 1: DISCIPLINING THE GLOBAL SOUTH

1. Henry Kissinger, *White House Years* (New York: Little, Brown, 1979), ebook; "The CIA and Chile: Anatomy of an Assassination," National Security Archive, October 22, 2020.

2. "Kissinger and Chile: The Declassified Record," National Security Archive Electronic Briefing Book No. 437, ed. Peter Kornbluh, National Security Archive, September 11, 2013; Peter Kornbluh, *The Pinochet File: A Declassified Dossier on Atrocity and Accountability* (New York: New Press, 2003); David E. Sanger, "Henry Kissinger Is Dead at 100; Shaped the Nation's Cold War History," *New York Times*, December 1, 2023; Peter Kornbluh, "Kissinger's Bloody Paper Trail in Chile," *Nation*, May 15, 2023; "Allende and Chile: 'Bring Him Down,'" National Security Archive, November 3, 2020; David Schmitz, *Thank God They're on Our Side* (Chapel Hill, NC: University of North Carolina Press, 1999).

3. "Memorandum of Conversation of a Meeting of the National Security Council," November 6, 1970, *Foreign Relations of the United States, 1969–1976, Chile, 1969–1973 Vol. XXI* (Washington, DC: U.S. Government Printing Office, 2014); "Telegram from the Central Intelligence Agency to the Station in Chile," October 16, 1970, *Foreign Relations of the United States, 1969–1976, Vol. XXI*.

4. "Kissinger and Chile: The Declassified Record"; Stephen M. Streeter, *"Uncool and Incorrect" in Chile: The Nixon Administration and the Downfall of Salvador Allende* (Jefferson, NC: McFarland, 2023). A Kissinger staffer said: "Henry saw Allende as being a far more serious threat than Castro. . . . Allende was a living example of democratic social reform in Latin America."

5. One aspect of suppressing the anti-fascist resistance was the recruitment of war criminals like Klaus Barbie, an SS officer nicknamed the "Butcher of Lyon." Although he was responsible for many hideous crimes, the U.S. Army employed him as a spy and helped him escape to Bolivia to avoid prosecution for war crimes. Later on, when it became difficult or impossible to protect these useful folks in Europe, many of them (including Barbie) were spirited off, including to the U.S. itself, which became a "safe haven" for Nazis. In fact, "we welcomed approximately 10,000 Nazis, some of whom had played pivotal roles in the genocide." A National Archives report on how "American counterintelligence recruited former Gestapo officers, SS veterans and Nazi collaborators" concluded that "tracking and punishing war criminals were not high among the Army's priorities" after the war. Instead, the Army's Counterintelligence Corps "spied on suspect

groups ranging from German Communists to politically active Jewish refugees in camps for displaced people," believing that "some war crimes by former Nazis and their collaborators should be overlooked because the suspects could be transformed into valuable assets" in the power struggle with the Soviet Union. Sam Roberts, "Declassified Papers Show U.S. Recruited Ex-Nazis," *New York Times*, December 11, 2010. See Richard Breitman and Norman J. W. Goda, "Hitler's Shadow: Nazi War Criminals, U.S. Intelligence, and the Cold War," National Archives, 2010; Martin Lee, "The CIA's Worst-Kept Secret: Newly Declassified Files Confirm United States Collaboration with Nazis," *Foreign Policy in Focus*, Institute for Policy Studies, May 1, 2001; Stuart Taylor Jr., "U.S. Army Shielded Barbie; Offers 'Regrets' to the French," *New York Times*, August 17, 1983; Tom Bower, *The Paperclip Conspiracy: The Battle for the Spoils and Secrets of Nazi Germany* (London: Michael Joseph, 1987); Eric Lichtblau, *The Nazis Next Door: How America Became a Safe Haven for Hitler's Men* (Boston: Mariner, 2015); Deborah E. Lipstadt, "'The Nazis Next Door,' by Eric Lichtblau," *New York Times*, October 31, 2014; Billie Anania, "Why Monuments to Nazi Collaborators Are All Over America," *ARTNews*, November 1, 2022; Eric Lichtblau, "Nazis Were Given 'Safe Haven' in U.S., Report Says," *New York Times*, November 13, 2010.

6. See Frank Kofsky, *Harry S. Truman and the War Scare of 1948: A Successful Campaign to Deceive the Nation* (New York: St. Martin's, 1993), 268. Kofsky shows Truman "deceived Congress and the public about the intentions of the Soviet Union and the likelihood of war" and "rebuffed all efforts by the Soviets to reach an accommodation with the United States." Kennan quoted in John Lewis Gaddis, *Strategies of Containment: A Critical Appraisal of American National Security Policy During the Cold War* (1982, rev. ed.: New York: Oxford University Press, 2005), 39; Melvyn Leffler, *A Preponderance of Power: National Security, the Truman Administration, and the Cold War* (Redwood City, CA: Stanford University Press, 1992).

7. Thomas Boghardt, "'By All Feasible Means': New Documents on the American Intervention in Italy's Parliamentary Elections of 1948," *Sources and Methods* blog, Cold War International History Project, Wilson Center, May 1, 2017. The American public was kept in the dark. The Truman administration was "worried about the consequences at home were word to leak that the U.S. was carrying out secret operations of dubious legal and moral rectitude in a country where thousands of American soldiers lay buried in solemn testimony to U.S. efforts to free Italy from authoritarian rule," especially given that some of the funding for the operation came from seized Nazi assets, including "wealth stolen, from, among others, the murdered Jews of Europe." Robert A. Ventresca, *From Fascism to Democracy: Culture and Politics in the Italian Election of 1948* (Toronto: University of Toronto Press, 2004), 95–96.

8. "Report by the National Security Council," November 14, 1947, *Foreign Relations of the United States, 1948, Western Europe, Vol. III*; Alan A. Platt and Robert Leonardi, "American Foreign Policy and the Postwar Italian Left," *Political Science Quarterly* 93, no. 2 (1978); 197–215; Michael Peck, "Declassified: How America Planned to

Invade Italy (to Save It from Russia)," *National Interest*, February 12, 2017; "CIA Covert Aid to Italy Averaged $5 Million Annually from Late 1940s to Early 1960s, Study Finds," National Security Archive, February 7, 2017; "Interview with Mark Wyatt," National Security Archive, February 15, 1996. See also John L. Harper, *America and the Reconstruction of Italy* (Cambridge, UK: Cambridge University Press, 1986); James E. Miller, *The United States and Italy 1940–1950* (Chapel Hill: University of North Carolina Press, 1986).

9. Dov H. Levin, "Partisan Electoral Interventions by the Great Powers: Introducing the PEIG Dataset," *Conflict Management and Peace Science* 36, no. 1 (2019): 88–106; Scott Shane, "Russia Isn't the Only One Meddling in Elections. We Do It, Too," *New York Times*, February 17, 2018. The CIA officer bragging about this activity was accurately reflecting the organization's culture. Mike Pompeo has confessed: "What's the cadet motto at West Point? You will not lie, cheat, or steal, or tolerate those who do. I was the CIA director. We lied, we cheated, we stole. We had entire training courses. It reminds you of the glory of the American experiment." Mike Pompeo, "Why Diplomacy Matters," speech at Texas A&M University, April 15, 2019.

10. On "reeducation," see Lawrence Wittner, *American Intervention in Greece, 1943–1949* (New York: Columbia University Press, 1982), 164, which notes the plan met with "hearty approval" from the State Department. Wittner notes that "haunted by their fear of revolution and determined, at all costs, to destroy its constituency, American officials joined the Greek right in fostering policies of repression," 166. "Text of Stevenson's Speech at UN and Excerpts from Fedorenko's Reply," *New York Times*, May 22, 1964. Other officials similarly cited Greece as a model for Vietnam, see Wittner, 308. Wittner notes that the major consequences of the war were "reducing much of Greece to ruin, establishing the United States as the dominant power in Greek affairs, and inspiring a growing pattern of American overseas intervention," 312.

11. John W. Dower and Hirata Tetsuo, "Japan's Red Purge: Lessons from a Saga of Suppression of Free Speech and Thought," *Asia-Pacific Journal: Japan Focus* 5, no. 7 (2007); Joe Moore, *Japanese Workers and the Struggle for Power, 1945–1947* (Madison: University of Wisconsin Press, 1983); Christopher Reed, "The United States and the Japanese Mengele: Payoffs and Amnesty for Unit 731," *Asia-Pacific Journal: Japan Focus* 4, no. 8 (2006); John W. Dower, *Embracing Defeat: Japan in the Wake of World War II* (New York: W. W. Norton, 1999), 525.

12. Donald Kirk, "Is the U.S. to Blame for the Massacre on Jeju?," InsideSources .com, April 25, 2018; Anthony Kuhn, "Survivors of a Massacre in South Korea Are Still Seeking an Apology from the U.S.," NPR, September 7, 2022. For background, see Bruce Cumings, *Origins of the Korean War, Vol. 1: Liberation and the Emergence of Separate Regimes, 1945–1947* (Princeton, NJ: Princeton University Press, 1981); Bruce Cumings, *Origins of the Korean War, Vol. 2: The Roaring of the Cataract, 1947–1950* (Princeton, NJ: Princeton University Press, 1992).

13. Remarks by the Honorable Dean Acheson, *Proceedings of the American Society of*

International Law (1963): 13–14; Michael Grow, *U.S. Presidents and Latin American Interventions: Pursuing Regime Change in the Cold War* (Lawrence: University Press of Kansas, 2008).

14. Stephen G. Rabe, *U.S. Intervention in British Guiana: A Cold War Story* (Chapel Hill: University of North Carolina Press, 2005). Arthur Schlesinger notes that John F. Kennedy had an "absolute determination to prevent any new state from going down the Castro road," regardless of what that state's own people had to say, Arthur Schlesinger, Jr., *A Thousand Days: John F. Kennedy in the White House* (Greenwich, CT: Fawcett Publications, 1965), 712. Lyndon Johnson, similarly, felt that "any man who permitted a second communist state to spring up in this hemisphere would be impeached and ought to be," Eric F. Goldman, *The Tragedy of Lyndon Johnson* (New York: Dell Publishers, 1969), 451.

15. Although it was attempting to have Lumumba killed, the United States did not directly arrange the assassination. Nevertheless, as Stuart Reid writes, the U.S. "played a role in every event leading up to Lumumba's downfall and death." Emmanuel Gerard and Bruce Kuklick, *Death in the Congo: Murdering Patrice Lumumba* (Cambridge, MA: Harvard University Press, 2015); Stuart A. Reid, *The Lumumba Plot: The Secret History of the CIA and a Cold War Assassination* (New York: A. A. Knopf, 2023); Sean Kelly, *America's Tyrant: The CIA and Mobutu of Zaire* (Washington, DC: American University Press, 1993); Susan Williams, *White Malice: The CIA and the Covert Recolonization of Africa* (New York: PublicAffairs, 2021), 509. Williams notes that "America's deliberate violation of democracy in African nations where people had struggled against all odds to free themselves from colonial occupation and to achieve majority rule" was done "in the name of American democracy," 517. Mobutu had more influence with American presidents than any other African leader and was the first foreign leader George H. W. Bush met with in office. Ronald Reagan called Mobutu "a man of good sense and goodwill," while Bush described him as "one of our most valued friends" and said that "we support him as he strives to peacefully resolve problems." Mobutu was a despot who stole billions from the impoverished people of his country and "often was compared to King Leopold II of Belgium, who in 1876 claimed the Congo as private property to be exploited for his private gain." After his death, *The Washington Post* noted that his "peculation and abuse of human rights counted for less in Washington than his anticommunist credentials." J. Y. Smith, "Congo Ex-Ruler Mobutu Dies in Exile," *Washington Post*, September 8, 1997; George H. W. Bush, "Remarks Following Discussions with President Mobutu Sese Seko of Zaire," June 29, 1989; Howard W. French, "Mobutu Sese Seko, 66, Longtime Dictator of Zaire," *New York Times*, September 8, 1997.

16. Maureen Dowd, "War in the Gulf: White House Memo; Bush Moves to Control War's Endgame," *New York Times*, February 23, 1991.

17. "Minutes of Telephone Conversations of John Foster Dulles and Christian Herter," June 19, 1958, Dwight D. Eisenhower Library, Abilene, Kansas, cited in

"A View from Below," *Diplomatic History* (Winter 1992); Lars Schoultz, *Human Rights and United States Policy Toward Latin America* (Princeton, NJ: Princeton University Press, 1981), 7.

18. George Gedda, "50 Years Ago in Guatemala," *Foreign Service Journal* (June 2004); Charles R. Burrows, quoted in Piero Gleijeses, *Shattered Hope: The Guatemalan Revolution and the United States, 1944–54* (Princeton, NJ: Princeton University Press, 1991), 365.

19. Arthur M. Schlesinger, Jr., *Robert Kennedy and His Times* (Boston: Houghton Mifflin Harcourt, 1978). The phrase "terrors of the earth" is Schlesinger's. Louis A. Pérez, Jr., "Fear and Loathing of Fidel Castro: Sources of U.S. Policy Toward Cuba," *Journal of Latin American Studies* 34, no. 2 (2002): 227–54; "Kennedy and Cuba: Operation Mongoose," National Security Archive, October 3, 2019.

20. Christian Appy, *American Reckoning: The Vietnam War and Our National Identity* (New York: Viking, 2015), 193fn. The Joint Chiefs of Staff produced a document laying out possible "pretexts which would provide justification for U.S. military intervention in Cuba," including the possibility of staging attacks on U.S. targets and blaming Cuba. Even neoconservative writer Max Boot comments that "it is hard to imagine a more outlandish or distasteful document, redolent of the ruse that Hitler used on August 31, 1939, to start World War II," Max Boot, "Operation Mongoose: The Story of America's Efforts to Overthrow Castro," *Atlantic*, January 5, 2018; Taylor Branch and George Crile III, "The Kennedy Vendetta: How the CIA Waged a Silent War Against Cuba," *Harper's Magazine*, August 1975; Aviva Chomsky, *A History of the Cuban Revolution* (Hoboken, NJ: Wiley-Blackwell, 2010); Keith Bolender, *Voices from the Other Side: An Oral History of Terrorism Against Cuba* (London: Pluto Press, 2010).

21. "We were hysterical about Castro at the time of the Bay of Pigs and thereafter," Robert McNamara recalled. Internal records from the Kennedy administration describe an atmosphere of what was called "fanaticism" over the failure of the U.S. to reconquer Cuba. Louis A. Pérez, Jr., "Change Through Impoverishment: A Half-Century of Cuba-U.S. Relations," North American Congress on Latin America (NACLA), December 14, 2015; Louis A. Pérez, Jr., "The Personal Is Political: Animus and Malice in the U.S. Policy Toward Cuba, 1959–2009," in Soraya M. Castro Marino and John S. Reitan, eds., *Fifty Years of Revolution: Perspectives on Cuba, the United States, and the World* (Gainesville, FL: University Press of Florida, 2012); Document 270, *Foreign Relations of the United States, 1961–1963, Cuba, January 1961–September 1962, Vol. X.*

22. Salim Lamrani, *The Economic War Against Cuba: A Historical and Legal Perspective on the U.S. Blockade* (New York: Monthly Review Press, 2013).

23. *Denial of Food and Medicine: The Impact of the U.S. Embargo on Health and Nutrition in Cuba*, American Association for World Health, Executive Summary, March 1997, Washington, DC; Maria C. Werlau, "The Effects of the U.S. Embargo on Health and Nutrition in Cuba: A Critical Analysis," *Cuba in Transition*, 1998; Amnesty International, "The U.S. Embargo Against Cuba: Its Impact on Economic

and Social Rights," 2009; "Research-Based Progress Report of the Human Rights Council Advisory Committee Containing Recommendations on Mechanisms to Assess the Negative Impact of Unilateral Coercive Measures on the Enjoyment of Human Rights and to Promote Accountability," United Nations Human Rights Council, February 10, 2015.

24. Lars Schoultz, *That Infernal Little Cuban Republic: The United States and the Cuban Revolution* (Chapel Hill: University of North Carolina Press, 2009), 561.

25. Anna Samson, "A History of the Soviet-Cuban Alliance (1960–1991)," *Politeja*, no. 10/2 (2008): 89–108.

26. The term "successful defiance" is from a National Intelligence Estimate done by the CIA in March 1960; Remarks of Senator John F. Kennedy at Democratic Dinner, Cincinnati, Ohio, October 6, 1960; "Summary of conversation between the Vice President and Fidel Castro," April 19, 1959.

27. "Memorandum from the President's Special Assistant (Schlesinger) to President Kennedy," March 10, 1961, *Foreign Relations of the United States, 1961–1963, American Republics, Vol. XII*; Stephen G. Rabe, *The Most Dangerous Area in the World: John F. Kennedy Confronts Communist Revolution in Latin America* (Chapel Hill: University of North Carolina Press, 1999); Piero Gleijeses, "The Cuban Revolution: The First Decade," in *The Cambridge History of Communism, Vol. 2*, eds., Norman Naimark et al. (Cambridge, UK: Cambridge University Press, 2017), 364–87.

28. John Quincy Adams, *Writings of John Quincy Adams, Vol. VII*, ed. Chauncey Ford Worthington (Boston: Adamant Media, 2001), 372; Ada Ferrer, *Cuba: An American History* (New York: Scribner, 2021), 179; Bolender, *Voices from the Other Side*.

29. Ernest R. May and Philip D. Zelikow, eds., *The Kennedy Tapes: Inside the White House During the Cuban Missile Crisis* (New York: W. W. Norton, 2002), xi; Michael J. Strauss, *The Leasing of Guantanamo Bay* (Westport, CT: Praeger Security International, 2009). The George H. W. Bush and Clinton administrations kept Haitian refugees in Guantánamo. See "Haitians and GTMO," Guantánamo Public Memory Project. In a shameful forgotten incident, Clinton kept HIV-positive Haitians in Guantánamo for up to twenty months, even though they were "credible candidates for political asylum," because immigrants with the virus were barred from entry, turning Guantánamo into an "HIV prison camp." Refugees became sicker in Guantánamo, where there was inadequate medical care, and one died shortly after release. Lynne Duke, "U.S. Ordered to Free HIV-Infected Haitians," *Washington Post*, June 9, 1993; George J. Annas, "Detention of HIV-Positive Haitians at Guantanamo—Human Rights and Medical Care," *New England Journal of Medicine* 329, no. 8 (August 1993). The Biden administration has considered reviving the practice of imprisoning fleeing Haitians at Guantánamo, Priscilla Alvarez, "Biden Administration Discussing Using Guantanamo Bay to Process Possible Influx of Haitian Migrants," CNN, March 13, 2024.

30. Roosevelt quoted in A. G. Hopkins, *American Empire: A Global History* (Princeton, NJ: Princeton University Press, 2019), 559; Lamrani, *The Economic War Against Cuba*, 75.

31. The United States encouraged and supported but did not directly participate in this coup. It was prepared to aid the generals in seizing power if necessary and had worked to undermine the moderate leftist government of João Goulart, who had declined to support Kennedy's planned invasion of Cuba. "Brazil Marks 40th Anniversary of Military Coup: Declassified Documents Shed Light on U.S. Role," James G. Hershber and Peter Kornbluh, eds., National Security Archive; John DeWitt, "The Alliance for Progress: Economic Warfare in Brazil (1962–64)," *Journal of Third World Studies* 26, no. 1 (2009): 57–76; Matias Spektor, "The United States and the 1964 Brazilian Military Coup," Oxford Research Encyclopedia of Latin American History, 2018; Anthony W. Pereira, "The U.S. Role in the 1964 Coup in Brazil: A Reassessment," *Bulletin of Latin American Research* 37, no. 1 (January 2018).

32. "Statement of Policy by the National Security Council," March 18, 1953, *Foreign Relations of the United States, 1952–1954, The American Republics, Vol. IV* (Washington, DC: U.S. Government Printing Office, 1983).

33. Office of Intelligence Research Report, 1949, quoted in Walter LaFeber, *Inevitable Revolutions: The United States in Central America* (New York: W. W. Norton, 1993), 97–98; John Foster Dulles, telephone call to Allen Dulles, June 19, 1958, Minutes of Telephone Conversations of John Foster Dulles and Christian Herter, Eisenhower Presidential Library, Abilene, KS; William Y. Elliott, ed., *The Political Economy of American Foreign Policy* (New York: Henry Holt & Co., 1955), 42. Kennedy quoted in Russell Crandall, *The Salvador Option: The United States in El Salvador 1977–1992* (Cambridge, UK: Cambridge University Press, 2011), 501.

34. National Intelligence Estimate, May 19, 1953, *Foreign Relations of the United States, 1952–1954, The American Republics, Vol. IV*; Daniel Denvir, interview with Greg Grandin, "The United States Has Used Latin America as Its Imperial Laboratory," *Jacobin*, March 23, 2023.

35. Grandin, "The United States Has Used Latin America as Its Imperial Laboratory." The classic study of the coup is Stephen Schlesinger and Stephen Kinzer, *Bitter Fruit: The Untold Story of the American Coup in Guatemala* (1982; repr: Cambridge, MA: Harvard University Press, 2005). See also Nick Cullather, *Secret History: The CIA's Classified Account of Its Operations in Guatemala 1952–1954* (Redwood City, CA: Stanford University Press, 2006).

36. Kirsten Weld, *Paper Cadavers: The Archives of Dictatorship in Guatemala* (Durham, NC: Duke University Press, 2014), 117; Greg Grandin, *The Last Colonial Massacre: Latin America in the Cold War* (Chicago: University of Chicago Press, 2004), 99; Schlesinger and Kinzer, *Bitter Fruit*, 254, note the terrible lasting effects of U.S. actions on both the country and the region. The coup "has remained the central episode in the modern history of that country." It meant that "movements toward peaceful reform in the region were set back, dictators were strengthened and encouraged, and activists [looked] to guerrilla warfare rather than elections as the only way to produce change."

37. "Did Reagan Finance Genocide in Guatemala?," ABC News, May 14, 2013;

"Question-and-Answer Session with Reporters on the President's Trip to Latin America," December 4, 1982, Ronald Reagan Presidential Library and Museum; Keane Bhatt, "This American Life Whitewashes U.S. Crimes in Central America, Wins Peabody Award," *North American Congress on Latin America* blog, July 29, 2013; Lou Cannon, "Reagan Praises Guatemalan Military Leader," *Washington Post*, December 5, 1982; Sibylla Brodzinsky and Jonathan Watts, "Former Guatemalan Dictator Convicted of Genocide and Jailed for 80 Years," *Guardian*, May 10, 2013; Julio Godoy, "Return to Guatemala: Unlike East Europe Fear Without Hope," *Nation* 250, no. 9, March 5, 1990.

38. Many such volumes do in fact exist. See, e.g., David Schmitz, *Thank God They're on Our Side: The United States and Right-Wing Dictatorships, 1921–1965* (Chapel Hill: University of North Carolina Press, 1999); David Schmitz, *The United States and Right-Wing Dictatorships, 1965–1989* (New York: Cambridge University Press, 2006); Stephen G. Rabe, *The Killing Zone: The United States Wages Cold War in Latin America* (New York: Oxford University Press, 2015).

39. Greg Grandin, *Empire's Workshop: Latin America, the United States, and the Rise of the New Imperialism* (New York: Henry Holt, 2007), 4; "Memorandum from the President's Assistant for National Security Affairs (Kissinger) to President Nixon," October 7, 1970; "Conversation Between the President's Assistant for National Security Affairs (Kissinger) and President Nixon," June 11, 1971, *Foreign Relations of the United States, 1969–1976, Documents on American Republics, 1969–1972, Vol. E-10*; Stephen G. Rabe, *Kissinger and Latin America: Intervention, Human Rights, and Diplomacy* (Ithaca, NY: Cornell University Press, 2020), 70–73.

40. John Dinges, *The Condor Years: How Pinochet and His Allies Brought Terrorism to Three Continents* (New York: New Press, 2004), 245; J. Patrice McSherry, *Predatory States: Operation Condor and Covert War in Latin America* (Lanham, MD: Rowman and Littlefield, 2005). Days before the assassination of Letelier, Henry Kissinger had rescinded a U.S. warning to Pinochet against engaging in assassinations, "New Docs Show Kissinger Rescinded Warning on Assassinations Days Before Letelier Bombing in DC," *Democracy Now!*, April 12, 2010. "Memorandum from the Assistant Secretary of State for Inter-American Affairs (Shlaudeman) to Secretary of State Kissinger," *Foreign Relations of the United States, 1969–1976, Documents on South America, 1973–1976, Vol. E-11, Part 2*. The memo frets about Operation Condor, but primarily because it will cause inconvenient blowback. It notes that there are "bothersome parallels" between the regimes we are supporting and Nazi Germany, and it is "technically accurate" to call them fascist. Indeed, the "National Security Doctrine" (NSD) adhered to by the military elites of these Latin American states was fascistic in its core tenets: (1) that the state is absolute and the individual is nothing; (2) that every state is involved in permanent warfare, at that time "Communism" versus the "Free World"; and (3) that control over "subversion" is possible only through domination by the natural leadership in the struggle against subversion. For more on the connection between European fascism and the U.S.-backed Latin American dictatorships,

including U.S. collaboration with former fascists after World War II because of their anti-communism, see Branko Marcetic, "The CIA's Secret Global War Against the Left," *Jacobin*, November 30, 2020.

41. Rabe, *The Killing Zone,* xxxix, 148. Rabe notes that even where there was civil unrest and killings conducted by multiple sides, "leaders and security forces supported by the United States carried out 90 percent or more of the killings in every Latin American country."

42. Lawrence Pezzullo quoted in William LeoGrande, *Our Own Backyard: The United States in Central America 1977–1992* (Chapel Hill: University of North Carolina Press, 2000), 26. Brzezinski quoted in Robert Pastor, *Not Condemned to Repetition: The United States and Nicaragua* (Boulder, CO: Westview Press, 2018), ebook. See also Morris H. Morley, *Washington, Somoza and the Sandinistas: State and Regime in U.S. Policy Toward Nicaragua 1969–1981* (Cambridge, UK: Cambridge University Press, 2002); Holly Sklar, *Washington's War on Nicaragua* (Boston: South End Press, 1988); Aviva Chomsky, *Central America's Forgotten History: Revolution, Violence, and the Roots of Migration* (Boston: Beacon Press, 2021).

43. Bernard Gwertzman, "Kissinger on Central America: A Call for U.S. Firmness," *New York Times,* July 19, 1983; "Notice of the Continuation of the National Emergency with Respect to Nicaragua," April 22, 1986, Ronald Reagan Presidential Library and Museum; "Address to the Nation on the Situation in Nicaragua," March 16, 1986, Ronald Reagan Presidential Library and Museum.

44. Further demonstrating its callous disregard for the Nicaraguan people, the U.S. withheld disaster relief in the wake of Hurricane Joan in 1988. (This decision starkly contrasted with the significant aid sent after the 1972 earthquake, which was largely embezzled by the Somoza regime.) By withholding aid during the Sandinista era, the U.S. ensured that any assistance would not bolster the government's efforts to aid its people, again prioritizing political objectives over humanitarian concerns; "U.S. Accused of Impeding Relief Effort for Nicaragua," *Los Angeles Times*, October 29, 1988.

45. Thomas W. Walker and Christine J. Wade, *Nicaragua: Living in the Shadow of the Eagle* (Boulder, CO: Westview Press, 2011), ebook; Greg Grandin, "Chomsky Listens: Latin America and the Ethics of Solidarity," in *The Cambridge Companion to Chomsky*, ed. James McGilvray (Cambridge, UK: Cambridge University Press, 2017), 295–313.

46. Archbishop Óscar Romero, "Letter to President Carter on Aid to Military in El Salvador," February 17, 1980, United States Conference of Catholic Bishops.

47. "From Madness to Hope: The 12-Year War in El Salvador," Report of the Commission on the Truth for El Salvador; Hilary Goodfriend, "30 Years Ago Today in El Salvador, U.S.-Trained Soldiers Murdered 6 Priests in Cold Blood," *Jacobin*, November 16, 2019; "Justice Remains Elusive to Survivors of Salvador's Sumpul River Massacre," Catholic News Service, May 18, 2021; LaFeber, *Inevitable Revolutions*, 250. A priest who went to the river the next day observed that "there were so many vultures picking at the bodies in the water that it looked like a black

carpet." For more background, see Raymond Bonner, *Weakness and Deceit: U.S. Policy and El Salvador* (New York: Times Books, 1984).

48. Danny Hajek, "'I Miss Them, Always': A Witness Recounts El Salvador's 1989 Jesuit Massacre," NPR, November 11, 2016; Carlos Dada, "The Beatification of Óscar Romero," *New Yorker*, May 19, 2015; Mary McGrory, "Salvador Murder and Resurrection," *Washington Post*, April 14, 1990. McGrory comments that "the Salvadoran military will do anything, it seems, to wipe out socially conscious church workers, especially Jesuits, in their country" with the aid of their "U.S.-supplied firepower."

49. Raymond Bonner, "In Salvador, a U.S.-Trained Unit at War," *New York Times*, July 13, 1981; Tracy Wilkinson, "Notorious Salvadoran Battalion Is Disbanded," *Los Angeles Times*, December 9, 1992; Nelson Rauda and John Washington, "The U.S. Role in the El Mozote Massacre Echoes in Today's Immigration," *Washington Post*, May 12, 2021; Leigh Binford, *The El Mozote Massacre: Human Rights and Global Implications* (Tucson: University of Arizona Press, 2016); Mark Danner, *Massacre at El Mozote: A Parable of the Cold War* (New York: Vintage, 1993); *El Salvador: The Making of U.S. Policy, 1977–1984*, National Security Archive; Dustin Hill, "Commitment Beyond Morality: American Complicity in the Massacre at El Mozote" (master's thesis, Eastern Kentucky University, 2011); John Beverley, "El Salvador," *Social Text* no. 5 (Spring 1982), 67–72; Mark Hertsgaard, *On Bended Knee: The Press and the Reagan Presidency* (New York: Farrar, Straus and Giroux, 1988). As Greg Grandin explains, the Reagan administration had a concerted campaign of trying to suppress reporting on the human consequences of its Central America policies: "In 1983, the Reagan administration set up the Office of Public Diplomacy. This was in direct violation of the National Security Act, which prohibited the use of propaganda and disinformation on the U.S. public. It was staffed by psyops operatives from the Department of Defense and used Republican-aligned advertising firms from Madison Avenue to run polls and focus groups so they could find out what language would play well with public opinion. If anyone reported a negative story about the U.S.-backed regime in El Salvador, the response wasn't necessarily to try to disprove it but rather to throw enough mud in the water so that nobody could form a clear opinion about what had happened," Grandin, "The United States Has Used Latin America as Its Imperial Laboratory."

50. For more on U.S. training of human rights abusers, particularly at the infamous "School of the Americas," see Lesley Gill, *The School of the Americas: Military Training and Police Violence in the Americas* (Durham, NC: Duke University Press, 2004). Gill's conclusion is forthright: "Ordinary people who desired land reform, better wages, improved health care, education, and the basic right of self-determination were labeled communists by U.S.-backed regimes and murdered, tortured, and disappeared by shadowy paramilitary death squads and state security forces trained by the United States," 2.

51. Central Intelligence Agency, Directorate of Intelligence, "Intelligence Report:

Indonesia 1965–The Coup That Backfired," 1968. The report called the coup and killings "one of the most significant events of the twentieth century, far more significant than many other events that have received much greater publicity," though did not comment on *why* other events receive "much greater publicity." Jess Melvin, *The Army and the Indonesian Genocide: Mechanics of Mass Murder* (New York: Routledge, 2018). Melvin argues persuasively that the killings constitute a case of genocide under the 1948 Genocide Convention.

52. Geoffrey B. Robinson, *The Killing Season: A History of the Indonesian Massacres, 1965–66* (Princeton, NJ: Princeton University Press, 2018), 122–23; Vincent Bevins, *The Jakarta Method: Washington's Anticommunist Crusade and the Mass Murder Program That Shaped Our World* (New York: PublicAffairs, 2020), 11. Bevins reminds us that "there's a reason we have to settle for estimates. Because, for more than fifty years, the Indonesian government has resisted any attempt to go out and record what happened, and no one around the world has much cared to ask, either."

53. "Indonesia: Vengeance with a Smile," *Time*, July 15, 1966; *The Atlantic* is quoted in Isabel Hilton, "Our Bloody Coup in Indonesia," *Guardian*, August 1, 2001; James Reston, "Washington: A Gleam of Light in Asia," *New York Times*, June 19, 1966; *The New York Times* reported in 1970 that Suharto was assuring the U.S. he "could avert any serious pressure for nationalization or other attacks upon North American, European or Japanese investments," Robert Walker, "Indonesia Assures U.S. on Investments," *New York Times*, July 9, 1970.

54. Robinson, *The Killing Season*, 198. Kathy Kadane, "U.S. Officials' Lists Aided Indonesian Bloodbath in '60s," *Washington Post*, May 21, 1990.

55. Reston, "Washington: A Gleam of Light in Asia"; Robinson, *The Killing Season*; Bevins, *The Jakarta Method*. Bevins notes: "As far as we know, this was at least the third time in history that U.S. officials had supplied lists of communists and alleged communists to allies, so that they could round them up and kill them. The first was in Guatemala in 1954, the second was in Iraq in 1963." "Telegram from the Embassy in Indonesia to the Department of State," April 8, 1958; "Memorandum from the Joint Chiefs of Staff to Secretary of Defense McElroy," April 8, 1958, *Foreign Relations of the United States, 1958–1960, Indonesia, Vol. XVII* (Washington, DC: U.S. Government Printing Office, 1994).

56. Kadane, "U.S. Officials' Lists Aided Indonesian Bloodbath in '60s."

57. Kadane, "U.S. Officials' Lists Aided Indonesian Bloodbath in '60s"; Brad Simpson, "Accomplices in Atrocity," *Inside Indonesia*, July–September 1996; Jaechun Kim, "U.S. Covert Action in Indonesia in the 1960s: Assessing the Motives and Consequences," *Journal of International and Area Studies* 9, no. 2 (2002): 63–85. Indeed, Robert McNamara, then secretary of defense, told Congress that U.S. military aid and training had "paid dividends." McNamara told Lyndon Johnson that U.S. military assistance "encouraged [the army] to move against the communist party when the opportunity was presented."

58. The United States is not the only Western power that bears responsibility. The

British helped with anticommunist propaganda, including newsletters exhorting the killers to continue. "Communism must be abolished in all its forms. The work started by the army must be carried on and intensified," said one of the British newsletters. "I am delighted that a good number of communists have been disposed of," said Norman Reddaway, Britain's "coordinator of political warfare" in Indonesia. Paul Lashmar, Nicholas Gilby, and James Oliver, "Slaughter in Indonesia: Britain's Secret Propaganda War," *Guardian*, October 17, 2021; "Survivors of 1965 Indonesia Massacres Urge UK to Apologise," *Observer*, October 24, 2021.

59. Daniel Patrick Moynihan, *A Dangerous Place* (Boston: Little, Brown, 1978), 247; Liechty quoted in John Pilger, "The Rape of East Timor," *Fair Observer*, February 25, 2016.

60. "Remarks by President Carter," December 6, 1978, *Foreign Relations of the United States, 1977–1980, Foundations of Foreign Policy, Vol. I* (Washington, DC: U.S. Government Printing Office, 2014); G. Taylor, "'Encirclement and Annihilation': The Indonesian Occupation of East Timor," in R. Gellately and B. Kiernan, eds., *The Specter of Genocide: Mass Murder in Historical Perspective* (Cambridge, UK: Cambridge University Press, 2003), 163–86; Hearings Before the Subcommittee on International Organizations of the Committee on International Relations, House of Representatives, Ninety-fifth Congress, First Session, June 28 and July 19, 1977.

61. S. Staveteig, "How Many Persons in East Timor Went 'Missing' During the Indonesian Occupation?: Results from Indirect Estimates," IIASA Interim Report, International Institute for Applied Systems Analysis, Laxenburg, Austria, 2007; Clinton Fernandes, *The Independence of East Timor: Multi-Dimensional Perspectives—Occupation, Resistance, and International Political Activism* (Durham, NC: Duke University Press, 2004), 48, 58; John Pilger, *Distant Voices* (New York: Vintage, 1994), 233.

62. Allan Nairn, a reporter who witnessed the 1991 massacre, vividly describes the "very organized, very systematic" attack in which the Timorese were "just torn apart by the bullets" until "no one was left standing"; "Amy Goodman Recounts the East Timor Massacre 15 Years Ago," *Democracy Now!*, November 13, 2006; Krithika Varagur, "Declassified Files Provide Insight into Indonesia's Democratic Transition," Voice of America, July 24, 2018; David E. Sanger, "Real Politics: Why Suharto Is In and Castro Is Out," *New York Times*, October 31, 1995; Jim Mann and Glenn F. Bunting, "Clinton Aided Indonesia Regime," *Los Angeles Times*, October 16, 1996; "U.S. Promoted Close Ties to Indonesian Military as Suharto's Rule Came to an End in Spring 1998," National Security Archive, July 24, 2018.

63. Brian Knowlton, "Albright Nudges Suharto to Resign: 'An Opportunity for Statesmanship,'" *New York Times*, May 21, 1998. "President Suharto has given much to his country over the past thirty years," Albright added. Notably she did not call for allowing the people of East Timor to enjoy the right of self-determination.

64. Dan Merica and Jason Hanna, "In Declassified Document, CIA Acknowledges Role in '53 Iran Coup," *CNN*, August 19, 2013.

65. Roham Alvandi and Mark J. Gasiorowski, "The United States Overthrew Iran's Last Democratic Leader," *Foreign Policy*, October 30, 2019; Tim Weiner, *Legacy of Ashes: The History of the CIA* (New York: Doubleday, 2007), 92.

66. Mostafa T. Zahrani, "The Coup That Changed the Middle East: Mossadeq v. the CIA in Retrospect," *World Policy Journal* 19, no. 2 (2002): 93–99; "Iranian Nuclear Scientists Studied in U.S.," NPR, March 12, 2007.

67. "The Iranian Accord," *New York Times*, August 6, 1954. To the *Times*, Mossadegh was a "lunatic Arab." Notably, *Times* coverage changed once the shah was in power. A plebiscite called by Mossadegh was denounced by *The New York Times* as "more fantastic and farcical than any ever held under Hitler or Stalin." A plebiscite conducted by the shah ten years later "under far more questionable circumstances," with a *99 percent vote in favor of the shah*, was lauded by the *Times* as "emphatic evidence" that "the Iranian people are doubtless behind the shah in his bold new reform efforts." The shah's fraudulent elections were lauded with equal enthusiasm. Richard W. Cottam, *Iran and the United States: A Cold War Case Study* (Pittsburgh, PA: University of Pittsburgh Press, 1989), 129. See also William A. Dorman and Mansour Farhang, *The U.S. Press and Iran: Foreign Policy and the Journalism of Deference* (Oakland: University of California Press, 1988).

68. Andrew Scott Cooper, "Declassified Diplomacy: Washington's Hesitant Plans for a Military Coup in Pre-Revolution Iran," *Guardian*, February 11, 2015; Ray Takeyh, "The Coup That Wasn't: Jimmy Carter and Iran," *Survival* 64, no. 4 (2022): 137–50; Mahan Abedin, "36 Years On, the U.S. Is Still Struggling to Understand Iran," *Middle East Eye*, February 20, 2015.

69. Gary Milhollin, "Building Saddam Hussein's Bomb," *New York Times*, March 8, 1992. Milhollin says that "American equipment went directly into the Iraqi mass-destruction weapon programs," "our officials knew it was going there." The U.S. government "continued to let sensitive American equipment flow to Iraqi front companies even after it knew that the equipment was likely to be diverted" to the production of weapons of mass destruction. Gary Milhollin, "Testimony: U.S. Exports to Iraq," Senate Committee on Banking, Housing, and Urban Affairs, October 27, 1992. The 1989 U.S. weapons conference was "very helpful to Iraq" in its pursuit of nuclear weapons. David Albright and Kevin O'Neill, "Iraq's Efforts to Acquire Information About Nuclear Weapons and Nuclear-Related Technologies from the United States," Institute for Science and International Security, November 12, 1999.

70. Farah Pandith, "Extremism Is Riyadh's Top Export," *Foreign Policy*, March 24, 2019; Sudarsan Raghavan, "An Unnatural Disaster: Yemen's Hunger Crisis Is Born of Deliberate Policies, Pursued Primarily by a Saudi-Led Coalition Backed by the United States," *Washington Post*, December 27, 2018. The *Post* notes that "one-third of the 18,000 airstrikes carried out by the coalition have targeted non-military sites, including factories, farms, markets, power plants and food ware-

houses." Radhya Almutawakel and Abdulrasheed Alfaqih, "Saudi Arabia and the United Arab Emirates Are Starving Yemenis to Death," *Foreign Policy*, November 8, 2019. Almutawakel and Alfaqih observe that "the Saudis and Emiratis couldn't continue their bombing campaign in Yemen without U.S. military support. Natasha Bertrand and Alex Marquardt, "U.S. Seeks Full Reset with Saudi Arabia, Effectively Moving On from the Murder of Jamal Khashoggi," CNN, June 10, 2022; "The AP Interview: Khashoggi Fiancee Criticizes Biden Visit," Associated Press, July 14, 2022; Ellen Knickmeyer and Matthew Lee, "U.S. Moves to Shield Saudi Crown Prince in Journalist Killing," Associated Press, November 18, 2022.

71. "Iran and Nuclear Weapons Production," Congressional Research Service, March 20, 2024.

72. Martin Van Creveld, "Sharon on the Warpath: Is Israel Planning to Attack Iran?," *International Herald Tribune*, August 21, 2004; Thomas Powers, "Iran: The Threat," *New York Review of Books*, July 17, 2008; "Tehran Accuses Netanyahu of Threatening to Nuke Iran in His UN Speech," *Times of Israel*, September 27, 2023; Ben Norton, "UN Votes 152 to 5 Telling Israel to Get Rid of Its Nuclear Weapons," *Monthly Review*, November 3, 2022.

73. "'Maximum Pressure': U.S. Economic Sanctions Harm Iranians' Right to Health," Human Rights Watch, October 29, 2019; Adam Dubard, "Biden Has Maintained Trump's Failed Sanctions Policy," *The Hill*, June 22, 2023; Michael D. Shear and Farnaz Fassihi, "Iran Releases 5 Americans as U.S. Unfreezes Billions in Oil Revenue for Tehran," *New York Times*, September 18, 2023, however, the administration ultimately reneged on the deal and kept Iran's money frozen; Nancy Cordes, "U.S. Reaches 'Quiet Understanding' with Qatar Not to Release $6 Billion in Iranian Oil Revenues," CBS News, October 12, 2023.

74. "U.S. State Department: Iran Remains 'World's Worst State Sponsor of Terrorism,'" Radio Free Europe, November 2, 2019; "Country Reports on Terrorism 2020: Iran," U.S. Department of State; "2023 Annual Threat Assessment of the U.S. Intelligence Community," Office of the Director of National Intelligence.

75. That attack disclosed the details of fifteen million bank debit cards, representing close to one fifth of the country's population, and was the "largest financial scam in Iran's history." *The New York Times* warned it was "likely to further rattle an economy already reeling from the effects of American sanctions."

76. Thomas Warrick, "U.S.-Iran Tensions: Implications for Homeland Security," Statement to the House Committee on Homeland Security, January 15, 2020; Paul Wagenseil, "Hard-Rocking Cyberattack Said to Strike Iranian Nuclear Plants," NBC News, July 23, 2012; Samore quoted in Edward Lucas, *Cyberphobia: Identity, Trust, Security, and the Internet* (New York: Bloomsbury, 2015), 137–38; David E. Sanger, "Obama Order Sped Up Wave of Cyberattacks Against Iran," *New York Times*, June 1, 2012; Idrees Ali and Phil Stewart, "U.S. Carried Out Secret Cyber Strike on Iran in Wake of Saudi Oil Attack: Officials," Reuters, October 16, 2019. Misha Glenny argues that the U.S.-Israeli deployment of Stuxnet "marked a significant and dangerous turning point in the militarization of the

internet," noting the difference between "locking [viruses] away safely for future use" and "deploy[ing] them in peacetime." Stuxnet has "fired the starting gun in a new arms race" and "all countries that possess an offensive cyber capability will be tempted to use it now that the first shot has been fired." Misha Glenny, "A Weapon We Can't Control," *New York Times*, June 24, 2012.

77. Archit Shukla, "The Killing of General Soleimani—A Blatant Violation of International Laws," *Jurist*, April 14, 2020; Nick Cumming-Bruce, "The Killing of Qassim Suleimani Was Unlawful, Says UN Expert," *New York Times*, July 9, 2020; Michael Crowley, "For Some Never Trumpers, Killing of Suleimani Was Finally Something to Like," *New York Times*, January 6, 2020; Mohammed Rasool, "New Call of Duty Starts with 'Assassination of Qassem Soleimani,'" *Vice*, October 24, 2022.

78. Quoted in LaFeber, *Inevitable Revolutions*, 107.

79. "Report by the Special Study Group," 1954, *Foreign Relations of the United States, 1950–1955, The Intelligence Community, 1950–1955* (Washington, DC: U.S. Government Printing Office, 2007); Lars Schoultz, U.S. Foreign Policy and Human Rights Violations in Latin America: A Comparative Analysis of Foreign Aid Distributions," *Comparative Politics* 13, no. 2 (1981): 149–70.

80. "U.S. Foreign Assistance to the Middle East: Historical Background, Recent Trends, and the FY2022 Request," Congressional Research Service, September 7, 2021; Philippe Nassif and Sara Salama, "Biden's Egypt Problem," *Just Security*, July 19, 2021, noting U.S. practice of "continuing to turn a blind eye and enabling al-Sisi's flagrant violations of human rights in his 'open air prison for critics'"; "Egypt: U.S. to Provide Security Assistance Despite Repression," Human Rights Watch, September 15, 2023; Alex Emmons, "State Department Fails to Vet or Monitor Military Aid to Egypt," *Intercept*, May 12, 2016; "The Questionable Legality of Military Aid to Egypt," *New York Times*, August 19, 2015.

81. Nazeeha Saeed and Vivian Nereim, "Mass Hunger Strike in Bahrain Prison Sets Off Rare Protests," *New York Times*, September 6, 2023; Brian Dooley, "Bahrain Faces New Crisis as Prison Protests Escalate," Human Rights First, August 18, 2023.

82. Barak Ravid, "U.S. and Bahrain to Sign Strategic Security and Economic Agreement," *Axios*, September 11, 2023; Vivian Nereim, "U.S. Deepens Security Pledge to Bahrain, an Adversary of Iran," *New York Times*, September 13, 2023; Karen DeYoung, "U.S. Pact with Bahrain Seen as Model for Strengthening Persian Gulf Ties," *Washington Post*, September 13, 2013; Paul R. Pillar, "Is Bahrain a Dry Run for Controversial U.S.-Saudi Pact?," Quincy Institute for Responsible Statecraft, September 18, 2023.

83. "Biden-Harris Administration Strengthens Partnership with Kingdom of Bahrain and Launches 'Comprehensive Security Integration and Prosperity Agreement,'" White House, September 13, 2023.

84. Leila Fadel, "The Family of a Jailed Bahrain Activist Says He Has Resumed a Hunger Strike," NPR, September 14, 2023.

85. Daniel Flatley, "Biden Signs Bipartisan Law Punishing China Over Uyghur Abuse," Bloomberg.com, December 23, 2021; Quint Forgey and Kelly Hooper, "Biden Fist Bump with MBS Triggers Backlash," *Politico*, July 15, 2022.

CHAPTER 2: THE WAR ON SOUTHEAST ASIA

1. Anthony Lewis, "Look on My Works . . . ," *New York Times*, May 1, 1975; John K. Fairbank, "Assigment for the '70s," presidential address, American Historical Association, New York City, December 29, 1968; Pete Buttigieg, *Shortest Way Home* (New York: Liveright, 2019), ebook; Max Hastings, *Vietnam: An Epic Tragedy, 1945–1975* (New York: Harper Collins, 2018), ebook.
2. Daniel Ellsberg, *Secrets: A Memoir of Vietnam and the Pentagon Papers* (New York: Penguin Books, ebook, 2003).
3. Hồ Chí Minh, "Declaration of Independence of the Democratic Republic of Viet-Nam," in *On Revolution: Selected Writings, 1920–66*, ed. Bernard B. Fall (New York: Frederick A. Praeger, 1967), 143–45.
4. Telegram from Hồ Chí Minh to President Harry Truman, February 28, 1946; Letter from Hồ Chí Minh to President Harry Truman, January 18, 1946.
5. Hastings, *Vietnam;* Murrey Marder, "When Ike Was Asked to Nuke Vietnam," *Washington Post*, August 22, 1982.
6. Michael Schaller, *The American Occupation of Japan* (New York: Oxford University Press, 1987), 151; "The Secretary of State to the Embassy in the United Kingdom," April 4, 1954, *Foreign Relations of the United States, 1952–1954, Indochina, Vol. XIII, Part 1* (Washington, DC: U.S. Government Printing Office, 1982); "Department of State Policy Statement on Indochina, September 27, 1948," *Foreign Relations of the United States, 1948, The Far East and Australasia, Vol. VI* (Washington, DC: U.S. Government Printing Office, 1974).
7. George Kahin, *Intervention: How America Became Involved in Vietnam* (New York: A. A. Knopf, 1986), 89, 60–66; Dwight D. Eisenhower, *The White House Years (1953–1956): Mandate for Change* (Garden City, NY: Doubleday, 1963), 372; Charles Mohr, "Nightmare for Saigon," *New York Times*, October 24, 1966.
8. Christian Appy, *American Reckoning: The Vietnam War and Our National Identity* (New York: Viking, 2015), ebook; Seth Jacobs, *Cold War Mandarin: Ngo Dinh Diem and the Origins of America's War in Vietnam, 1950–1963* (Lanham, MD: Rowman & Littlefield, 2006), 123–25; David Hotham, in *Viet-Nam: The First Five Years*, ed. R. Lindholm (Lansing: Michigan State University Press, 1959), 346.
9. Stanley Karnow, *Vietnam: A History* (London: Guild Publishing, 1985), 255.
10. Interview of General Nguyễn Khánh with German magazine *Stern*, reprinted in *Los Angeles New Advocate*, April 1–15, 1972; Paper "Prepared by the Ambassador in Vietnam (Taylor)," *Foreign Relations of the United States, 1964–1968, Vol. I, Vietnam, 1964* (Washington, DC: U.S. Government Printing Office, 1992).
11. Douglas Pike, *Viet Cong* (Cambridge, MA: MIT Press, 1966), 110; Vann quoted in

Eric M. Bergerud, *The Dynamics of Defeat: The Vietnam War in Hau Nghia Province* (Boulder, CO: Westview Press, 1993), ebook.

12. Bernard B. Fall and Marcus G. Raskin, eds., *The Viet-Nam Reader* (New York: Vintage Books, 1965); Bernard B. Fall, *Last Reflections on a War* (Garden City, NY: Doubleday, 1967). In *Vietnam Inc.*, Philip Jones Griffiths recounts being told by a pilot how impressive napalm was: "We sure are pleased with those backroom boys at Dow [Chemical Company]. The original product wasn't so hot—if the gooks were quick they could scrape it off. So the boys started adding polystyrene— now it sticks like shit to a blanket. But then if the gooks jumped under water it stopped burning, so they started adding Willie Peter [WP, white phosphorus] so's to make it burn better. It'll even burn under water now. And just one drop is enough, it'll keep on burning right down to the bone so they die anyway from phosphorous poisoning."

13. "Greatest bomber in history" was a phrase used by *The Washington Post*, soon also used by senators John V. Tunney (D-CA) and Frank Moss (D-UT), *Congressional Record–Senate*, April 17, 1972, p. 12817, and April 19, 1972, p. 13455; "Conversation Between President Nixon and His Assistant for National Security Affairs (Kissinger)," April 19, 1972, *Foreign Relations of the United States, 1969–1976, Soviet Union, October 1971–May 1972, Vol. XIV* (Washington, DC: U.S. Government Printing Office, 2006); Appy, *American Reckoning*; Martha Gellhorn, *The Face of War* (New York: Simon & Schuster, 1959), 224.

14. Facts in this paragraph from Nick Turse, *Kill Anything That Moves: The Real American War in Vietnam* (New York: Metropolitan Books, 2013). Turse's vital book is relied on *passim*; Truong Nhu Tang, *A Vietcong Memoir: An Inside Account of the Vietnam War and Its Aftermath* (New York: Vintage, 1986).

15. Quy-Toan Do, "Agent Orange and the Prevalence of Cancer Among the Vietnamese Population 30 Years After the End of the Vietnam War," Policy Research Working Paper no. 5041, World Bank Development Research Group, September 2009; "The U.S. Military and the Herbicide Program in Vietnam," in *Veterans and Agent Orange: Health Effects of Herbicides Used in Vietnam*, Institute of Medicine Committee to Review the Health Effects in Vietnam Veterans of Exposure to Herbicides (Washington, DC: National Academies Press, 1994); Arthur H. Westing, "'Agent Blue' in Vietnam," *New York Times*, July 12, 1971; John Milner, *Vietnam: After the Fire* (Acacia Productions, Channel Four, and Cinema Guild, 1988).

16. Gabriel Kolko, *Vietnam: Anatomy of a Peace* (New York: Routledge, 1997), 2; RAND quoted in Turse, *Kill Anything That Moves*, 95.

17. Guenter Lewy, *America in Vietnam* (New York: Oxford University Press, 1978), 226; Nick Turse, "The Ken Burns Vietnam War Documentary Glosses Over Devastating Civilian Toll," *Intercept*, September 28, 2017.

18. Geoffrey C. Ward and Ken Burns, *The Vietnam War: An Intimate History* (New York: A. A. Knopf, 2017), 153.

19. Lewy, *America in Vietnam*, 180–81; David Gates, "Transition: Westmoreland," *Newsweek*, July 31, 2005.

20. Lewy, *America in Vietnam*, 96. For a more thoroughgoing critique of Lewy's history, see Noam Chomsky, "On the Aggression of South Vietnamese Peasants Against the United States," in *Towards a New Cold War* (New York: Pantheon, 1982), 154–65.

21. Ward and Burns, *The Vietnam War*, 54; Lewy, *America in Vietnam*, 243.

22. Wallace Terry, *Bloods: An Oral History of the Vietnam War by Black Veterans* (New York: Presidio Press, 1984); Turse, *Kill Anything That Moves*, 28.

23. Peter Davis, *Hearts and Minds* (Culver City, CA: Columbia Pictures, 1974); John Mecklin, *Mission in Torment* (Garden City, NY: Doubleday, 1965), 76.

24. Andrew Preston, "How Vietnam Was America's Avoidable War," *New Statesman*, September 19, 2018; Tim O'Brien, *The Things They Carried* (Boston: Houghton Mifflin, 1990).

25. Deborah Nelson, *The War Behind Me: Vietnam Veterans Confront the Truth About U.S. War Crimes* (New York: Basic Books, 2008), 76; Lewy, *America in Vietnam*, 452.

26. Ward and Burns, *The Vietnam War*, 273; Nick Turse, "A My Lai a Month," *The Nation*, November 13, 2008; Turse, *Kill Anything That Moves*, 206.

27. Ward and Burns, *The Vietnam War*, 154.

28. Lewis M. Simons, "The U.S. Promised Ukraine Cluster Bombs. In Laos, They Still Kill Civilians," NPR, July 11, 2023; "War Legacy Issues in Southeast Asia: Unexploded Ordnance," Congressional Research Service, June 3, 2019.

29. Leah Zani, *Bomb Children: Life in the Former Battlefields of Laos* (Durham, NC: Duke University Press, 2019), 19; Joshua Kurlantzick, *A Great Place to Have a War: America in Laos and the Birth of a Military CIA* (New York: Simon & Schuster, 2017), 18.

30. Antonia Bolingbroke-Kent, "'I Don't Want More Children to Suffer What I Did': The 50-Year Fight to Clear U.S. Bombs from Laos," *Guardian*, April 27, 2023.

31. Thomas Fuller, "One Woman's Mission to Free Laos from Millions of Unexploded Bombs," *New York Times*, April 5, 2015; Stearns quoted in Kurlantzick, *A Great Place to Have a War*, 179, commenting that bombs were dropped "even without clear military targets, so the pilots would get some practice," and quoting another U.S. official joking that "we couldn't just let the planes rust" during halts on bombing North Vietnam; Fred Branfman, *Voices from the Plain of Jars: Life Under an Air War* (Madison: University of Wisconsin Press, 1972). See also Brett S. Morris, "Laos After the Bombs," *Jacobin*, July 3, 2015.

32. Bolingbroke-Kent, "'I Don't Want More Children to Suffer What I Did.'" On the upside, some peasants are now able to make a living collecting unexploded ordnance.

33. Elizabeth Becker, "Kissinger Tapes Describe Crises, War and Stark Photos of Abuse," *New York Times*, May 27, 2004; Taylor Owen and Ben Kiernan, "Bombs over Cambodia," *The Walrus*, October 2006.

34. Ben Kiernan, *The Pol Pot Regime: Race, Power, and Genocide in Cambodia Under the Khmer Rouge, 1975–79* (New Haven, CT: Yale University Press, 1998), 16. Similar conclusions are suggested by William Shawcross in *Sideshow: Kissinger, Nixon, and the Destruction of Cambodia* (London: Andre Deutsch, 1979); Taylor Owen and

Ben Kiernan, "Making More Enemies Than We Kill? Calculating U.S. Bomb Tonnages Dropped on Laos and Cambodia, and Weighing Their Implications," *Asia-Pacific Journal: Japan Focus* 13, no. 16 (April 27, 2015).

35. Elizabeth Becker, *When the War Was Over: The Voices of Cambodia's Revolution and Its People* (New York: Simon & Schuster, 1986), 440; Adam Jones, *Genocide: A Comprehensive Introduction* (London: Taylor & Francis, 2010), 302. Jones comments on the "anomalous sight, throughout the 1980s, of genocidal communists receiving some of their firmest backing from Washington, DC."

36. Don Oberdorfer, "U.S. to Support Pol Pot Regime for UN Seat," *Washington Post*, September 15, 1980; Elizabeth Becker, "Death of Pol Pot: The Diplomacy," *New York Times*, April 17, 1998; Ben Kiernan, *How Pol Pot Came to Power* (London and New York: Verso, 2008), xxix.

37. Shawcross, *Sideshow*, 395; William Shawcross, "Sihanouk's Case," *New York Review of Books*, February 22, 1979. For more on Kissinger specifically, see Nick Turse, "Blood on His Hands," *Intercept*, May 23, 2023; Reed Brody, "Is Henry Kissinger a War Criminal?," *Just Security*, June 27, 2023; René Rojas, Bhaskar Sunkara, and Jonah Walter, eds., *The Good Die Young: The Verdict on Henry Kissinger* (London and New York: Verso, 2024).

38. "Year Zero Author on Justice," *Phnom Penh Post*, April 11, 2013.

39. Christian Appy, *Patriots: The Vietnam War Remembered from All Sides* (New York: Penguin Books, 2003), 126.

40. Elizabeth Becker, "The Secrets and Lies of the Vietnam War, Exposed in One Epic Document," *New York Times*, June 9, 2021.

41. McNaughton quoted in Howard Zinn, *A People's History of the United States* (New York: HarperCollins, 1999), 499. Zinn's Vietnam chapter is vital for an understanding of the background to the war as well as the resistance movement that tried to stop it; "Conversation Among President Nixon, the Assistant to the President (Haldeman), and the President's Assistant for National Security Affairs (Kissinger)," May 5, 1972, *Foreign Relations of the United States, 1969–1976, Vietnam, January–October 1972, Vol. VIII* (Washington, DC: U.S. Government Printing Office, 1972).

42. William Ehrhart, "A Vietnam Vet," interview by David Hoffman, 1989, YouTube, https://www.youtube.com/watch?v=tixOyiR8B-8.

43. Jimmy Carter, The President's News Conference, March 24, 1977.

CHAPTER 3: 9/11 AND THE WRECKING OF AFGHANISTAN

1. George W. Bush, "President Bush Addresses the Nation," September 20, 2001; Osama bin Laden, *Messages to the World: The Statements of Osama bin Laden* (London and New York: Verso, 2005), 46–47.

2. "Victims Relive the Terror of Israel Attack on Lebanon," *Deseret News*, April 17, 1997; Associated Press reported that "no one knows the number for sure because many victims were blown apart when the 155mm shells rained down." Sam F. Ghattas, "A Year Later, Survivors Carry Scars of Qana Massacre," Associated

Press, April 16, 1997. The scars do not go away, as interviews with surviving victims reported twenty years later: Federica Marsi, "Two Decades of Pain: Lebanese Village Still Reeling from Israeli 'Massacre,'" *Middle East Eye*, August 1, 2016.

3. "Israel/Lebanon: Unlawful Killings During Operation 'Grapes of Wrath,'" Amnesty International, July 23, 1996; Human Rights Watch concluded that "the sustained firing of such shells, without warning, in close proximity to a large concentration of civilians—violated a key principle of international humanitarian law"; "Operation 'Grapes of Wrath': The Civilian Victims," Human Rights Watch, September 1997; "Qana Dead 'a Bunch of Arabs,'" *Independent*, May 10, 1996. The commander of the attack, Naftali Bennett, eventually became the prime minister of Israel.
4. Osama bin Laden, "Letter to America," *Guardian*, November 24, 2002.
5. See Scott D. Seligman, "The Franklin Prophecy," *Tablet*, August 4, 2021.
6. Peter Waldman et al., "The Moneyed Muslims Behind the Terror," *Wall Street Journal*, September 14, 2001; Peter Waldman and Hugh Pope, "Worlds Apart: Some Muslims Fear War on Terrorism Is Really a War on Them," *Wall Street Journal*, September 21, 2001. The *Journal* said that an "oft-heard lament from Arabs and Muslims is: Why, if equality and freedom are so important in the West, doesn't the U.S. stand up for them in the Muslim world?" The Arabic newspaper *al-Quds al-Arabi*, while condemning the September 11 attacks, nevertheless called "upon American citizens to ask, why among all the embassies, buildings and defense establishments of all the Western powers, it is theirs that are targeted by terrorist actions?"
7. Waldman and Pope, "Worlds Apart"; David Gardner, "The West's Role in Islam's War of Ideas," *Financial Times*, July 8, 2005.
8. Serge Schmemann, "War Zone; What Would 'Victory' Mean?," *New York Times*, September 16, 2001.
9. Or, more precisely, *re*launched. The original "global war on terror" was declared by the Reagan administration when it took office, using fevered rhetoric about what Reagan called a "plague spread by depraved opponents of civilization itself" and a "return to barbarism in the modern age" (the words of Secretary of State George Shultz). That "war on terror" has been quietly removed from history. It quickly turned into a murderous and destructive terrorist war afflicting Central America, southern Africa, and the Middle East, with grim repercussions to the present.
10. "Costs of War: Summary of Findings," Watson Institute for International and Public Affairs, Brown University, n.d.
11. "U.S. Tried for Years to Secure Bin Laden," *Orlando Sentinel*, October 29, 2001; Carter Malkasian, *The American War in Afghanistan: A History* (New York: Oxford University Press, 2021), ebook.
12. David B. Ottaway and Joe Stephens, "Diplomats Met with Taliban on Bin Laden," *Washington Post*, October 29, 2001; Mujib Mashal, "Taliban 'Offered bin Laden

Trial Before 9/11,'" *Al Jazeera English*, September 11, 2011; John Mueller, "What If the U.S. Didn't Go to War in Afghanistan After 9/11?," Cato Institute, September 3, 2021; Vahid Brown, "The Facade of Allegiance: Bin Ladin's Dubious Pledge to Mullah Omar," *CTC Sentinel* 3, no. 1 (January 2010).

13. John F. Burns, "Pakistan Antiterror Support Avoids Vow of Military Aid," *New York Times*, September 16, 2001; Samina Ahmed, "The United States and Terrorism in Southwest Asia: September 11 and Beyond," *International Security* 26, no. 3 (Winter 2001–2002): 92.

14. Patrick E. Tyler, "Bush Warns 'Taliban Will Pay a Price,'" *New York Times*, October 8, 2001; "Bush Announces Strikes Against Taliban," *Washington Post*, October 7, 2001; Alice Thomas, "Exercise Caution, Experts Say," *Columbus Dispatch*, September 16, 2001; Michael Howard, "What's in a Name? How to Fight Terrorism," *Foreign Affairs*, January/February 2002; Robert Kagan, "It Wasn't Hubris That Drove America into Afghanistan. It Was Fear," *Washington Post*, August 26, 2021; Dan Balz, Bob Woodward, and Jeff Himmelman, "Afghan Campaign's Blueprint Emerges," *Washington Post*, January 28, 2002; Carlos Lozada, "9/11 Was a Test. The Books of the Last Two Decades Show How America Failed," *Washington Post*, September 3, 2021.

15. Malkasian, *The American War in Afghanistan*, 60–61; Patrick Cockburn, "Who Killed 120 Civilians? The U.S. Says It's Not a Story," *Independent*, May 10, 2009.

16. Rory McCarthy, "New Offer on Bin Laden," *Guardian*, October 16, 2001; Carl Conetta, "Strange Victory: A Critical Appraisal of Operation Enduring Freedom and the Afghanistan War," Project on Defense Alternatives Research Monograph 6, January 30, 2002; "Afghanistan: New Civilian Deaths Due to U.S. Bombing," Human Rights Watch, October 30, 2001; "U.S. Planes Bomb a Red Cross Site," *New York Times*, October 27, 2001; "A Future for the Afghans," *Guardian*, October 16, 2001.

17. Sarah Chayes, "Spinning the War in Afghanistan," *Bulletin of the Atomic Scientists* 62, no. 5 (2006): 54–61.

18. "Pentagon: Afghan Village a 'Legitimate Target,'" CNN, November 2, 2001; Jason Burke, "U.S. Admits Lethal Blunders," *Guardian,* October 13, 2001; Robert Nickelsberg with Jane Perlez, "Survivors Recount Fierce American Raid That Flattened a Village," *New York Times*, November 2, 2001.

19. Barry Bearak, "Leaders of the Old Afghanistan Prepare for the New," *New York Times*, October 25, 2001; Anatol Lieven, "On the Road: Interview with Commander Abdul Haq," Carnegie Endowment for International Peace, October 14, 2001. Haq commented that "Afghans are now being made to suffer for these Arab fanatics, but we all know who brought these Arabs to Afghanistan in the 1980s." Haq is making reference to the period where religious fundamentalist extremists in Afghanistan were recruited, armed, and financed by the CIA and their allies in Pakistani intelligence to cause maximal harm to the Russians during the Soviet occupation. For the Reaganites, "the single aim" was "bleeding the Russians and pillorying the Soviets in world opinion." The immediate result was a war

that devastated Afghanistan, with even worse consequences after the Russians withdrew and Reagan's jihadis took over. The long-term result was two decades of terror and civil war. See Steve Coll, *Ghost Wars: The Secret History of the CIA, Afghanistan, and bin Laden, from the Soviet Invasion to September 10, 2001* (New York: Penguin Press, 2004).

20. "RAWA Statement on the U.S. Strikes on Afghanistan," Revolutionary Association of the Women of Afghanistan, October 11, 2001, http://www.rawa.org/us-strikes.htm.

21. Donald Rumsfeld news conference, October 29, 2001; Leslie Rose, "U.S. Bombing of Afghanistan Not Justified as Self-Defense Under International Law," 59 Guild Prac. 65 (2002); Alfred W. McCoy, "You Must Follow International Law (Unless You're America)," *Nation*, February 24, 2015.

22. Craig Whitlock, *The Afghanistan Papers* (New York: Simon & Schuster, 2021), 28.

23. "Not Inviting Taliban to Bonn Conference Was a Historic Mistake," *South Asia Monitor* (December 31, 2020); Malkasian writes that Rumsfeld "may have even threatened to pull U.S. support if any deal went through."

24. Except as otherwise noted, all quotations from Malkasian, *The American War in Afghanistan*, and Whitlock, *The Afghanistan Papers*.

25. Joel Roberts, "Plans for Iraq Attack Began on 9/11," CBS News, September 4, 2002; Maura Reynolds, "Bush 'Not Concerned' About Bin Laden in '02," *Los Angeles Times*, October 14, 2004.

26. Office of the Secretary of Defense, Donald Rumsfeld "snowflake" to [redacted], Subject: "Meetings with President," October 21, 2002, 5:50 p.m., National Security Archive.

27. James Risen, "A War's Epitaph," *Intercept*, August 26, 2001; "The United States' Response to Corruption in Afghanistan," Institute of World Politics, May 1, 2018.

28. Rodric Braithwaite, "New Afghan Myths Bode Ill for Western Aims," *Financial Times*, October 15, 2008.

29. "Dexter Filkins on the Fall of Afghanistan," *New Yorker Radio Hour*, August 20, 2021; Patrick Cockburn, "Return to Afghanistan: A Report from Kabul," *London Review of Books,* June 11, 2009.

30. Sarah Chayes, *The Punishment of Virtue: Inside Afghanistan After the Taliban* (New York: Penguin Books, 2007), ebook.

31. Luke Harding, "Afghan Massacre Haunts Pentagon," *Guardian*, September 14, 2002. The White House resisted pressure from human rights groups to investigate the horrific Dostum massacre. James Risen, "U.S. Inaction Seen After Taliban P.O.W.'s Died," *New York Times*, July 10, 2009; Rod Nordland, "Accused of Rape and Torture, Exiled Afghan Vice President Returns," *New York Times*, July 22, 2018; Joshua Partlow, "Dostum, a Former Warlord Who Was Once America's Man in Afghanistan, May Be Back," *Washington Post*, April 23, 2014; Matthew Rosenberg, "Afghanistan's Vice President Is Barred from Entering U.S.," *New York Times*, April 25, 2016.

32. Hillary Clinton, "The Way Forward in Afghanistan," Testimony Before the Sen-

ate Foreign Relations Committee, Washington, DC, June 23, 2011, quoted in Whitlock, *The Afghanistan Papers.*

33. Nick Davies and David Leigh, "Afghanistan War Logs: Massive Leak of Secret Files Exposes Truth of Occupation," *Guardian*, July 25, 2010.

34. Peter Finn, "Staff Sgt. Robert Bales Admits to Killing 16 Afghans," *Washington Post*, June 5, 2013; Ben Doherty, "Ben Roberts-Smith Called Alleged Killing of Unarmed Afghan Teenager 'Beautiful Thing,' Court Hears," *Guardian*, February 11, 2022; "On 3 October 2015, U.S. Airstrikes Destroyed Our Trauma Hospital in Kunduz, Afghanistan, Killing 42 People," Médecins Sans Frontières; Spencer Ackerman, "Doctors Without Borders Airstrike: U.S. Alters Story for Fourth Time in Four Days," *Guardian*, October 6, 2015.

35. Risen, "A War's Epitaph."

36. Risen, "A War's Epitaph"; Scott Shane, "Drone Strikes Reveal Uncomfortable Truth: U.S. Is Often Unsure About Who Will Die," *New York Times*, April 23, 2015; Scott Shane, "Drone Strike Statistics Answer Few Questions, and Raise Many," *New York Times*, July 3, 2016; Ryan Bort, "The U.S. Government Just Killed 30 Innocent People," *Rolling Stone*, September 19, 2019; Peter Finn, "Rise of the Drone: From Calif. Garage to Multibillion-Dollar Defense Industry," *Washington Post*, December 23, 2011; the Costs of War project estimates seventy thousand civilians were killed across the Afghanistan/Pakistan war zone over the course of U.S. involvement.

37. Gopal cited in Malkasian, *The American War in Afghanistan*, 113.

38. "U.S. Drops Its Biggest Non-Nuclear Bomb on Afghans, Already Traumatized by Decades of War," *Democracy Now!*, April 14, 2017; Alex Emmonds, "'Mother of All Bombs' Never Used Before Due to Civilian Casualty Concerns," *Intercept*, April 13, 2017; U.S. official quoted in Dexter Filkins, "Last Exit from Afghanistan," *New Yorker*, March 1, 2021.

39. "Dexter Filkins on the Fall of Afghanistan," *New Yorker Radio Hour*; Eliza Griswold, "The Afghans America Left Behind," *New Yorker*, December 20, 2021.

40. Matthew Aikins et al., "In U.S. Drone Strike, Evidence Suggests No ISIS Bomb," *New York Times*, September 20, 2021; Eric Schmitt, "No U.S. Troops Will Be Punished for Deadly Kabul Strike, Pentagon Chief Decides," *New York Times*, December 13, 2021.

41. "15 Million Afghans Receive WFP Food Assistance So Far in 2021; Massive Uplift Needed as Economy Disintegrates," World Food Program, December 14, 2021; Saeed Shah, "As Afghanistan Sinks into Destitution, Some Sell Children to Survive," *Wall Street Journal*, October 16, 2021; Sune Engel Rasmussen, "'No Father Wants to Sell His Son's Kidney.' Afghans Pushed to Desperate Measures to Survive," *Wall Street Journal*, April 19, 2022; "Afghanistan: WFP Forced to Cut Food Aid for 2 Million More," *UN News*, September 5, 2023; Mansoor Khosrow, "'Life of Toil': Growing Number of Starving Afghan Families Send Children to Work," Radio Free Europe, May 17, 2023.

42. Ellen Ioanes, "U.S. Policy Is Fueling Afghanistan's Humanitarian Crisis," *Vox*,

January 22, 2022; Charlie Savage, "Spurning Demand by the Taliban, Biden Moves to Split $7 Billion in Frozen Afghan Funds," *New York Times*, February 11, 2022; Ruth Pollard, "Joe Biden's $7 Billion Betrayal of Afghanistan," Bloomberg, February 13, 2022.

43. Afghanistan is *one* of the poorest countries in the world but not the absolute poorest.

44. Quoted in Sima Samar, *Outspoken: My Fight for Freedom and Human Rights in Afghanistan* (Toronto: Random House Canada, 2024), 290–91.

45. Baheer quoted in Pollard, "Joe Biden's $7 Billion Betrayal of Afghanistan"; Lynne O'Donnell, "Afghanistan Still Wants Its Frozen Funds," *Foreign Policy*, July 21, 2022; "The Biden Administration Frees Up $7 Billion in Afghan Assets Frozen in the U.S.," NPR, February 14, 2022; Javed Ahmad Kakar, "Biden Extends Freeze on Afghan Central Bank's Assets," *Pajhwok Afghan News*, February 8, 2024.

46. Laurel Miller, "Afghanistan Is in Meltdown, and the U.S. Is Helping to Speed It Up," *New York Times*, January 11, 2022; David Miliband, "The Afghan Economy Is a Falling House of Cards. Here Are 5 Steps to Rebuild It," CNN, January 20, 2022; Mark Weisbrot, "Biden's Sanctions on Afghanistan Threaten to Kill More Civilians Than Two Decades of War," *USA Today*, March 10, 2022.

47. Camilo Montoya-Galvez, "U.S. Is Rejecting over 90% of Afghans Seeking to Enter the Country on Humanitarian Grounds," CBS News, June 20, 2022; Dan De Luce, "Afghans Subject to Stricter Rules Than Ukrainian Refugees, Advocates Say," NBC News, April 29, 2022; Claire Adida et al., "Americans See Afghan and Ukrainian Refugees Very Differently. Why?," *Washington Post*, April 29, 2022; Alice Speri, "The Biden Administration Is Keeping Thousands of Afghans in Limbo Abroad," *Intercept*, September 13, 2023; Moustafa Bayoumi, "They Are 'Civilised' and 'Look Like Us': The Racist Coverage of Ukraine," *Guardian*, March 2, 2022.

48. Miller, "Afghanistan Is in Meltdown, and the U.S. Is Helping to Speed It Up."

49. "Taliban Diplomat Condemns Attacks," CNN, September 12, 2001; Rajiv Chandrasekaran, *Little America: The War Within the War for Afghanistan* (New York: Vintage, 2013), 22; "Human and Budgetary Costs to Date of the U.S. War in Afghanistan, 2001–2022," Costs of War Project, Watson Institute for International and Public Affairs, Brown University; Nitin J. Ticku, "Taliban Says They Condemned 9/11 Terror Attacks in 2001, Were Ready to Cooperate with the U.S.," *Eurasian Times*, September 12, 2021.

50. Howard, "What's in a Name?"

51. Patrick Cockburn, "Wasn't Bin Laden the Reason We Went to War?," *Independent*, May 8, 2011.

52. Patrick Cockburn, *The Age of Jihad* (London and New York: Verso, 2016), ebook. For further details and sources on the Afghanistan war, see Scott Horton, *Fool's Errand: Time to End the War in Afghanistan* (independently published, 2017).

CHAPTER 4: IRAQ: THE CRIME OF THE CENTURY

1. The other major contender is U.S. climate policy.
2. Bryan Pietsch, "George W. Bush Called Iraq War 'Unjustified and Brutal.' He Meant Ukraine," *Washington Post*, May 19, 2022; Meredith Clark, "The War Killed 500,000 Iraqis," NBC News, October 16, 2013; "Iraqi Civilians," Costs of War Project, Watson Institute for International and Public Affairs, Brown University. Note that casualty estimates vary widely.
3. Dahr Jamail, "Iraq: War's Legacy of Cancer," *Al Jazeera English*, March 15, 2013; Aaron Rupar, "Red Cross: Iraq Situation Getting Worse," ThinkProgress.com, April 11, 2007; "Iraq Conflict: Crisis of an Orphaned Generation," BBC News, November 28, 2012. In 2005, the head of Iraq's Association of University Lecturers estimated that "about 300 academics and university administrators have been assassinated in a mysterious wave of murders since the American occupation of Iraq began in 2003," while "about 2,000 others . . . have fled the country in fear for their lives," Charles Crain, "Approximately 300 Academics Have Been Killed," *USA Today*, January 17, 2005. *Time* magazine reported on the consequences in 2006: "The exodus has forced many universities to fast-track underqualified teachers to full professorship, or simply to suspend entire departments. This means Iraq's students are getting a poor education, with disastrous consequences for the country's future. It's hard to believe now, but in the 1960s and '70s, Iraq's academia was the envy of the Arab world. Now, it lies in tatters." Aparisim Ghosh, "Baghdad Bulletin: Death Stalks the Campus," *Time*, November 2, 2006.
4. William Kristol, "We Were Right to Fight in Iraq," *USA Today*, May 20, 2015. In 2003, Kristol had said: "I would be shocked if we don't find weapons of mass destruction. . . . I expect us to find them and if we don't find them, that would undercut in part the rationale for the war." Nevertheless, when Bernie Sanders asked if Kristol would apologize for the horrific war he boosted, Kristol refused, saying that he "dislike[s] quasi-Stalinist demands for apologies." See Jon Schwarz, "Bernie Sanders Asked Bill Kristol to Apologize for Pushing the Iraq War. Guess What Happened Next," *Intercept*, May 28, 2019. Andrew Sullivan, *I Was Wrong* (independently published, 2013), ebook.
5. David Ignatius, "A War of Choice, and One Who Chose It," *Washington Post*, November 2, 2003. Incidentally, Wolfowitz, ever the idealist, had served as U.S. ambassador to Indonesia during the Reagan administration, and used his post to help protect the Reagan administration from being embarrassed by Suharto's human rights record. After Suharto was finally ousted, Wolfowitz wrote an editorial arguing that it was "too early to render the verdict" on the mass-murdering dictator. Paul Wolfowitz, "The Tragedy of Suharto," *Wall Street Journal*, May 27, 1998.
6. "Obama Says His Position on Iraq Is Unchanged," NPR, July 3, 2008. The Obamas maintain warm relations with George W. Bush, with Michelle Obama telling the *Today* show, "I love him to death. He's a wonderful man," and "He is my partner in crime." Hannah Yasharoff, "George W. Bush Thinks It's a 'Prob-

lem' That People Can't Understand His Friendship with Michelle Obama," *USA Today*, April 19, 2021.

7. Incidentally, the initial ascent of Hussein's Ba'ath Party was supported by the CIA, which had been working to facilitate a coup against the nationalist government of Abd al-Karim Qasim, after Qasim expropriated British and American holdings in the Iraq Petroleum Company. As historian Eric Jacobsen explains, U.S. policymakers feared that Qasim could threaten to inspire nationalist uprisings elsewhere in the region and undermine "the postwar neocolonial social order." Eric Jacobsen, "A Coincidence of Interests: Kennedy, U.S. Assistance, and the 1963 Iraqi Ba'th Regime," *Diplomatic History* 37, no. 5 (2013): 1029–59. It remains in dispute whether the CIA actively assisted in the Ba'ath coup or was merely plotting its own coup at the time, but there is evidence that in the aftermath, "the CIA provided the submachine-gun-toting Iraqi National Guardsmen with lists of suspected communists who were then jailed, interrogated, and summarily gunned down." We know that "at the very least currently declassified documents reveal that U.S. officials were actively considering various plots against Qasim and that the CIA was building up assets for covert operations in Iraq." Kenneth Osgood, "Eisenhower and Regime Change in Iraq: The United States and the Iraqi Revolution of 1958," in David Ryan and Patrick Kiely, eds., *America and Iraq: Policy-making, Intervention and Regional Politics* (New York: Routledge, 2008). Brandon Wolfe-Hunnicutt says there is "compelling evidence of an American role in the coup," Brandon Wolfe-Hunnicutt, "Oil Sovereignty, American Foreign Policy, and the 1968 Coups in Iraq," *Diplomacy & Statecraft* 28, no. 2 (2017): 235–53. See also Richard Sale, "Saddam Key in Early CIA Plot," United Press International, April 10, 2003.

8. Ian Black, "Iran and Iraq Remember War That Cost More Than a Million Lives," *Guardian,* September 23, 2010; "Only thing standing" quoted from Kenneth Pollack, *The Threatening Storm: The Case for Invading Iraq* (New York: Random House, 2002), ebook; Matt Kelley, "U.S. Supplied Germs to Iraq in '80s," Associated Press, October 1, 2002; Julian Borger, "Rumsfeld 'Offered Help to Saddam,'" *Guardian*, December 31, 2002. The U.S. also sold arms to Iran at the same time, in what eventually became known as the "Iran-Contra" affair, perhaps operating on the principle Harry Truman once suggested should be applied to Nazi Germany and the Soviet Union: "If we see that Germany is winning we ought to help Russia and if Russia is winning we ought to help Germany and that way let them kill as many as possible," David McCullough, *Truman* (New York: Simon & Schuster, 1992), 262.

9. James Gerstenzang, "U.S. Sinks or Damages 6 Iran Ships in Persian Gulf Clashes: Tehran Strikes Back After Oil Rig Shellings," *Los Angeles Times*, April 19, 1988; International Court of Justice, *Case Concerning Oil Platforms (Islamic Republic of Iran v. United States of America)*, judgment of November 6, 2003. Though virtually forgotten in the U.S., the shootdown "remains one of the moments the Iranian government points to in its decades-long distrust of America." Further inflaming

Iranian anger, the U.S. gave the captain who shot down the airliner a Legion of Merit award. Jon Gambrell, "30 Years Later, U.S. Downing of Iran Flight Haunts Relations," Associated Press, July 3, 2018. An Iranian professor told NBC News in 2020 (after two U.S. fighter jets had a near-miss encounter with another Iranian passenger jet) that the 1988 shootdown has contributed to a widespread impression among Iranians that "the United States does not care for the lives of innocent people." Amin Hossein Khodadadi and Isobel van Hagen, "Iranian Passenger Flight Incident a Grim Echo of U.S. Downing of Airliner in 1988," NBC News, July 25, 2020. Marty Steinberg, "'Kinder, Gentler,' and Other George HW Bush quotes," CNBC, December 1, 2018.

10. Robert Fisk, *The Great War for Civilization: The Conquest of the Middle East* (New York: A. A. Knopf, 2005), ebook; Julian Borger, "Rumsfeld 'Offered Help to Saddam,'" *Guardian*, December 31, 2022. Borger notes that in 1983 "the secretary of state, George Shultz, was passed intelligence reports of 'almost daily use of CW [chemical weapons]' by Iraq," but just weeks later, "Ronald Reagan signed a secret order instructing the administration to do 'whatever was necessary and legal' to prevent Iraq losing the war." Patrick E. Tyler, "Officers Say U.S. Aided Iraq in War Despite Use of Gas," *New York Times*, August 18, 2002; Shane Harris and Matthew M. Aid, "CIA Files Prove America Helped Saddam as He Gassed Iran," *Foreign Policy*, August 26, 2013.

11. Tyler, "Officers Say U.S. Aided Iraq in War Despite Use of Gas." The U.S. allegedly removed thousands of pages from Iraq's weapons declaration report to the United Nations, some of which "implicated twenty-four U.S.-based corporations and the successive Ronald Reagan and George Bush Sr. administration in connection with the illegal supplying of Saddam Hussein government with myriad weapons of mass destruction and the training to use them," "U.S. Illegally Removes Pages from Iraq UN Report," ProjectCensored.org, April 29, 2010; "President Bush: Monday 'Moment of Truth' for World on Iraq," White House, Office of the Press Secretary, March 16, 2003.

12. Joost R. Hiltermann, "Halabja: America Didn't Seem to Mind Poison Gas," *New York Times*, January 17, 2003; Peter W. Galbraith, "The True Iraq Appeasers," *New York Times*, September 4, 2006.

13. Steven A. Holmes, "Congress Backs Curbs Against Iraq," *New York Times*, July 28, 1990; John Edward Wilz, "The Making of Mr. Bush's War: A Failure to Learn from History?," *Presidential Studies Quarterly* 25, no. 3 (1995): 525.

14. There is controversy over whether Hussein interpreted the remark as an indication that the United States would not intervene, and Kenneth Pollack writes that the ambassador effectively "assured Saddam that the United States did not intend to intercede in Iraq's dispute with Kuwait, while urging him to find a peaceful solution." Years later in captivity, Hussein would ask U.S. investigators: "If you didn't want me to go in, why didn't you tell me?," Steve Coll, *The Achilles Trap: Saddam Hussein, the C.I.A., and the Origins of America's Invasion of Iraq* (New York: Penguin Press, 2024), 174. Coll says that Hussein even thought "Bush might *want*

him to take Kuwait," because he was not hiding his preparations and the U.S. "delivered no direct or forceful warning against an attack."

15. Elaine Sciolino, "U.S. Gave Iraq Little Reason Not to Mount Kuwait Assault," *New York Times,* September 23, 1990; Pollack, *The Threatening Storm.*

16. R. W. Apple Jr., "Standoff in the Gulf: U.S. 'Nightmare Scenario': Being Finessed by Iraq," *New York Times,* December 19, 1990.

17. William Drozdiak, "Arab Nations Break Silence, Condemn Iraq," *Washington Post,* August 4, 1990; George H. W. Bush, "Remarks to Community Members at Fort Stewart, Georgia," February 1, 1991; "Confrontation in the Gulf; Proposals by Iraqi President: Excerpts from His Address," *New York Times,* August 13, 1990; "Bush Tabbed for 'Nobel War Prize,'" *Greensboro News and Record,* February 26, 1991; *Times of India* cited by William Dalrymple, *Spectator,* February 23, 1991.

18. As a 1990 op-ed in the *Orlando Sentinel* put it: "For a decade, the United States has watched Saddam Hussein's aggression and atrocities—and, by deliberate policy, fed him, lent him money, ignored his attacks on U.S. ships and protected his cash flow. It is hard, therefore, to swallow President Bush's explanation that we have gone to war in the Persian Gulf because we suddenly object, as a matter of principle, to Iraq's aggression, or because we are suddenly horrified by his atrocities, or because we want 'to serve the cause of justice and freedom'"; Joshua Holland, "The First Iraq War Was Also Sold to the Public Based on a Pack of Lies," BillMoyers.com, June 27, 2014. For more on how easily false stories about the enemy spread during war, see Arthur Ponsonby's *Falsehood in War-Time,* published in 1928 about the First World War but still highly relevant.

19. The phrase, familiar to us from the Vietnam context and Kissinger's infamous remark, should be understood as a genocidal call to ignore ordinary rules of engagement.

20. "Hussein to 'Get Ass Kicked' in War—Bush," *Los Angeles Times,* December 20, 1990; "Needless Deaths in the Gulf War: Civilian Casualties During the Air Campaign and Violations of the Laws of War," Human Rights Watch, 1991; Noura Boustany, "Bombs Killed Victims as They Slept," *Washington Post,* February 14, 1991; Al Kamen, "Iraqi Factory's Product: Germ Warfare or Milk?," *Washington Post,* February 8, 1991; "No Justice for the Victims of Al-Amiriyah," Geneva International Center for Justice, February 13, 2019; Ray Howze, "'Highway of Death' Still Stands Out for One Gulf War Veteran," *Leaf Chronicle,* February 26, 2016; Patrick Cockburn, "In Middle East Wars It Pays to Be Skeptical," *CounterPunch,* April 23, 2018; Tim Arango, "After 25 Years of U.S. Role in Iraq, Scars Are Too Stubborn to Fade," *New York Times,* February 16, 2016; Eric Schmitt, "U.S. Army Buried Iraqi Soldiers Alive in Gulf War," *New York Times,* September 15, 1991; "Army Tanks Buried Iraqi Soldiers Alive in Trenches," *Deseret News,* September 12, 1991; Col. Lon Maggart, who led the 1st Brigade in the assault, defended the practice: "I know burying people like that sounds pretty nasty. . . . But it would be even nastier if we had to put our troops in the trenches and clean them out with bayonets." For more on how the slaughter went unreported, see Patrick J.

Sloyan, "'What I Saw Was a Bunch of Filled-In Trenches with People's Arms and Legs Sticking Out of Them. For All I Know, We Could Have Killed Thousands,'" *Guardian*, February 14, 2003.

21. Barton Gellman, "Allied Air War Struck Broadly in Iraq: Officials Acknowledge Strategy Went Beyond Purely Military Targets," *Washington Post*, June 23, 1991.

22. Mehdi Hasan, "The Ignored Legacy of George H. W. Bush: War Crimes, Racism, and Obstruction of Justice," *Intercept*, December 1, 2018; George H. W. Bush, "Remarks to Community Members at Fort Stewart, Georgia, February 1, 1991; George H. W. Bush, "Remarks to the American Legislative Exchange Council," March 1, 1991.

23. George H. W. Bush, The President's News Conference on the Persian Gulf Conflict, March 1, 1991.

24. Note that atrocities become mere "sins" when they are being discussed as the drawback to our support for a dictator, because to say *however many his atrocities, he was the best hope for stability* would make the U.S. position sound reprehensible. Once the term "stability" is also translated into English—in this case, it means "subordination to U.S. interests," the correct interpretation of the sentence is: *No amount of horror and repression could persuade Washington to consider the human rights of Iraqis over the self-interest of Washington.* Thomas L. Friedman, "A Rising Sense That Iraq's Hussein Must Go," *New York Times*, July 7, 1991; Carole O'Leary of American University, who studies Iraqi opposition groups, claims Bush effectively told the rebels: "You do it and we're going to help you," quoted in Jason Embry, "Uprising in Iraq May Be Slow Because of U.S. Inaction in 1991," Cox News Service, April 4, 2003; Tim Arango, "A Long-Awaited Apology for Shiites, but the Wounds Run Deep," *New York Times*, November 8, 2011; Alan Cowell, "Kurds Assert Few Outside Iraq Wanted Them to Win," *New York Times*, April 11, 1991.

25. U.S. support for Saddam during his worst atrocities created complications when Saddam was ultimately put on trial, and the tribunal was tailored specifically to "block Mr. Hussein from trying to call witnesses like Defense Secretary Donald H. Rumsfeld to testify about the United States' earlier cooperation with the Hussein government," Neil A. Lewis and David Johnston, "U.S. Team Is Sent to Develop Case in Hussein Trial," *New York Times*, March 7, 2004.

26. On the bombings, "the longest sustained U.S. air operations since the Vietnam War," see Chip Gibbons, "When Iraq Was Clinton's War," *Jacobin*, May 6, 2016; Halliday quoted in Anthony Arnove, ed., *Iraq Under Siege: The Deadly Impact of Sanctions and War* (Boston: South End Press, 2003); H. C. von Sponeck, *A Different Kind of War: The UN Sanctions Regime in Iraq* (Oxford, UK, and New York: Berghahn Books, 2006). Reports of the sanctions' effects on child mortality specifically were later disputed as having been based on manipulated statistics, Tim Dyson and Valeria Cetorelli, "Changing Views on Child Mortality and Economic Sanctions in Iraq: A History of Lies, Damned Lies and Statistics," *British Medical Journal, Global Health*, 2017. However, at the time, without contesting the

claim that five hundred thousand Iraqi children may have died as a result, Secretary of State Madeleine Albright said such a "price" was "worth it." One's relief that the deaths of children were overestimated should not diminish one's horror that a high U.S. official rationalized policies that she had reason to believe were causing the widespread deaths of children, "Madeleine Albright Saying Iraqi Kids' Deaths 'Worth It' Resurfaces," *Newsweek*, March 23, 2022.

27. Yasmin Husein Al-Jawaheri, *Women in Iraq: The Gender Impact of International Sanctions* (Boulder, CO: Lynne Rienner, 2008); Joy Gordon, *Invisible War: The United States and the Iraq Sanctions* (Cambridge, MA: Harvard University Press, 2010), 2–3, 102; Lisa Blaydes, *State of Repression: Iraq Under Saddam Hussein* (Princeton, NJ: Princeton University Press, 2020), 25.

28. "Comical Ali/Baghdad Bob," KnowYourMeme.com.

29. Thom Shanker, "Rights Group Faults U.S. Over Cluster Bombs," *New York Times*, December 12, 2003; Peter Maass, "Good Kills," *New York Times*, April 20, 2003.

30. See Ali A. Allawi, *The Occupation of Iraq: Winning the War, Losing the Peace* (New Haven, CT: Yale University Press, 2007).

31. George F. Will, "A Report Overtaken by Reality," *Washington Post*, December 7, 2006.

32. *Winter Soldier: Iraq and Afghanistan: Eyewitness Accounts of the Occupations* (Chicago: Haymarket Books, 2008), ebook.

33. Christian Appy, *American Reckoning* (New York: Penguin Books, 2015), 309. Rumsfeld denied that what had taken place was torture, saying that it was "abuse, which I believe technically is different from torture," "U.S. Avoiding 'Torture' to Describe Soldiers' Actions," CBC News, May 14, 2004. While the Bush administration tried to deny or downplay the crimes, some on the American right forthrightly defended the practices, with Rush Limbaugh saying that soldiers who were "being fired at every day" deserved to "have a good time" for "emotional release," and Michael Savage saying that he wished the torture had been worse: "I would have liked to have seen dynamite put in their orifices. . . . We need more of the humiliation tactics, not less," Andrew Sullivan, "Limbaugh on Torture: A Recap," DailyDish.com, July 28, 2009; Nicole Casta and Shant Mesrobian, "Savage Nation: It's Not Just Rush; Talk Radio Host Michael Savage: 'I Commend' Prisoner Abuse; 'We Need More,'" MediaMatters.org, May 13, 2004; Abu Ghraib torture victims were never given their day in court, see Elise Swain, "Iraqis Tortured by the U.S. in Abu Ghraib Never Got Justice," *Intercept*, March 17, 2023.

34. Mike Hoyt and John Palattella, eds., *Reporting Iraq: An Oral History of the War by the Journalists Who Covered It* (Hoboken, NJ: Melville House, 2007), 21, 62, 65–66. Translator Ali Fadhil recounts having to reassure two young U.S. soldiers who were alarmed when they heard the daily call to prayer and thought it was a signal for insurgents to rise up and kill Americans.

35. Hoyt and Palattella, *Reporting Iraq*, 65–66; Jason Burke, *The 9/11 Wars* (New York: Penguin Books, 2012), ebook.

36. Ali Fadhil, "City of Ghosts," *Guardian*, January 11, 2005.

37. Joe Carr, "A Drive Through Devastated Fallujah," *National Catholic Reporter*, June 17, 2005.

38. In 2003, for instance, a U.S. tank opened fire on the Baghdad hotel where all of the international press were staying, killing two journalists. Giles Tremlett, "Tank Captain Admits Firing on Media Hotel," *Guardian*, April 23, 2003.

39. The dialogue is, as a Reuters colleague of the dead journalists said, the "sort of language that kids would use on video games." ("Look at those dead bastards." "Nice.") The military lied repeatedly about the circumstances of the journalists' deaths and covered up what had been done, Paul Daley, "'All Lies': How the U.S. Military Covered Up Gunning Down Two Journalists in Iraq," *Guardian*, June 14, 2020.

40. Remarks by the Vice President to the Veterans of Foreign Wars 103rd National Convention, White House, August 26, 2002; "We don't know exactly the true dimension of the threat," confessed State Department director of policy Richard Haass, quoted in Bob Roberts and Richard Wallace, "Blair: I Have No Idea What Saddam's Up To," *Mirror*, September 9, 2002.

41. Zinni quoted in David Corn, "'Hubris': New Documentary Reexamines the Iraq War 'Hoax,'" *Mother Jones*, February 16, 2013. The so-called Downing Street memos "show[ed] that British officials at the highest levels believed that President Bush had decided to invade Iraq almost a year before he told the American public of his decision." As paraphrased by *Sunday Times* reporter Michael Smith, the memos showed British government officials concluding that "the evidence against Saddam Hussein is thin . . . regime change is illegal under international law so we are going to have to go to the UN to get an ultimatum, not as a way of averting war but as an excuse to make war legal, and . . . we aren't preparing for what happens after and no-one has the faintest idea what Iraq will be like after a war." Joseph Cirincione, "The Media and the Downing Street Memos," Carnegie Endowment for International Peace, June 21, 2005; Richard Clarke, *Against All Enemies: Inside America's War on Terror* (New York: Free Press, 2004), ebook.

42. Importantly, while it is often said that no weapons of mass destruction were found in Iraq, this is not strictly true. A number of abandoned stockpiles of chemical weapons from before 1991 were uncovered. The Bush administration actually worked to conceal the discovery, because these "filthy, rusty, or corroded" weapons were clearly "long-abandoned." However, they did cause serious injuries to U.S. soldiers and Iraqi police, and the U.S. "lost track of chemical weapons that its troops found, left large caches unsecured, and did not warn people—Iraqis and foreign troops alike—as it hastily exploded chemical ordnance in the open air." Secrecy about the discoveries "prevented troops in some of the war's most dangerous jobs from receiving proper medical care and official recognition of their wounds." One reason the Bush administration did not wish to publicize the discoveries was that in "five of six incidents in which troops were wounded by chemical agents, the munitions appeared to have been designed in the United

States, manufactured in Europe and filled in chemical agent production lines built in Iraq by Western companies," C. J. Chivers, "The Secret Casualties of Iraq's Abandoned Chemical Weapons," *New York Times*, October 14, 2014.

43. Barton Gellman and Walter Pincus, "Depiction of Threat Outgrew Supporting Evidence," *Washington Post*, August 10, 2003. The only report making such an allegation had been released in the early 1990s and concerned a nuclear weapons program that was known to have been subsequently destroyed. In fact, the IAEA's conclusion at the time was that there was "no indication of resumed nuclear activities . . . nor any indication of nuclear-related prohibited activities. See "In a Chief Inspector's Words: 'A Substantial Measure of Disarmament,'" *New York Times*, March 8, 2003. The IAEA spokesman said in 2003: "There's never been a report like that issued from this agency. . . . If anybody tells you they know the nuclear situation in Iraq right now, in the absence of four years of inspections, I would say that they're misleading you because there isn't solid evidence out there," quoted in Mehdi Hasan, "Blair: Truth and Lies," *Guardian*, January 29, 2010. Hasan documents a similar pattern of outright deception from British prime minister Tony Blair, including assertions about the certainty ("beyond doubt") of an active weapons program that directly contradicted the conclusions of British intelligence ("sporadic and patchy" evidence). Blair has since, while expressing a vague contrition, said that "there were no lies, there was no deceit," which is an additional lie. "Tony Blair: 'I Express More Sorrow, Regret and Apology Than You Can Ever Believe,'" *Guardian*, July 6, 2016. "Powell '01: WMDs Not 'Significant,'" CBS News, September 28, 2003. In 2003, Powell would tell the UN Security Council, "The gravity of this moment is matched by the gravity of the threat that Iraq's weapons of mass destruction pose to the world. Let me now turn to those deadly weapons programs and describe why they are real and present dangers to the region and to the world." He later falsely insisted that "I didn't change my assessment." "Lies and More Lies," *Outlook India*, February 3, 2022. There was little discussion of why even if a dictatorial rule *did* possess weapons of mass destruction, this justified inflicting misery on the citizenry through war. There was certainly no public debate on the question of why Hussein had no right to possess WMDs, but the United States (a country that has used them repeatedly against civilian populations, including chemical weapons in Vietnam and nuclear weapons in Japan) does. Interestingly, at one point Bush said the following: "Year after year, Saddam Hussein had gone to elaborate lengths, spent enormous sums, taken great risks to build and keep weapons of mass destruction. But why? The only possible explanation, the only possible use he could have for those weapons, is to dominate, intimidate, or attack." If the only possible explanation for the possession of such weapons is domination, intimidation, and attack, one might wonder why the United States possesses them in vastly greater quantities than Hussein ever did—not a question that will ever get an airing in the U.S. press.

44. "In Their Own Words: Iraq's 'Imminent' Threat," Center for American Progress, 2004; "Iraq on the Record: The Bush Administration's Public Statements on Iraq," U.S. House of Representatives Committee on Government Reform, March 16, 2004; Jeffrey Lewis, "Rumsfeld on the Imminent Threat from Iraq," Arms Control Wonk, March 18, 2004; Dylan Matthews of *Vox* cites many more specific egregious examples, Dylan Matthews, "No, Really, George W. Bush Lied About WMDs," *Vox*, July 9, 2016; Barton Gellman and Walter Pincus, "Depiction of Threat Outgrew Supporting Evidence," *Washington Post*, August 9, 2003.

45. "Official's Key Report on Iraq Is Faulted: 'Dubious' Intelligence Fueled Push for War," *Washington Post*, February 9, 2007. A classified President's Daily Brief on September 21, 2001, told Bush "there was scant credible evidence that Iraq had any significant collaborative ties with Al Qaeda." Nevertheless, he proceeded to spend the next year and a half repeating the exact opposite, knowing that the public would hear his voice and not see the content of his intelligence reports.

46. Joseph Cirincione, "Let's Go to the Videotape," Carnegie Endowment for International Peace, March 22, 2006; "Communication from the President of the United States Transmitting a Report Consistent with the War Powers Resolution That He Directed U.S. Armed Forces, Operating with Other Coalition Forces, to Commence Combat Operations on March 19, 2003, Against Iraq," March 21, 2003; "President Bush Announces Major Combat Operations in Iraq Have Ended," Office of the Press Secretary, White House, May 1, 2003.

47. Pollack, *The Threatening Storm*, xxi.

48. Mattathias Schwartz, "Secret 9/11 Memo Reveals Bush Rewriting the History of the 9/11 Attacks and the Warnings He'd Tuned Out," *Business Insider*, November 30, 2022; "O'Neill: Bush Planned Iraq Invasion Before 9/11," CNN, January 10, 2004; letter to William J. Clinton, Project for the New American Century, January 26, 1998.

49. Once the justifications were switched from preventing a threat to performing a service for Iraqis, Ken Roth of Human Rights Watch gave a detailed explanation of why the war did not, even assuming this was not a dishonest pretext, meet the standards necessary for a military action to be considered "humanitarian." "War in Iraq, Not a Humanitarian Intervention," Human Rights Watch, January 25, 2004. Despite the failure to find weapons of mass destruction, Bush simply lied and insisted the opposite had happened: "We found the weapons of mass destruction. We found biological laboratories." Nevertheless, Bush would later participate in a skit at the White House Correspondents' Dinner in which he joked about the failure to find WMDs. The skit featured Bush wandering around the White House and making comments like "Those weapons of mass destruction have got to be here somewhere," or "Maybe under here." Given the number of people who died horrific violent deaths as a result of the deception, the skit was deemed by some to be "tasteless and ill-judged." David Teather, "Bush Jokes About Search for WMD, But It's No Laughing Matter for Critics," *Guardian*, March 26, 2004. On the "single question," see "President George Bush Discusses

Iraq in National Press Conference," Office of the Press Secretary, March 6, 2003; Augustus Richard Norton, "The United States in the Middle East: Grand Plans, Grand Ayatollahs and Dark Alleys," Middle East Policy Council, September 5, 2004.

50. Walter Pincus, "Skepticism About U.S. Deep, Iraq Poll Shows," *Washington Post*, November 12, 2003; "Poll: U.S. Are Occupiers, Not Liberators," *Al Jazeera English*, May 20, 2004; Tom Hayden, "What Iraqis Really Think About the Occupation," *Nation*, October 11, 2005; Jane Arraf, "Iraqi Parliament Votes to Expel U.S. Troops, Trump Threatens Sanctions," NPR, January 6, 2020.

51. Don van Natta, Jr., "U.S. Recruits a Rough Ally to Be a Jailer," *New York Times*, May 1, 2005; Matt Bivens, "Uzbekistan's Human Rights Problem," *Nation*, November 12, 2001.

52. Alison Langley, "Readying Relief for Iraqis," *New York Times*, February 17, 2003; Kenneth H. Bacon, "Iraq: The Humanitarian Challenge," *Bulletin of the Atomic Scientists*, January 1, 2003; Ed Vulliamy, Burhan Wazir, and Gaby Hinsliff, "Aid Groups Warn of Disaster in Iraq," *Guardian*, December 22, 2002.

53. "Powell to UN: Butt Out," *New York Post*, March 27, 2003; Peter W. Galbraith, *The End of Iraq: How American Incompetence Created a War Without End* (New York: Simon & Schuster, 2007), 142; Walter Gibbs, "Scowcroft Urges Wide Role for the UN in Postwar Iraq," *New York Times*, April 9, 2003.

54. David Rohde, "Iraqis Were Set to Vote, but U.S. Wielded a Veto," *New York Times*, June 19, 2003.

55. John D. Colgan, "Oil, Conflict, and U.S. National Interests," *International Security*, October 2013; a balanced discussion of the role of oil in the U.S. decision to go to war can be found in John S. Duffield, "Oil and the Decision to Invade Iraq," in Jane K. Cramer and A. Trevor Thrall, eds., *Why Did the United States Invade Iraq?* (New York: Routledge, 2012); "Address by President Carter on the State of the Union Before a Joint Session of Congress," January 23, 1980.

56. "Bush Says Iraqi Aggression Threatens 'Our Way of Life,'" *New York Times*, August 16, 1990; "Bush: Out of These Troubled Times, a New World Order," *Washington Post*, September 12, 1990. George H. W. Bush said that in addition to matters of principle, "vital economic interests are at risk as well. Iraq itself controls some ten percent of the world's proven oil reserves. Iraq plus Kuwait controls twice that. An Iraq permitted to swallow Kuwait would have the economic and military power, as well as the arrogance, to intimidate and coerce its neighbors—neighbors who control the lion's share of the world's remaining oil reserves," Address Before a Joint Session of the Congress on the Persian Gulf Crisis and the Federal Budget Deficit," September 11, 1990; John Abizaid, "Courting Disaster: The Fight for Oil, Water and a Healthy Planet," panel discussion, Stanford University, October 13, 2007; Richard Haass, *War of Necessity, War of Choice: A Memoir of Two Iraq Wars* (New York: Simon & Schuster, 2009), ebook. Haass says this fact "does not support the contention that either [Iraq] war was about oil" because "U.S. interest in the region's oil is strategic . . . not tied in any

way to gaining financial advantage." But the fact that the interest is "strategic" in nature makes no difference to the question of whether the war was "about" oil.

57. However, Frum also recounted seeing Ahmed Chalabi and Dick Cheney. "He and Cheney spent long hours together, contemplating the possibilities of a Western-oriented Iraq: an additional source of oil, an alternative to U.S. dependency on an unstable-looking Saudi Arabia," quoted in Jillian Rayfield, "David Frum on Iraq: There Was No WH Debate," *Salon*, March 19, 2013.

58. Pollack, *The Threatening Storm*, 152, 272.

59. Michael Moore, "Six Years Ago, Chuck Hagel Told the Truth About Iraq," *Huff-Post*, January 5, 2013; Peter Beaumont and Joanna Walters, "Greenspan Admits Iraq Was About Oil, as Deaths Put at 1.2m," *Guardian*, September 16, 2007; Clarke, *Against All Enemies*.

60. Kim Cobb, "Writer Says Bush Talked About War in 1999," *Houston Chronicle*, November 1, 2004.

61. Scott McClellan, "George W. Bush, the Great Pretender," *Sunday Times*, June 1, 2008.

62. Monica Prasad, "Republicans Play Dirty Because Republican Policies Are Unpopular," *Economic Sociology* 21, no. 2 (March 2020); Richard Perle, "Thank God for the Death of the UN," *Guardian*, March 20, 2003; Roger Owen, "War by Example," *Al-Ahram Weekly*, April 3–9, 2003; "Interview: Richard Perle," PBS, *Frontline*.

63. Quoted in Thomas Ricks, *Fiasco: The American Military Adventure in Iraq, 2003–2005* (New York: Penguin Books, 2006), 87.

64. Riverbend, *Baghdad Burning: Girl Blog from Iraq* (New York: Feminist Press at the City University of New York, 2005), 251; Kim Sengupta, "How the Iraq War Unleashed Jihad and the Rise of Isis," *Independent*, March 20, 2023. Those who waged the war never acknowledged having made the world less safe, with Donald Rumsfeld insisting in his memoir that "ridding the region of Saddam's brutal regime has created a more stable and secure world."

65. Ben Terris, "George W. Bush's Wars Are Now Over. He Retreated a While Ago," *Washington Post*, September 1, 2021; Peter Schjeldahl, "George W. Bush's Painted Atonements," *New Yorker*, March 3, 2017; Jonathan Alter, in a similarly generous *New York Times* review titled "Bush Nostalgia Is Overrated, but His Book of Paintings Is Not," agreed: Bush is "an evocative and surprisingly adept artist." As Michael Moore darkly observed, "Only in America can a war criminal reinvent himself as the new Bob Ross."

66. Sheehan, a principled opponent of war viciously smeared in the right-wing press, was equally critical of Barack Obama, whom she called "that war criminal in the White House," Stephen L. Carter, "Cindy Sheehan Antiwar Activism Continues Despite Being Used by the Democrats," *Daily Beast*, May 16, 2011; Anna Iovine, "The Iraqi Man Who Threw His Shoes at George W. Bush Is a Twitter Hero for Today's Protesters," *Mashable*, June 4, 2020.

67. Robert D. McFadden, "Donald H. Rumsfeld, Defense Secretary During Iraq War, Is Dead at 88," *New York Times*, June 30, 2021; Eric Schmitt, "Colin Powell, Who Shaped U.S. National Security, Dies at 84," *New York Times*, October 18,

2021. The more accurate headline would, of course, be "Colin Powell, Whose Falsehoods Justified a Major Crime Against Humanity, Dies at 84." Benjamin Hart, "Paul Bremer Is Alive and Well and Teaching Skiing in Vermont," *New York*, March 2003; Emily Cochrane, "The Cheneys, Once Despised by the Left, Are Welcomed Warmly by Democrats at a January 6 Observance," *New York Times*, January 6, 2022.

68. Jonathan Snyder, "USS *Fallujah*: Future Navy Amphibious Assault Ship Will Honor Marine Battles in Iraq," *Stars and Stripes*, December 14, 2022; Nabil Salih, "U.S. Empire's Legacy: Fallujah and Football Played in a Graveyard," *Al Jazeera English*, January 5, 2023.

69. Peter Bergen and Paul Cruickshank, "The Iraq Effect: War Has Increased Terrorism Sevenfold Worldwide," *Mother Jones*, March 1, 2007; "Declassified Key Judgments of the National Intelligence Estimate on Global Terrorism," *New York Times*, September 27, 2006; Carter Malkasian, *The American War in Afghanistan: A History* (New York: Oxford University Press, 2021), 79.

70. J. M. Berger, *Jihad Joe: Americans Who Go to War in the Name of Islam* (Lincoln, NE: Potomac Books/Nebraska Press, 2011), 351. The thirty-year-old Pakistani American who tried to set off a car bomb in Times Square in 2010 said he was "motivated by opposition to U.S. policy in the Muslim world" and that Americans "don't care about the people elsewhere in the world when they die." When asked about how he could justify potentially killing civilians, he replied that when "the drone hits in Afghanistan and Iraq . . . they kill women, they kill children, they kill everybody. It's a war. . . . I am part of the answer to the U.S. terrorizing the Muslim nations and the Muslim people. . . . I'm avenging the attack." *The New York Times* reported that even though he had been "thriving in the West," his "argument with American foreign policy grew after 9/11." Similar testimony is heard from others who planned attacks. Najibullah Zazi, the Afghan American man who planned to bomb the New York City subway in 2009, said his plan was "because of my feelings about what the United States was doing in Afghanistan." Similar explanations would be given by Richard Reid, the "shoe bomber" who tried to blow up an American Airlines flight in December 2001, who said his "motivation for turning to violence . . . was the foreign policy of the U.S. government, which, he said, had resulted in the murder of thousands of Muslims and oppressed people around the world from Vietnam to southern Africa to Afghanistan and Palestine." Fort Hood shooter Nidal Hasan held a "deep and public opposition to the wars in Iraq and Afghanistan" and produced a PowerPoint presentation, 'Why the War on Terror Is a War on Islam.'" The "underwear bomber," Umar Farouk Abdulmutallab, said the act was motivated by U.S. support for Israel and "in retaliation of the killing of innocent and civilian Muslim populations in Palestine, especially in the blockade of Gaza, and in retaliation for the killing of innocent and civilian Muslim populations in Yemen, Iraq, Somalia, Afghanistan and beyond, most of them women, children, and noncombatants." The surviving Boston Marathon bomber told his interrogators "that the Ameri-

can wars in Iraq and Afghanistan motivated him and his brother to carry out the attack." Radical cleric Anwar Al-Awlaki, whose sermons encouraged violence against the United States, was an American citizen who was born in New Mexico and had been a doctoral student at George Washington University. But Al-Awlaki—who was extrajudicially executed by the Obama administration in 2011—said that "with the American invasion of Iraq and continued U.S. aggression against Muslims, I could not reconcile between living in the U.S. and being a Muslim, and I eventually came to the conclusion that jihad against America is binding upon myself just as it is binding on every other Muslim."

CHAPTER 5: THE UNITED STATES, ISRAEL, AND PALESTINE

1. Noam Chomsky, "Palestine 2012—Gaza and the UN Resolution," Chomsky.info, 2012.
2. Ronald Reagan, "Remarks at the Welcoming Ceremony for Prime Minister Menachem Begin of Israel," September 9, 1981; Crossman quoted in Amy Kaplan, *Our American Israel: The Story of an Entangled Alliance* (Cambridge, MA: Harvard University Press, 2018), ebook.
3. Avi Shlaim, "Britain and the Arab-Israeli War of 1948," *Journal of Palestine Studies* 16, no. 4 (1987): 70; "Paper Prepared by the National Security Council Planning Board," July 29, 1958, *Foreign Relations of the United States, 1958–1960, Near East Region; Iraq; Iran; Arabian Peninsula, Vol. XII* (Washington, DC: U.S. Government Printing Office, 1956).
4. Biden specifically said that "were there not an Israel, the United States of America would have to invent an Israel to protect her interest in the region." M. Muhannad Ayyash, "Biden Says the U.S. Would Have to Invent an Israel if It Didn't Exist. Why?," TheConversation.com, July 24, 2023; Henry Jackson, *Congressional Record*, May 21, 1973, S9446.
5. All quotes from victims in this section are taken from Maram Humaid, "'Blood, Body Parts, Screams': Gaza Reels After Israeli Strikes," *Al Jazeera English*, August 7, 2022.
6. See, for instance, Andrew Carey and Abeer Salman, "More Than 40 People Killed in Gaza in Weekend of Violence," CNN, August 7, 2022. The article notes the deaths of numerous Gazans, as well as the accompanying humanitarian crisis, including the shortage of fuel, the shutting down of water treatment facilities, and the lack of electricity in Gazan households. But Israel's blockade of Gaza is undiscussed.
7. As of 2020, Israel's air force had "324 fighter and ground attack aircraft, all of U.S. origin: 83 Boeing F-15s, 224 Lockheed Martin F-16s, and 16 Lockheed Martin F-35s." Salih Booker and William D. Hartung, "Israel's Military, Made in the USA," *Nation*, May 21, 2021.
8. Fawaz Turki, *The Disinherited: Journal of a Palestinian Exile* (New York: Monthly Review Press, 1972), ebook.

9. Israel Zangwill famously used the phrase "a land without a people for a people without a land" in 1901. Zangwill later acknowledged that "Palestine proper already has its inhabitants. The pashalik of Jerusalem is already twice as thickly populated as the United States." Zangwill thereby concluded that "[we] must be prepared either to drive out by the sword the [Arab] tribes in possession as our forefathers did or to grapple with the problem of a large alien population, mostly Mohammedan and accustomed for centuries to despise us," and "it is utter foolishness to allow it to be the country of two peoples . . . a different place must be found either for the Jews or their neighbors." Quoted in Nur Masalha, *Expulsion of the Palestinians: The Concept of "Transfer" in Zionist Political Thought, 1882–1948*, (Beirut, Lebanon: Institute for Palestine Studies, 1992), 6, 10; Smilansky quoted in Benny Morris, *Righteous Victims: A History of the Zionist-Arab Conflict, 1881–1999* (New York: A. A. Knopf, 1999), 42. Morris (654) says that "Zionist leaders and settlers" largely "managed to avoid 'seeing' the Arabs," often simply leaving them unmentioned, which he suggests was in part "the routine European colonist's mental obliteration of the 'natives,'" partly to avoid confronting the practical difficulties of what became known as the "Arab problem," and partly to avoid feeling "guilt" over the "moral dubiousness" of an expansionist enterprise. *Kol Kitve Ahad Ha'am* (Tel Aviv: Hotsaat Dvir, 1947), 23, quoted in Rashid Khalidi, "Palestinian Peasant Resistance to Zionism Before World War I," in Edward W. Said and Christopher Hitchens, eds., *Blaming the Victims: Spurious Scholarship and the Palestinian Question* (London and New York: Verso, 1988), 216.

10. Hillel Zeitlin, "Ha-mashber" ("The Crisis"), *Ha-Zman* 3 (July-September 1905), quoted in Anita Shapira, *Land and Power: The Zionist Resort to Force, 1881–1948* (Redwood City, CA: Stanford University Press, 1999), 46; Yitzhak Epstein, "She'ela Ne'elama" ("A Hidden Question"), *Ha-Shilo'ah* 17 (November-April 1907/8), quoted in Shapira; letter from Yusuf Diya Pasha al-Khalidi, Pera, Istanbul to Chief Rabbi Zadok Kahn, March 1, 1899, Central Zionist Archives, H1\197 [Herzl Papers], quoted in Rashid Khalidi, *The Hundred Years' War on Palestine* (New York: Metropolitan Books, 2020), 10; Theodor Herzl, *Complete Diary*, ed. Raphael Patai, trans. Harry Zohn (New York: Herzl Press and T. Yoseloff, 1960), 1:88; Edward W. Said, *The Question of Palestine* (New York: Vintage, 1980), 13.

11. Vladimir Jabotinsky, "The Iron Wall," trans. L. Brenner, 1923.

12. Weizmann quoted in Ann Moseley Lesch, "The Palestine Arab Nationalist Movement Under the Mandate," in William B. Quandt, Fuad Jabber, and Ann Mosely Lesch, eds., *The Politics of Palestinian Nationalism* (Berkeley: University of California Press, 1973), 12; Joseph Weitz, *My Diary and Letters to the Children* (Masada: Ramat Gan, 1965), 2:181–82, quoted in Said, *The Question of Palestine*, 100; Morris, *Righteous Victims*, 654.

13. E. L. Woodward and R. Butler, eds., *Documents on British Foreign Policy, 1919–1939*, first series, 1919–1929 (London: Her Majesty's Stationery Office, 1952), 340–48, quoted in Khalidi, *The Hundred Years' War on Palestine*, 47; Michael Cohen, *Churchill and the Jews 1900–1948* (New York: Routledge, 2003), 62–63;

Isaiah Friedman, *The Question of Palestine: 1914–1918: British-Jewish-Arab Relations* (New York: Schocken Books, 1973), 7.

14. The King-Crane Commission Report, August 28, 1919.

15. See Masalha, *Expulsion of the Palestinians*; Protocol of the Meeting of the Jewish Agency Executive with the Political Committee of the Zionist Actions Committee (June 2, 1938), CZA, quoted in Benny Morris, "Refabricating 1948," *Journal of Palestine Studies* 27, no. 2 (Winter, 1998), 86; Benny Morris, article in *Ha'aretz*, May 9, 1989, quoted in Masalha, "A Critique of Benny Morris," *Journal of Palestine Studies* 21, no. 1 (Autumn 1991), 92; in "Refabricating 1948," Morris says there are "mountains of evidence" that "the majority of the movement's leaders" supported transfer (ethnic cleansing). See also the extensive discussion in chapter 2 of Benny Morris, *The Birth of the Palestinian Refugee Problem Revisited* (Cambridge, UK: Cambridge University Press, 2004).

16. Vincent Sheean, *Personal History* (New York: Doubleday, Doran & Co., 1935, sections reprinted in Walid Khalidi, ed., *From Haven to Conquest* [Institute for Palestine Studies, Beirut, 1971]). Theodor Herzl, *The Jewish State* (New York: American Zionist Emergency Council, 1946), 15; Herzl also expected the state to be "a wall of defense for Europe in Asia." Amira Hass, "Barak's Jargon Is Identical to That of Gush Emunim," *Haaretz*, December 21, 1999; Said, *The Question of Palestine*, 8.

17. Instead, the Arab High Committee called for an independent Palestine "with protection of all legitimate Jewish and other minority rights and safeguarding of reasonable British interests," quoted in Sumantra Bose, *Contested Lands: Israel-Palestine, Kashmir, Bosnia, Cyprus, and Sri Lanka* (Cambridge, MA: Harvard University Press, 2007), 223–24.

18. Special issue of *Filastin* (May 19, 1914), 1, quoted in Khalidi, *The Hundred Years' War on Palestine*, 34; Abba Eban, *Personal Witness: Israel Through My Eyes* (New York: Putnam, 1992), 49–50.

19. Morris, *Righteous Victims*, 136–37; Rashid Khalidi, interview with *Current Affairs*, July-August 2022; "The Case Against a Jewish State in Palestine: Albert Hourani's Statement to the Anglo-American Committee of Enquiry of 1946," *Journal of Palestine Studies* 35, no. 1 (2005–2006), 80–90. On the expansionist character of early Zionism, and reasons Palestinian Arabs had for fearing partition was a "stepping-stone," see discussion in chapter 3 of Jerome Slater, *Mythologies Without End: The U.S., Israel, and the Arab-Israeli Conflict, 1917–2020* (New York: Oxford University Press, 2020).

20. There have been efforts to portray the Palestinian departure as voluntary, but these do not hold up. Benny Morris comments that "above all . . . the refugee problem was caused by attacks by Jewish forces on Arab villages and towns and by the inhabitants' fear of such attacks, compounded by expulsions, atrocities, and rumors of atrocities—and by the crucial Israeli cabinet decision in June 1948 to bar a refugee return," leaving the Palestinians "crushed, with some 700,000 driven into exile and another 150,000 left under Israeli rule." Even if Palestinians had fled voluntarily, it is unclear why this would justify barring them from re-

turning to their homes or claiming their property. Ben-Gurion said in 1948 that the return of refugees "must be prevented . . . at all costs." "[W]e should frustrate their re-entry . . . I shall also favour denying their reappearance after the war," Yoav Gelber, *Palestine 1948: War, Escape, and the Emergence of the Palestinian Refugee Problem* (Liverpool, UK: Liverpool University Press, 2006), 283.

21. Sharett quoted in Mark Tessler, *A History of the Israeli-Palestinian Conflict* (Bloomington: Indiana University Press, 2009), 298; "Human dust" quoted in Avi Shlaim, *Collusion Across the Jordan: King Abdullah, the Zionist Movement, and the Partition of Palestine* (Oxford: Clarendon Press, 1988), 491.

22. Ari Shavit, "Interview with Ehud Barak," *Haaretz*, February 2, 2001; David Ben-Gurion, "Speech at the Mapai Political Committee," June 7, 1938, quoted in Simha Flapan, *Zionism and the Palestinians* (New York: Harper & Row, 1979), 141–42. Ben-Gurion also said: "If I were an Arab leader, I would never sign an agreement with Israel. It is normal; we have taken their country. It is true God promised it to us, but how could that interest them? Our God is not theirs. There has been Anti-Semitism, the Nazis, Hitler, Auschwitz, but was that their fault? They see but one thing: we have come and we have stolen their country. Why would they accept that?," quoted by Nahum Goldmann in *Le Paradoxe Juif* (*The Jewish Paradox*) (New York: Grosset & Dunlap, 1978), 121.

23. Frank Giles, "Golda Meir: 'Who Can Blame Israel,'" *Sunday Times*, June 15, 1969, 12. Some have even fabricated evidence to suggest that the Arab inhabitants of Palestine at the time of the establishment of the state of Israel were recent immigrants. See Norman G. Finkelstein, "A Land Without a People: Joan Peters' 'Wilderness' Image," in *Image and Reality of the Israel-Palestine Conflict* (London and New York: Verso, 2003). It is common to claim that while Palestinians may have lived in Palestine, they did not have a "Palestinian identity" (the implication being that they were therefore not entitled to national self-determination). Ironically, the Zionist project itself was an effort to construct a new national identity, not just an effort to procure land for an existing people. Begin quoted in Israeli newspaper *Yediot Aharanot*, October 17, 1969, quoted in Slater, *Mythologies Without End*, 108.

24. "Israel's Occupation: 50 Years of Dispossession," Amnesty International, June 7, 2017.

25. Eqbal Ahmad, "Pioneering in the Nuclear Age: An Essay on Israel and the Palestinians," in Carollee Bengelsdorf, Margaret Cerullo, and Yogesh Chandrani, eds., *The Selected Writings of Eqbal Ahmad* (Pakistan: Oxford University Press, 2006), 313; Morris, *Righteous Victims*, 341. The day-to-day experience of occupation is well captured in Nathan Thrall, *A Day in the Life of Abed Salama* (New York: Metropolitan Books, 2023).

26. The withdrawal was not a benevolent recognition of Palestinian autonomy. Dov Weissglas, a confidant of then Prime Minister Ariel Sharon, who was in charge of negotiating and implementing it, explained the cynical calculations underlying the move to *Haaretz*: "The significance of the disengagement plan is the

freezing of the peace process. And when you freeze that process, you prevent the establishment of a Palestinian state, and you prevent a discussion on the refugees, the borders and Jerusalem. Effectively, this whole package called the Palestinian state, with all that it entails, has been removed indefinitely from our agenda. And all this with authority and permission. All with a [U.S.] presidential blessing and the ratification of both houses of Congress. . . . The disengagement is actually formaldehyde. It supplies the amount of formaldehyde that is necessary so there will not be a political process with the Palestinians." The presence of the blockade means that the United Nations still considers Gaza occupied territory despite the military pullback. As Israeli journalist Gideon Levy notes, what should be relevant is not the question of whether Israel controls Gaza with a military stationed outside or within, but how Israel's actions create the conditions within Gaza: "The fact that it is more convenient for the occupier to control it from outside has nothing to do with the intolerable living conditions of the occupied." Gideon Levy, *The Punishment of Gaza* (London and New York: Verso, 2010).

27. "Gaza in 2020: A Liveable Place?," United Nations Relief and Works Agency for Palestine Refugees in the Near East, 2012. Even conservative British prime minister David Cameron has described Gaza as a "prison camp," Nicholas Watt and Harriet Sherwood, "David Cameron: Israeli Blockade Has Turned Gaza Strip into a 'Prison Camp,'" *Guardian*, July 27, 2010. Israeli human rights organization B'Tselem said in 2005 that the area had become "one gigantic prison," saying that Israel's "policies have reduced many human rights—among them the right to freedom of movement, family life, health, education, and work—to 'humanitarian gestures' that Israel sparingly provides," "One Big Prison: Freedom of Movement to and from the Gaza Strip," B'Tselem.org, 2005; Weisglass quoted in Conal Urquhart, "Gaza on Brink of Implosion as Aid Cut-Off Starts to Bite," *Guardian*, April 15, 2006.

28. Juan Cole, "Top 10 Myths About Israel's Attack on Gaza," *Arab American News*, November 23, 2012. Cole cites "Gaza's Children: Falling Behind, the Effect of the Blockade on Child Health in Gaza," Save the Children, 2012; "Trapped: The Impact of 15 Years of Blockade on the Mental Health of Gaza's Children," Save the Children, 2022; "Gaza Children Living in 'Hell on Earth,' UN Chief Says, Urging Immediate End to Fighting," UN News, May 20, 2021; Rajaie Batniji, "Searching for Dignity," *Lancet* 380, issue 9840 (August 4, 2012): 466–67.

29. Suzanne Goldenberg, "U.S. Plotted to Overthrow Hamas After Election Victory," *Guardian*, March 3, 2008; Levy, *The Punishment of Gaza*. Hillary Clinton said the U.S. should not have allowed a Palestinian election to take place if it could not fix the outcome, and "if we were going to push for an election, then we should have made sure that we did something to determine who was going to win," "Recording Released of Clinton Suggesting Rigging 2006 Palestinian Election," *Jerusalem Post*, October 29, 2016. On the extreme violence deployed during Cast Lead, see "Breaking the Silence: Soldiers' Testimonies from Operation Cast Lead, Gaza,

2009," documenting use of "white phosphorus ammunition in densely inhabited neighborhoods, massive destruction of buildings unrelated to any direct threat to Israeli forces, and permissive rules of engagement that led to the killing of innocents," including the use of "insane" amounts of firepower. See also Norman G. Finkelstein, *Gaza: An Inquest into Its Martyrdom* (Berkeley: University of California Press, 2018). For more details on this period, filling in gaps, see Noam Chomsky, "Ceasefires in Which Violations Never Cease: What's Next for Israel, Hamas, and Gaza?," TomDispatch, September 9, 2014; Noam Chomsky, "Guillotining Gaza," InformationClearingHouse.info, July 30, 2007; Noam Chomsky, interview by Solomon Eppel and Tushar Khadloya, "Contradictions in U.S. Foreign Policy," *Brown Journal of World Affairs* 14, no. 2 (Spring/Summer 2008): 229–39.

30. Sara Roy, "A Deliberate Cruelty: Rendering Gaza Unviable," Said Memorial Lecture, 2012; see also Sara Roy, *Unsilencing Gaza: Reflections on Resistance* (London: Pluto Press, 2021).

31. "Desmond Tutu: Israel Guilty of Apartheid in Treatment of Palestinians," *Jerusalem Post*, March 10, 2014; Hirsh Goodman, *Let Me Create a Paradise, God Said to Himself: A Journey of Conscience from Johannesburg to Jerusalem* (New York: PublicAffairs, 2009), 78; Goodman is recalling a Ben-Gurion radio address from 1967; "In 1976 Interview, Rabin Likens Settler Ideologues to 'Cancer,' Warns of 'Apartheid,'" *Times of Israel*, September 25, 2015. "Olmert Warns of 'End of Israel,'" BBC News, November 29, 2007. Within Israel's legally recognized borders, there is severe discrimination against the Israeli Arab population, but it does not rise to the level of apartheid. This is sometimes erroneously used to prove that Israel does not enforce an apartheid.

32. Tom Perry, "Israel Is Imposing 'Apartheid Regime' on Palestinians, UN Agency Says," *Independent*, March 16, 2017; Mehdi Hasan, "Top Israelis Have Warned of Apartheid, so Why the Outrage at a UN Report?," *Intercept*, March 22, 2017.

33. "A Threshold Crossed: Israeli Authorities and the Crimes of Apartheid and Persecution," Human Rights Watch, April 27, 2021.

34. "Israel's Apartheid Against Palestinians: A Look into Decades of Oppression and Domination," Amnesty International, February 2022; "A Regime of Jewish Supremacy from the Jordan River to the Mediterranean Sea: This Is Apartheid," B'Tselem.org, January 12, 2021.

35. Observe that while there are consistent demands on Palestinians to recognize the state of Israel's "right to exist," there is no such demand for Israel to recognize a state of Palestine's "right to exist." Furthermore, to demand that the Palestinians, or for that matter anyone, accept Israel's "right to exist" is to grant Israel something that no state in the international system has. They are given recognition, but no state is granted a "right to exist." In the case of Israel, that would require the Palestinians to recognize the legitimacy of their expulsion. It is as if Mexico were required to accept the right of the United States to exist on half of Mexico, gained by conquest. Mexicans do not and should not accept that. Almost every border in the world is the result of conquest. The borders are recognized,

but nobody goes on to demand that the legitimacy be recognized, especially by a population that was driven out.

36. "Judea and Samaria" is an Israeli term for the occupied West Bank of Palestine.

37. Israeli Government Election Plan, Jerusalem, May 14, 1989, official text distributed by the Embassy of Israel in Washington, reprinted in the *Journal of Palestine Studies* XIX, no. I (Autumn 1989): 145–48; Yitzhak Rabin, "Speech to Knesset on Ratification of Oslo Peace Accords," October 5, 1995; Liel Leibovitz, "Fibi Netanyahu," *Tablet*, July 15, 2010. Netanyahu was speaking without realizing he was being recorded. He explained his methods: "They asked me before the election if I'd honor [the Oslo accords]. I said I would, but . . . I'm going to interpret the accords in such a way that would allow me to put an end to this galloping forward to the sixty-seven borders. How did we do it? Nobody said what defined military zones were. Defined military zones are security zones; as far as I'm concerned, the entire Jordan Valley is a defined military zone. Go argue." In the video he also says that the way to deal with Palestinians is to "beat them up, not once but repeatedly, beat them up so it hurts so badly, until it's unbearable." Michael Hirsh and Colum Lynch, "The Long Game of Benjamin Netanyahu," *Foreign Policy*, April 9, 2019; the quote is Hirsh and Lynch's paraphrase of Netanyahu's position. "Netanyahu: No Palestinian State on My Watch," *Times of Israel*, March 16, 2015. He has also said: "I never agreed to return to '67 lines, I never agreed to recognize the right of return and I never agreed to forgo our presence in the Jordan Valley. Never," "Netanyahu Agreed to Withdraw to '67 Lines, Document Confirms," *Haaretz*, March 8, 2015. "Likud—Platform," 1999; the platform promises "stringent measures" if there should ever be a "unilateral Palestinian declaration of the establishment of a Palestinian state." Ron Pundak, "From Oslo to Taba: What Went Wrong?," *Survival* 43, no. 3 (Autumn 2001), 33; David Matz, "Why Did Taba End? (Part 2)," *Palestine-Israel Journal* 2, no. 3 (2003); at their final press conference, the two parties issued a joint statement declaring that they "have never been closer to reaching an agreement and it is thus our shared belief that the remaining gaps could be bridged with the resumption of negotiations following the Israeli elections."

38. Reuven Pedatzur, "No One Is Blameless," *Haaretz*, February 25, 2005.

39. Greg Myre, "4 Israeli Ex-Security Chiefs Denounce Sharon's Hard Line," *New York Times*, November 15, 2003; Joel Greenberg, "Yeshayahu Leibowitz, 91, Iconoclastic Israeli Thinker," *New York Times*, August 19, 1994.

40. Moshe Gorali, "'The Lines Between Good and Evil Have Blurred,'" *Haaretz*, March 31, 2004; Morris, *Righteous Victims*, 342. Eldar and Zartel quoted in Reuven Pedatzur, review of Akiva Eldar and Idit Zartel, *Adonei Ha'aretz (Lords of the Land)*, *Ha'aretz*, February 21, 2005.

41. "U.S. Foreign Aid to Israel," Congressional Research Service, February 18, 2022; Josh Ruebner, Salih Booker, and Zaha Hassan, "Bringing Assistance to Israel in Line with Rights and U.S. Laws," Carnegie Endowment for International Peace, May 12, 2021.

42. A phrase *The New York Times* used to describe Yasser Arafat.

43. Jacob Magin, "UN Panel Votes 163–5 in Support of Palestinian Statehood, End of Occupation," *Times of Israel*, November 20, 2020.

44. Elaine Sciolino, "Self-Appointed Israeli and Palestinian Negotiators Offer a Plan for Middle East Peace," *New York Times*, December 2, 2003; "From Oslo to Taba: What Went Wrong?," 41; Aaron David Miller, *The Much Too Promised Land: America's Elusive Search for Arab-Israeli Peace* (New York: Bantam Books, 2008), 243. In 2005, Miller acknowledged that "many American officials involved in Arab–Israeli peace-making, myself included, have acted as Israel's attorney, catering and coordinating with the Israelis at the expense of successful peace negotiations," Aaron David Miller, "Israel's Lawyer," *Washington Post*, May 23, 2005. John Crowley, "Israel Rejects Arab Peace Initiative," *Telegraph*, March 29, 2007; Barak Ravid, "Netanyahu: Israel Will Never Accept Arab Peace Initiative as Basis for Talks with Palestinians," *Haaretz*, June 13, 2016.

45. Shlomo Shamir, "United States Vetoes Anti-Israel Security Council Resolution," *Haaretz*, March 26, 2004.

46. Barack Obama, Speech to AIPAC, March 4, 2012; Ben Rhodes, *The World as It Is: A Memoir of the Obama White House* (New York: Random House, 2018), 162–63; Jeffrey Goldberg, "Obama to Iran and Israel: 'As President of the United States, I Don't Bluff,'" *Atlantic*, March 2, 2012.

47. Adam Entous, "The Maps of Israeli Settlements That Shocked Barack Obama," *New Yorker*, June 11, 2018; Natasha Mozgovaya, "Lieberman Praises Obama's UN General Assembly Speech," *Haaretz*, September 21, 2011, quoted in Rashid Khalidi, *Brokers of Deceit* (Boston: Beacon Press, 2014), 145. For background on Lieberman's racism, see Samah Salaime, "This Election, Lieberman's Racism Is Going Mainstream," *+972 Magazine*, January 17, 2015; David Gardner, "Israeli Hardliners Sense an Opportunity in Donald Trump's Victory," *Financial Times*, December 7, 2016.

48. "Greenlighting De Facto Annexation: A Summary of Trump's Impact on the Settlements," Peace Now, September 11, 2020; Slater, *Mythologies Without End*, 595.

49. Slater, *Mythologies Without End*, 338; "Kushner: Palestinians Showing They Aren't Ready for Statehood," *Times of Israel*, January 29, 2020; Jonathan Swan, "Kushner Uncertain Palestinians Are Capable of Governing Themselves," *Axios*, June 2, 2019. Notably, Kushner thought that Obama had "tried to beat up on Israel and give the Palestinians everything," a remarkable statement of how little the Trump administration intended to give the Palestinians, because Obama had given them precisely nothing, Adam Entous, "Donald Trump's New World Order," *New Yorker*, June 11, 2018.

50. Alexander Ward, Nahal Toosi, and Jonathan Lemire, "The One Word Biden Won't Say in Israel," *Politico*, July 13, 2022.

51. Note that Israel's ability to declare "no-go zones" within Gaza undermines its claim not to occupy the area. The UN Office for the Coordination of Humanitarian Affairs (UNOCHA) notes that Israel enforces these "Access Restricted

Areas" within Gaza "through the firing of live ammunition, land leveling, destruction of property, arrests, and the confiscation of equipment." See "2015 Overview: Movement and Access Restrictions," UNOCHA.

52. "Report of the Independent International Commission of Inquiry on the Protests in the Occupied Palestinian Territory," United Nations Human Rights Council, 2019, 11.

53. Rosie Perper, "120 Countries Voted to Condemn Israel for Using 'Excessive' Force in Gaza Clashes That Killed over 100 People," *Business Insider,* June 13, 2018; Report of the Independent International Commission of Inquiry.

54. Noa Landau, "UN Council: Israel Intentionally Shot Children and Journalists in Gaza," *Haaretz,* February 28, 2019.

55. Isabel Kershner and David M. Halbfinger, "Israelis Reflect on Gaza: 'I Hope at Least That Each Bullet Was Justified,'" *New York Times,* May 15, 2018; Declan Walsh and Isabel Kershner, "After Deadly Protests, Gazans Ask: What Was Accomplished?," *New York Times,* May 18, 2018; Shmuel Rosner, "Israel Needs to Protect Its Borders. By Whatever Means Necessary," *New York Times,* May 18, 2018. For a full analysis of the arguments made in the op-ed, see Nathan J. Robinson, "Propaganda 101: How to Defend a Massacre," *Current Affairs,* May 21, 2018.

56. "UN General Assembly Urges Greater Protection for Palestinians, Deplores Israel's 'Excessive' Use of Force," *UN News,* June 13, 2018.

57. John Fetterman, Democratic senator from Pennsylvania, said, "Whenever I'm in a situation to be called on to take up the cause of strengthening and enhancing the security of Israel or deepening our relationship between the United States and Israel, I'm going to lean in." In 2021, members of the Democratic Socialists of America considered expelling Congressman Jamaal Bowman, a DSA member, after he voted in favor of continued military aid to Israel, a decision that did not prevent the director of Pro-Israel America from saying that Bowman "cannot be trusted" on Israel and supports a "hateful" agenda.

58. Bret Stephens, "Ilhan Omar Knows Exactly What She Is Doing," *New York Times,* March 7, 2019; Liam Quinn, "Meghan McCain Slams Rep. Ilhan Omar's 'Blatantly Anti-Semitic Rhetoric' Amid Bitter Twitter Spat," Fox News, March 8, 2019; Kevin D. Williamson, "Anti-Semitism's Collaborators," *National Review,* March 6, 2019.

59. The writer Ta-Nehisi Coates described a similar revelation after visiting the Occupied Territories, realizing that what was described as a complicated conflict was actually quite straightforward: "I think what shocked me the most was, in any sort of opinion piece or reported piece . . . that I've read about Israel and about the conflict with the Palestinians, there's a word that comes up all the time, and it is 'complexity' . . . what I expected was that I would find a situation in which it was hard to discern right from wrong, it was hard to understand the morality at play, it was hard to understand the conflict. [But] I immediately understood what was going on over there. . . . And I have to say it was quite familiar. Again, I was in a territory where your mobility is inhibited, where your voting rights are in-

hibited, where your right to the water is inhibited, where your right to housing is inhibited. And it's all inhibited based on ethnicity. . . . And so, the most shocking thing about my time over there was how uncomplicated it actually is."

60. "The Perle-Chomsky debate," Ohio State University, 1988.

61. "Israeli Forces Open Fire to Stop People Returning to North Gaza," *Al Jazeera English*, November 24, 2023.

62. Maayan Lubell et al., "Israel Vows 'Mighty Vengeance' After Surprise Attack," Reuters, October 7, 2023; "Gaza: 3,195 Children Killed in Three Weeks Surpasses Annual Number of Children Killed in Conflict Zones Since 2019," Save the Children International, October 29, 2023; Nicholas Kristof, "So Many Child Deaths in Gaza, and for What?," *New York Times*, December 6, 2023; Allegra Goodwin, et al., "Infants Found Dead and Decomposing in Evacuated Hospital ICU in Gaza," CNN, December 8, 2023. The IDF promised evacuating medical staff that it would send ambulances for the infants, but did not.

63. "'Are You Seriously Asking Me About Palestinian Civilians?': Ex-Israeli PM," *TRT World*, October 2023.

64. Yuval Abraham, "'A Mass Assassination Factory': Inside Israel's Calculated Bombing of Gaza," *+972 Magazine*, November 30, 2023; Yuval Abraham, "'Lavender': The AI Machine Directing Israel's Bombing Spree in Gaza," *+972 Magazine*, April 3, 2024. There are plenty of specific examples of Israeli strikes on civilian infrastructure that had no obvious military purpose, see, e.g., "Gaza: Israeli Strike Killing 106 Civilians an Apparent War Crime," Human Rights Watch, April 4, 2024.

65. John Paul Rathbone, "Military Briefing: The Israeli Bombs Raining on Gaza," *Financial Times*, December 5, 2023; Julian Borger, "Civilians Make Up 61% of Gaza Deaths from Airstrikes, Israeli Study Finds," *Guardian*, December 9, 2023; "'Pallywood Propaganda': Pro-Israeli Accounts Online Accuse Palestinians of Staging Their Suffering," France 24, November 21, 2023. Omar Shakir, "While a Fire Rages in Gaza, the West Bank Smolders," Human Rights Watch, November 22, 2023.

66. Ryan Grim, "Netanyahu's Goal for Gaza: 'Thin' Population 'to a Minimum,'" *Intercept*, December 3, 2023; Aurora Almendral and Yasmine Salam, "A Forced Exodus from Gaza to Egypt? Israeli 'Concept Paper' Fuels Outrage," NBC News, November 2, 2023; "PM Warns Ministers to Pipe Down After Comments on New 'Nakba' and Nuking Gaza," *Times of Israel*, November 12, 2023; "Israel's Unfolding Crime of Genocide of the Palestinian People & U.S. Failure to Prevent and Complicity in Genocide," Center for Constitutional Rights, October 8, 2023; Neil Vigdor, "Republican Congressman Says of Gaza: 'It Should Be Like Nagasaki and Hiroshima,'" *New York Times*, March 31, 2024. There is no shortage of such quotes. For more, see Nathan J. Robinson, "My Date with Destiny," *Current Affairs*, March 28, 2024.

67. "Former Israel General Says 'Severe Epidemics' in Gaza Would Help Israel Win the War," *Middle East Eye*, November 21, 2023; Gretchen Stenger, "Infectious

Disease Specialist with UVA Health Explains Effects of Water Crisis in Gaza," CBS-19 News, April 1, 2024.

68. Mitchell McCluskey and Richard Allen Greene, "Israel Military Says 2 Civilians Killed for Every Hamas Militant Is a 'Tremendously Positive' Ratio Given Combat Challenges," CNN, December 6, 2023; Yaniv Kubovich, "Israel Created 'Kill Zones' in Gaza. Anyone Who Crosses into Them Is Shot," *Haaretz*, March 31, 2024; @DavidKlion, Twitter (X) post, December 22, 2023, https://twitter.com /DavidKlion/status/1738387640817197241.

69. Steve Holland and Jeff Mason, "U.S. Not Drawing Red Lines for Israel, White House Says," Reuters, October 27, 2023, Biden later revised this, saying that an invasion of Rafah would cross a "red line." Israel subsequently invaded Rafah anyway, with the U.S. denying this had crossed a "red line"; Benjamin Q. Huỳnh et al., "No Evidence of Inflated Mortality Reporting from the Gaza Ministry of Health," *Lancet*, vol. 403, 10421 (2024): 23–24; "U.S. State Dept Human Rights Officer Latest to Resign in Gaza Protest," *Al Jazeera English*, March 27, 2024; Maria Abi-Habib et al., "More Than 500 U.S. Officials Sign Letter Protesting Biden's Israel Policy," *New York Times*, November 14, 2023.

70. "'Please Stop This War Against Us': Gaza Doctor Begs for World's Help as Hunger & Disease Spread," *Democracy Now!*, April 4, 2024; Irfan Galarian, "I'm an American Doctor Who Went to Gaza. What I Saw Wasn't War—It Was Annihilation," *Los Angeles Times*, February 16, 2024; Jason Burke, "UNICEF Official Tells of 'Utter Annihilation' After Travelling Length of Gaza," *Guardian*, March 22, 2024.

71. Alexander Ward, Adam Cancryn, and Jonathan Lemire, "Biden Admin Officials See Proof Their Strategy Is Working in Hostage Deal," *Politico,* November 21, 2023; Emily Rauhala, "U.S. Backs Israel Before UN Court as Biden-Netanyahu Tension Simmers," *Washington Post*, February 21, 2024.

72. John Hudson, "U.S. Approved More Bombs to Israel on Day of World Central Kitchen Strikes," *Washington Post*, April 4, 2024; Isaac Chotiner, "Biden's Increasingly Contradictory Israel Policy," *New Yorker*, April 2, 2024. The best available book on the post–October 7 situation is Jamie Stern-Weiner, ed., *Deluge: Gaza and Israel from Crisis to Cataclysm* (New York and London: OR Books, 2024).

CHAPTER 6: THE GREAT CHINA THREAT

1. Trump Twitter Archive; *The Situation Room with Wolf Blitzer*, CNN, January 20, 2011; Hui Feng, "Trump Took a Sledgehammer to U.S.-China Relations. This Won't Be an Easy Fix, Even If Biden Wins," TheConversation.org, October 19, 2020; Barbara Plett Usher, "Why U.S.-China Relations Are at Their Lowest Point in Decades," BBC, July 24, 2020; Adam Shaw, "Pompeo Says Chinese Threat 'Inside the Gates' Amid Rising Fears About Risk to U.S. Data, Economic Security," Fox News, July 9, 2022; Stephen K. Bannon, "We're in an Economic War with China. It's Futile to Compromise," *Washington Post*, May 6, 2019; Christopher

Wray, "The Threat Posed by the Chinese Government and the Chinese Communist Party to the Economic and National Security of the United States," Hudson Institute, Washington, DC, July 7, 2020.

2. "Attorney General William P. Barr Delivers Remarks on China Policy at the Gerald R. Ford Presidential Museum," Office of Public Affairs, U.S. Department of Justice, July 16, 2020.

3. "National Security Strategy of the United States of America," December 2017.

4. "U.S. Strategic Framework for the Indo-Pacific," National Archives (declassified 2021).

5. Edward Wong et al., "Joe Biden's China Journey," *New York Times*, October 6, 2021; Nahal Toosi, "Biden Ad Exposes a Rift over China on the Left," *Politico*, April 23, 2020; Joe Leahy and Demetri Sevastopulo, "China Hits Out at U.S. After Joe Biden Calls Xi Jinping a 'Dictator,'" *Financial Times*, June 21, 2023; Joseph R. Biden Jr., "Why America Must Lead Again," *Foreign Affairs*, March/April 2020.

6. Jennifer Conrad, "A Year In, Biden's China Policy Looks a Lot Like Trump's," *Wired*, December 30, 2021; Gavin Bade, "'A Sea Change': Biden Reverses Decades of Chinese Trade Policy," *Politico*, December 26, 2022; Michael Schuman, "China Will Get Stronger," *Atlantic*, January/February 2024; Didi Tang and Ken Moritsugu, "China Sees Two 'Bowls of Poison' in Biden and Trump and Ponders Who Is the Lesser of Two Evils," Associated Press, January 29, 2024.

7. Michael Hirsh, "The Big, Quiet Issue Biden and Xi Are Avoiding," *Politico*, November 14, 2023; Ivana Saraci, "Blinken: China Poses 'Most Serious, Long-Term Challenge' to World Order," *Axios*, May 26, 2022; "Fact Sheet: 2022 National Defense Strategy," Department of Defense; Van Jackson, "America Is Turning Asia into a Powder Keg," *Foreign Affairs*, October 22, 2021; Edward Wong, "On U.S. Foreign Policy, the New Boss Acts a Lot Like the Old One," *New York Times*, July 24, 2022; "Fact Sheet: Advancing the Rebalance to Asia and the Pacific," Office of the Press Secretary, White House, November 16, 2015; "Obama Tells Asia U.S. 'Here to Stay' as a Pacific Power," *Guardian*, November 16, 2011.

8. For background, see Robert P. Newman, *Owen Lattimore and the "Loss" of China* (Berkeley: University of California Press, 1992).

9. Michael T. Klare, "Welcome to the New Cold War," *Nation*, January 14, 2022; Demetri Sevastopulo, "Joe Biden Announces U.S., UK and Australia Co-Operation on Hypersonic Weapons," *Financial Times*, April 5, 2022; "U.S. Dept. of Defense, Military and Security Developments Involving the People's Republic of China 2021," USC U.S.-China Institute, November 2, 2021.

10. Deb Riechmann, "U.S. Intelligence Director Says China Is Top Threat to America," AP News, December 30, 2020; "Safeguarding Our Future: Protecting Government and Business Leaders at the U.S. State and Local Level from People's Republic of China (PRC) Influence Operations," National Counterintelligence and Security Center, July 2022; Burgess Everett, "Schumer Presses Trump to Label China a Currency Manipulator," *Politico*, January 24, 2017; "Attorney Gen-

eral William P. Barr Delivers Remarks on China Policy at the Gerald R. Ford Presidential Museum," July 16, 2020.

11. Deborah Brautigam and Meg Rithmire, "The Chinese 'Debt Trap' Is a Myth," *Atlantic*, February 6, 2021.

12. See Rob Larson, "The IMF's Bottomless Bottom-Line Cruelty," *Current Affairs*, February 2, 2022.

13. Paul Wiseman, "In Trade Wars of 200 Years Ago, the Pirates Were Americans," Associated Press, March 28, 2019. "Trade Secrets: Intellectual Piracy and the Origins of American Industrial Power," Working Knowledge, Harvard Business School, June 21, 2004; Jack Goldsmith, "Does the U.S. Still Interfere in Foreign Elections?," Project-Syndicate.org, October 28, 2020. Another example: the U.S. routinely accuses other powers of running meddlesome online influence campaigns. But during the COVID-19 pandemic, the Pentagon tried to undermine China's international vaccination campaigns by deliberately spreading anti-vaccine misinformation online, attempting to worsen COVID-19 in order to subvert China. Chris Bing and Joel Schectman, "Pentagon Ran Secret Anti-Vax Campaign to Undermine China During Pandemic," Reuters, June 14, 2024.

14. Kyle Haynes, "Would China Be a Benign Hegemon?," *Diplomat*, June 2, 2017; Ha-Joon Chang, *Kicking Away the Ladder: Development Strategy in Historical Perspective* (London: Anthem Press, 2002).

15. "Statement by PJ Keating," September 28, 2021.

16. Cobus van Staden, "Fears of a Chinese Naval Base in West Africa Are Overblown," *Foreign Policy*, March 3, 2022; Phelim Kine, "U.S. Turns the Screws on Solomon Islands to Counter China," *Politico*, April 28, 2022.

17. "We Shouldn't Underestimate the Incredible Danger Posed by the Taiwan Crisis," interview with Lyle Goldstein, *Jacobin*, August 6, 2022.

18. "U.S. Poses Most Serious Long-Term Challenge to International Order: Spokesperson," *Xinhua*, May 31, 2022.

19. Chris Buckley, "After China's Military Spectacle, Options Narrow for Winning Over Taiwan," *New York Times*, August 7, 2022.

20. Nathaniel Sher, "Why We Shouldn't Declare Taiwan an Independent Country," Quincy Institute for Responsible Statecraft, October 9, 2023.

21. Kyle Mizokami, "The U.S. Military 'Failed Miserably' in a Fake Battle over Taiwan," *Popular Mechanics*, August 2, 2021.

22. Kathrin Hille and Demetri Sevastopulo, "Taiwan: Preparing for a Potential Chinese Invasion," *Financial Times*, June 6, 2022; Kathrin Hille and Demetri Sevastopulo, "U.S. Accused of Undermining Taiwan Defences by Focusing on 'D-day' Scenario," *Financial Times*, May 17, 2022; Richard C. Bush, "What the Historic Ma-Xi Meeting Could Mean for Cross-Strait Relations," Brookings Institution, November 9, 2015.

23. Chris Horton, "Taiwan's Status Is a Geopolitical Absurdity," *Atlantic*, July 8, 2019.

24. Jack Detsch, "The U.S. Is Getting Taiwan Ready to Fight on the Beaches," *Foreign*

Policy, November 8, 2021; Christina Lu, "Biden Vows to Defend Taiwan," *Foreign Policy*, May 24, 2022; Ben Burgis, "Nancy Pelosi Is Rolling the Dice on World War III," *Jacobin*, August 4, 2022.

25. Chris Buckley and Steven Lee Myers, "'Starting a Fire': U.S. and China Enter Dangerous Territory over Taiwan," *New York Times*, October 9, 2021.

26. Paul Godwin, "Asia's Dangerous Security Dilemma," *Current History* 109, no. 728 (September 2010), 264–66; Stephen Walt, "Does Anyone Still Understand the 'Security Dilemma'?," Quincy Institute for Responsible Statecraft, July 26, 2022; Roger Cohen, "In Submarine Deal with Australia, U.S. Counters China but Enrages France," *New York Times*, September 16, 2021; Stavros Atlamazoglu, "The U.S. Navy Is Training for War in the South China Sea," *1945*, July 18, 2022; Takahashi Kosuke, "U.S.-Led RIMPAC, World's Largest Maritime Exercise, Starts Without China or Taiwan," *Diplomat,* July 1, 2022; Stavros Atlamazoglu, "What Is RIMPAC 2022? Simple: A Warning to China," *1945*, July 18, 2022.

27. Hal Brands, "Containment Can Work Against China, Too," *Wall Street Journal*, December 3, 2021; S.2226–National Defense Authorization Act for Fiscal Year 2024; Alexa Fee, "Romney Calls for a Change of Course Concerning China," *Daily Caller*, February 16, 2012; Jackie Calmes, "Trans-Pacific Partnership Text Released, Waving Green Flag for Debate," *New York Times*, November 5, 2015.

28. M. Taylor Fravel, "China's Misunderstood Nuclear Expansion," *Foreign Affairs*, November 10, 2023.

29. John Mearsheimer, "The Rise of China Will Not Be Peaceful at All," *Australian*, November 18, 2005.

30. Richard Stone, "'National Pride Is at Stake.' Russia, China, United States Race to Build Hypersonic Weapons," *Science*, January 8, 2020; Peter Martin, "Kissinger Warns Biden of U.S.-China Catastrophe on Scale of WWI," November 16, 2020.

31. Gordon Corera, "China: MI5 and FBI Heads Warn of 'Immense' Threat," BBC, July 7, 2022; Tom Mitchell, "China Blasts 'Extremely Dangerous' U.S. Policy at High-Level Talks," *Financial Times,* July 25, 2021; John Kuo Wei Tchen and Dylan Yeats, eds., *Yellow Peril! An Archive of Anti-Asian Fear* (London and New York: Verso, 2014).

32. Cindy Wang and Isabel Reynolds, "China Likely Fired Missiles over Taiwan in High-Risk Milestone," Bloomberg, August 3, 2022; Stuart Lau, "China Suspends Climate Talks with U.S.," *Politico*, August 5, 2022.

CHAPTER 7: NATO AND RUSSIA AFTER THE COLD WAR

1. Strobe Talbott, introduction, in John Norris, *Collision Course: NATO, Russia, and Kosovo* (Westport, CT: Praeger, 2005).

2. J. de Hoop Scheffer, AP/Novum, *Trouw* (Netherlands), June 29, 2007.

3. Kennan quoted in Thomas L. Friedman, "Now a Word from X," *New York*

Times, May 2, 1998; Richard Sakwa, *Frontline Ukraine* (London: I. B. Tauris & Co., 2015), 4.

4. Charles A. Kupchan, "Expand NATO—and Split Europe," *New York Times*, November 27, 1994; Michael Mandelbaum, "Preserving the New Peace: The Case Against NATO Expansion," *Foreign Affairs*, May/June 1995; Ted Galen Carpenter, "Ignored Warnings: How NATO Expansion Led to the Current Ukraine Tragedy," Cato Institute, February 24, 2022. Galen Carpenter himself had written at the time: "It would be extraordinarily difficult to expand NATO eastward without that action's being viewed by Russia as unfriendly. Even the most modest schemes would bring the alliance to the borders of the old Soviet Union. Some of the more ambitious versions would have the alliance virtually surround the Russian Federation itself . . . [Expansion] would constitute a needless provocation of Russia."

5. "'We're Fundamentally at War': Rep. Moulton Says U.S. in Proxy War with Russia," *Democracy Now!*, May 9, 2022; Susan B. Glasser, "What If We're Already Fighting the Third World War with Russia?," *New Yorker*, September 29, 2022.

6. This was Bill Clinton's own description of his motivation for ordering the bombings. "Clinton's Statements on Kosovo," *Washington Post*, June 1, 1999.

7. "A Cash-Starved Peace in Kosovo," *New York Times*, March 7, 2000; Javier Solana, "NATO's Success in Kosovo," *Foreign Affairs*, November/December 1999; Samantha Power, *"A Problem from Hell": America and the Age of Genocide* (New York: Basic Books, 2002), ebook.

8. Michael Mandelbaum, "A Perfect Failure: NATO's War Against Yugoslavia," *Foreign Affairs* 78, no. 5 (1999): 2–8.

9. Christopher Layne and Benjamin Schwarz, "Was It a Mistake?," *Washington Post*, March 26, 2000.

10. Wesley Clark, *Waging Modern War* (New York: PublicAffairs, 2001), 171; Elaine Sciolino and Ethan Bronner, "Crisis in the Balkans: The Road to War," *New York Times*, April 18, 1999; Jeremy Hammond, "Syria and Lessons Unlearned from the U.S./NATO Bombing of Kosovo," *Foreign Policy Journal*, September 6, 2013; "Kosovo: Civilian Deaths in the NATO Air Campaign," Human Rights Watch, February 1, 2000. China's ambassador to the UN described the embassy bombing as a "barbarian act" and "a gross violation of the United Nations charter, international law and the norms governing international relations" as well as "a violation of the Geneva convention." NATO cast doubt on its responsibility for the bus bombing, calling reports a "deliberate distortion" and saying it had no evidence of its own involvement. Human Rights Watch, however, received additional evidence pointing to NATO responsibility and counted the victims as casualties of NATO's bombing. Paul Watson in the *Los Angeles Times* gave a harrowing account of the bus bombing: "Nada was among 43 civilians who survived Monday's bombing. In the room of 10 women and children where she lay in Pec's main hospital, one of the wounded was a blond girl about 4 years old. The wedding Nada and her mother had set out to plan must have seemed so far away.

A piece of shrapnel had severed Nada's spine like a knife, and the director of Pec's hospital, Dr. Miodrag Jasovic, judged the girl's chances of walking again at zero. . . . The thought of being attacked by NATO while riding a bus was so remote to passenger Sladjana Prascevic, 25, of Decani that she first thought it was an ambush by the guerrilla Kosovo Liberation Army. . . . Paralyzed and covered in blood, Nada was caught in a panicked tangle of people trying to escape. Frantic, her mother grabbed the girl by both hands and dragged her out of the bus, past the corpses of passengers, police and soldiers. Then, witnesses said, a NATO warplane dropped a cluster bomb. It released dozens of bomblets that exploded into bits of shrapnel and blew holes about the size of baseballs into the asphalt. One of the yellow canisters failed to detonate. It sat, threatening to go off, just a few feet from the corpse of a police officer in blue camouflage who died flat on his back, far behind the bus. A metal label riveted to a round piece of the main cluster bomb landed in the middle of the road and provided these details on the bomb's origins and type: "Sensor proximity FZU 39/B," the metal plate said. The lot number was MN89F005-010, and the part number was 77757-10. It was made in the U.S. and the manufacturer was listed as Magnavox. Nada's mother was dragging the girl into a forest nearby when the cluster bomblets exploded along the road, forcing dazed survivors to flee deeper into the trees, Matanovic and other witnesses said. Police and soldiers later arrived to transport survivors to the hospital. When a small group of journalists reached the scene about 3:15 p.m., police were loading the last corpses into a truck." Paul Watson, "NATO Bombs Kill 17 More Civilians," *Los Angeles Times*, May 4, 1999.

11. Thomas L. Friedman, "Stop the Music," *New York Times*, April 23, 1999.
12. "No Justice for the Victims of NATO Bombings," Amnesty International, April 23, 2009; "Serb Media Battles NATO with Scenes of Destruction," CNN, April 9, 1999; Richard Norton-Taylor, "Serb TV Station Was Legitimate Target, Says Blair," *Guardian*, April 23, 1999.
13. Bradley Graham, "Report Says NATO Bombing Killed 500 Civilians in Yugoslavia," *Washington Post*, February 7, 2000.
14. Susan Sontag, "Why Are We in Kosovo?," *New York Times*, May 2, 1999; *The Kosovo Report*, The Independent International Commission on Kosovo (New York: Oxford University Press, 2000).
15. Michael MccGwire, "Why Did We Bomb Belgrade?," *International Affairs* (Royal Academy of International Affairs, London), 76.1 (January 2000); "Bombing of Yugoslavia Awakens Anti-U.S. Feeling Around World," *Washington Post*, May 18, 1999. The *Post* reported that global opposition to NATO's conduct was widespread and spanned Latin America, Asia, and Africa, and that it could be seen "in newspaper editorials, opinion polls, public protests, Internet banter and street graffiti." Anthony Sampson, "Mandela Accuses 'Policeman' Britain," *Guardian*, April 4, 2000.
16. Likewise, Tony Blair cited the "credibility of NATO" as a core issue that meant "we couldn't lose"; "Moral Combat: NATO at War," BBC Two, March 12, 2000.

17. All quotations from Norris, *Collision Course.* Note that Norris's book carries a foreword from Clinton's own deputy secretary of state, Strobe Talbott.

18. Patrick Wintour, "War Strategy Ridiculed," *Guardian,* July 20, 2000.

19. Yeltsin quoted by Norris; "Yeltsin Sees War Threat in NATO Enlargement," *Monitor* 1, no. 91, September 8, 1995.

20. Albright quoted in Galen Carpenter; Strobe Talbott, "Why NATO Should Grow," *New York Review of Books*, August 10, 1995.

21. Paul Taylor, "Ukraine: NATO's Original Sin," *Politico,* November 23, 2021; Branko Marcetic, "Diplomatic Cables Show Russia Saw NATO Expansion as a Red Line," American Committee for U.S.-Russia Accord, January 16, 2023.

22. According to the National Security Archive, the UK government gave similar assurances: "As late as March 1991, according to the diary of the British ambassador to Moscow, British prime minister John Major personally assured Gorbachev, 'We are not talking about the strengthening of NATO.' Subsequently, when Soviet defense minister Marshal Dmitri Yazov asked Major about East European leaders' interest in NATO membership, the British leader responded, 'Nothing of the sort will happen'"; "NATO Expansion: What Gorbachev Heard," National Security Archive, December 12, 2017. Robert M. Gates, *Duty: Memoirs of a Secretary at War* (New York: Vintage, 2015), 157. A similar judgment was voiced by Steven Pifer, who was ambassador to Ukraine from 1998 to 2000: "That was a real mistake. . . . It drove the Russians nuts. It created expectations in Ukraine and Georgia, which then were never met."

23. Horace Campbell and Ali A. Mazrui, *Global NATO and the Catastrophic Failure in Libya* (New York: New York University Press, 2013); Ian Martin, *All Necessary Measures? The United Nations and International Intervention in Libya* (London: Hurst, 2022); Joe Dyke, "NATO Killed Civilians in Libya. It's Time to Admit It," *Foreign Policy*, March 20, 2021.

24. "This Man Predicted Russia-Ukraine War in 2015: The West Is Leading Ukraine Down the Primrose Path," *India Times*, February 27, 2022; Shane Harris et al., "Road to War: U.S. Struggled to Convince Allies, and Zelensky, of Risk of Invasion," *Washington Post*, August 16, 2022.

25. "On Launching a Special Military Operation in Ukraine," Address by the President of the Russian Federation, February 24, 2022.

26. Thomas L. Friedman, "This Is Putin's War. But America and NATO Aren't Innocent Bystanders," *New York Times*, February 21, 2022. In 1996, Friedman had described NATO expansion as "the most ill-conceived project of the post-cold-war era." Noor Ibrahim, "Biden Tells Putin Where to Shove His 'Red Lines,'" *Daily Beast*, December 7, 2021.

27. Anatol Lieven, "Ukraine: The Most Dangerous Problem in the World," *Nation*, November 15, 2021.

28. Jack F. Matlock, Jr., "I Was There: NATO and the Origins of the Ukraine Crisis," Quincy Institute for Responsible Statecraft, February 15, 2022.

29. Michael Schwirtz, "NATO Signals Support for Ukraine in Face of Threat from

Russia," *New York Times*, December 16, 2021; Samuel Charap, "NATO Honesty on Ukraine Could Avert Conflict with Russia," *Financial Times*, January 13, 2022.

30. John R. Deni, "The Strategic Case for Risking War in Ukraine," *Wall Street Journal*, December 22, 2021.

31. Interview with Zbigniew Brzezinski, *Le Nouvel Observateur* (France), January 15–21, 1998, 76.

32. Quoted in Andrew Van Wagner, "Stopping the Killing," *Join Andrew* Substack, January 19, 2023.

33. Alexander Ward, "Tell Us How the Ukraine War Ends," *Politico*, March 1, 2022; Daniel W. Drezner, "What Is the Plan Behind Sanctioning Russia?," *Washington Post*, April 25, 2022; Natasha Bertrand et al., "Austin's Assertion That U.S. Wants to 'Weaken' Russia Underlines Biden Strategy Shift," CNN, April 26, 2022.

34. Congressional Progressive Caucus letter, October 24, 2022; Alexander Ward et al., "House Progressives Retract Russia-Diplomacy Letter amid Dem Firestorm," *Politico*, October 25, 2022; Michael Birnbaum and Missy Ryan, "NATO Says Ukraine to Decide on Peace Deal with Russia—Within Limits," *Washington Post*, April 5, 2022.

35. Peter Baker, "Top U.S. General Urges Diplomacy in Ukraine While Biden Advisers Resist," *New York Times*, November 10, 2022; Kylie Atwood and Oren Liebermann, "Biden Admin Divided over Path Ahead for Ukraine as Top U.S. General Milley Pushes for Diplomacy," CNN, November 11, 2022.

36. Yasmeen Serhan, "Why Germany Agonized over Sending Tanks to Ukraine," *Time*, January 25, 2023; "Germany Is Refusing to Send Tanks to Ukraine. Biden Cannot Let This Stand," *Washington Post*, January 21, 2023.

37. Graham E. Fuller, "Washington Denies Reality of 'Spheres of Influence'—a New Pinnacle of Hypocrisy," Graham E. Fuller's blog, February 6, 2022; Fiona Harrigan, "Don't Kick Russian Students Out of the U.S.," *Reason*, March 1, 2022; Jim Lobe, "Networks Covered the War in Ukraine More Than the U.S. Invasion of Iraq," Quincy Institute for Responsible Statecraft, April 9, 2022. Indeed, many in the media were quite open about being more sympathetic to European victims, with one CBS correspondent saying: "You know, this is a relatively civilized, relatively European—I have to choose those words carefully, too—city [Kyiv] where you wouldn't expect that or hope that it's going to happen." H. A. Hellyer, "Coverage of Ukraine Has Exposed Long-Standing Racist Biases in Western Media," *Washington Post*, February 28, 2022.

38. Timothy Ash, "It's Costing Peanuts for the U.S. to Defeat Russia," Center for European Policy Analysis, November 18, 2022; Dennis Romboy, "Mitt Romney Says U.S. Support of Ukraine Is Good for Americans," *Deseret News*, January 26, 2023.

39. Samuel Charap and Miranda Piebe, "Avoiding a Long War: U.S. Policy and the Trajectory of the Russia-Ukraine Conflict," RAND Research & Commentary, January 25, 2023.

40. Alistair MacDonald and Daniel Michaels, "BAE, U.S. in Talks to Restart M777

Howitzer Production After Ukraine Success," *Wall Street Journal*, October 9, 2022; Eric Lipton et al., "Military Spending Surges, Creating New Boom for Arms Makers," *New York Times*, December 18, 2022; David Ignatius, "The West Feels Gloomy About Ukraine. Here's Why It Shouldn't," *Washington Post*, July 18, 2023; Taras Kuzio, "The West Reaps Multiple Benefits from Backing Ukraine Against Russia," Atlantic Council, January 12, 2023. Ukraine's defense minister actually pitched the country's war as an ideal "testing ground" for Western weapons, Roman Olearchyk, "Military Briefing: Ukraine Provides Ideal 'Testing Ground' for Western Weaponry," *Financial Times*, July 5, 2023.

41. Eliot A. Cohen, "Western Aid to Ukraine Is Still Not Enough," *Atlantic*, January 17, 2023; Eliot A. Cohen, "Cut the Baloney Realism," *Atlantic*, November 21, 2023; Eliot A. Cohen, "Let's Use Chicago Rules to Beat Russia," *Atlantic*, July 6, 2023; Aaron Maté, "U.S. Fighting Russia 'to the Last Ukrainian': Veteran U.S. Diplomat," TheGrayzone.com, March 24, 2022; Aaron Maté, "U.S., UK Sabotaged Peace Deal Because They 'Don't Care About Ukraine': Fmr. NATO Adviser," TheGrayzone .com, September 27, 2022; Branko Marcetic, "Ukraine's Tragedies: A 'Good Deal' for Some War Supporters," Quincy Institute for Responsible Statecraft, February 26, 2025.

42. Barbara Moens et al., "Europe Accuses U.S. of Profiting from War," *Politico*, November 24, 2022; "Ukraine Crisis: List of Countries That Have Imposed Sanctions on Russia," BusinessToday.in, February 23, 2022; Howard W. French, "Why Ukraine Is Not a Priority for the Global South," *Foreign Policy*, September 19, 2022.

43. Sakwa, *Frontline Ukraine*; Oli Brown et al., "The Consequences of Russia's War on Ukraine for Climate Action, Food Supply and Energy Security," Chatham House, September 13, 2023.

44. For detailed responses to common criticisms, see Noam Chomsky, "The Ukraine War: Chomsky Responds," CounterPunch.org, June 3, 2022. For a discussion of the idea that questioning the U.S. stance fails to respect Ukrainian agency, see Branko Marcetic, "Free Agents?," *New Left Review*, November 23, 2023.

45. "Head of Ukraine's Leading Party Claims Russia Proposed 'Peace' in Exchange for Neutrality," *Ukrainska Pravda*, November 24, 2023; Robert Semonsen, "Former Israeli PM: West Blocked Russo-Ukraine Peace Deal," *European Conservative*, February 7, 2023; Catherine Belton, "Russia Will Stop 'in a Moment' if Ukraine Meets Terms—Kremlin," Reuters, March 7, 2022; Anton Troianovski, "Putin Quietly Signals He Is Open to a Cease-Fire in Ukraine," *New York Times*, December 23, 2023; "Putin Says Russia Does Not Reject Talks with Ukraine," Reuters, July 29, 2023; Ben Aris, "Lavrov Confirms Ukraine War Peace Deal Reached Last April, but Then Abandoned," Intellinews, September 27, 2023; "Russia Has Shown No Interest in Negotiations to End War Despite Putin's Words, U.S. Officials Say," Radio Free Europe, December 23, 2022; Kaitlin Lewis, "Russia Offered to End War if Ukraine Dropped NATO Bid: Kyiv Official," *Newsweek*, November 27, 2023; "Blinken: 'Kiev Willing to Negotiate if Russia Shows Interest in a Diplomatic Solution,'" *Agenzia Nova*, September 11, 2023.

46. Helene Cooper et al., "Troop Deaths and Injuries in Ukraine War Near 500,000, U.S. Officials Say," *New York Times*, August 18, 2023; Erin Snodgrass, "The Average Age of Ukrainian Soldier Is Older Than 40 as the Country Grapples with Personnel Problems," *Business Insider*, November 6, 2023.

47. Oliver Milman, "How the Gas Industry Capitalized on the Ukraine War to Change Biden Policy," *Guardian*, September 22, 2022; Tom Fairless, "How War in Europe Boosts the U.S. Economy," *Wall Street Journal*, February 18, 2024.

48. James Mattis, "National Defense Strategy and Nuclear Posture Review," Committee on Armed Services, U.S. House of Representatives, February 6, 2018.

CHAPTER 8: NUCLEAR THREATS AND CLIMATE CATASTROPHE

1. Alvin Powell, "Pinker Explains the Long Peace," *Harvard Gazette*, March 30, 2012; Steven Pinker, *The Better Angels of Our Nature: Why Violence Has Declined* (New York: Viking, 2011); Paul Thomas Chamberlain notes that "between the end of World War II and 1990, more than 20 million people died in violent conflicts. Broken down, that means that an average of more than 1,200 people died in wars of one type or another, every day, for forty-five years. Most of them were civilians. In raw numerical terms, this death toll equals more than three My Lai massacres every day for forty-five years. Nearly all of them have been forgotten," Paul Thomas Chamberlain, *The Cold War's Killing Fields: Rethinking the Long Peace* (New York: Harper, 2018). For a more detailed response to Pinker, see Edward S. Herman and David Peterson, *Reality Denial: Steven Pinker's Apologetics for Western-Imperial Violence*, Znetwork.org, July 24, 2012, and Nathan J. Robinson, "The World's Most Annoying Man," *Current Affairs*, May 29, 2019.

2. For example, merely counting the number of lynchings in the Jim Crow South does not accurately measure the system's violence, because the *threat* of lynching was ubiquitous—again, it is like counting as armed robberies only those instances in which somebody was actually shot.

3. On the horrors of the firebombing and analysis of the justifications for it, see Edwin P. Hoyt, *Inferno: The Fire Bombing of Japan, March 9–August 15, 1945* (Montebello, NY: Madison Books, 2000).

4. See Greg Mitchell, "The Great Hiroshima Cover-Up—and the Greatest Movie Never Made," *Asia-Pacific Journal* 9, no. 21 (August 2011). Mitchell documents the suppression of the most graphic footage of atomic bomb victims by the U.S. authorities, quoting the director of the army's filmmaking team saying of the footage: "[U.S. officials] wanted it buried. . . . They were fearful because of the horror it contained . . . because it showed effects on men, women and children. . . . They didn't want that material out because they were sorry for their sins—and because they were working on new nuclear weapons." The footage was eventually exposed thanks to the efforts of Japanese antinuclear activists.

5. J. Robert Oppenheimer, *Atom and Void: Essays on Science and Community* (Princeton, NJ: Princeton University Press, 2014), 141; Harold P. Green, "The Oppenheimer

Case: A Study in the Abuse of Law," *Bulletin of the Atomic Scientists* 33, no. 7 (September 1977): 12; Holcomb B. Noble, "Joseph Rotblat, 96, Dies; Resisted Nuclear Weapons," *New York Times*, September 2, 2005.

6. Mainau Declaration, 5th Lindau Nobel Laureate Meeting, July 15, 1955; "The Russell-Einstein Manifesto," Atomic Heritage Foundation, July 9, 1955.

7. "Nuclear Weapons," United Nations Office for Disarmament Affairs. Address by the Soviet Representative (Gromyko) to the United Nations Atomic Energy Commission, June 19, 1946, in *Documents on Disarmament, Vol. 1* (Washington, DC: United States Arms Control and Disarmament Agency, 1960), 19–21.

8. Michio Kaku and Daniel Axelrod, in *To Win a Nuclear War: The Pentagon's Secret War Plans* (Boston: South End Press, 1999), 30; Henry Stimson, diary entries, May 14–15, 1945.

9. Lawrence S. Wittner, *One World or None: A History of the World Nuclear Disarmament Movement Through 1953* (Redwood City, CA: Stanford University Press, 1993), 79.

10. Marion Lloyd, "Soviets Close to Using A-Bomb in 1962 Crisis, Forum Is Told," *Boston Globe*, October 13, 2002.

11. Christian Appy, *American Reckoning* (New York: Penguin Books, 2015), 76.

12. See also Sheldon M. Stern, *The Cuban Missile Crisis in American Memory: Myths versus Reality* (Redwood City, CA: Stanford University Press, 2012); Noam Chomsky, "Cuban Missile Crisis: How the U.S. Played Russian Roulette with Nuclear War," *Guardian*, October 15, 2012.

13. "President Reagan's Plan to Deploy 572 Intermediate Range Missiles," United Press International, September 13, 1983; Ewa Pieta, "The Red Button and the Man Who Saved the World" (Ithaca, NY: Log In Productions, 2006), documentary.

14. George Lee Butler, "General Lee Butler Addresses the Canadian Network Against Nuclear Weapons," Nuclear Age Peace Foundation, March 11, 1999; Daniel Ellsberg, *The Doomsday Machine: Confessions of a Nuclear War Planner* (New York: Bloomsbury, 2017), ebook. Ellsberg found it, and our present nuclear plans, "dizzyingly insane and immoral in its almost-incalculable and inconceivable destructiveness and deliberate murderousness." He argues that "no stake whatever, no cause, no principle, no consideration of honor or obligation or prestige or maintaining leadership in current alliances . . . can justify maintaining any risk whatever of causing the near extinction of human and other animal life on this planet."

15. More incidents are documented in Eric Schlosser, *Command and Control: Nuclear Weapons, the Damascus Accident, and the Illusion of Safety* (New York: Penguin Books, 2013). See also "Accidental Nuclear War: A Timeline of Close Calls," Future of Life Institute, February 23, 2016.

16. "Essentials of Post–Cold War Deterrence," STRATCOM, 1995.

17. Alex Emmons, "Obama's Russian Rationale for $1 Trillion Nuke Plan Signals New Arms Race," *Intercept*, February 23, 2016; Hans M. Kristensen, "How U.S. Nuclear Force Modernization Is Undermining Strategic Stability," *Bulletin of the Atomic Scientists*, March 1, 2017.

18. 2022 Nuclear Posture Review, Department of Defense; David A. Koplow, "Parsing Good Faith: Has the United States Violated Article VI of the Nuclear Non-Proliferation Treaty," *Wisconsin Law Review* 301 (1993).

19. Liu Zhen, "China Warns U.S. Nuclear Policy Will Fuel Arms Race and Threaten Peace," *South China Morning Post*, October 28, 2022.

20. Lawrence S. Wittner, *Confronting the Bomb: A Short History of the World Nuclear Disarmament Movement* (Redwood City, CA: Stanford University Press, 2009), 79; "Memorandum of Discussion at the 277th Meeting of the National Security Council," February 27, 1956, *Foreign Relations of the United States, 1955–1957, National Security Policy, Vol. XIX* (Washington, DC: U.S. Government Printing Office, 1990).

21. Wittner, *Confronting the Bomb*, 166.

22. "The Women Who Took on the British Government's Nuclear Programme," Imperial War Museum, London.

23. Elaine Scarry, *Thermonuclear Monarchy: Choosing Between Democracy and Doom* (New York: W. W. Norton, 2014); George Lee Butler, "The Risks of Nuclear Deterrence: From Superpowers to Rogue Leaders," National Press Club, February 2, 1998.

24. Lisbeth Gronlund et al., "An Expert Proposal: How to Limit Presidential Authority to Order the Use of Nuclear Weapons," *Bulletin of the Atomic Scientists*, January 8, 2021; Anthony Summers, *The Arrogance of Power: The Secret World of Richard Nixon* (New York: Penguin Books, 2001). Summers also quotes a Kissinger aide who heard a drunken Nixon on a different occasion tell Kissinger, "Henry, we've got to nuke them." Nixon himself admitted having considered using nuclear weapons in Vietnam. See "Nixon Proposed Using A-Bomb in Vietnam War," Associated Press, March 1, 2002. Nixon is commonly portrayed as subscribing to what he called his "madman theory," a kind of bluff of appearing insane enough to inflict horrific violence. ("I want the North Vietnamese to believe I've reached the point where I might do *anything* to stop the war," including putting "his hand on the nuclear button," i.e., to portray himself as potentially genocidal.) In fact, the record shows that the madness was no bluff, and nuclear annihilation of Vietnamese targets was seriously considered. See "Nixon White House Considered Nuclear Options Against North Vietnam, Declassified Documents Reveal," National Security Archive, July 31, 2006. In any case, as Le Duc Tho told Kissinger, Vietnam had already been hit with the equivalent of hundreds of atomic bombs. Criminal insanity was not a mere threat or diplomatic tactic. It was official policy.

25. William Perry, interviewed on PBS. "75 Years After Hiroshima, Should U.S. President Have Authority to Launch Nuclear Attack?," PBS *Newshour*, August 5, 2020; Julian Borger, "Ex-Intelligence Chief: Trump's Access to Nuclear Codes Is 'Pretty Damn Scary,'" *Guardian*, August 23, 2017.

26. William J. Perry and Tom Z. Collina, *The Button: The New Nuclear Arms Race and Presidential Power from Truman to Trump* (Dallas, TX: BenBella Books, 2020); Garrett M. Graff, "The Madman and the Bomb," *Politico*, August 11, 2017.

27. "Netanyahu Thanks U.S. for Blocking Push for Middle East Nuclear Arms Ban," *Guardian*, May 23, 2015; "Public Opinion in Iran and America on Key International Issues," WorldPublicOpinion.org, Program on International Policy Attitudes, January 24, 2007; "Iranian Public Opinion Under 'Maximum Pressure,'" Center for International & Security Studies, University of Maryland, October 16, 2019. Even the Israeli public has voiced majority support for a nuclear-free Middle East in previous years, Michael Felsen, "Finding the Way to Helsinki," *Jerusalem Post*, December 13, 2012.

28. "No First Use FAQs," Global Zero; "Treaty on the Prohibition of Nuclear Weapons (TPNW)," entered into force January 22, 2021, Nuclear Threat Initiative.

29. James M. Acton, "The U.S. Exit from the Anti-Ballistic Missile Treaty Has Fueled a New Arms Race," Carnegie Endowment for International Peace, December 13, 2021; Paul Meyer, "Is There Any Fizz Left in the Fissban? Prospects for a Fissile Material Cutoff Treaty," Arms Control Association, 2007; Kingston Reif, "Biden Continues Trump Nuclear Funding," *Arms Control Today*, July/August 2021.

30. Mohamed ElBaradei, "Towards a Safer World," *Economist*, October 16, 2003; Jimmy Carter, "Saving Nonproliferation," *Washington Post*, March 27, 2005.

31. Harry S. Truman, "Annual Message to the Congress on the State of the Union," January 7, 1953; Robert S. McNamara, "Apocalypse Soon," *Foreign Policy*, October 21, 2009; Julian Borger, "Nuclear Weapons Risk Greater Than in Cold War, Says Ex-Pentagon Chief," *Guardian*, January 7, 2016; Sam Nunn, "The Cold War's Nuclear Legacy Has Lasted Too Long," *Financial Times*, December 5, 2004; Michael MccGwire, "Shifting the Paradigm," *International Affairs* 78, no. 1 (2002).

32. Alexandra Topping, "Heatwave Led to London Firefighters' Busiest Day Since Second World War," *Guardian*, July 20, 2022; Aspen Pflughoeft, "'Busiest Day Since World War II' Sends Firefighters Rushing to 1,100 Fires in London," *Miami Herald*, July 20, 2022; "Fire Which Swept Through Village 'Like a Scene from the Blitz,'" Says Resident," *Independent*, July 20, 2022.

33. Claire M. Belcher et al., *UK Wildfires and Their Climate Challenges*, University of Exeter Global Systems Institute, 2021. Researchers found that "the projected increase in fire danger is predominantly due to hotter temperatures, less rainfall, lower humidity and stronger winds expected across the UK in future decades due to climate change."

34. "Up to 4 Million Children in Pakistan Still Living Next to Stagnant and Contaminated Floodwater," UNICEF, January 9, 2023; "Devastating Floods in Pakistan," UNICEF, 2023; Leo Sands, "Pakistan Floods: One Third of Country Is Under Water—Minister," BBC News, August 29, 2022; "'It Was Just the Perfect Storm for Malaria'—Pakistan Responds to Surge in Cases Following the 2022 Floods," World Health Organization, April 18, 2023.

35. John Schwartz, "A Million Years of Data Confirms: Monsoons Are Likely to Get Worse," *New York Times*, June 4, 2021; Benji Jones, "How Melting Glaciers Fueled Pakistan's Fatal Floods," *Vox*, August 30, 2022.

36. Damian Carrington, "Climate Crisis: 11,000 Scientists Warn of 'Untold Suffering,'" *Guardian*, November 5, 2019.

37. Henry Fountain, "Climate Change Is Accelerating, Bringing World 'Dangerously Close' to Irreversible Change," *New York Times*, December 4, 2019; Jason P. Dinh, "Climate Scientists Fear the 'Uncharted Territory' Earth Has Entered," Atmos, November 13, 2023; Raymond Pierrehumbert, "There Is No Plan B for Dealing with the Climate Crisis," *Bulletin of the Atomic Scientists* 75, no. 5 (2019): 215–21; Ammar Frangoul, "'We're on a 'Highway to Climate Hell,' UN Chief Guterres Says, Calling for a Global Phase-Out of Coal," CNBC, November 7, 2022; Oded Carmeli, "'The Sea Will Get as Hot as a Jacuzzi': What Life in Israel Will Be Like in 2100," *Haaretz*, August 17, 2019.

38. Cristian Román-Palacios and John J. Wiens, "Recent Responses to Climate Change Reveal the Drivers of Species Extinction and Survival," *PNAS*, 2020; Betsy Mason, "Spiders Might Be Quietly Disappearing," *Atlantic*, October 28, 2023; Chi Xu et al., "Future of the Human Climate Niche," *PNAS*, 2019.

39. Timothy M. Lenton, "Climate Tipping Points—Too Risky to Bet Against," *Nature*, November 27, 2019; Oana A. Dumitru, "Constraints on Global Mean Sea Level During Pliocene Warmth," *Nature*, August 30, 2019; William J. Ripple et al., "The 2023 State of the Climate Report: Entering Uncharted Territory," *BioScience*, October 24, 2023; Jeremy Lent, "What Will It Really Take to Avoid Collapse?," *Patterns of Meaning*, December 19, 2017.

40. Hannah Ritchie and Max Roser, "Pakistan: CO2 Country Profile," Our World in Data; Jason Hickel, "Degrowth," in *The Climate Book* by Greta Thunberg (New York: Penguin Books, 2022), 310.

41. "Richest 1% Emit as Much Planet-Heating Pollution as Two-Thirds of Humanity," Oxfam, November 19, 2023; "Global Carbon Inequality," World Inequality Report, 2022; Solomon Hsiang, "Warming and Inequality," in *The Climate Book*.

42. Laurie Parsons, *Carbon Colonialism: How Rich Countries Export Climate Breakdown* (Manchester, UK: Manchester University Press, 2023); see also Jag Bhalla, "We Can't Have Climate Justice Without Ending Computational Colonialism," *Current Affairs*, February 4, 2023.

43. See https://fossilfueltreaty.org/.

44. Robert Pollin, "How to Pay for a Zero Emissions Economy," *American Prospect*, December 5, 2019; see also Noam Chomsky and Robert Pollin, *Climate Crisis and the Global Green New Deal* (London and New York: Verso, 2020).

45. Lisa Friedman, "Trump Rule Would Exclude Climate Change in Infrastructure Planning," *New York Times*, January 3, 2020; Juliet Eilperin et al., "Trump Administration Sees a 7-Degree Rise in Global Temperatures by 2100," *Washington Post*, September 28, 2019.

46. Maxime Joselow, "Bills in Red States Punish Climate-Conscious Businesses," *Washington Post*, June 1, 2022; Saul Elbein, "Documents Reveal How Fossil Fuel Industry Created, Pushed Anti-ESG Campaign," *Hill*, May 18, 2023.

47. Branko Marcetic, "The Democrats Are Climate Deniers," *Jacobin*, January 28, 2019; "Remarks by the President on American-Made Energy," March 22, 2012, Office of the Press Secretary, White House; "Barack Obama's Remarks in St. Paul," *New York Times*, June 3, 2008; George Monbiot, "If You Want to Know Who's to Blame for Copenhagen, Look to the U.S. Senate," *Guardian*, December 21, 2009; Mark Hertsgaard, "The Ugly Truth About Obama's 'Copenhagen Accord,'" *Vanity Fair*, December 21, 2009; Robert Rapier, "The Irony of President Obama's Oil Legacy," *Forbes*, January 15, 2016; Nathan J. Robinson, "We Now Know the Full Extent of Obama's Disastrous Apathy Toward the Climate Crisis," *Current Affairs*, June 5, 2023.

48. Chris Cillizza, "Nancy Pelosi Just Threw Some Serious Shade at Alexandria Ocasio-Cortez's 'Green New Deal,'" CNN, February 8, 2019; Lois Beckett, "'You Didn't Vote for Me': Senator Dianne Feinstein Responds to Young Green Activists," *Guardian*, February 23, 2019.

49. Nathan J. Robinson, "Exxon Admits Capitalism Created the Climate Crisis," *Current Affairs*, July 5, 2021; see also Kate Aronoff, *Overheated: How Capitalism Broke the Planet—and How We Fight Back* (New York: Bold Type Books, 2021).

50. Sammy Westfall, "Why Has It Been So Hard to Get Fossil Fuels Mentioned in UN Climate Deals?," *Washington Post*, November 10, 2021; Ruth Michaelson, "'Explosion' in Number of Fossil Fuel Lobbyists at Cop27 Climate Summit," *Guardian*, November 10, 2022; Hiroko Tabuchi, "Files Suggest Climate Summit's Leader Is Using Event to Promote Fossil Fuels," *New York Times*, November 28, 2023; Julia Conley, "Outrage After Kerry Backs UAE Oil Exec as President of UN Climate Summit," Common Dreams, January 16, 2023; Peter Kalmus, "The Climate Summit Is a Sick Joke. You Should Be Angry and Afraid," *Newsweek*, December 1, 2023.

51. Kelsey Vlamis, "Despite Biden Climate Change Pledges and Conservative Complaints About a War on Energy, the U.S. Is on Pace for Record Oil and Gas Production in 2023," *Business Insider*, November 29, 2023.

52. Kejal Vyas, "Global Conflicts Stir Sleeping Energy Giant in South America," *Wall Street Journal*, December 21, 2023; Vlamis, "Despite Biden Climate Change Pledges and Conservative Complaints About a War on Energy."

53. Clifford Krauss, "Surging U.S. Oil Production Brings Down Prices and Raises Climate Fears," *New York Times*, December 1, 2023; Rachel Frazin and Zack Budryk, "Biden's First-Ever UN Climate Summit Snub Carries Symbolic Weight," *Hill*, November 28, 2023; Timothy Puko and Katy Stech Ferek, "Climate Bill Is Boon for Fossil-Fuel Sector," *Wall Street Journal*, July 28, 2022; James Bikales, "Biden's Latest China Crackdown Puts His EV Ambitions at Risk," *Politico*, December 1, 2023; see Nathan J. Robinson, "Can a 'Boon for the Fossil Fuel Sector' Really Be Called a Climate Bill?," *Current Affairs*, July 29, 2022; Oliver Milman and Nina Lakhani, "Biden Backtracks on Climate Plans and 'Walks Tightrope' to Court Both Young Voters and Moderates," *Guardian*, March 8, 2024.

54. Jim Takersley and Lisa Friedman, "Biden's Absence at Climate Summit High-

lights His Fossil Fuel Conundrum," *New York Times*, November 27, 2023; Seth Borenstein, "U.S. Oil Production Hits All-Time High, Conflicting with Efforts to Cut Heat-Trapping Pollution," Associated Press, October 20, 2023; Nathan J. Robinson, "A Climate Scientist on Why the Global Climate Summit Is a Disaster and a 'Sick Joke,'" *Current Affairs*, December 8, 2023.

55. See Nathan J. Robinson, "Turning Down the Money," *Current Affairs*, May 16, 2019; Robert Sanders, "In Media Coverage of Climate Change, Where Are the Facts?," *Berkeley News*, September 19, 2019.

56. See Nathan J. Robinson, "The Media's Climate Coverage Is Indefensible," *Current Affairs*, January 5, 2019; Simon Romero and Giulia Heyward, "Colorado Wildfire Inquiry Focuses on Christian Sect," *New York Times*, January 3, 2022; Sam Brasch, "Why a Fire Scientist Sees Climate Fingerprints on the Suburban Boulder County Fires," *CPR News*, January 3, 2022.

57. Fiona Harvey, "Scientists Deliver 'Final Warning' on Climate Crisis: Act Now or It's Too Late," *Guardian*, March 20, 2023; Sarah Kaplan, "World Is on Brink of Catastrophic Warming, UN Climate Change Report Says," *Washington Post*, March 20, 2023.

CHAPTER 9: THE DOMESTIC ROOTS OF FOREIGN POLICY

1. Hans Morgenthau, "Defining the National Interest—Again: Old Superstitions, New Realities," *New Republic*, January 22, 1977.

2. "Americans Continue to Say the U.S. Should Stay Impartial in Israeli-Palestinian Conflict," Chicago Council on Global Affairs, February 28, 2024; Brendan Rascius, "Should U.S. Keep Arming Israel? Poll Finds Most Americans Want Weapon Shipments to Stop," *Miami Herald*, March 12, 2024.

3. David Shribman, "Poll Finds a Lack of Public Support for Latin Policy," *New York Times*, April 29, 1984; Anthony Leiserowitz, "International Public Opinion, Perception, and Understanding of Global Climate Change," Yale Program on Climate Change Communication, July 17, 2009; "Growing Public Support for U.S. Ties with Cuba—and an End to the Trade Embargo," Pew Research Center, July 21, 2015; Nomaan Merchant and Hannah Fingerhut, "Democrats and Republicans Are Skeptical of U.S. Spying Practices, an AP-NORC Poll Finds," Associated Press, June 8, 2023; "Voters Want the U.S. to Call for a Permanent Ceasefire in Gaza and to Prioritize Diplomacy," DataforProgress.org, December 5, 2023.

4. "Jeffrey Sachs w/John Mearsheimer—a Missed Opportunity for Peace," YouTube, November 16, 2023.

5. "Jeffrey Sachs w/John Mearsheimer—a Missed Opportunity for Peace."

6. Quoted in Christian Appy, *American Reckoning* (New York: Penguin Books, 2015).

7. Benjamin I. Page and Marshall M. Bouton, *The Foreign Policy Disconnect: What Americans Want from Our Leaders but Don't Get* (Chicago: University of Chicago Press, 2006).

8. Carroll Doherty and Jocelyn Kiley, "A Look Back at How Fear and False Beliefs

Bolstered U.S. Public Support for War in Iraq," Pew Research Center, March 14, 2023.

9. Alex Koppelman, "You Don't Care What the American People Think?," *Salon*, March 19, 2008.

10. "The CIA's Secret Quest for Mind Control: Torture, LSD and a 'Poisoner in Chief,'" NPR's *Fresh Air*, September 9, 2019; "The U.S. Has a History of Testing Biological Weapons on the Public—Were Infected Ticks Used Too?," TheConversation .com, July 22, 2019; George Lardner, "Army Report Details Germ War Exercise in N.Y. Subway in '66," *Washington Post*, April 21, 1980; "How the U.S. Government Exposed Thousands of Americans to Lethal Bacteria to Test Biological Warfare," *Democracy Now!*, July 13, 2005; John Hendren, "Cold War Bioweapon Tests Included California," *Los Angeles Times*, October 10, 2002; Andrew Prokop, "Read the Letter the FBI Sent MLK to Try to Convince Him to Kill Himself," *Vox*, January 15, 2018; see also Tim Weiner, *Enemies: A History of the FBI* (New York: Random House, 2013).

11. Bernard Gwertzman, "Kissinger on Central America: A Call for U.S. Firmness," *New York Times*, July 19, 1983.

12. Lawrence R. Jacobs and Benjamin I. Page, "Who Influences U.S. Foreign Policy?," *American Political Science Review* 99, no. 1 (2005): 107–23.

13. Thomas Ferguson, *Golden Rule: The Investment Theory of Party Competition and the Logic of Money-Driven Political Systems* (Chicago: University of Chicago Press, 1995); see also Martin Gilens, *Affluence and Influence: Economic Inequality and Political Power in America* (Princeton, NJ: Princeton University Press, 2014); Benjamin Page and Martin Gilens, *Democracy in America? What Has Gone Wrong and What We Can Do About It* (Chicago: University of Chicago Press, 2017); Larry Bartels, *Unequal Democracy: The Political Economy of the New Gilded Age* (Princeton, NJ: Princeton University Press, 2018).

14. Robert Weissman, "Americans Widely Reject Proposals for More Pentagon Spending—so Should Congress," DataforProgress.org, June 7, 2022.

15. Richard J. Barnet, *The Economy of Death* (New York: Atheneum, 1969), 9.

16. Edward K. Hall, "Remarks on Public Relations of Utility Companies," Telephone Society of New England, reprinted in *Public Service*, March 1910.

17. Thomas E. Mann and Norman Jay Ornstein, "Finding the Common Good in an Era of Dysfunctional Governance," *Daedalus* (Spring 2013).

18. For more on the illusions of "free trade," see Noam Chomsky, *Profit over People: Neoliberalism and the Global Order* (New York: Seven Stories Press, 1999).

19. See Noam Chomsky, "Reinhold Niebuhr," *Grand Street* 6, no. 2 (Winter 1987).

20. Edward Bernays, *Propaganda* (New York: Horace Liveright, 1928).

21. Walter Lippmann, *The Phantom Public* (New York: Harcourt, Brace and Company, 1925).

22. On this commission, see Holly Sklar, ed., *Trilateralism* (Boston: South End Press, 1980).

23. Kevin D. Williamson, "Election 2024: You Asked for It, America," *Wall Street Journal*, December 15, 2023.

24. Vandenburg quoted in Walter LaFeber et al., *The American Century* (New York: Taylor & Francis, 2015), 227; summary of conversation between the vice president and Fidel Castro, April 19, 1959.

25. H. Bruce Franklin shows in *War Stars: The Superweapon and the American Imagination* that one major theme in popular literature is that we are about to face destruction from some terrible, awesome enemy, and at the last minute we are saved by a superhero or a superweapon.

26. Larry Bartels, "Ethnic Antagonism Erodes Republicans' Commitment to Democracy," *PNAS*, August 31, 2020; Daniel A. Cox, "After the Ballots Are Counted: Conspiracies, Political Violence, and American Exceptionalism," American Enterprise Institute, February 11, 2021.

27. Dwight D. Eisenhower, "The Chance for Peace," speech before the American Society of Newspaper Editors, April 16, 1953.

28. William Hartung, "Biden's New Whopping $886B Defense Budget Request," Quincy Institute for Responsible Statecraft, March 10, 2023.

CHAPTER 10: INTERNATIONAL LAW AND THE "RULES-BASED ORDER"

1. "Panama Sets National Holiday for Victims of 1989 U.S. Invasion," Associated Press, March 31, 2022; Jeff Cohen and Mark Cook, "How Television Sold the Panama Invasion," FAIR, January 1, 1990; Belén Fernández, "The Truth Behind U.S.' Operation Just Cause in Panama," *Al Jazeera English*, January 31, 2016; for a full discussion of the background to the invasion, see Noam Chomsky, *Deterring Democracy* (New York: Hill and Wang, 1992).

2. Thomas Powers, "Panama: Our Dangerous Liaison," *New York Times*, February 18, 1990.

3. Don Shannon, "UN Assembly Condemns U.S. Invasion," *Los Angeles Times*, December 30, 1989; Carl T. Bogus, "The Invasion of Panama and the Rule of Law," *International Lawyer* 26, no. 3 (1992): 781–87; George H. W. Bush, "Address to Nation on Panama Invasion," December 20, 1989.

4. Howard Friel and Richard Falk, *The Record of the Paper: How the 'New York Times' Misreports U.S. Foreign Policy* (London and New York: Verso, 2004), ebook.

5. International Court of Justice Reports, 1949, 35.

6. "Adopting Annual Resolution, Delegates in General Assembly Urge Immediate Repeal of Embargo on Cuba, Especially amid Mounting Global Food, Fuel Crises," United Nations, November 3, 2022.

7. Stuart Taylor, Jr., "Nicaragua Takes Case Against U.S. to World Court," *New York Times*, April 10, 1984.

8. "Countries Opposed to Signing a U.S. Bilateral Immunity Agreement (BIA):

U.S. Aid Lost in FY04 & FY05 and Threatened in FY06," Coalition for the International Criminal Court, November 2006; David A. Koplow, "Indisputable Violations: What Happens When the United States Unambiguously Breaches a Treaty?," *Fletcher Forum of World Affairs* 37, no. 1 (Winter 2013); Steven Mufson and Alan Sipress, "UN Funds in Crossfire over Court," *Washington Post*, August 15, 2001; "U.S.: 'Hague Invasion Act' Becomes Law," Human Rights Watch, 2002.

9. Christopher J. Dodd and John B. Bellinger III, "How the U.S. Can Support a War Crimes Investigation into Russia," *Washington Post*, April 5, 2022.

10. Noam Chomsky, Amy Goodman, and Jeremy Scahill, "The Truth About America's Secret, Dirty Wars," panel discussion, Harvard University, April 27, 2013.

11. "Cluster Munitions: Background and Issues for Congress," Congressional Research Service, March 20, 2024; see "U.S.: Commit to Joining Cluster Munitions Ban," Human Rights Watch, September 15, 2021, HRW points out that "the U.S. has a terrible history of using cluster munitions around [the] world."; Tom Fawthorp, "The Curse of Cluster Bombs," Institute for Policy Studies, September 30, 2011; "U.S. Amends UN Ambassador's Condemnation of Russia's Use of Cluster Bombs," *Democracy Now!*, March 10, 2022.

12. "U.S. Against 180+: Washington the Solo Dissenter to Biological Weapons Verification Regime in Intl Community," *Global Times*, April 8, 2022; "International Criminal Court: U.S. Efforts to Obtain Impunity for Genocide, Crimes Against Humanity and War Crimes," Amnesty International, September 1, 2002; Samantha Power, "The United States and Genocide Prevention: No Justice Without Risk," *Brown Journal of World Affairs* 6, no. 1 (1999): 19–31.

13. Sam Pope Brewer, "U. S., in First Veto in U.N., Backs Britain on Rhodesia," *New York Times*, March 18, 1970; Edith M. Lederer, "U.S. Vetoes UN Resolution Condemning All Violence Against Civilians in Israel-Hamas War," AP News, October 18, 2023.

14. David Kaye, "Stealth Multilateralism," *Foreign Affairs,* September/October 2013.

15. Despite these guarantees, the domestic U.S. court system is still stacked in the prosecutor's favor. It is a sign of the extraordinary weakness of U.S. cases against Guantánamo prisoners that they could not be tried in the domestic courts. See Stephen Bright and James Kwak, *The Fear of Too Much Justice: Race, Poverty, and the Persistence of Inequality in the Criminal Courts* (New York: New Press, 2023).

16. Marian Wang, "What Exactly Is the War Powers Act and Is Obama Really Violating It?," *ProPublica*, June 17, 2011.

17. Jo Becker and Scott Shane, "Secret 'Kill List' Proves a Test of Obama's Principles and Will," *New York Times*, May 29, 2012.

18. "The United States Must Stop Providing Weapons Used to Repress Colombia's Protests," Amnesty International, May 20, 2021; "Colombia Panel's Report Is a Step Toward Mending a Civil War's Scars," *New York Times*, June 28, 2022; Stephen Zunes, "The United States and the Kurds: A Brief History," *Common Dreams*, October 25, 2007; Michelle Ciarrocca, "U.S. Arms for Turkish Abuses," *Mother Jones*, November 17, 1999.

19. "Meeks Leads Letter Urging Administration Not to Certify Certain Foreign Military Financing for Egypt," House Foreign Affairs Committee, August 10, 2023; Michael Crowley and Vivian Yee, "Choosing Security over Rights, U.S. Approves $235 Million in Egypt Aid," *New York Times*, September 14, 2023. Incredibly, the *Times* reminds us that "the remaining $980 million in annual U.S. military aid [to Egypt] is not subject to human rights conditions." This means that the Biden administration wasn't even being asked to withhold *all* aid, just *the part of the aid that is legally subject to human rights conditions*.

20. "NSA Surveillance Exposed by Snowden Was Illegal, Court Rules Seven Years On," *Guardian*, September 3, 2020. The case of Julian Assange, whose WikiLeaks organization exposed multiple U.S. war crimes, has been similarly egregious. See Noam Chomsky and Alice Walker, "Julian Assange Is Not on Trial for His Personality—but Here's How the U.S. Government Made You Focus on It," *Independent*, September 9, 2020; Chomsky, Goodman, and Scahill, "The Truth About America's Secret, Dirty Wars."

21. Nina Tannenwald, *The Nuclear Taboo: The United States and the Non-Use of Nuclear Weapons Since 1945* (New York: Cambridge University Press, 2007), 80.

22. Blaine Harden, "The U.S. War Crime North Korea Won't Forget," *Washington Post*, March 24, 2015; Max Fisher, "Americans Have Forgotten What We Did to North Korea," *Vox*, August 3, 2015; "Strategic Air Warfare: An Interview with Generals Curtis E. LeMay, Leon W. Johnson, David A. Burchinal, and Jack J. Catton," Richard H. Kohn and Joseph P. Harahan, eds., Office of Air Force History, Washington, DC, 1988.

23. David Coleman, ed., National Security Archive Electronic Briefing Book No. 513, National Security Archive, April 28, 2015.

24. Ishaan Tharoor, "The Bengali Blood on Henry Kissinger's Hands," *Washington Post*, December 1, 2023; see also Gary J. Bass, *The Blood Telegram: Nixon, Kissinger, and a Forgotten Genocide* (New York: A. A. Knopf, 2013).

25. Dana Milbank, "1975 East Timor Invasion Got U.S. Go-Ahead," *Washington Post*, December 6, 2001; David F. Schmitz, *The United States and Right-Wing Dictatorships 1965–1989* (New York: Cambridge University Press, 2006), 129–30; Gerald R. Ford, "Letter to the Chairman and Members of the Senate Select Committee to Study Governmental Operations with Respect to Intelligence Activities," November 4, 1975.

26. Note that the U.S. vetoed an 11–1 Security Council resolution condemning the Grenada invasion, Richard Bernstein, "U.S. Vetoes UN Resolution 'Deploring' Grenada Invasion," *New York Times*, October 29, 1983. For information on Reagan's 1986 bombing of Libya, see Noam Chomsky et al., "The First Prime Time Bombing in History," *MERIP Middle East Report* 140 (986): 12–14; Reagan's CIA director, William Casey, is also reported to have arranged a Beirut car bombing that killed eighty people, "Interview: Bob Woodward," PBS *Frontline*, September 2001; Robert Windrem, "U.S. Government Considered Nelson Mandela a Terrorist Until 2008," NBC News, December 7, 2013.

27. John Lancaster and Barton Gellman, "U.S. Calls Baghdad Raid a Qualified Success," *Washington Post*, June 28, 1993; Dino Kritsiotis, "The Legality of the 1993 U.S. Missile Strike on Iraq and the Right of Self-Defence in International Law," *International and Comparative Law Quarterly* 45, no. 1 (1996): 162–77; Marc Lacey, "Sudan Says, 'Say Sorry,' but U.S. Won't," *New York Times*, October 20, 2005.

28. "Bringing George W. Bush to Justice: International Obligations of States to Which Former U.S. President George W. Bush May Travel," Amnesty International, 2011; note that the Amnesty report, documenting serious international crimes by a U.S. president, went uncovered by the U.S. media.

29. "Getting Away with Torture: The Bush Administration and Mistreatment of Detainees," Human Rights Watch, July 12, 2011; David Hicks, *Guantanamo: My Journey* (New York: Random House, 2010), ebook.

30. Christopher Hitchens, "Believe Me, It's Torture," *Vanity Fair*, July 2, 2008; see Carol Rosenberg, "What the C.I.A.'s Torture Program Looked Like to the Tortured," *New York Times*, December 4, 2019.

31. Obama's defenders blame Congress for this, but the White House declined to put effort into pursuing the prison's closure. The attitude among White House officials was, one told *The New Yorker*, "Why are we going to waste our political capital on detainees? No one is going to give you any credit for closing Guantánamo," Connie Bruck, "Why Obama Has Failed to Close Guantánamo," *New Yorker*, July 25, 2016.

32. Josh Gerstein, "Obama: We Tortured Some Folks," *Politico*, August 2, 2014; David Johnston and Charlie Savage, "Obama Reluctant to Look into Bush Programs," *New York Times*, January 11, 2009; Murtaza Hussain, "Report to UN Calls Bullshit on Obama's Look Forward, Not Backwards Approach to Torture," *Intercept*, October 30, 2014.

33. "Malala to Obama: Drone Strikes 'Fueling Terrorism,'" CNN, October 12, 2013; "Living Under Drones: Death, Injury, and Trauma to Civilians," Stanford International Human Rights and Conflict Resolution Clinic/NYU Global Justice Clinic, September 2012; "Yemeni Man Brings the Horror of Drone Strikes Home to U.S. Senate," *Independent*, April 24, 2013. Note that the Obama administration pressured the government of Yemen to keep a journalist in prison who had reported on the effects of drone strikes, "Prominent Yemeni Journalist Lands in Jail; U.S. Wants Him to Stay There," *World*, April 6, 2012.

34. Karen McVeigh, "Drone Strikes: Tears in Congress as Pakistani Family Tells of Mother's Death," *Guardian*, October 29, 2013; Matthew Byrne, "Drone Skies," *Current Affairs*, June 22, 2022.

35. Tim Dickinson, "Trump Claims—and Celebrates—Extrajudicial Killing of Antifa Activist," *Rolling Stone*, October 15, 2020; Stephanie Nebehay, "UN Expert Deems U.S. Drone Strike on Iran's Soleimani an 'Unlawful' Killing," Reuters, July 6, 2020.

36. Mark Weisbrot and Jeffrey Sachs, "Economic Sanctions as Collective Punishment: The Case of Venezuela," Center for Economic and Policy Research, April 2019.

37. Mike Pompeo, *Never Give an Inch: Fighting for the America I Love* (New York: Broadside Books, 2023), ebook.

38. Adil Ahmad Haque, "Biden's First Strike and the International Law of Self-Defense," JustSecurity.org, February 26, 2021; William Partlett, "Does It Matter That Strikes Against Syria Violate International Law?," *Pursuit*, April 16, 2018; Julia Conley, "Biden's Expansion of Title 42 Violates International Law: UN," Common Dreams, January 6, 2023.

39. Stephen M. Walt, "Some Rules of Global Politics Matter More Than Others," *Foreign Policy*, March 27, 2023; Dominic Tierney, "What 'All Options Are on the Table' with Iran Actually Means," *Atlantic*, August 10, 2012.

40. Michael Byers, *War Law: Understanding International Law and Armed Conflict* (New York: Grove, 2007).

41. On the structural unfairness of the Security Council, see Julian Borger et al., "Vetoed! What's Wrong with the UN Security Council—and How It Could Do Better," *Guardian*, September 23, 2015.

CHAPTER 11: HOW MYTHOLOGIES ARE MANUFACTURED

1. George Orwell, "The Freedom of the Press," *Times Literary Supplement*, September 15, 1972; Orwell Foundation.

2. Jo Ann Boydston, ed., *John Dewey: The Later Works*, Vol. 2, from *Common Sense*, November 1935.

3. Matthew Yglesias, *One Billion Americans: The Case for Thinking Bigger* (New York: Portfolio/Penguin, 2020). Because the premise is uncontroversial in the United States, Yglesias treats it as *true* and reaches the bizarre conclusion that we should aim to populate the world with "one billion Americans" so that we do not become the "little dog" to China.

4. Anthony DiMaggio, *Mass Media, Mass Propaganda: Understanding the News in the "War on Terror"* (Lanham, MD: Rowman & Littlefield, 2008); Bob Herbert, "Dangerous Incompetence," *New York Times*, June 30, 2005; "A Failed Presidency," *Los Angeles Times*, November 1, 2004; *Crossfire*, CNN, October 19, 2004.

5. "To Save the Future," *New York Times*, April 5, 1975.

6. Julian E. Zelizer, "Why U.S. Presidents Really Go to War," *Foreign Policy*, September 10, 2023.

7. "Is There a Chance in Nicaragua?," *Washington Post*, March 14, 1986.

8. Hena Ashraf, "Narrow Afghan Debate on Cable's 'Liberal' Channel," FAIR, May 1, 2011; *The Rachel Maddow Show*, MSNBC, July 15, 2010, transcript.

9. Nicholas D. Kristof, "Saving the Iraqi Children," *New York Times*, November 27, 2004.

10. "U.S. Media's 5 Most Popular Revisionist Tropes About the Iraq and Vietnam Wars," *Citations Needed*, May 10, 2023.

11. Haley Britzky and Natasha Bertrand, "U.S. Kills 5 Iran-Backed Militia Members in Drone Strike in Iraq," CNN, December 4, 2023. On Haiti specifically, see

Noam Chomsky, introduction, in Paul Farmer, *The Uses of Haiti* (Monroe, ME: Common Courage Press, 1994); Noam Chomsky and Paul Farmer, "The Uses of Haiti," MIT Technology and Culture Forum, 2004; Cécile Accilien, "U.S. Media Have Distorted Narratives on Haiti Since 1804. It's Still Happening," Truthout .org, September 29, 2021.

12. Terrorism has also been defined as "the use or threat of action designed to influence the government or an international governmental organization or to intimidate the public, or a section of the public; made for the purposes of advancing a political, religious, racial or ideological cause; and it involves or causes: serious violence against a person; serious damage to a property; a threat to a person's life; a serious risk to the health and safety of the public; or serious interference with or disruption to an electronic system," UK Terrorism Act, 2000.

13. In the end, the same terms were offered as before, leading a Kissinger aide to conclude that "we bombed the North Vietnamese into accepting our concessions."

14. "Hospital Deaths," *New York Times*, December 24, 1972; Brad Lendon, "'Like Walking on Missiles': U.S. Airman Recalls the Horror of the Vietnam 'Christmas Bombings' 50 Years On," CNN, December 17, 2022.

15. "State Sponsors of Terrorism," U.S. Department of State; Ryan Grim, "State Department Stuns Congress, Saying Biden Is Not Even Reviewing Trump's Terror Designation of Cuba," *Intercept*, July 6, 2020; Mariakarla Nodarse Venancio and Alex Bare, "The Human Cost of Cuba's Inclusion on the State Sponsor of Terrorism List," Washington Office on Latin America, March 28, 2023.

16. "Russia's Terror Bombing Will Fail if NATO Helps Ukraine Withstand It," *Washington Post*, October 10, 2022.

17. Avishay Artsy, "Israeli Settler Violence Against Palestinians in the West Bank, Briefly Explained," *Vox*, December 2, 2023; Michael Kinsley, "Down the Memory Hole with the Contras," *Wall Street Journal*, March 26, 1987.

18. John F. Burns, "Ringleader of '85 Achille Lauro Hijacking Says Killing Wasn't His Fault," *New York Times*, November 8, 2002. Klinghoffer's killer stated that he had deliberately selected "an invalid, so that they would know that we had no pity for anyone, just as the Americans, arming Israel, do not take into consideration that Israel kills women and children of our people." The killer was apparently unmoved by the argument that Israel only ever drives tanks over invalids *negligently* rather than *deliberately*. Justin Huggler and Phil Reeves, "Why Israel Dreads a Full Investigation," *Arab News*, April 28, 2002.

19. In *Root Causes of Terrorism: Myths, Realities, and Ways Forward*, ed. Tore Bjorgo (New York: Routledge, 2005), 208–9.

20. Marro quoted in DiMaggio, *Mass Media, Mass Propaganda*, 183; Harper Lambert, "CBS Reporter Calls Ukraine 'Relatively Civilized' as Opposed to Iraq and Afghanistan, Outrage Ensues," TheWrap.com, February 26, 2022.

21. For a more detailed case study, see Edward S. Herman and Noam Chomsky, *Manufacturing Consent: The Political Economy of Mass Media* (New York: Pantheon, 2002).

22. Steve Rendell and Tara Broughel, "Amplifying Officials, Squelching Dissent," FAIR, May 1, 2003.

23. Adam Johnson, "On 50th Anniversary of Israeli Occupation, Palestinian Opinions Largely Ignored," FAIR, June 7, 2017; Conor Smyth, "For Cable News, a Palestinian Life Is Not the Same as an Israeli Life," FAIR, November 17, 2023; Gregory Shupak, "When They Don't Ignore, U.S. Media Often Disparage Palestinians' Right of Return," FAIR, March 20, 2019.

24. Gregory Shupak, "To U.S. Papers, Iranian Weapons Far More Newsworthy Than Those Made in USA," FAIR, January 27, 2023.

25. Adam Johnson, "'Renouncing Violence' Is a Demand Made Almost Exclusively of Muslims," FAIR, March 29, 2019.

26. Joshua Cho, "Chinese 'Imperialism' in Hong Kong Concerns U.S. Media; Puerto Rican, Palestinian Colonies, Not So Much," FAIR, July 24, 2020.

27. Bryce Greene, "NPR Devotes Almost Two Hours to Afghanistan over Two Weeks—and 30 Seconds to U.S. Starving Afghans," FAIR, September 2, 2022; Julie Hollar, "Biden's Multi-Billion Afghan Theft Gets Scant Mention on TV News," FAIR, February 15, 2022.

28. Adam Johnson, "Out of 26 Major Editorials on Trump's Syria Strikes, Zero Opposed," FAIR, April 18, 2018; Adam Johnson, "Few to No Anti-Bombing Voices as Trump Prepares to Escalate Syria War," FAIR, April 13, 2018; *The New York Times* headline was later changed after being ridiculed; Margaret Sullivan, "The Media Loved Trump's Show of Military Might. Are We Really Doing This Again?," *Washington Post*, April 8, 2017.

29. Ben Norton, "MSNBC Ignores Catastrophic U.S.-Backed War in Yemen, Finds Russia 5000% More Newsworthy," FAIR, January 8, 2018.

30. Matthew Kimball, "To Corporate Media, an Exercise Bike Ad Is More Newsworthy Than ¾ of a Trillion for the Pentagon," FAIR, December 19, 2019.

31. See, for example, Damien Dave, "U.S. Pursues Defense Partnership with India to Deter Chinese Aggression," *New York Times*, October 17, 2023; Edward Wong and Steven Lee Myers, "Officials Push U.S.-China Relations Toward Point of No Return," *New York Times*, July 25, 2020.

32. Nathan J. Robinson, "Why This Foreign Policy Expert Thinks Americans Dangerously Misunderstand China," *Current Affairs*, May 16, 2023.

33. Natalie Khazaal, "Bias Hiding in Plain Sight: Decades of Analyses Suggest U.S. Media Skews Anti-Palestinian," TheConversation.com, February 29, 2024; Adam Johnson and Othman Ali, "Coverage of Gaza War in *The New York Times* and Other Major Newspapers Heavily Favored Israel, Analysis Shows," *Intercept*, January 9, 2024; "Off the Charts: Accuracy in Reporting of Israel/Palestine," IfAmericansKnew.org, 2004; Laura Albast and Cat Knarr, "How Media Coverage Whitewashes Israeli State Violence Against Palestinians," *Washington Post*, April 28, 2022; further examples of prevailing assumptions are provided in Norman Solomon, *War Made Easy: How Presidents and Pundits Keep Spinning Us to Death*

(Nashville, TN: Turner, 2005), and Norman Solomon, *War Made Invisible: How America Hides the Human Toll of Its Military Machine* (New York: New Press, 2023).

34. Orwell's concept of doublethink: "Freedom is slavery: to hold simultaneously two opinions that cancel out, knowing them to be contradictory and believing in both of them . . . to forget whatever it [is] necessary to forget, then to draw it back into memory again at the moment it [is] needed, and then promptly forget it again." A quote from George W. Bush illustrates the concept nicely: "I just want you to know that, when we talk about war, we're really talking about peace."

35. James Chace, "How 'Moral' Can We Get?," *New York Times*, May 22, 1977.

36. Alan MacLeod, "Russia Has 'Oligarchs,' the U.S. Has 'Businessmen,'" FAIR, September 14, 2019; Alan MacLeod, "Dictator: Media Code for 'Government We Don't Like,'" FAIR, April 11, 2019.

37. Edward Herman, *The Real Terror Network* (Boston: South End Press, 1982), 139.

38. "Some Critical Media Voices Face Censorship," FAIR, April 3, 2003; Chris Hedges, *The Greatest Evil Is War* (New York: Seven Stories Press, 2022), ebook. Both the authors of this book have personally experienced this form of corporate censorship. Noam Chomsky's *Counterrevolutionary Violence* (coauthored with Edward Herman) was canceled and pulped by the publisher in 1973, after a top executive deemed it a "scurrilous attack on respected Americans." Nathan J. Robinson was fired as a *Guardian* political columnist after writing a tongue-in-cheek tweet critical of U.S. military aid to Israel.

39. John Plunkett, "CNN Star Reporter Attacks War Coverage," *Guardian*, September 16, 2003; Eric Alterman, "The Buck Stops Where?," Center for American Progress, September 29, 2005.

40. Interview with Dan Rather, *Larry King Live*, CNN, April 14, 2003.

41. Michael Massing, "Now They Tell Us," *New York Review of Books*, February 26, 2004.

42. In November 2023, for instance, MSNBC canceled the program of Mehdi Hasan, the network's most outspoken critic of U.S. support for Israel; Erum Salam, "Dismay as Mehdi Hasan's MSNBC and Peacock news show cancelled," *Guardian*, November 30, 2023; Glenn Greenwald, "The Spirit of Judy Miller Is Alive and Well at the *NYT*, and It Does Great Damage," *Intercept*, July 21, 2015; Julie Hollar, "Afghanistan Withdrawal: Sundays with the Military Industrial Complex," FAIR, October 20, 2021.

43. David Hume, "Of the First Principles of Government," in *Essays, Moral, Political, and Literary*, Hume Texts Online.

44. Harold Pinter, "Art, Truth & Politics," Nobel Literature Prize Lecture, 2005.

45. For clear proposals on how to reform journalism to be more democratic and better serve the social good, see Victor Pickard, *Democracy Without Journalism? Confronting the Misinformation Society* (New York: Oxford University Press, 2019); Victor Pickard, *America's Battle for Media Democracy: The Triumph of Corporate Libertarianism and the Future of Media Reform* (New York: Cambridge University Press, 2015); Robert W. McChesney, "Rejuvenating American Journalism: Some

Tentative Policy Proposals," presentation to Workshop on Journalism, Federal Trade Commission, Washington, DC, March 10, 2010.

CONCLUSION: HEGEMONY OR SURVIVAL?

1. "Introducing Our Special Issue on America at War," *Smithsonian,* January 2019; "U.S. Periods of War and Dates of Recent Conflicts," Congressional Research Service, February 5, 2024; letter from George Washington to Lafayette, August 15, 1786; Barack Obama, "State of the Union Address," Washington, DC, January 12, 2016. The conquest of the territory was horrific. The English colonists in North America had no doubts about what they were doing. One of the leading diplomatic histories of the United States, by Thomas Bailey, said that the colonists confidently set forth on their mission "of felling trees and Indians." Revolutionary War hero General Henry Knox, the first secretary of war in the newly liberated American colonies, described "the utter extirpation of all the Indians in most populous parts of the Union" by means "more destructive to the Indian natives than the conduct of the conquerors of Mexico and Peru," which was no small achievement. George Washington said the Indians were like wolves, savages in human form, "beasts" that had to be driven into the wilderness. Washington, known to us as the father of the country, was known by the Iroquois as the "town destroyer"—because even before the Revolutionary War was over, he launched a major campaign of destruction among the Iroquois nations. In orders to one of his generals, Washington wrote: "The immediate objects are the total destruction and devastation of their settlements and the capture of as many prisoners of every age and sex as possible. It will be essential to ruin their crops now in the ground and prevent their planting more." Washington saw strategic necessity in "the total ruin of their settlements" because "our future security will be . . . in the terror" experienced by the Indians. Indeed, Seneca chief Cornplanter told Washington: "When your army entered the country of the Six Nations, we called you Town Destroyer and to this day when your name is heard our women look behind them and turn pale, and our children cling close to the necks of their mothers."

2. Bertrand Russell, Nobel Lecture, December 11, 1950; on the conquest of the Americas, David E. Stannard, *American Holocaust* (New York: Oxford University Press, 1993).

3. Thomas Carothers, "The Reagan Years" in A. Lowenthal, ed., *Exporting Democracy* (Baltimore, MD: Johns Hopkins University Press, 1991). See also his *In the Name of Democracy* (Berkeley: University of California Press, 1991).

4. Robert Pastor, *Not Condemned to Repetition: The United States and Nicaragua* (Boulder, CO: Westview Press, 2018), ebook.

5. See Nathan J. Robinson, "The Great American World War II Story," *Current Affairs,* January/February 2022; John W. Dower, *War Without Mercy: Race & Power in the Pacific War* (New York: W. W. Norton, 1986); David Fedman and Cary

Karacas, "A Cartographic Fade to Black: Mapping the Destruction of Urban Japan During World War II," *Journal of Historical Geography* 38 (2012): 306–28; Edwin P. Hoyt, *Inferno: The Fire Bombing of Japan, March 9–August 15, 1945* (Montebello, NY: Madison Books, 2000); Telford Taylor, *Nuremberg and Vietnam* (Chicago: Quadrangle Books, 1970); A. C. Grayling, *Among the Dead Cities: The History and Moral Legacy of the WWII Bombing of Civilians in Germany and Japan* (London: Walker Books, 2006).

6. Edward Wong, "On U.S. Foreign Policy, the New Boss Acts a Lot Like the Old One," *New York Times*, July 24, 2022.

7. Indeed, as Mengele tortured and murdered twins, he appeared to have convinced himself he was doing legitimate scientific research, telling a friend that "it would be a sin, a crime . . . and irresponsible not to utilize the possibilities that Auschwitz had for twin research," Robert Jay Lifton, "Who Made This Man? Mengele," *New York Times*, July 21, 1985.

8. John C. Calhoun, "On the Reception of Abolition Petitions," February 6, 1837, in *The Senate, 1789–1989: Classic Speeches, 1830–1993*, Robert C. Byrd, ed., U.S. Government Printing Office, 1988.

9. Samuel P. Huntington, "The Lonely Superpower," *Foreign Affairs* 78, no. 2 (1999): 35–49; Robert Jervis, "Weapons Without Purpose? Nuclear Strategy in the Post–Cold War Era," *Foreign Affairs* 80, no. 4 (2001): 143–48.

10. Review of the U.S. Department of Defense Air, Space, and Supporting Information Systems Science and Technology Program (Washington, DC: National Academies Press, 2001); Dave Lawler, "U.S. Spent More on Military in 2022 Than Next 10 Countries Combined," *Axios*, April 24, 2023; the UN General Assembly "by a recorded vote of 175 in favor to none against, with 2 abstentions (Israel and United States) . . . approved the draft resolution 'Prevention of an Arms Race in Outer Space'"; Sa'id Mosteshar, "Space Law and Weapons in Space," *Planetary Science*, 2019.

11. See Norman Ware, *The Industrial Worker, 1840–1860: The Reaction of American Industrial Society to the Advance of the Industrial Revolution* (Chicago: Ivan R. Dee, 1990); David Milton, *The Politics of U.S. Labor: From the Great Depression to the New Deal* (New York: Monthly Review Press, 1982).

12. On the hysterical response to Zinn, see David Detmer, *Zinnophobia: The Battle over History in Education, Politics, and Scholarship* (Winchester, UK: Zero Books, 2018); Nicole Gaudiano, "Trump Creates 1776 Commission to Promote 'Patriotic Education,'" *Politico*, November 2, 2020; Caleb Ecarma, "From Florida to Oklahoma, PragerU's Propaganda Project Isn't Slowing Down," *Vanity Fair*, September 6, 2023. See also Nathan J. Robinson, "Why Critical Race Theory Should Be Taught in Schools," *Current Affairs*, July 27, 2021.

13. Tim Adams, "'A Beautiful Outpouring of Rage': Did Britain's Biggest Ever Protest Change the World?," *Guardian*, February 11, 2023.

14. Chiara Eisner, "The U.S. Military Trained Him. Then He Helped Murder Berta Cáceres," *Guardian*, December 21, 2021.

15. See Noam Chomsky, "The Revolutionary Pacifism of A. J. Muste," in *American Power and the New Mandarins* (New York: Pantheon, 1969).

16. "It Is Still 90 Seconds to Midnight, 2024 Doomsday Clock Statement," *Bulletin of the Atomic Scientists*, January 23, 2024.

17. "Economy Remains the Public's Top Policy Priority; COVID-19 Concerns Decline Again," Pew Research Center, February 6, 2023.

Index

Abalos, Victor, 46
Abdulmutallab, Umar Farouk,
    343n70
Abedin, Mahan, 54
Abizaid, John, 129
Abu Ghraib, 120
Acheson, Dean, 29, 31, 246
Achille Lauro hijacking, 278–79
activist movements, 214–15, 295–98
Adams, John Quincy, 37
Afghanistan
    bin Laden extradition and, 90
    corruption in, 96–97
    democracy and, 98
    drone bombings in, 100–101
    frozen assets and, 102–3
    Iraq War priority over, 95–96
    liberal critics of war in, 275
    Operation Enduring Freedom and,
        91–94
    quality of life in, 99, 102–3
    refugees from, 104
    Soviet invasion of, 196, 328n19
    Taliban and, 90–95, 101–3, 106
    torture and, 100
    U.S. invasion of, 94–95, 105–6
    U.S. withdrawal from, 101–2
    warlords in, 98–99
Afghan War Logs, 99
African Nuclear-Weapon-Free
    Zone, 217
Ahmad, Eqbal, 146
Ahmed, Samina, 91
Albright, Madeleine, 52, 190–91, 304n4,
    319n63, 336n26
Alfaqih, Abdulrasheed, 320n70
Alian, Ghassan, 162
Allende, Salvador, 23–25
Almutawakel, Radhya, 320n70
Alvandi, Roham, 53
Amanpour, Christiane, 284
"American exceptionalism," 4
American Service-Members Protection
    Act, 253
Amnesty International, 60, 145–46, 149,
    187, 263
Andreas, Peter, 171–72
Animal Farm (Orwell), 271

Annan, Kofi, 188
anti-fascist resistance, 25–28
Anti-Personnel Mine Ban
    Convention, 255
anti-Semitism, 87, 144
Appy, Christian, 68, 70, 210
Arab League, 114, 153
Arab nationalism, 136
Arakhamia, David, 202
Árbenz, Jacobo, 39–40
Argentina, 42–43, 315n40
Ash, Timothy, 198–99
Assange, Julian, 373n20
Atlacatl Battalion, 46
d'Aubuisson, Roberto, 45
Augustine, 276
Australia, 178
Al-Awlaki, Anwar, 343n70
Axelrod, Daniel, 208
Ayalon, Ami, 151

Ba'ath Party, 119, 333n7
Bacon, Kenneth, 127
Baheer, Obaidullah, 103
Bahrain, 60–62
Bai, Akbar, 98
Bailey, Thomas, 379n1
Baker, James, 192
Bakunin, Mikhail, 233
Balch, Jennifer, 230
Balfour Declaration, 141
Banfield, Ashleigh, 12–13
Bannon, Steve, 167
Banzer, Hugo, 41–42
Barak, Ehud, 142, 144, 148, 151
Barbie, Klaus, 308n5
Barnet, Richard, 240–41
Barr, William, 167–68, 171
Bay of Pigs, 33
Bearden, Milton, 90
Begala, Paul, 273
Begin, Menachem, 144–45
Bellinger, John B., III, 253

Ben-Gurion, David, 141–42, 144, 148,
    346n20, 347n22
Bennett, Naftali, 160, 202
Ben-Yair, Michael, 149
Bergen, Peter, 133
Berger, J. M., 134
Berger, Sandy, 186
Bernays, Edward, 243–44
Bevins, Vincent, 47, 50, 318n52, 318n55
Biden, Joe
    Afghanistan exit and, 101–2
    Bahrain and, 61–62
    China and, 168–69
    Cuba and, 277
    Egypt aid and, 258
    Inflation Reduction Act and, 229
    international law violations by, 267
    Iran approach of, 57
    Israel and, 136, 156, 163–65, 344n4
    labor movements and, 298
    military budget of, 248
    nuclear weapons and, 212–13, 218
    oil production and, 228–29
    Saudi Arabia and, 55
    Taiwan and, 177
    Trump's foreign policy and, 291
    on Ukraine and NATO, 194
    Ukraine war and, 196–97
Biegun, Stephen E., 169
bin Laden, Osama, 85–88, 90, 134
bin Salman, Mohammed, 55
Biological Weapons Convention, 255
Blair, Tony, 187, 339n43
Blaydes, Lisa, 117–18
Blinken, Antony, 169
Bohlen, Charles, 3
Bolender, Keith, 33–34, 37
Bolivia, 41–42
Boot, Max, 312n20
Borger, Julian, 334n10
Born, Max, 208
Bosch, Juan, 260
Bosnia bombing, 190

Bouton, Marshall, 237
Bowles, Chester, 33
Bowman, Jamaal, 352n57
Braithwaite, Rodric, 97
Branfman, Fred, 78
Brazil, 38, 314n31
Bremer, L. Paul, 118–19, 128, 133
British Guiana, 29–30
Bronson, Rachel, 116
Bryant, Brandon, 100–101
Brzezinski, Zbigniew, 43, 80, 196
B'Tselem, 146, 149, 348n27
Bulletin of the Atomic Scientists, 212, 300
Bumiller, Elisabeth, 284
Burke, Jason, 121
Burnham, Forbes, 30
Burns, John, 279
Burns, Ken, 63, 74, 275
Burns, William, 191–92
Bush, George H. W., 55
    Gulf War and, 113–17, 129, 335n18,
        341n56
    international law violations by, 262
    Iraq's invasion of Iran and, 111–12
    Panama invasion and, 250
Bush, George W., 2–3
    Afghanistan and, 91–96, 106
    bin Laden extradition and, 90
    climate crisis and, 226
    "Coalition Provisional Authority"
        and, 118–19
    dictatorships and, 126–27
    "global war on terror" and, 90, 133–34
    international law violations by, 263–64
    Iraq War and, 95–96, 129–31, 340n49
    Israel and, 154
    mass murder and, 132–33
    on 9/11 attacks, 85, 124
    nostalgia for, 132–33
    Obama, M.'s, friendship with, 132,
        332n6
    Operation Enduring Freedom and,
        91–94

    torture techniques and, 263–64
    on war and greatness, 130
Butler, Lee, 211, 215
Buttigieg, Pete, 63
Byers, Michael, 268

Cáceres, Berta, 297
Calhoun, John C., 292
Cambodia, Vietnam War and, 79–81
Campbell, Kurt, 57
Capone, Al, 200, 305n11
Caputo, Philip, 76
"carbon colonialism," 224
Carothers, Thomas, 288
Carr, Joe, 121
Carter, Jimmy, 41, 43, 129, 196
    El Salvador and, 45
    on human rights, 51, 60
    international law violations by,
        261–62
    nuclear weapons and, 219
    Vietnam War and, 83–84
Castro, Fidel, 33–37, 52, 246, 312n20
CDA (Cuban Democracy Act), 35
CEDAW (Convention on the
        Elimination of All Forms of
        Discrimination Against
        Women), 255
Central Intelligence Agency (CIA)
    Ba'ath Party and, 333n7
    Bolivia coup and, 41–42
    British Guiana operation of, 29–30
    Castro and, 33, 312n20
    Chilean coup and, 24–25
    election interference by, 27–28, 310n9
    Guatemalan coup and, 40
    Iranian coup and, 53–54
    Lumumba and, 30–31, 311n15
    MK-ULTRA project of, 238
Chamberlain, Paul Thomas, 363n1
Chandrasekaran, Rajiv, 105
Chayes, Sarah, 92, 98
Cheju Island massacre, 28–29

chemical weapons, 72, 74, 110–12, 338n42
Cheney, Dick, 122, 124, 133, 237–38
Chhit Do, 79
Chiang Kai-shek, 174
Chile, 23–25, 32
China
  currency manipulation and, 171
  economic threats of, 167–69
  famine of 1958–61 in, 291–92
  human rights abuses in, 170–71
  Inflation Reduction Act and, 229
  intellectual property theft and, 171–72
  Japan in, 1–2
  Kosovo bombings and, 186
  National Security Strategy warning on, 168
  NATO criticism from, 192–93
  nuclear weapons and, 213
  Solomon Islands and, 172–73
  spy balloon from, 281–82
  Taiwan and, 173–77
  tech development in, 169
  U.S. "security dilemma" with, 177–80
  vaccination campaigns of, 356n13
Chirac, Jacques, 191
Church Committee, 261
Churchill, Winston, 9, 67, 141
CIA. See Central Intelligence Agency
City of God (Augustine), 276
Clapper, James, 216
Clark, Wesley, 186
Clarke, Richard, 123, 130
climate crisis, 205, 267
  activist movements and, 298
  "carbon colonialism" and, 224
  Democratic Party and, 226–29
  examples of, 220–21
  future impact of, 221–22, 231
  Kyoto Protocol and, 236, 255–56
  media coverage on, 229–30
  oil lobbyists and, 227–28
  Paris Agreement and, 225, 227

  plans for, 224–25
  Republican Party and, 225–26
  responsibility for, 222–24, 230–31
Clinton, Bill, 35
  international law violations by, 262–63
  Kosovo bombings and, 186, 188
  nuclear weapons and, 212
  Suharto and, 52
Clinton, Hillary, 99, 278, 348n29
cluster bombs, 254
"Coalition Provisional Authority," 118–19
Coates, Ta-Nehisi, 352n59
Cockburn, Patrick, 92, 97–98, 105–6
Cohen, Eliot, 199–200
Cohn, Carol, 12
Cold War
  fearmongering in, 246–47
  NATO after, 183–85
  nuclear weapons and, 208–12
  power systems during, 18
Cole, Juan, 146–47
Coll, Steve, 334n14
Colombia, 257–58
Communism
  "domino theory" of, 31–32, 311n14
  Guatemala and, 39–40
  Indonesia and, 47–50
  propaganda against, 318n58
  terminology of, 39, 59
Confronting the Bomb (Wittner), 214
Convention on Cluster Munitions, 254
Convention on the Elimination of All Forms of Discrimination Against Women (CEDAW), 255
Convention on the Rights of Persons with Disabilities, 255
Convention on the Rights of the Child (CRC), 255
COP28, 228–29
Copenhagen climate summit, 226
Cornplanter, 379n1

Corrie, Rachel, 297
Costs of War project, 90
Cotton, Tom, 15
Council on Foreign Relations, 9–10
Cowell, Alan, 117
Crain, Charles, 332*n*3
Cranston, Alan, 217
CRC (Convention on the Rights of the Child), 255
The Crisis of Democracy report, 245
critical race theory, 296
Crocker, Ryan, 95
Crossman, Richard, 136
Cruickshank, Paul, 133
Cuba
    Bay of Pigs and, 33
    CIA assassination attempts in, 33, 312*n*20
    Guantánamo Bay and, 37–38, 256, 263–64, 313*n*29
    Latin America, Castro, and, 36–37
    Soviet Union's ties to, 36
    terrorism and, 277–78
    U.S. embargo of, 34–35, 236, 251
Cuban Democracy Act (CDA), 35
Cuban Missile Crisis, 7, 209–10
Cumings, Bruce, 29
Curtis, Mark, 6
cyberweapons, 58, 320*n*76

D'Alema, Massimo, 186
de Hoop Scheffer, Jaap, 183
democracy, 4–5, 17
    Afghanistan and, 98
    citizen resistance in, 294–95
    foreign policy and, 245–46
    "intelligent minorities" in, 243–44
    international law and, 294
    in Iraq, 126–28
    Israel and, 151–52
    monarchy compared to, 233
    nuclear weapons and, 215–17
    Orwell on, 271

public opinion in, 242–43
public participation in, 247–48
U.S. acceptance of certain, 288–89
Democratic Party, 226–29, 241–42
Democratic Republic of Congo, 30–31
Deni, John, 195
Dewey, John, 241, 271–72
dictatorships, 15, 38, 45, 60–61, 126–27, 315*n*40
DiMaggio, Anthony, 273
Dinges, John, 42
The Disinherited (Turki), 139
Djibouti, 172
Dodd, Chris, 253
Domínguez, Jorge, 7
"domino theory," 31–32, 311*n*14
Donahue, Phil, 284
Doolittle Report, 59–60
"Doomsday Clock," 300
Do Quy, 72
Dostum, Abdul Rashid, 98–99
"doublethink," 378*n*34
Dower, John, 28
Downing Street memos, 338*n*41
Drezner, Daniel, 196–97
drone bombings, 100–101, 265
Dulles, Allen, 30
Dulles, John Foster, 32, 39

East Timor, 50–53, 319*n*63
Eban, Abba, 143
Egypt, 60, 151, 217, 258, 373*n*19
Ehrhart, W. D., 83
Eiland, Giora, 162–63
Einstein, Albert, 208
Eisenhower, Dwight, 67–68, 214, 248, 260
ElBaradei, Mohamed, 219
Eldar, Akiva, 152
election interference, 27–28, 310*n*9
Elkins, Caroline, 307*n*35
Ellsberg, Daniel, 64–65, 211, 364*n*14
El Salvador, 32, 45–46, 316*n*47, 317*n*48

The Encyclopedia of the Social Sciences, 244

"Energy Discrimination
    Elimination," 226

Epstein, Yitzhak, 139

Ericsson, 34

d'Escoto, Miguel, 252

Esposito, John, 88

"exceptionalism" of U.S., 2–3, 20

ExxonMobil, 227

Fadhil, Ali, 121, 337*n*34

Fairbank, John King, 63

Fairness and Accuracy in Reporting
    (FAIR), 280–81

Falk, Richard, 251

Fall, Bernard, 70

Fallujah, USS, 133

Federspiel, Howard, 49

Feinstein, Dianne, 227

Ferguson, Thomas, 240

"Fermi paradox," 300

Fernandes, Clinton, 51

Ferrer, Ada, 37

Fetterman, John, 352*n*57

"Fifth Freedom," 5

Fiji Anti-Nuclear Group, 215

Filkins, Dexter, 97, 102, 120–21

"First Principles of Government"
    (Hume), 285

fissionable materials for weapons
    purposes (FISSBAN), 218

Ford, Gerald, 261

foreign policy. *See also* international law
    business steering, 239–42
    democracy and, 245–46
    idealism in, 290
    public opinion and, 235–39
    torture and, 257
    of Trump and Biden, 291

The Foreign Policy Disconnect (Page and
    Bouton), 237

Fossil Fuel Non-Proliferation Treaty
    initiative, 224

Four Freedoms, 5

France, 2, 65–67

Franklin, Benjamin, 87

Franklin, H. Bruce, 371*n*25

Freeman, Chas, 200

Friedman, Thomas, 116, 187, 194

Friel, Howard, 251

Frum, David, 129, 342*n*57

Fuller, Graham E., 198

Galen Carpenter, Ted, 184, 358*n*4

Gardner, David, 88, 155

Garrels, Anne, 121

Gasiorowski, Mark J., 53

Gates, Robert, 192, 254

Gaza. *See also* Palestine/Palestinians
    civil protests of 2018–19 in, 156–57
    "de-development" of, 147–48
    elections in, 147, 348*n*29
    Hamas attacks from, 160
    Israel strikes in, 137–38, 156–59,
        160–65
    living conditions in, 146–47, 348*n*27
    "no-go zones" in, 351*n*51
    Operation Cast Lead and, 147
    Oslo Accords and, 148, 350*n*37
    Rafah invasion in, 354*n*69
    Trump's plan for, 155–56

Gellhorn, Martha, 70–71

Geneva Accord, 153

Georgia, 191–92

Gerard, Emmanuel, 30

Gergen, David, 214

Germany, 197–98, 274

Gilbert, Lord, 190

Gill, Lesley, 317*n*50

Glenny, Misha, 320*n*76

"global war on terror," 90, 133–34,
    327*n*9

Godoy, Julio, 41

Godwin, Paul, 177

Golden Rule (Ferguson), 240

Goldstein, Lyle, 173–74, 177, 180

Gopal, Anand, 101
Gorbachev, Mikhail, 192
Gordon, Lincoln, 38
Goulart, João, 314n31
Graham, Lindsey, 200
"Grand Area" planning, 9–10
Grandin, Greg, 40–41, 44–45, 317n49
Grayling, A. C., 290
Great March of Return, 298
Greece, 27–28, 259–60, 305n15, 310n10
Greene, Graham, 63–64
Greenham Common Women's Peace
    Camp, 214
Green New Deal, 224–25
Greenspan, Alan, 130
Greentree, Todd, 95
Grenada invasion, 262
Griffiths, Philip Jones, 324n12
Grow, Michael, 29
Guantánamo Bay, 37–38, 256, 263–64,
    313n29
Guatemala, 32, 39–41, 314n36
Gulf War, 113–17, 129, 335n18, 341n56
Guterres, António, 147, 221

Ha'Am, Ahad, 139
Haass, Richard, 129, 341n56
Hagel, Chuck, 130
Hague Invasion Act, 253
Haig, Alexander, 79
Haines, Gerald, 11, 306n24
Haiti, 278, 313n29
Halliday, Denis, 117
Hamada, Khalil, 137–38
Hamada, Najwa Abu, 137–38
Hamas, 147, 160–65
Hamilton, Alexander, 171, 243
Haq, Abdul, 93, 106, 328n19
Harden, Blaine, 260
Hare, Bill, 229
Hasan, Mehdi, 339n43, 378n42
Hasan, Nidal, 343n70
Hassol, Susan Joy, 221

Hastings, Max, 64
Haynes, Kyle, 172
Hedges, Chris, 13, 284
Heisenberg, Werner, 208
Herbert, Bob, 273
Herman, Edward, 283
Hertsgaard, Mark, 46
Herzl, Theodor, 139
Hickel, Jason, 223
Hicks, David, 263–64
Hiltermann, Joost, 112
Himmler, Heinrich, 1
Hirata Tetsuo, 28
Hirohito, Emperor, 1–2
Hiroshima bombings, 205, 207, 259
Hirsh, Michael, 169, 179
Hitler, Adolf, 1, 114–15, 274
Hồ Chí Minh, 65–68
Honduras, 32, 45, 297
Hoover, J. Edgar, 260
Hotham, David, 68
Hourani, Albert, 143
Howard, Michael, 3, 91, 105
Hsiang, Solomon, 223
human rights, 4–5, 17
    Carter on, 51, 60
    China's abuses of, 170–71
    Colombia's abuses of, 257–58
    Egypt's abuses of, 60, 258, 373n19
    Guatemala and abuses of, 41
    international law and abuse of,
        257–58
    Israel's abuses of, 60
    political economy of, 59–62
Human Rights Watch, 56–57, 60, 92,
    118, 149, 187, 263–64, 327n3,
    358n10
Hume, David, 285
Huntington, Samuel, 3, 245, 293
Hurricane Joan, 316n44
Hussain, Murtaza, 265
Hussein, Saddam, 108, 333n7, 334n14,
    336n25

Hussein, Saddam, (*cont.*)
  chemical weapons and, 110–12,
    338*n*42
  civilian uprisings against, 116
  Gulf War and, 113–17
  Iran invasion by, 54–55, 110–12
  9/11 attacks and, 124–25
  rise of, 110, 113
  WMDs and, 123–24, 339*n*43, 340*n*49

IAEA (International Atomic Energy
  Agency), 57, 339*n*43
ICC (International Criminal Court), 253
ICPPED (International Convention for
    the Protection of All Persons from
    Enforced Disappearance), 255
IDF (Israel Defense Forces), 85–86, 165
Ignatius, David, 109, 199
IMF (International Monetary Fund), 52
imperialism, 1–2, 8–11, 307*n*35
Indonesia, 31, 47–53, 318*n*53, 319*n*63
Indonesian Communist Party (PKI),
    47–50
Inflation Reduction Act, 229
intellectual property theft, 171–72
International Atomic Energy Agency
    (IAEA), 57, 339*n*43
International Convention for the
    Protection of All Persons from
    Enforced Disappearance
    (ICPPED), 255
International Criminal Court (ICC), 253
international law
  Biological Weapons Convention
    and, 255
  cluster bombs and, 254
  democracy and, 294
  fairness of, 268–69
  Guantánamo Bay and, 256, 263–64
  human rights abuse and, 257–58
  ICC and, 253
  Law of the Sea Convention and, 254–55
  NATO violations of, 192
  Obama, B., Libya, and, 256–57
  United Nations Charter and, 250–51,
    267–68
  U.S. undermining, 251–67
  whistleblowers and, 258–59
International Monetary Fund (IMF), 52
international security, U.S. and, 3–4
Iran, 8
  coup in, 53–54
  Iraq's invasion of, 54–55, 110–12
  Israel and, 56, 217–18
  nuclear weapons and, 55–57, 217–18
  plebiscites in, 320*n*67
  Stuxnet and, 58, 320*n*76
  terrorism and, 57–59
  U.S. 1988 shootdown and, 333*n*9
  U.S. sanctions against, 56–57
Iran-Contra affair, 333*n*8
Iraq
  chemical weapons of, 110–12
  civilian uprisings in, 116
  Clinton's missile strike in, 262
  "Coalition Provisional Authority" in,
    118–19
  democracy in, 126–28
  education in, 332*n*3
  elections in, 128
  ethnic conflict in, 131–32
  Gulf War and, 113–17, 129, 335*n*18,
    341*n*56
  Iran invaded by, 54–55, 110–12
  9/11 attacks and, 123–25
  al-Qaeda and, 340*n*45
  U.S. sanctions against, 117–18,
    336*n*26
Iraq Veterans Against the War, 119–20
Iraq War, 12–13
  Abu Ghraib, torture, and, 120
  activist movements against, 297
  Afghanistan war ignored for, 95–96
  "Coalition Provisional Authority"
    and, 118–19
  critics of, 109, 272–73

dehumanization in, 119–22
devastation of, 107–8, 131–32
Downing Street memos on, 338*n*41
extreme force used in, 118
justification and motivations of, 108–
    9, 122–32
media's hierarchy of victims in, 279
morality and motives of, 273
oil and, 128–30
public opinion on, 126, 237–38
terrorism and, 133–34
WMD falsehoods and, 122–24,
    339*n*43, 340*n*49
al-'Isa, 'Isa, 143
Islamic State, 132
Israel, 351*n*49
    activist movements in, 297
    anti-Semitism and criticism of, 144
    apartheid accusations against, 148–49
    Arab portrayals in, 142
    Balfour Declaration and, 141
    colonialism and, 140, 144, 159
    democracy and, 151–52
    Gaza strikes by, 137–38, 156–59,
        160–65
    Hamas attacks against, 160
    human rights abuses of, 60
    Iran and, 56, 217–18
    media on military acts of, 138, 158
    media's nationalistic bias and, 282
    military aid for, 152
    "nakba" and, 143–44, 346*n*20
    Operation Cast Lead and, 147
    Oslo Accords and, 148, 350*n*37
    Palestine occupation by, 86–87,
        145–46, 148–50, 347*n*22
    Palestinian statehood and, 150, 153,
        347*n*26, 349*n*35
    Qana massacre and, 85–86
    Rafah invasion by, 354*n*69
    security decisions of, 159–60
    Six-Day War and, 136
    state formation of, 138–44, 345*n*9

Stuxnet and, 58, 320*n*76
Taba negotiations and, 150–51
"A Threshold Crossed" report and, 149
"transfer" policy of, 141–42
two-state solution and, 150, 153–55
U.S. relationship with, 135–37, 152–
    56, 164–65, 235–36, 344*n*4, 352*n*57
West Bank illegal settlements of, 148,
    151, 161
World Central Kitchen workers killed
    by, 165
Israel Defense Forces (IDF), 85–86, 165
Italy, 26–27, 309*n*7

Jabotinsky, Ze'ev, 140–41
Jackson, Henry, 136–37
Jagan, Cheddi, 29–30
Jamaica, 34
Japan
    in China, 1–2
    election interference in, 28
    Hiroshima and Nagasaki bombings
        in, 205, 207, 259
    Taiwan and, 174
    U.S. firebombings in, 289–90
Jay, John, 243
Jefferson, Thomas, 65–66
Jervis, Robert, 293
Jihad Joe (Berger), 134
Johnson, Adam, 275–76
Johnson, Boris, 202
Johnson, Lyndon B., 68, 78
    on Communism, 311*n*14
    Greece and, 305*n*15
    international law violations by, 260
    Vietnam War and, 81, 304*n*9
Jones, Adam, 326*n*35

Kagan, Robert, 91
Kahin, George, 67
Kaku, Michio, 208
Kalmus, Peter, 228, 229
Karnow, Stanley, 69

Karzai, Hamid, 95, 101
Kaye, David, 255
Keating, Paul, 172
Kennan, George, 9–10, 25–26, 59, 184
Kennedy, John F., 7, 33–34, 36, 210, 260
Kennedy, Robert, 33
Kerry, John, 228
Khalidi, Rashid, 143
al-Khalidi, Yusuf Diya, 139
Khalilzad, Zalmay, 95
Khamvongsa, Channapha, 78–79
Khashoggi, Jamal, 55
al-Khawaja, Abdulhadi, 60–61
al-Khawaja, Maryam, 61
Khirbet Khizeh (Yizhar), 143–44
Khmer Rouge, 79–81
Khrushchev, Nikita, 209–10
Kiernan, Ben, 79–80
Killgore, Andrew, 53
The Killing Season (Robinson), 47
King, Martin Luther, Jr., 180
King-Crane Commission, 141
Kinsley, Michael, 278
Kinzer, Stephen, 238
Kirkpatrick, Jeane, 307n34
Kissinger, Henry, 261
    Argentina and, 43, 315n40
    Bolivian coup and, 41–42
    Cambodia and, 79–80
    Chilean coup and, 23–25
    on China, 180
    Nicaragua and, 44, 238–39
    on nuclear weapons, 216
    Vietnam War and, 83
"Kissingerian realism," 290
Klare, Michael, 170
Klinghoffer, Leon, 278–79, 376n18
Klion, David, 163
Knox, Henry, 379n1
Kofsky, Frank, 309n6
Kopkind, Andrew, 2
Korea, 28–29
Kornbluh, Peter, 24

Kosovo bombings, 185–90, 358n10
Kristof, Nicholas, 160, 275
Kristol, William, 108, 332n4
Kroizer, Yitzhak, 162
Kuklick, Bruce, 30
Kupchan, Charles, 184
Kurlantzick, Joshua, 77–78
Kushner, Jared, 155–56, 351n49
Kuwait, 6–7, 113–17, 341n56
Kyoto Protocol, 236, 255–56

labor movements, 295, 298
Lamrani, Salim, 34–36, 38
Laos, Vietnam War and, 77–79
Lasswell, Harold, 244
Latin America. *See also specific countries*
    Cuba, Castro, and, 36–37
    dictatorships in, 38, 315n40
    "domino theory" and, 32
    mass murder in, 41–42
    nationalism and, 11, 38–39
Law of the Sea Convention, 178,
    254–55
Layne, Christopher, 186
Lebanon, 85–86
Leffler, Melvyn, 26
Leibowitz, Yeshayahu, 151
LeMay, Curtis, 71, 260, 290
Lemieux, Jason Wayne, 119–20
Lent, Jeremy, 222
Letelier, Orlando, 42, 315n40
Levy, Gideon, 147, 347n26
Lewis, Anthony, 63
Lewy, Guenter, 73–74
Libya, 192–93, 256–57
Lie, Alon, 149
Lieberman, Avigdor, 155
Liechty, C. Philip, 51
Lieven, Anatol, 194–96
Limbaugh, Rush, 337n33
Lippmann, Walter, 244
Lodge, Henry Cabot, Jr., 214
Lumumba, Patrice, 30–31, 311n15

The Lumumba Plot (Reid), 31
lynchings, 363n2

Maddow, Rachel, 275
Madison, James, 243
Mafia Doctrine, 5–8, 17, 30, 305n11
Maggart, Lon, 335n20
Mainau Declaration, 208
Major, John, 360n22
Malkasian, Carter, 90–91, 95, 101,
    105–6, 134
Mandela, Nelson, 189, 262
Mandelbaum, Michael, 184, 185
Mann, Thomas E., 241
Manning, Chelsea, 122, 297
"manufacture of consent," 244
Marcetic, Branko, 193
Markey, Ed, 224
Marro, Anthony, 279
Martens, Robert, 49
mass murder
    Bush, G. W., and, 132–33
    in Cambodia, 79
    Cheju Island massacre, 28–29
    in Chile, 23
    East Timor invasion and, 51
    in El Salvador, 45–46
    every day, 363n1
    in Gaza, 160–65
    "global war on terror" and, 90
    Hamas attacks and, 160
    of Hiroshima and Nagasaki
        bombings, 207
    human costs of, 12–13
    Iraq War and, 107–8
    justifications for, 1–2, 13–15
    Kosovo bombings and, 187–88
    in Laos, 78
    in Latin America, 41–42
    lynchings and, 363n2
    in Nicaragua, 44–45
    Operation Enduring Freedom and,
        93–94

    of PKI in Indonesia, 47–50
    Qana massacre and, 85–86
    Ukraine war and, 201
    in Vietnam War, 70, 72, 76–77, 81
Mathews, Jessica T., 304n7
Matlock, Jack, 195
Mattis, James, 203
May, Ernest, 37
McCain, Meghan, 158
MccGwire, Michael, 188, 190, 219
McFarlane, Robert, 214
McGrory, Mary, 317n48
McNamara, Robert, 209–10, 219, 237,
    312n21, 318n57
McNaughton, John, 82–83
Mearsheimer, John, 179, 193, 236
Mecklin, John, 75
media
    on climate crisis, 229–30
    freedom and, 271–72
    hierarchy of victims in, 279–81
    on Israel military actions, 138, 158
    nationalistic bias in, 281–82
    self-reflection in, 285
    state propaganda and, 19, 283–85
    on terrorism, 278–79
    on Ukraine war, 198
Meir, Golda, 144, 151
Merkel, Angela, 191
Mexico, 298
Milhollin, Gary, 320n69
Miliband, David, 104
military budget, U.S., 240, 248
Mill, John Stuart, 307n35
Miller, Aaron David, 153–54, 351n44
Miller, Judith, 284–85
Miller, Laurel, 104
Milley, Mark, 197
Milošević, Slobodan, 186, 189–90
Minsk II agreement, 195, 201
Mitchell, Greg, 363n4
MK-ULTRA, 238
Mobutu Sese Seko, 31, 311n15

Moghrabi, Ahmed, 164
monarchy, 233
Morgenthau, Hans, 4
Morris, Benny, 140–43, 146, 152, 345*n*9, 346*n*15, 346*n*20
Mosaddegh, Mohammad, 53, 260, 320*n*67
Moulton, Seth, 163
Moynihan, Daniel Patrick, 51
Al-Muslimi, Farea, 265
Muslims, 88, 134, 343*n*70
Muste, A. J., 299
My Lai massacre, 77

Nagasaki bombings, 205, 207, 259
al-Nairab, Umm Mohammad, 138
Nairn, Allan, 319*n*62
"nakba," 143–44, 346*n*20
Nanjing Massacre, 1–2
Nasser, Gamal Abdel, 6
National Defense Authorization Act, 178
"national interest" concept, 7–8, 19
nationalism
    Arab, 136
    in Iran, 53, 54
    Latin America and, 11, 38–39
    U.S. opposing, 288
    in Vietnam, 67
National Security Council (NSC), 6–7, 27, 38–39, 246
National Security Strategy, 168
NATO. *See* North Atlantic Treaty Organization
Nazi refugees, in U.S., 308*n*5
Negbi, Moshe, 151–52
Netanyahu, Benjamin, 56, 150, 158, 162, 217, 350*n*37
Ngô Đình Diệm, 64, 67–69
Nguyễn Cao Kỳ, 69
Nguyễn Văn Thiệu, 69
Nicaragua, 43–45, 125, 236, 238–39, 252, 261–62, 274–75, 278, 289, 316*n*44

Nicaragua v. United States, 262
Niebuhr, Reinhold, 243
The 9/11 Wars (Burke), 121
9/11 attacks, 85–90, 123–25
Nixon, Richard
    Cambodia and, 79–80
    Castro and, 36, 246
    Chilean coup and, 23–25
    international law violations by, 261
    on nuclear weapons, 216–17
    on presidential power, 256
    terrorism and, 277
    Vietnam War and, 70, 83, 365*n*24
Nobel Peace Prize, 264
Noble Intent, mythology of, 20
Non-Proliferation of Nuclear Weapons Treaty, 213, 218–19
Noriega, Manuel, 249–50
Norris, John, 189
North Atlantic Treaty Organization (NATO)
    in Afghanistan, 98
    Bosnia bombing by, 190
    China's criticism of, 192–93
    Georgia membership in, 191–92
    international law violations of, 192
    Kosovo bombings and, 185–90, 358*n*10
    Libya bombing by, 192–93
    post–Cold War mission of, 183–85
    Russia threatened by, 184, 190–93, 266
    Ukraine and, 185, 191–94, 266
    Ukraine war and, 193–202
North Korea, 260
Norton, Augustus Richard, 125–26
NSC (National Security Council), 6–7, 27, 38–39, 246
Nuclear Freeze movement, 214
Nuclear Posture Review, 212–13
Nuclear-Weapon-Free Zones, 217
nuclear weapons
    activism against, 214–15
    China and, 213

Cold War and, 208–12
Cuban Missile Crisis and, 7, 209–10
democracy threatened by, 215–17
Hiroshima and Nagasaki bombings
    and, 205, 207, 259
Iran and, 55–57, 217–18
Mainau Declaration and, 208
"no first use" policy for, 218
Non-Proliferation Treaty on, 213,
    218–19
pressing challenges of, 300–301
of Soviet Union and U.S., 208–12
suppression of victim footage and,
    363n4
terminal war and, 206–7
threats of, 205–6
United Nations Charter and, 250
Vietnam War and, 365n24
Nunn, Sam, 219

Obama, Barack, 2
    Afghanistan and, 101, 105
    climate crisis and, 226
    Cuba and, 277
    cyberattacks on Iran by, 58
    international law violations by, 264–65
    Iraq War criticism of, 109
    Israel and, 154–55, 351n49
    Libya attack and, 256–57
    Nobel Peace Prize and, 264
    nuclear weapons and, 212
    "pivot to Asia" of, 169
    Trans-Pacific Partnership and, 178–79
    whistleblowers and, 259
Obama, Michelle, 132, 332n6
O'Brien, Tim, 75
Ocasio-Cortez, Alexandria, 224
oil, 129, 227–30
Olmert, Ehud, 146, 149
Omar, Ilhan, 158
"One China" policy, 177
O'Neill, Paul, 125
Operation Allied Force, 189

Operation Cast Lead, 147, 348n29
Operation Condor, 42, 261, 315n40
Operation Enduring Freedom, 91–94
Operation Just Cause, 249–50
Oppenheimer, J. Robert, 207
Ornstein, Norman, 241
Orwell, George, 6, 271, 282, 378n34
Oslo Accords, 148, 350n37
outer space, U.S. goals, 293–94
Outer Space Treaty of 1967, 293
Owen, Roger, 131
Owen, Taylor, 79

Page, Benjamin, 237
Pahlavi, Reza, 53
Pakistan, 220–21, 223, 261
Palau, 215
Palestine/Palestinians. See also Gaza;
    West Bank
    Balfour Declaration and, 141
    Great March of Return and, 298
    identity of, 347n23
    Israeli occupation of, 86–87, 145–46,
        148–50, 347n22
    Israel state formation and, 138–44,
        345n9
    King-Crane Commission and, 141
    media's nationalistic bias and, 282
    "nakba" and, 143–44, 346n20
    Oslo Accords and, 148, 350n37
    Peel Commission and, 143
    self-determination of, 145
    statehood for, 150, 153, 347n26,
        349n35
    Taba negotiations and, 150–51
    two-state solution and, 150, 153–55
Palestinian Authority, 147
Palestinian Liberation Front, 278–79
Palestinian Liberation Organization
    (PLO), 153
Palestinian National Council (PNC), 150
Panama, U.S. invasion of, 249–50, 262
Paris Agreement, 225, 227

Pastor, Robert, 288

patriotism, war crimes dismissed and, 13–15

Pearl Harbor attacks, 89

Pedatzur, Reuven, 151

Peel Commission, 143

Pelosi, Nancy, 135, 177, 181, 226

Pentagon Papers, 65, 82

A People's History of the United States (Zinn), 296, 326n41

Perle, Richard, 131

Perón, Isabel, 42

Perry, William J., 216, 219

Petrov, Stanislav, 211

Pezzullo, Lawrence, 43

Pfeiffer, E. W., 72

Pierrehumbert, Raymond, 221

Pike, Douglas, 69

Pilger, John, 51–52

Pinker, Steven, 206

Pinochet, Augusto, 23–25, 315n40

The Pinochet File (Kornbluh), 24

Pinter, Harold, 286

PKI (Indonesian Communist Party), 47–50

PLO (Palestinian Liberation Organization), 153

PNC (Palestinian National Council), 150

Pollack, Kenneth, 113, 124–25

Pollard, Ruth, 103

Pollin, Robert, 224–25

Pol Pot, 80

Pompeo, Mike, 57, 167, 266–67, 310n9

Ponchaud, Francois, 80–81

Popiełuszko, Jerzy, 280

"popular organizations," 45

Powell, Colin, 90–91, 116, 123, 128, 133, 339n43

power
    justifying, 1–2
    presidential, 256
    systems of, 17–18, 26
    wealth and, 239–42

Power, Samantha, 13–15, 185–86, 189, 306n32

Powers, Thomas, 56, 249

presidential power, 256

press. *See* media

propaganda
    against Communism, 318n58
    language of, 282–86
    media and state, 19, 283–85
    terrorism and, 276–82
    of war, 274–76

public opinion
    on defense spending, 240
    in democracy, 242–43
    fearmongering and, 246–47
    foreign policy and, 235–39
    freedom and, 271–72
    on Iraq War, 126, 237–38
    on Israel and Gaza, 165
    "manufacture of consent" and, 244
    on refugees, 104
    on Vietnam War, 82, 237

Puerto Rico, 175

Pundak, Ron, 150, 153

Putin, Vladimir, 8, 27, 193, 199, 201–2, 266, 274, 278

al-Qaeda, 124–25, 340n45

Qana massacre, 85–86

The Quiet American (Greene), 63–64

Rabe, Stephen, 30, 43, 316n41

Rabin, Yitzhak, 148–50

racism, 74–76, 245, 296, 363n2

Raddatz, Martha, 237–38

Rafah invasion, 354n69

RAND Corporation, 198–99

Ratcliffe, John, 171

Rather, Dan, 284

RAWA (Revolutionary Association of the Women of Afghanistan), 93–94

Reagan, Ronald, 41, 55
    El Salvador and, 45–46

"global war on terror" and, 327n9
international law violations by, 262
Iraq's invasion of Iran and, 111
Israel and, 136
on Mobutu, 311n15
Nicaragua and, 43–45, 125, 236, 275
nuclear weapons and, 211
Reddaway, Norman, 318n58
Rehman, Zubair uh, 265
Reid, Harry, 132
Reid, Richard, 343n70
Reid, Stuart, 31, 311n15
Republican Party, 225–26, 241, 247
Revolutionary Association of the Women
    of Afghanistan (RAWA), 93–94
"revolutionary pacifism," 299
Rhodes, Ben, 154, 216
Rice, Condoleezza, 123
"right to dominate," U.S. and, 272–73
Rinkevich, Baruch, 221
Ríos Montt, Efraín 41
Ripple, William, 222
Risen, James, 100–101
Robespierre, Maximilien, 2
Robinson, Geoffrey, 47, 49–50
Romero, Óscar, 45, 280
Romney, Mitt, 179, 198
Roosevelt, Franklin D., 5, 298
Roosevelt, Theodore, 38
Rostow, Walt, 81
Rotblat, Joseph, 207–8
Roth, Ken, 340n49
Roy, Sara, 147–48
Rubio, Marco, 14–15
Rumsfeld, Donald, 93–96, 120, 123–24,
    129, 133, 337n33
Rusk, Dean, 29–30, 260
Russell, Bertrand, 208, 287
Russia, 8
    cluster bombs and, 254
    Minsk II agreement and, 195, 201
    NATO as threat to, 184, 190–93, 266
    Ukraine invasion by, 193–203, 274, 278

Sachs, Jeffrey, 236, 266
Said, Edward, 2, 142
Sakwa, Richard, 201
Salih, Nabil, 133
Samore, Gary, 58
Sanders, Bernie, 298, 332n4
Sandinistas, 43–45, 275
Saudi Arabia, 55, 171, 320n70
Scahill, Jeremy, 259
Scarry, Elaine, 215
Schlesinger, Arthur, Jr., 36–37, 311n14
Schmemann, Serge, 89
Schneider, René, 24
"School of the Americas," 317n50
Schoultz, Lars, 32, 35, 60
Schumer, Chuck, 171
Schwarz, Benjamin, 186
Scowcroft, Brent, 128
Shahalemi, Naser, 103
Shaked, Ayelet, 162
Shamir, Yitzhak, 150
Shane, Scott, 27
Sharett, Moshe, 144
Sharon, Ariel, 151, 279
Sheean, Vincent, 142
Sheehan, Casey, 132
Sheehan, Cindy, 132–33, 342n66
Sheehan, Neil, 73
Shepard, William, 244
Al-Shifa plant bombing, 262–63
Shirazi, Nima, 275–76
Shirzai, Gul Agha, 98
Shlaim, Avi, 136
Shultz, George, 250, 334n10
Sihanouk, Norodom, 80
Simpson, Bradley, 49
Siracusa, Ernest, 42
Six-Day War, 136
Slater, Jerome, 155
Smilansky, Moshe, 139
Smith, Adam, 12, 239, 242
Smith, Michael, 338n41
Smuggler Nation (Andreas), 172

Snowden, Edward, 258–59, 297
Solana, Javier, 185
Soleimani, Qassim, 59, 266
Solomon Islands, 172–73
South Africa, 262
South America, oil in, 228
Soviet Union
    Afghanistan invaded by, 196, 328n19
    Cuba's ties to, 36
    power structure of, 18, 26
    U.S. nuclear weapons and, 208–12
Sponeck, Hans von, 117
Stanekzai, Masoom, 94–95
State Department, U.S., 9–11, 42,
    315n40
State of Repression (Blaydes), 117–18
Stearns, Monteagle, 78–79
Stephens, Bret, 158
Stevenson, Adlai, 28
Stimson, Henry, 11, 209, 227
Stohl, Michael, 279
Strategic Command (STRATCOM),
    211–12
Streeter, Stephen M., 25
Stuxnet, 58, 320n76
Sudan, 262–63
Suharto, 47–53, 318n53, 332n5
Sullivan, Andrew, 108–9
Summers, Anthony, 365n24
Sunrise Movement, 298
Swalwell, Eric, 198

Taalas, Petteri, 221
Taba negotiations, 150–51
Taguba, Antonio, 263
Tahiti, 215
Taiwan, 173–77
Talbott, Strobe, 183, 191
Taliban, 90–95, 101–3, 106
Taqi, Lina, 86
Taylor, Maxwell, 69
Taylor, Paul, 191
Taylor, Telford, 290

terminal war, nuclear weapons and,
    206–7
terrorism, 17. *See also* 9/11 attacks
    Cuba and, 277–78
    definitions of, 276–77, 376n12
    "global war on," 90, 133–34, 327n9
    Gulf War and, 115–16
    Iran and, 57–59
    Iraq War effect on, 133–34
    motivations for, 343n70
    Operation Enduring Freedom and,
        92–93
    propaganda and, 276–82
    roots of, 89
    in Ukraine, 278
Thailand, 31
Tharoor, Ishaan, 261
Tharoor, Shashi, 307n35
The Things They Carried (O'Brien), 75
The Threatening Storm (Pollack),
    124–25
"A Threshold Crossed" report, 149
Thucydides, 21
Torres, Juan José, 41–42
torture, 100, 120, 257, 263–65
To Win a Nuclear War (Kaku and
    Axelrod), 208
"transcendent purpose," of U.S., 4
Trans-Pacific Partnership, 178–79
Treaty of Pelindaba, 217
Treaty on the Prohibition of Nuclear
    Weapons, 218
Trenin, Dimitry, 191
Trilateral Commission, 245
Truman, Harry, 66, 219, 309n7, 333n8
Trump, Donald, 13, 55, 126
    Afghanistan and, 101
    Biden's foreign policy and, 291
    China and, 167
    on climate crisis, 225
    Cuba and, 277
    cyberattacks on Iran by, 58
    fearmongering by, 247